D1488481

Future Focus

FUTURE FOCUS

HOW 21 COMPANIES ARE CAPTURING 21ST CENTURY SUCCESS

THEODORE B. KINNI

with introduction and commentary by Al Ries

CAPSTONE

First published 2000 by
Capstone Publishing, Inc.   Capstone Publishing Limited
40 Commerce Park   Oxford Centre for Innovation
Milford   Mill Street
CT 06460   Oxford OX2 0JX
USA   United Kingdom
Contact: info@capstonepub.com   http://www.capstone.co.uk

CIP catalogue records for this book are available from the British Library and the US Library of Congress, Library of Congress Card Number: 00-104762

ISBN 1-900961-65-2

Typeset in 11/14 pt Caslon by
Sparks Computer Solutions Ltd, Oxford, UK
http://www.sparks.co.uk
Printed and bound in the USA by
Sheridan Books, Ann Arbor, Michigan

This book is printed on acid-free paper

Substantial discounts on bulk quantities of Capstone books are available to corporations, professional associations and other organizations. If you are in the USA or Canada, phone the LPC Group, Special Sales Department for details on (1-800-626-4330) or fax (1-800-334-3892). Everywhere else, phone Capstone Publishing on (+44-1865-811113) or fax (+44-1865-240941).

Contents

Acknowledgments

As always thanks are due to superagent John Willig, whose judgement and support remain constants in the ever-changing publishing world. And to Donna Greiner. There would be no books without her research efforts and motivational support.

TK

Introduction

by Al Ries

Future Focus is our attempt to predict the future. It's a difficult task because you obviously cannot study the future. To predict the future, you have no choice. You have to study the past. Some people might dismiss such research as hopelessly inadequate to shed much light in the darkness of the decades ahead. But one example might show the power of the historical approach to predicting the future.

The most valuable company in the world in the year 2000 is the General Electric Company. Will GE repeat in the year 2100?

Not a chance.

The most valuable company in America in the year 1900 was International Harvester. But Harvester was in the process of becoming an unfocused company. Over the years, Harvester developed a leadership position in three major lines of business: trucks, farm machinery and construction equipment.

It takes time to screw up a company as large as International Harvester. But it always happens to a firm that loses its focus.

At the halfway mark in the 20th century, International Harvester was still ahead of its specialist competition. In 1954, for example, Harvester was No. 22 on *Fortune*'s list of the 500 largest industrial companies in America. Harvester sales of about $1 billion were greater than the combined sales of its three specialist competitors. Caterpillar (construction equipment) was No. 75, Deere (farm equipment) was No. 296 and Pacific Car & Foundry (trucks) was No. 356.

So where is International Harvester today? Exactly where you would expect to find them. A company, no matter how large and profitable, cannot possibly manage to stay on top of three major industries: trucks, construction equipment and farm machinery.

During the 1950s, International Harvester lost its leadership in farm machinery to Deere. In the 1960s, Harvester lost its leadership in construction equipment to Caterpillar. Along the way it also lost out in heavy-duty trucks to Pacific Car & Foundry (PACCAR) and medium-duty trucks to Ford.

In the 1980s, teetering on the edge of bankruptcy, International Harvester sold its construction equipment division to Dresser Industries and its farm machinery division (along with the International Harvester name) to Tenneco.

Renamed Navistar and focused on trucks and school buses, the company dropped to No. 256 on the latest Fortune 500 list. Well ahead of the former conglomerate are the three specialist competitors. Caterpillar, No. 66. Deere, No. 119 and PACCAR, No. 237. As a matter of fact, the combined annual sales of Caterpillar, Deere and PACCAR are six times the annual sales of Navistar. And combined profits are 20 times that of Navistar.

Now let's look at General Electric. GE, for the most part, is in mature businesses where it competes with other conglomerates. In aircraft engines, the competitor is United Technologies. In diesel-electric locomotives, it's General Motors. In electrical equipment, it's Westinghouse. In medical systems, it's Siemens. In lighting, it's Philips. What saves GE is the lack of specialist competition.

Nor would you expect such competition to develop in the years to come. Would you want to start a company making light bulbs? Or refrigerators? Or electric motors? Or distribution transformers? Not if you could start an Internet company. Or a telecommunications company. Or a computer company. Or a software company. Or any company focused on tomorrow-type products and services. What you can expect is a slow decline in GE sales and profits. You can only squeeze a lemon so much.

The one area where GE can expect more specialist competition is in their biggest moneymaker, financial services. And so we predict that GE will become the International Harvester of the 21st century. It may be around to celebrate the year 2100 but its executives won't be drinking too much champagne.

The *Future Focus 21*

The *Future Focus 21*

The future comes one day at a time, so said Dean Acheson, who served as US Secretary of State while the post-World War II world hardened into shape. "One days" pile up until suddenly, tick tock, we cross the doorstep into a new millenium.

That first new millenium day, unless you believe the world will end on the movement of a clock hand, won't be all that different from the day before. Business people around the world – at least the smart ones – will continue to ask, what do we have to do today to prosper tomorrow, next month, next year?

That's the question that started us working on *Future Focus* and conveniently, we get to frame it around the biggest day on the calendar in about 1000 years. So, we ask, what will it take to succeed in business in the new century and new millenium?

Since, as Acheson reminds us, the present is only one day away from the future, we started in search of the answer to that question by studying who is succeeding today.

Who has the numbers?

The bottom line of business success is in the numbers. There are many reasons to be in business, often wonderfully altruistic ones, but without profit they will certainly be short-lived.

Business, at its core, is about profit and profit is counted in numbers. Success means higher revenues and earnings, and above-average returns to investors. It also means a history of such numbers. After all, a single number can be misleading, such as the spectacular ones that result when one good year pops up after a long line of losers.

Happily, there are plenty of numbers available from distinguished corporate scorekeepers, including *Hoover's*, *Forbes*, *Business Week*, *Fortune*, *IndustryWeek*, and others. They provided our first long list of candidates.

The numbers also eliminated many companies you might expect to see in a book about business success in the new millenium. They cut out the companies in the emerging Internet industry. None have long financial histories; only a few have started earning significant profits; and, most of them are busier building their burn rates – the rate at which they can consume investor capital – than their profits. They are not yet successful in the full sense of the word. Intriguing, but not successful.

That said, you will find several companies that are successfully using the Internet in this book. Dell Computer, with an enviable numbers history, set up its computer-direct shop on the Net and generates sales at rates exceeding $40 million each day. Dell made our list.

Of course, as financial advisors are so fond of saying, past results are not indicative of future performance. If they were, the Dow Jones Industrial Average would surely contain more than one company from its original group. (Interestingly, that one company is General Electric, which didn't make our cut.)

Conversely, there are few companies in this book whose stock you couldn't have picked up at bargain-basement prices at one time or another. After telecom giant LM Ericsson fell into the clutches of Ivar Krueger, the notorious Swedish Match King of the 1920s, it was on the ropes for years.

But downturns happen in every company. They challenge and they test. So, a period of less-than-stellar results is also no guarantee of failure. Ericsson, which passed its greatest test, has staying power and the company made our list.

Who has staying power?

First, what is staying power? It is as unscientific a term as you are likely to run across in a business book and it's doubtful that it will qualify as the next corporate buzzword. But, in *Future Focus*, it stands for a combination of qualities that make a company a long-term winner ... and make it worth studying.

When an athlete is said to have staying power, it usually means he or she has physical stamina and knows, better than most, how to play the game.

- Athletes with staying power are intense and completely focused on their sport. Think about Monica Seles' concentration on the tennis court.
- Athletes with staying power are constantly improving their performance. They innovate. Think about Muhammad Ali's incredible boxing.
- Athletes with staying power are still playing when their contemporaries have disappeared. They change their style and their strategy, and they keep playing. Think of Nolan Ryan's seemingly endless summer in baseball.

When a company has staying power, it has these same characteristics. It is focused. It is innovative. And, it is *protean* – it can embrace and adapt to the inevitable challenges that confront it without losing its identity.

Focused. It feels presumptuous to talk about focus when Al Ries, the world's leading authority on the concept, is already providing a running commentary throughout this book. Let's keep it simple:

"When you focus a company," Al says, "you create a powerful, laserlike ability to dominate a market."

When Toyota's name comes up, what do you think of? How about Nokia? Heineken? That is the staying power of focus and those are more companies that made our list.

Innovative. When you focus, you start to hone in on your work and your customers. You can figure out what they need before they do and you can create it. You become innovative.

"Every organization – not just business – needs one core competency: innovation," writes Peter Drucker.

Thirty-five years ago, a steel joist fabricating business run by a guy named Ken Iverson was having a hard time turning a profit because of the cost of the steel. So, Iverson did a little innovating and Nucor was born. That is the staying power of innovation and Nucor made the list.

Protean. Nothing stays the same. Never has, never will. This point has been repeated *ad nauseam* in the 1990s, but it does not mean that companies that stick to their knitting can't succeed over the long haul.

"A visionary company carefully preserves and protects its core ideology, yet all the specific manifestations of its core ideology must be open to change and evolution," wrote Jim Collins and Jerry Porras in *Built to Last*, the conclusion of their six-year study of companies that have enjoyed long-term success.

Tomorrow, in Dean Acheson's future, the barriers between communications networks will disappear. We will effortlessly transmit and receive video, voice, and data from anywhere at any time. Cisco Systems has made 30 acquisitions – $7 billion worth – in six years to remain a leader in the emerging technologies that will demolish those barriers. That is the staying power of the protean company and Cisco made our list.

Focused, innovative, protean: these are qualitative words and subjective traits. You can count how many new products a company releases each year or what percentage of revenues derive from its core business, but ultimately they are reduced to a judgement call.

Which of the *Future Focus* candidates, we asked, have staying power? Which are focused? Which are innovative? And which are protean? We studied their histories, their strategies, their leaders. The list got a lot shorter.

We got a little tougher. How did they stand in their industry? How did their industry stand in the greater economic picture? The list got shorter still.

So, who's left?

There were more than 21 companies left when we got done with our search, but somewhat surprisingly, not a lot more. Forty-six to be exact. We wrangled those down to just over half and during the writing of the book, a few disappeared into mergers and couple more started moving in directions that don't look very promising to us.

We eventually hit our imposed, but fitting, final number of 21. Twenty-one focused, innovative, and protean companies that can teach us about what it will take to succeed tomorrow, in the 21st century.
Here they are:

The *Future Focus 21*

Applied Materials	Bertelsmann	Cisco Systems
Dell Computer	LM Ericsson	Glaxo Wellcome
Heineken	HSBC Holdings	Intel
Interface	Microsoft	Nestle
Nintendo	Nokia	Nucor
Quebecor	Royal Dutch/Shell	Sensormatic Electronics
Tellabs	Toyota Motor	3Com

The *Future Focus 21* are an extraordinarily diverse lot. They range in annual revenues from just under $1 billion to over $100 billion. They are headquartered on three different continents and in nine different countries (although just under half are US-based). They operate in a broad range of industries ranging from games to food to pharmaceuticals (with small concentrations in the computer and communications industries). Their workforces range from 5000 to 185,000 people.

What can we learn from them?

Predicting the future is a fuzzy business, but as the saying goes, hindsight is 20/20. The *Future Focus 21* give us the benefit of their experience. We are privy to their reasoning and follow their successes and failures, often for well over a century.

For all their physical differences, the companies of *Future Focus* also have a few interesting themes in common. It is at these convergence points between the companies that the larger lessons about success in tomorrow's business world emerge.

There are four themes that run through these companies, including the exception or two that prove the rule.

21st-century success is focused

Over and over, the *Future Focus* companies got in trouble when they diversified their businesses. Some diversify sooner and some later, but it rarely fails to happen.

There are a couple of common scenarios: in one, a company creates a product and starts to do well, really well. It feels confident, invincible even. If it can sell widgets so well, just think what it can do with thingamajigs.

In another common scenario: market "X" is hot and our company has some extra cash. Let's grab another piece of the action. Or, the opposite: our company's market is in the doldrums. Let's grab some other piece of the action.

One example in this book bridges two *Future Focus* companies. In 1980, telecom giant LM Ericsson couldn't resist the siren call of computers. It bought a struggling computer maker named Datasaab and took a bath. In 1988, it sold Datasaab at a loss to telecom giant Nokia, which couldn't resist the siren call of computers. Three years later, guess what Nokia does with its losing proposition?

Almost all of the *Future Focus 21* have flirted with diversification. Almost all have lost money on the outside ventures and are extremely focused as of today. Those that continue to operate outside their core businesses are usually in related businesses and are building a vertically integrated operation.

Learn from them. The lesson: get and stay focused.

21st-century success is innovative

The *Future Focus 21* are innovators. They are busy searching out original products and services or they are busy introducing existing products and services in markets that have never seen them before. Either way, they are innovators in the marketplace.

Thirty-five years ago, a supermarket manager named Ron Assaf was running down a shoplifter. Today, the billion-dollar company he founded is selling electronic security labels in over 90 countries.

German soldier Reinhard Mohn is in a US prison camp after being captured in World War II when he learns about book clubs. He is struck by the idea and when the war is over, takes it home with him. Fifty-five years later, Bertelsmann, the company his family founded, is the world's largest direct marketer of books.

The stories go on, but the point remains the same. The lesson: be innovative.

21st-century success is global

With a single exception, every *Future Focus* is a global company and is trying to get more global. A well-focused company replaces the urge to diversify its businesses with the drive to diversify its markets.

Some are early in the push beyond their home countries. When US-based Tellabs started out, "Ma Bell" was the telephone business and their biggest customer. Today, telecom is spilling over geographic borders and the company is following.

Others were born international companies and never looked back. One hundred and ten years ago, an English trader in Russia and a Dutch plantation manager in Sumatra were both bitten by the oil bug. Today, their two companies comprise the Royal Dutch/Shell Group and are at work in over 120 nations.

The world is the market. The lesson: go global.

21st-century success has speed bumps

There isn't a single, sustained upward ride in any of the *Future Focus* histories. Sooner or later, a competitor beats you to the next best thing or the bottom drops out of your customer's market or the whole economy heads south for a breather.

Over half of the *Future Focus 21* have ridden out catastrophic events. They have been through the worldwide Great Depression of 1930s and two world wars. In 1945, the workers at Toyota were rebuilding their bombed out auto plant when they got the news their emperor had surrendered unconditionally. Thirty years later, the same plant was turning out the best-selling car in the world.

Others have faced more common challenges, such as the unexpected demise of their cash cows, their best customers, or their vision of the future. All of them embraced the challenge and battled back.

Their examples prove that business success is not a smooth ride. The lesson: be prepared for hard times.

What's ahead?

The rest of the book explores each of the 21 companies of *Future Focus* in turn. Since each chapter is a portrait of a company, they are organized using photographic metaphors.

Each company is introduced by a quote from one of its leaders, an *Executive snapshot* that offers a fast insight into the strategic vision of the company.

The expert commentary of Al Ries follows. Early in the writing of the profiles Al said, you take care of the trees and I'll take care of the forest. And he has. Al pulls the lessons of each company out front in a style that makes it clear why he is internationally respected. A word to readers who work at these companies and in the same industries: in light of Al's usual consulting rates, his section of the profiles represents a spectacular bargain.

After Al's commentary comes the trees. The company *backdrop* relates its history. Many of these corporate stories have never been published in a book before and all of them contain the fascinating twists and turns that make success in business such a challenge.

The *backdrop* gives way to the company *close-up*. Here is what the *Future Focus* companies look like today, the day before the future. You get a look at how they are structured, their major products, customers, and markets, and where they make money. The *close-up* also offers a glimpse at the future by showing the direction in which each company is moving and the strategies they have adopted to get there.

The final section is company *contacts*, a listing of the contact points for each. If you need to know more, the best place to start is with the companies themselves.

3Com Corporation –
Santa Clara, California, USA

Executive snapshot

Faced with a fast-changing market driven by converging technologies, 3Com is broadening its focus to serve customers no matter what networks they choose.

"We will concentrate on delivering personalized information access to our customers. The Internet has enabled the mass customization of goods and services. The same will be true of information access capabilities," says Eric Benhamou, chairman, 3Com.

3Com backdrop

The value of a network equals the square of the number of its users. That is Metcalfe's Law and it explains that even though a single telephone, fax machine, or connected computer has no value in networking terms, each additional machine added to the network increases its value exponentially. 3Com, founded by Bob Metcalfe to build networks for computers, has reaped the rewards of his law.

In search of a thesis

Harvard "forced me to create Ethernet," says Bob Metcalfe. Late in 1972, in the search for a doctoral thesis that Harvard would accept,

Future focus

Focus. Focus. Focus

If 3Com represents computers, compatibility and communications, then 3Com's success represents focus, focus, focus.

Not that the company didn't make many focusing mistakes. Quite the contrary. Over the years 3Com committed every mistake in the book. What counts, however, is not how many mistakes you make, but whether or not you learn from your mistakes.

3Com learned the hard way. Founded by Bob Metcalfe, inventor of Ethernet, the first practical computer networking system, the company quickly lost its way. Founded to commercialize Ethernet technology, 3Com rapidly moved into both the computer hardware and software businesses.

Only three years after its start-up, 3Com entered the computer market, first with a network server and then with a workstation line. They also bought a personal computer hardware company (Convergent Technologies), which pushed 3Com to the verge of bankruptcy. To make matters worse, 3Com partnered with Microsoft to develop network operating system software to compete with industry leader Novell.

Today, of course, all of these diversification moves look extremely foolish. But in the early eighties, one can understand 3Com's thinking. The network market is small; if 3Com is to grow the company has to branch out into related products and services. This approach might work, if the market remains small and consequently attracts few competitors. But this is self-defeating thinking. If the market is going to remain small, then why would you want to stay in it?

The first question any company that wants to be a 21st-century leader has to ask itself is, "Will this market take off like a rocket?" Very few companies have any control over the future size of their markets. They are passive passengers on the market trains they choose to board. If the train isn't going anywhere, get off. Try to select the fastest market train you can find. Get on it and try to dominate the other passengers. You don't have to do anything more. The train will take you for the ride of your life.

A decade after its founding, 3Com reaches a fork in the road. Metcalfe and the CEO Bill Krause want to concentrate on 3Com's computer business. Eric Benhamou, who came aboard courtesy of an acquisition, wants to turn 3Com into a network company. The board side with Benhamou. Shortly thereafter both Metcalfe and Krause leave the company and Benhamou takes over as CEO. Focus becomes the order of the day. 3Com leaves the network software business and shuts down its workstation operations. 3Com would become a pure network hardware company.

Focus works in the long term but not necessarily in the short term. The year following its focus decision, 3Com revenues drop by 9% and the company loses $28 million. The short-term loss rapidly turns into a long-term gain. In just seven years, revenues at 3Com exploded from $400 million to more than $5 billion. Instead of an also-ran in network software or computer hardware, 3Com became a dominant, if not the dominant, player in network hardware.

Along the way, 3Com made numerous acquisitions to bolster its narrowly focused product line. It was a good strategy, kind of like getting ahead of the pack and then buying all the companies coming up behind you. Key purchases included: BICC Data Networks, Star-Tek, Synernetics, Centrum Communications, NiceCom, AccessWorks, Sonix Communications, Chipcom, Axon Networks, OnStream Networks, Lanworks Technologies.

3Com's biggest buy, of course, was US Robotics for $8.5 billion. The deal included the phenomenally successful electronic organizer, the Palm Pilot. What is more likely to unfocus a company in the long run, the acquisition of a so-so product in a different category or a hot-seller like the Palm Pilot?

The so-so product will gradually fade away leaving the company focused on its core product line. A hot-seller is more dangerous. It can tempt the company to see itself as a major player in "several related lines of businesses." A conglomerate in the making.

As successful as the Palm Pilot is, 3Com wisely decided to spin off its Palm Computing subsidiary into a separate company returning 3Com to its original network hardware focus.

Old Chinese proverb: Man who chases two rabbits, catches neither.

Metcalfe stumbles across an article about Alohanet, a simple, not-very-robust network of computers developed by Norm Abramson at the University of Hawaii. Metcalfe, then working at Xerox's famous Palo Alto Research Center (PARC), adds a retransmission feature to the system, dramatically boosting its delivery reliability.

The revamped Alohanet earns Metcalfe his PhD and in a memo written on May 23, 1973, he names the improved network structure EtherNet, soon to be altered to Ethernet. Along with PARC colleague David Boogs, Metcalfe spends the next couple of years creating the first Ethernet at PARC. They publish a paper on the technology in July 1976, and in December 1977 Xerox is granted a patent on Ethernet.

In January 1979, Metcalfe leaves PARC for consulting. Along with MIT and Digital Equipment Corp., he starts work on establishing Ethernet as an open industry standard. In June that year, he and co-founder Greg Shaw start 3Com to make and market Ethernet networking tools. The company headquarters is Metcalfe's Palo Alto apartment.

Fits and starts

Born ahead of the leading edge of networking, 3Com spends its first year as a consulting firm. Projects for companies, such as General Electric and Exxon, give the start-up $281,000 in revenues for its first full year.

The company's third employee is Howard Charney, the lawyer who filed the company's incorporation papers. Charney joins up in February 1980 and 3Com leaves Metcalfe's apartment for a home of its own in Menlo Park, California.

By September 1980, with the support of Intel, DEC, and Xerox, Ethernet is accepted as the *de jure* standard for computer networks and 3Com is ready to roll. In January 1981, it ships its first commercial product, UNET software, for networking UNIX-based computers.

With one product out and more on the way, 3Com scares up $1.1 million in venture capital in February. In return for the funding, Metcalfe agrees to add an experienced manager to the 3Com team. In March, Bill Krause, a former GM at Hewlett-Packard, joins 3Com as its first president.

That same month, the company's second product – the Ethernet transceiver – ships. The transceiver is produced in a makeshift plant, which is carved out of existing office space. For fiscal 1981, the company's second year, 3Com records $506,000 in revenues and employs 22 people.

New products notwithstanding, 3Com is outrunning its financing and has yet to turn a profit. In late 1981, it adopts the "Four Month Survival Plan." Its main tenets: a quantum increase in sales and distribution, a hiring freeze, and restrictions on spending.

In October 1981, 3Com ships the Q-Bus Ethernet controller, the first non-custom hardware controller offered by the company. Combined with the company's transceiver and cables, the Q-Bus controller provides customers with the first off-the-shelf network-in-a-box. The company moves to new digs in Mountain View, featuring 14,000 square feet and real manufacturing capabilities.

Turning the corner

In the beginning of 1982, 3Com gains some much needed breathing space when it raises another $2.1 million in venture capital. In February, the company's shipments exceed $250,000 per month for the first time. The first shipment of Unibus Ethernet (UE) controllers hits the market in April of 1982. By fiscal year-end '82, sales have more than tripled to $1.8 million and 32 people work at 3Com.

Bob Metcalfe does not come through the company's early trials quite as well. The company's board forces him to step down as CEO and chairman of the company, giving those jobs to Bill Krause. Calling it "the hardest thing I ever did," Metcalfe stays with the company and takes over as head of sales and marketing.

The first network adapter for an IBM personal computer ships in September 1982. Called the I.E., the card combines a controller and transceiver on one board. 3Com also enters the computer market with its first EtherSeries network server. Built on PARC's Altos computer platform, the server offers shared printing, file access, and e-mail.

The business is growing, with especially rapid gains in its Ethernet adapter and transceiver business. 3Com sales for fiscal 1983 hit $4.7 million; employee headcount rises to 48. In March 1984, the company successfully launches its IPO. Shares are offered at $6 each. Within the year, revenues grow to $16.7 million and headcount rises to 136 employees.

In late 1984, 3Com introduces its first internally designed network server, the 3Server. Sporting a 40Mb hard disk, 30286 processor, Ethernet connections, and a proprietary operating system, the 3Server is on the cutting edge. In early 1985, a second shift is added in manufacturing to keep up with customer demand. The fiscal year ends with revenues more than tripling again, to $46.3 million.

The company's growth spurt slows in 1986 as 3Com almost disappears in a merger with Convergent Technologies. In March 1986, the "last 3Com" party is thrown just 2 days before the financing collapses. Revenues still increase almost 50 percent to $64 million, but it is a big drop from the exponential growth of the previous three years.

In late 1986, the company moves once again, this time into two buildings occupying 160,000 square feet. Early in 1987, 3Com ships its 500,000th network adapter on the 15th anniversary of Metcalfe's formal announcement of Ethernet. The company also enters a co-development agreement with Microsoft to develop network operating-system software based on Microsoft's OS/2. The software will compete head-to-head against Novell's market-leading system.

The company expands into workstations with the launch of 3Station in May 1987. 3Station is a stripped-down PC with a hard disk, designed specifically for use in networks. The new business is headed up by Metcalfe and operates off-site as a separate business unit. In fiscal '87, 3Com breaks $100 million in revenues for the first time and brings its total installed base to 32,500 systems that connect more than 400,000 desktops.

3Com Corporation expands further into network infrastructure products with the acquisition of Bridge Communications, Inc. in September 1987. The internetworking market is just emerging and is growing at 75 percent a year. Communications servers, bridges, and gateways, the main products of the Bridge Communications, account for 34 percent of 3Com's total sales within the year.

The company also restructures as it absorbs the Bridge acquisition. It begins integrating its direct major accounts and reseller sales forces. It increases the size of the direct sales organization by 17 percent and adds 124 resellers to its VAR base. Direct sales to large customers account for 26 percent of total sales, VARs 57 percent and OEMs 17 percent.

Three of Bridge's four co-founders leave 3Com to form a new company, as 3Com itself restructures into three divisions. Eric Benhamou, the fourth Bridge founder, heads Software Products, Howard Charney leads Hardware Products, and Metcalfe runs Distributed Systems Division.

In July, 3Com expands its work-group software with the acquisition of Communications Solutions Inc. At the same time, it releases the first shipments of the developers' version of 3+Open LAN Manager, created under its agreement with Microsoft. LAN Manager begins volume shipments in October and 3+Open Mail and 3+Open Internet begin shipping later in the year.

The fight for focus

By the end of fiscal 1988, 3Com is ready for a new goal – its first billion-dollar year. It ships its 1000,000th Ethernet adapter and records its first $100 million quarter in the third quarter of fiscal 1989. In the light of its rapid revenue growth and fiscal 1989 sales of $385 million, 3Com projects it will hit the billion dollar mark in fiscal 1992.

The goal proves to be further from the company's reach as 3Com starts to flounder in fiscal 1990. Internally, the management team is divided with no clear vision for the company. Metcalfe and Krause see 3Com as a computer company along the lines of Sun Microsystems. Benhamou favors concentrating on network infrastructure: "I thought 3Com should revamp into a full network company with a coordinated architecture that included a hub, router, and switches," says Benhamou. "As for the workstation business, I proposed to either sell it or wind it down."

Even though computers account for a hefty portion of 3Com's revenues, external developments support Benhamou's vision. The partnership with Microsoft collapses as Microsoft begins selling LAN Manager directly to customers, bypassing established licensed distributors such as 3Com. Novell's Netware emerges as the clear winner in the battle over network management software. (Metcalfe later describes working with Microsoft as "mating with a black widow spider.")

Growth stalls and fiscal 1990 revenues rise slightly to $419 million. The company's board endorses Benhamou's plan, appointing him president in April 1990. Metcalfe leaves the company 30 days later.

Benhamou immediately begins repositioning 3Com as "the leading independent global data networking company." In August, Krause resigns the CEO spot and Benhamou takes full control of 3Com. The new CEO leaves the network software business and begins downsizing the workgroup systems hardware business, reducing the workforce by 12 percent and taking a $67 million restructuring charge. (Unable to find a buyer for the workstation business, 3Com eventually discontinues the operation.)

The new 3Com returns to its roots in networking hardware and focuses on four product lines: network adapters, terminal servers, wiring hubs, and internetworking platforms. At the same time the company moves to open systems announcing that its products will run Novell as well as Microsoft software.

In August 1990, 3Com begins building its infrastructure product depth by expanding into intelligent wiring hubs through a strategic alliance with SynOptics. The company also begins shipping the MultiConnect hub and has a stackable hub technology under development. The EtherLink 16TP is introduced in early 1991 and quickly becomes the best-selling adapter in 3Com's history. In a move designed to bolster customer confidence, 3Com becomes the first manufacturer to offer a lifetime warranty on its Ethernet adapters.

In the fall of 1990, the company moves to the new Great America Campus in Santa Clara. It uses the move to reduce costs by updating its manufacturing lines and processes with new and more automated equipment. By the end of the fiscal year, Benhamou is announcing the completion of the restructuring. Revenues drop nine percent for fiscal 1991 to just under $400 million and the company records a loss of $27.7 million.

The race for market share

With its direction clear, in fiscal 1992 3Com starts a run of growth using new products and acquisitions that drives the company from $400 million in annual revenues to over $5.7 billion in 1999.

In September 1991, the company launches a joint venture in Japan, 3Com Kabushiki Kaisha (K.K.). In January, it purchases BICC Data Networks, a $75 million hub maker in the UK, the largest in Europe. 3Com now offers the broadest range of structured wiring hubs and networking products available from a single vendor.

The company also opens parts banks and service centers in Europe and the Asia-Pacific region, and begins construction on a 60,000-square-foot manufacturing plant in Ireland. 3Com extends its presence into China with an agreement with Tsinghua University Science and Technology Development Corporation to operate a service and repair center on mainland China.

In November 1991, the company ships its 2000,000th Ethernet adapter. By the end of fiscal year 1992, 3Com ships more than 3 million of the boards. The company begins its recovery with $4.2 million in profits on $408 million in sales.

In fiscal 1993, 3Com launches a bombardment of new products that will drive growth and serve as the basis for further innovations for the next several years. These include its second-generation stackable hubs, the LinkBuilder FMS, new TokenLink token ring adapters based on IBM's Tropic ASIC, and the NETBuilder II token ring router. It also introduces the EtherLink III, the industry's first ASIC-based, third-generation adapters. The new adapters are the price and performance leaders in the marketplace and precipitate a minor crisis as orders overwhelm production capacity.

The company continues its expansion into Europe, opening its Irish manufacturing facility in September 1992. The new plant doubles 3Com's adapter manufacturing capacity and makes it the only major networking company to support customers with development, manufacturing, distribution, service and support operations in Europe. The company also opens new offices in Japan, Spain and the United Arab Emirates, bringing the number of countries in which 3Com has a direct presence to 18.

In February 1993, 3Com expands its product depth in hubs even further when it acquires Star-Tek, Inc., a maker of token ring hubs and network management products. Sales hit a record $617.2 million and net income is $38.6 million, also a new record.

In fiscal 1994, growth through acquisition continues as the company acquires two more companies: Synernetics, the company's long-time switching partner for the LinkBuilder, and Centrum Communications, a leading remote access firm that brings with it the AccessBuilder product line.

Continuing its new product run, 3Com introduces the NETBuilder Remote Office family and PCMCIA Ethernet/modem adapters for laptops, which within the year lead the market. The company also launches the SuperStack line in May 1994.

The company earns a spot on the *Fortune 500* for the first time as revenues hit $827 million.

In October 1994, 3Com acquires NiceCom, an Israel-based leader in ATM switching. As usage on the Internet begins to explode, the company also undertakes a major expansion into the remote access market with two additional deals: AccessWorks, a maker of ISDN modems, and Sonix Communications, an ISDN internetworking products manufacturer.

Strong demand for adapters translates into expanded manufacturing capacity. Both the Santa Clara and Ireland plants are operating three lines almost continuously in order to ship 8 million cards.

The demand for adapters and the added revenues of acquired companies gives 3Com its overdue billion-dollar year. In fiscal 1995, the company records $125 million in profits on almost $1.3 billion in sales.

At the start of fiscal 1996, 3Com makes its biggest acquisition yet when it buys Chipcom for $775 million in stock. Chipcom's high-end chassis hubs and switches extend 3Com's product line making it the second largest vendor in the intelligent hub market. In March 1996, the company acquires AXON Networks and its remote network management software for $65 million.

The OfficeConnect product line for small businesses is launched. Consisting of ISDN routers, manageable hubs and print/fax servers, OfficeConnect provides a complete LAN/WAN connectivity system. With the help of Chipcom, sales almost double to $2.3 billion and profits grow to $178 million. 3Com employs 5190 people.

3Com ships its new Ethernet and Fast Ethernet NICs at the start of fiscal 1997. By year-end, the new Fast Ethernet card will push the company past Intel into the leading market slot for those adapters.

In October 3Com acquires broadband ATM supplier, OnStream Networks, for $245 million. Within a month of the acquisition, 3Com launches the first new products created with OnStream's expertise, AccessBuilder 9300 and AccessBuilder 9010 ATM systems for small businesses and Web sites.

Global expansion continues as the company breaks ground for a manufacturing and distribution facility in Singapore. The new operation will serve Asia.

In June 1997, 3Com more than doubles its revenues, jumping into the second slot in the worldwide data networking market behind Cisco Systems, on the power of the company's largest purchase to date, the acquisition of the world's leading modem maker, US Robotics. The deal is valued at $8.5 billion and gives 3Com leadership in modems and remote access technology, as well as the leading handheld connected organizer, PalmPilot. Not yet content, in the fourth quarter of fiscal 1998, the company also acquires Lanworks Technologies, Inc., a provider of PC network boot technologies and products. The acquisition is valued at $13 million.

3Com also boosts its manufacturing capacity, bringing online an additional 170,000 square feet in Ireland and completing the new manufacturing facility in Singapore. It starts construction on a 525,000-square-foot research, development and manufacturing facility in Marlborough, Massachusetts.

3Com translates its newfound clout into some high-profile alliances with companies such as Siemens and Newbridge Networks Corporation. The Palm Computing business unit establishes a strategic alliance with IBM to manufacture the WorkPad PC companion and with Qualcomm to develop wireless communications products that build off the Palm Computing platform. Revenues for fiscal 1998 hit $5.4 billion.

In 1999, the company acquires a French communications software maker Smartcode and Interactive Web Concepts, a maker of e-business technology. 3Com also signs a $1 billion technology sharing alliance with IBM, and computer telephony pacts with Alcatel and Microsoft. The Palm VII, featuring wireless Internet access, is released.

In March 2000 3Com sells a minority stake in the Palm computing division to the public in a $875 million offering in one of the hottest IPOs of the year. The company says it will refocus on its core business and sell its modem business.

3Com close-up

One of the most compelling of today's trends is the growth of networks. Data, voice, and video-based networks are not only expanding their reach, they are themselves converging into a seamless structure of links spanning the globe. The business of building and connecting these networks is a growth industry and Silicon Valley-based 3Com Corporation is one of its primary players.

Computers, **Com**patibility, and **Com**munication are the three "coms" behind the company name. The founding player in the global market for data networking products, 3Com is the second largest company in the overall industry, and the largest in local and wide area network (LANs and WANs) hardware market.

The network market is among the fastest growing in the world, exceeding $50 billion in 2000. In addition to the continuing need for the corporate computer networks that created the industry, huge new markets, such as network equipment for Internet service providers, telecommunications companies, small businesses, and consumers, have emerged in the past decade.

With $5.77 billion in annual revenues, 3Com delivers end-to-end connectivity solutions to every major segment of these markets. The company's installed base totals over 100 million network connections worldwide, more than any of its competitors.

At the end of fiscal 1999, 3Com had 13,027 full-time employees. Of that total, 3184 were employed in engineering, 4141 in sales, marketing and customer service, 3465 in manufacturing, and 2237 in finance and administration.

3Com is a global company. It has offices and plants in 49 countries and on 6 continents. The company maintains dedicated research and development, manufacturing, and sales and service organizations worldwide. Roughly 47 percent of its fiscal 1999 sales were generated internationally.

3Com conducts high-volume manufacturing in the US, Ireland, Israel, and Singapore. The Singapore facility opened in fiscal 1998 and is 3Com's first production site in the Asia-Pacific region. In the US, 3Com has manufacturing operations in California, Illinois, Massachusetts, and Utah. Purchasing, mechanical assembly, burn-in, testing, final assembly, and quality assurance functions are performed at all of these plants.

The company's customer support operations are as extensive as the networks built with its products. Support facilities are located in the US, Asia-Pacific, Europe and Latin America. These include 140 parts and logistics centers and 8 technical call centers, which communicate with customers in more than 15 languages.

3Com's worldwide service and support organization is able to provide 7×24 customer support. Customer services include design, installation and maintenance on-site, by phone, or online via the Internet. Customer-specific support is built into 3Com's Internet site. Additionally, 3Com provides a variety of training services, including on-site and computer-based training courses.

Unlike its major competitors, the company sells its products via every conceivable distribution channel. 3Com has approximately 180 sales offices in 49 countries. The direct sales organization is focused on large enterprise and carrier/service provider customers worldwide. Indirect sales channels include systems integrators, VARs, distributors, national dealers and resellers, and OEMs. Many products are also sold through electronics catalogs and retailers. 3Com also counts some of the world's largest PC manufacturers among their industry partners. Gateway and Dell, for example, offer 3Com network products in their custom-made computers. IBM is selling the company's PalmPilot handheld organizer as the IBM WorkPad.

In 1997, with the acquisition of US Robotics, 3Com restructured into three major units based on its major customer and product segments. These are Carrier Systems, Enterprise Systems, and Client Access.

- *Carrier Systems* designs, sells, and maintains the communications networks used by 3Com's carrier and service provider customers, companies such as traditional telecommunications providers, local exchange carriers, and Internet service providers. Among its customers are nine of the ten largest North American ISPs, including America Online and CompuServe. This market is served directly by the company.
- *Enterprise Systems* creates the intranet and extranet infrastructures in use by large companies and institutions. Typically, these networks have more than 500 users and include organizations in the corporate, education, retail, health care and government sectors. 3Com enterprise customers include NationsBank, GMAC Commercial Mortgage, Stanford University, Nagasaki Institute and the US Federal Court system. The company also serves this market directly.
- *Client Access* provides 3Com products for the small and medium business, consumers, and home office segments. The company reaches these markets through independent distributors, resellers, and retailers.

During the 1990s, 3Com has purposely extended its product lines to become a broad-based supplier of all the building blocks of network systems. The company sells more than 800 hardware and software networking products. These include switches, hubs, remote access systems, routers, network management software, network interface cards (NICs), modems, and handheld organizers.

The company's products are valued in the field for their quality and particularly, for their compatibility with other hardware and software. In 1997, major industry publications bestowed more than 60 best-in-class awards on 3Com products. The 3Com name ranks in the top three, with Microsoft and Hewlett-Packard, in corporate and distribution channel brand recognition.

3Com's product lines fall into two major categories: systems products, which make up the physical structure of networks; and client access products, which connect people to those networks. A third category, handheld connected organizers, was acquired along with US Robotics in 1997 and spun off in 1999.

Systems products

Sales of systems products contributed $2.61 billion, or 45 percent, of 3Com's total sales in fiscal 1999. These products include switches, hubs, routers, and remote access products.

A switch is a device that filters and forwards packets of information between the segments of a network. LANs (local area networks) that use switches to join segments are called switched LANs. Switches can also provide direct links to either the desktop or server. Application-specific integrated circuits (ASICs) can be embedded into switches to improve their performance and reliability.

3Com switches are available in chassis form or stacks, which allow network expansion. The company's desktop switching devices are first in the market. The LAN switching devices are ranked second.

The company switch brands include OfficeConnect Ethernet/Fast Ethernet switches and SuperStack II switches for smaller networks. For large enterprise LANs, 3Com sells the CoreBuilder series. The PathBuilder series is designed for the WANs (wide area networks) market.

Hubs provide a common connection point for the devices in a network or to connect segments of a LAN. A hub contains multiple ports. When data arrives at a port, it is copied to the other ports so that all segments of the LAN can see it. 3Com's Fast Ethernet, Ethernet, and stackable hubs are all ranked first in the market.

3Coms hub brands include OfficeConnect for small networks, SuperStack II hubs for medium and large enterprises, mixed Ethernet, Fast Ethernet, and Token Ring workgroup hubs, and Gigabit Ethernet workgroup hubs.

Routers connect LANs and are used extensively on the Internet, where they forward packets of information from one host to another. The company offers SuperStack II, NETBuilder, and OfficeConnect NETBuilder routers.

Remote access products enable external logon to networks. They give remote users, such as telecommuters, Internet and online users, corporate suppliers, and a host of other users access to the network from a distance. 3Com's remote access equipment utilizes the company's proprietary HiPer Digital Signaling Processing (DSP) technology.

3Com's remote access products include three lines: SuperStack II Remote Access series for mid-sized enterprises and service providers; the AccessBuilder series for service providers with large dial-up networks and large corporate intranets; and the Total Control Remote Access series for the carrier level of network access.

Client access products

Client access products are the devices that users need to connect to networks. These encompass two main product groups: NICs (network interface cards) and modems. In fiscal 1999, 3Com sold $2.59 billion of these products, which represents 45 percent of total sales. The company is ranked first in the worldwide markets for both of these product groups.

NICs are expansion cards that are installed in computers so they can be connected to a network. NICs are used in network servers, personal computers, portable computers, and workstations. 3Com offers NICs for various networking technologies, including Ethernet, Fast Ethernet, Gigabit Ethernet, Token Ring, FDDI, and ATM connectivity.

Modems enable computers to transmit information over telephone lines by converting data from digital to analog form, and vice versa. They have, with the rise of the Internet, become an essential component of the personal computer.

3Com makes and markets modems for desktop and mobile users. It also provides the software used to install and use modems. The company's desktop modems include the US Robotics, Courier, and 3ComImpact brands.

For portable computers, the company makes smaller PC cards. These offer access to LANs in the form of NICs, modems for WANs, and cards that combine the two functions. This family is sold under the Megahertz brand name.

Handheld connected organizers

3Com acquired PalmPilot, the leading brand in handheld connected organizers, in its merger with US Robotics. These organizers represent a relatively new category of computing: electronic personal organizers, which act as companion products to desktop and laptop computers. In 1999, prior to the spin-off, these products contributed $569 million in revenues.

Electronic organizers help people keep track of a variety of information, such as daily appointments and phone numbers. They can also be connected to networks, allowing mobile retrieval of information from LANs and, with add-ons, connection to the Internet.

A docking cradle is used to pass information between personal organizers the user's computer. The handhelds also include character recognition software that allows users to input information by "writing" with a stylus.

3Com's organizers include the PalmPilot, Palm, and new wireless models. These use the Palm Computing operating system software, which now competes with a scaled-down Windows CE software from Microsoft and is supported by over 7500 independent software developers who are producing a variety of applications, utilities and games for the organizers.

Income statement

Year	Revenue ($m)	Net income ($m)	Net profit margin	Employees
1999	5,772.1	403.9	7.0%	13,027
1998	5,420.4	30.2	0.6%	12,920
1997	3,147.1	374.0	11.9%	7,109
1996	2,327.1	177.9	7.6%	5,190
1995	1,295.3	125.7	9.7%	3,072
1994	827.0	(28.7)	—	2,306
1993	617.2	38.6	6.3%	1,971
1992	408.4	4.2	1.0%	1,963
1991	398.6	(27.7)	—	1,731
1990	419.1	20.5	4.9%	2,008

Stock history

Year	Stock price ($) FY High	FY Low	FY Close	P/E High	Low	Per share ($) Earns	Div.	Book value
1999	51.13	20.00	27.31	47	18	1.09	0.00	8.74
1998	59.69	25.25	25.38	746	316	0.08	0.00	7.82
1997	81.38	24.00	48.50	57	17	1.42	0.00	8.51
1996	53.63	30.44	49.25	53	30	1.02	0.00	5.80
1995	34.63	10.06	32.00	52	15	0.66	0.00	3.36
1994	15.94	4.91	11.75	—	—	(0.23)	0.00	2.16
1993	10.00	2.41	6.75	33	8	0.30	0.00	2.09
1992	3.75	1.69	2.94	91	42	0.04	0.00	1.80
1991	4.75	1.34	2.16	—	—	(0.25)	0.00	1.75
1990	6.97	2.50	3.44	39	14	0.18	0.00	2.00

1999 year-end financials

Debt ratio	0.9%
Return on equity	13.5%
Cash ($m)	952.2
Current ratio	2.85
Long-term debt ($m)	30.4
Shares Outstanding ($m)	365.8
Dividend yield	0.0%
Dividend payout	0.0%
Market value ($m)	9,990.1

Financial data provided by Hoover's Online (www.hoovers.com) and Media General Financial Services, Inc.

3Com contacts

3Com Corporation   Phone: 408–326–5000
5400 Bayfront Plaza   Fax: 408–326–5001
Santa Clara, CA 95052–8145, USA URL: www.3com.com

CEO: Eric Benhamou   CFO: Christopher Paisley   HR: Eileen Nelson

Applied Materials, Inc. – Santa Clara, California, USA

Executive snapshot

The semiconductor industry is cyclical, but over the long haul, demand grows steadily. And that's what Applied Materials is banking on.

"As the market for computing, consumer, communications and Internet-related products continues to grow, we believe Applied Materials, with our technology leadership and global infrastructure, will have an excellent opportunity to capitalize on this growth," says CEO and chairman, James Morgan.

Applied Materials backdrop

The funny thing about gold rushes is that while most people are intensely focused on striking the mother lode, a myriad of opportunities to get rich by outfitting the miners themselves are often overlooked. That is one lesson that Michael McNeilly had already figured out by the time the silicon gold rush of the late 1960s was dawning.

Supplying the innovators

The first semiconductor manufacturers, as we'll see later with *Future Focus* company Intel, have a monumental challenge on their hands.

Future focus

Putting all your chips into one basket

"The hottest high-tech company you never heard of." That's the moniker that insiders use when they talk about Applied Materials, Inc.

James Morgan, Applied Materials CEO, calls his organization, "A very unique corporation that has the real potential to become one of the great global corporations of the 21st century."

We agree. And James Morgan is the primary reason why.

When you study successful companies, you will usually find that one decision is responsible for most of the organization's success. Many times that key decision was made by the founders when the company was launched. It's rare to find a company where a crucial strategic decision was made in midstream.

Applied Materials is the exception. When Morgan took over the 8-year-old, money-losing company in 1976, he promptly dropped five businesses to focus on the sixth: chip-making equipment for the semiconductor industry. This was the key decision that set the stage for "one of the great global corporations of the 21st century."

The rest was execution. But management in most companies places far too much emphasis on the power of pure execution. Without the right strategy, you cannot execute your way to success. With the right strategy, you greatly improve your ability to execute well. Putting all your chips in one basket automatically makes your company an expert in that business.

Customers cannot be experts in every supplier's business. Expertise is often the most important ingredient of the purchase. Companies depend on their suppliers to supply them with the right equipment for the job to be done.

By narrowing its focus, Applied Materials became "the expert" in chip-making equipment for wafer-fabricating systems. Over the years Applied eventually became more than three times larger than its nearest domestic competitor.

When you are the leader, you have the resources to outspend your competitors in research and development, the key area for a high-tech company. For a number of years, Applied Materials spent more in R&D than its nearest competitor received in revenue. How can you compete with that?

When you are the leader, your chances are better to pioneer the new technologies that could threaten your leadership. Technology is like a horse race. If there are five potential winners in a technology race, the leader often has the resources to bet on them all. A smaller company with limited resources, on the other hand, has to pick and choose only one or two.

That's why it's not surprising that the leader is usually the first to introduce technological winners. Applied Materials was first in the "dry etching" process where it remains the leader today. First in processing systems for the 200 mm silicon wafer. First in processing systems for the 300 mm wafer.

Having a narrow focus should not be confused with having a narrow line of products. Applied Materials in focused on chip-making equipment, period. On the other hand, it markets the broadest line of chip-making equipment in the industry. (Starbucks has a narrow focus, too. It's a retail establishment that focuses on coffee, but not just one kind of coffee. Starbucks has 32 different kinds of coffee from six countries around the world. In the same way, Toys "R" Us is focused on toys, but also carries the broadest line of toys in the retail world.)

How narrow is too narrow? That's a judgment call. Any category can be divided into an infinite number of categories. Take the shoe category. Shoes can be divided into athletic shoes (Nike's focus) and many other types of shoes. Athletic shoes can be divided into tennis shoes (K-Swiss's focus) and many other types of athletic shoes.

Applied Materials has a chip-making equipment focus. But the company is in nine different segments of the chip-making market. In six of these segments Applied Materials is the leader with an average market share of 53 percent. In one segment the company is in second place with 31 percent of the market. And in two segments Applied is in third place with an average market share of 15 percent. (Key question: Unless the last two segments are vital elements in a full-line strategy, why not drop them?)

> One blemish on Applied Materials' track record is its joint venture with Komatsu that cost the company upwards of $58 million. The reason is simple: lack of focus. Unless the company is in the same industry, any joint venture with an outside-the-industry firm is automatically suspect. What does a tractor company know about silicon-wafer manufacturing equipment?
>
> And if the company is in the same industry, why not buy them and increase your focus? The larger the market share of an industry a company has on a worldwide basis, the more powerful the company is.

Not only do they have to invent new products, such as memory chips and microprocessors, they also have to create the manufacturing processes and equipment to produce them successfully. And, that is where McNeilly sees his opening.

The young engineer quickly realizes that a chip maker's profitability is highly dependent on manufacturing yields and that yields are dependent on reliable, high-quality production equipment. So, McNeilly raises $100,000 in seed capital and starts Applied Materials, Inc. In 1967, with a staff of five, the company opens for business in Mountain View, California.

Within the year, Applied's first product, a machine capable of depositing a very thin film of silicon dioxide on a wafer, is complete. Revenues are a modest $110,000 in the company's first full year, losses are almost 3 times that high at $300,000. In 1969, Applied adds the first CVD reactor to its product line. The company still loses $300,000, but this time on revenues of $2.7 million.

As the 1970s dawn, Applied continues to expand its product lines. In 1970, it produces the first commercial production system for depositing the films used in LED displays and, in 1971, the first epitaxial reactor. Revenues grow to $7.2 million in 1970 and shrink in 1971 to $4.2 million. The red ink continues.

In 1972, however, McNeilly's ship comes in and the company goes public. The cash infusion puts the company on an even keel and by year-end, it is shipping systems to every major semiconductor manufacturer. That year, with sales of $6.3 million and 155 employees, Applied turns its first profit recording a gain of $700,000.

Misadventures in diversity

Applied uses its newfound wealth to diversify into varied supply segments including raw materials, chemistries, and equipment. Over the next two years, Applied jumps into five new ventures, including the acquisition of silicon wafer maker Galamar in 1974.

"The business of support products and services to the semiconductor seemed boundless to McNeilly," writes longtime CEO and chairman James Morgan in *Cracking the Japanese Market*, "and he wanted it all." And, up until year-end 1974, it seems he might get it. Applied records a $2.3 million profit on sales of $20 million.

A nationwide recession in 1975 puts an end to McNeilly's expansionist dreams. Applied's sales drop 45 percent to $13 million and the company loses $500,000. The company's lack of focus hinders its ability to weather the storm and in 1976, it loses $3.3 million on sales of $17 million. Applied's board revolts and James Morgan, a venture capitalist, is brought in as the new CEO.

Morgan is an early and ardent advocate of focus. He looks over the company and finds five of its six businesses are, in his words, "either marginal or outright liabilities." He decides to put all of Applied's chips on one bet, its core business: semiconductor manufacturing equipment.

It takes two years to right the company. Galamar and other non-core units are sold, and restructuring costs mount. In 1977, sales recover to $23.7 million, but losses remain high at $4.2 million. In 1978, the Intel 8086 creates a small but fast-growing market for personal computers and a corresponding need for more chip-making equipment. Sales grow to $27.8 million and profits explode to $4 million. Applied is back on track.

Focused expansion

As Applied regains its health, Morgan turns his gaze outward. If the company focuses on semiconductor manufacturing equipment, he reasons, it must aggressively sell its products in the US, Europe, and Japan – the major chip-making regions of the world.

In 1979, the company ends its distribution agreement with Kanematsu, a Japanese trading company. It forms Applied Materials Japan, a joint venture to directly market the company's products, which is run by seven former Kanematsu employees. The venture makes Applied the first US company in its industry to have a direct sales organization in Japan and revenues from the country double to over $6 million in its first full year.

The company also begins to expand its product lines to cover additional operations in the manufacture of semiconductors. Dan Maydan leaves Bell Labs to join the company. He is followed by Sasson Somekh and David N.K. Wang. The trio forms the core of Applied's new product development effort. In 1981, the company takes the first step in developing turnkey chip manufacturing systems and introduces the first commercially successful plasma etch system.

Applied also restructures its Japanese joint venture into a wholly owned subsidiary, another first for the US industry, in 1981. The Japanese expansion effort proves a fortuitous strategy when, in the early 1980s, the country's government targets semiconductors as a strategic industry and economically supports the growth of Applied's customer base. In 1983, Applied becomes the first non-Japanese company ever to receive funding from the Japan Development Bank. The bank loans the company money to develop a Japanese Technology Center. That year, Japan accounts for 33 percent of the company's sales, which break the $100 million revenue mark for the first time.

Applied opens the 65,000 square foot Narita Technology Center in 1984. Japanese revenues climb from 1982's $34 million, to $52 million. In 1985, Applied is able to boast that it is the first company in its industry to manufacture, market, and support its products in the US, Europe, and Japan. The expansion quickly pays off, helping Applied weather, with only a short stumble in its growth, a major recession brought on by overcapacity and a price war among chip makers in late 1984, 1985, and 1986.

Growing through innovation

During the lull, Applied records a host of firsts: it opens its first service center in China; becomes the first company to offer performance guarantees on its equipment; and, growing into another front-end manufacturing market, it introduces the first fully automated ion implanter.

More significantly, the company begins development of an innovative new design platform in chip manufacturing intended to replace traditional batch processing with a higher-yield, customizable design: the single-wafer, multi-chamber system.

In 1987, Applied releases its first product on the new platform, the Precision 5000 dielectric CVD system. It quickly gains industry-wide acceptance. Industry observers label it "the most successful product introduction in the history of the semiconductor equipment industry." In the next year, Applied adds etch processes to the platform and sales take off. By year-end, sales more than double to $362 million. It is the beginning of a growth trend that will not slow for the next decade.

In 1989, CVD tungsten processes are added to the Precision platform and Applied becomes the first company to release a system capable of processing the larger, new 200 mm silicon wafers. Annual revenues break over $500 million.

As the 1990s dawn, Applied Materials joins the ranks of the *Fortune 500*. In 1990, it expands its core technologies and introduces a second single-wafer, multi-chamber platform, called the Endura PVD (physical vapor deposition) system. In 1991, company revenues hit $638 million, with over $250 million coming from its Japanese subsidiary. Applied also takes an early step toward realizing the paperless business when it eliminates paper in its customers' clean-room environments and puts its equipment manuals on CD-ROMs.

Applied becomes the leading semiconductor equipment manufacturer in the world in 1992, a position it still holds. The company introduces a third single-wafer, multi-chamber platform, the Centura system aimed at high-temperature thin-film markets. Revenues hit $750 million.

In 1993, product diversity and global sales earn Applied its first $1 billion year, the first in its industry. In March, the first Precision 5000 system is inducted into the Smithsonian Institution's permanent collection of Information Age technology. It is installed next to the first semiconductor chip.

The company, seeing big future markets for the thin-film transistor and liquid crystal display manufacturing equipment used to produce flat panel displays, forms a joint venture corporation with Japan's Komatsu Ltd., to target the market. Each owns 50 percent of Applied Komatsu Technology.

Within two years, Applied has doubled its revenues again to just over $3 billion; net income exceeds $450 million. That year (1995), the company ships its 1000th dielectric CVD system and enters the rapid thermal processing (RTP) market.

In 1996, the company releases a fourth single-wafer, multi-chamber platform, the Optima which is intended for high-volume CVD applications. It becomes the first in the industry to open full-blown technology centers in Korea and Taiwan. It also receives its biggest single order ever, for equipment worth $153 million for Hyundai Electronics for a new fab (chip fabrication plant) in South Korea.

Preparing for slow times

Although the company's winning streak continues through year-end with $4.1 billion in revenues and income of $600 million, in the second half of the year, over-production and slashed memory chip prices cause the cyclical semiconductor industry to turn down once again. The company reacts quickly, reducing its workforce by 800 employees and consolidating facilities. These actions produce a restructuring charge of $25.1 million.

In 1997, Applied ships its 5000th single-wafer, multi-chamber system. It also becomes the first company to ship systems capable of processing the newly enlarged 300 mm silicon wafer that promises to become the new industry standard. To help support the full conversion to 300 mm program, Applied invests $430 million in research and product development facilities, including a dedicated 300 mm development and applications center in Santa Clara, California.

The company's Austin, Texas manufacturing center expansion is also completed as part of a master plan to build a manufacturing infrastructure capable of supporting at least $10 billion in annual revenues.

Applied enters the process diagnostics and control equipment market in 1997, building the industry's first complete in-house metrology lab for 300 mm wafers. It acquires two companies, Opal, Inc. and Orbot Instruments, Ltd for $300 million. Applied adds its lines of CD-scanning electron microscopes and wafer and reticle inspection systems to its existing products.

On October 24, 1997, $1000 invested in Applied stock 20 years ago is worth $563,831. Company revenues, however, are down slightly for the first time in 10 years and net income falls below $500 million.

In 1998, Applied opens its Equipment and Process Integration Center to help chip makers create and test the manufacturing processes for the new copper-based circuitry that may well be the next standard for chips. EPIC's first product module, the Copper Interconnect Equipment Set Solution, allows the company's customers to test copper interconnect designs quickly before installing equipment in their fabs, dramatically reducing start-up time and accelerating time to market for their product introductions. Building its diagnostics and control business, Applied acquires Consilium, Inc., a leading supplier of integrated semiconductor and electronics manufacturing software and services, in a stock-for-stock merger.

Year-end sales continue to languish at $4.04 billion. Net income takes a big hit, dropping over 50 percent to $231 million because of continuing contractions in the marketplace. The company records $170 million in non-recurring operating expenses, including $50 million for severance costs of 2000 employees and another $50 million for consolidation of facilities.

Applied also records costs of $58 million for the discontinued operations of its 50/50 joint venture, Applied Komatsu Technology, Inc. (AKT). The venture has not performed to expectations and will drop all of its product lines, except a CVD chip-fabrication system. Applied buys Komastu's stake in the remaining business.

In 1999, Applied buys Obsidian, a maker of chemical mechanical polishing systems, and in early 2000 announces it will expand into the photolithography market with the $2 billion acquisition of equipment maker Etec Systems.

Applied Materials close-up

The transformation of silicon into semiconductors is 20th-century alchemy and it has proven much more profitable than medieval efforts to turn lead into gold. Why have the new alchemists succeeded where the old failed? Perhaps the secret to their success lies in their lab equipment. Today's equipment is a far cry from the mortar and pestle, and more often than not it comes from a Santa Clara, California-based company named Applied Materials, Inc.

Fortune has dubbed Applied Materials "the no-name high-tech star," saying its dominance in the low-profile production equipment niche of the computer industry is as strong as Microsoft's and Intel's in software and microprocessors. Applied is the 800 lb gorilla of the semiconductor capital equipment market. It is the largest producer of wafer fabrication systems and services for the worldwide semiconductor industry.

The company's 1999 annual sales were $4.85 billion and their customer list reads like a who's who of the global chip business. In fact, the company has the highest level of globalization in its industry. Applied Materials' geographic sales diversity illustrates the point with North American sales contributing 34 percent of revenue, Taiwan 20 percent, Japan 17 percent, Europe 16 percent, South Korea 7 percent, and Asia-Pacific (China and Singapore) 6 percent.

Because of the highly technical knowledge required to sell its products, Applied has established its own direct sales force, with sales, service, and spare parts offices in each of its largest market regions. The company has over 80 sales and service offices worldwide, with 26 offices located in the US, 16 in Europe, 27 in Japan, 7 in Korea, 2 in Taiwan and 6 in Asia-Pacific.

Existing customers are served by the Installed Base Support Services (IBSS) Group, which provides service, parts, training, and upgrades. IBSS employs over 2500 customer and process support engineers who are stationed near or in customer plants in a dozen countries.

Working closely with customers to design unique production systems, the company's research and development operations are also conducted internationally. Engineering divisions are located in the United States, the UK, Israel and Japan, and there are process support and customer demonstration laboratories in the United States, the UK, Israel, Japan, Korea and Taiwan. During fiscal 1999, Applied spent over $682 million on R&D.

Manufacturing is primarily conducted in the US, at the company's Austin, Texas complex and in Santa Clara, California. There are additional manufacturing facilities in Israel, Japan, Korea, Taiwan, and the UK. In 1999 Applied Materials employed 12,755 people worldwide.

Chip making is a complex, technologically demanding business. Chips are made from silicon wafers and manufactured in layers. Depending on the design of the chip, each layer or "film" will undergo various operations, such as etching, deposition, heat treatments, or polishing. Throughout this cycle, testing is done to ensure the quality of the work.

Applied is notable for the expanse of its product lines. The company competes in so-called front-end processes of wafer fabrication. This is mainly process manufacturing as opposed to the back-end assembly and test operations. The company manufactures equipment for film deposition, etching, ion implantation, rapid thermal processing (RTP), chemical mechanical polishing (CMP), metrology and wafer/reticle inspection. This translates to a total worldwide market share of 15–20 percent. (All market-share data as of year-end 1998.)

Chip-making equipment is expensive. Over half the cost of a new chip fabrication plant, or fab, is in the equipment, and fabs usually cost between $1 billion and $2 billion to build.

Applied has organized itself into a series of five major product-based business groups that are loosely structured around the main technologies in the wafer fabrication process. These fabrication technologies are applied to chips in combinations. Each chip will pass through a variety of these machines on its way to final inspection and packaging.

Etch Product Business Group

In chip making, etching is a process that removes selected material from the layers of a chip. Today, dry (or plasma) etching is the standard technology used by chip makers and it is one of the most common processes in semiconductor manufacturing. In dry etching, an electrical field is applied to gases creating plasma energy, which in turn breaks the gases down into molecules capable of rapidly etching the film layer.

Applied Materials introduced its first dry etch equipment in 1981 and now holds 35 percent of the market, the leading share in the industry. The company produces systems in each of three main material applications: metal, silicon, and dielectric etch. This constitutes a complete line of dry etch processing solutions.

The company's etch systems process single wafers in a multi-chamber design. Metal etch systems include the Metal Etch DPS (decoupled plasma source) Centura, the Metal Etch MxP Centura, and the Precision

5000. Silicon etch tools feature the same DPS technology in a similarly named line of products. Dielectric products include the IPS Centura and the HDP (high-density plasma) Centura systems.

Metal Deposition Product (MDP) Business Group

Metal deposition processes add metals to chips. During deposition, a layer of electrically conductive metal is deposited to connect the films. The MPD group provides semiconductor manufacturers with the technology that is used to form these interconnects between the circuits. Two different technologies are used to create metal "wiring." They are physical vapor deposition (PVD) and chemical vapor deposition (CVD).

In PVD processes, pure metal targets are chipped away by argon gas ions. The resulting chips of aluminum, titanium, titanium nitride, and copper are deposited on the wafer. Applied owns a 74 percent share of the PVD equipment market.

In CVD processes, source gases that already contain metal atoms are injected into the deposition chamber and are bonded to the surface of a heated wafer. This process is used to deposit tungsten, titanium nitride, and aluminum. Applied leads this market with a 46 percent share.

The company's metal CVD products include the Precision 5000 and Centura MCVD. PVD products include the Endura HP and VHP PVD, Centura HP, and Endura Electra Cu. In 1996, Applied introduced a line of integrated metalization products. These are the Endura Advanced Liner, Liner TxZ Centura, and Endura Cool Al.

Planarization and Dielectric Disposition Business Group

Dielectric deposition is the placement of electrically insulating materials on wafers. These materials include silicon dioxide and silicon nitride. The process of dielectric disposition is similar to CVD metal disposition. Applied owns a 51 percent share of the market for DCVD equipment.

Introduced in 1998, the Producer platform is the group's latest DVCD system. It includes twin process chambers that allow simultaneous processing of two wafers in separate environments. Up to three twin chambers can be mounted to a single platform. Other products include: the Precision 5000, Centura, and Optima DCVD lines; the SACVD and Gigafill SCVD Centura; the Dielectric ARC Centura; and the Ultima NDP-CVD Centura.

Planarization is the act of grinding or polishing the surface of a wafer until it as flat as possible in order to create the best surface for the imprinting of chip circuitry and other manufacturing processes. The group's Mirra system is its current chemical mechanical polishing (CMP) platform. It is used to polish silicon dioxides, tungsten, and copper. The company is third in the CMP equipment market with a 15 percent share.

Process Diagnostics and Control Business Group

The PDC group is the home of the company's line of inspection and quality control products. This equipment, introduced in 1997 and 1998, is used in product development, process control, and defect reduction.

PDC's scanning electron microscopes (SEMs) use an electron beam to image and measure the features on a chip. Applied makes two kinds of SEMs: the Opal 7830 series, which measures critical dimensions in a chip's circuits after specific steps in production, and the SEMVision DR-SEM, which automatically examines, identifies, and classifies chip defects. The company is ranked third with a 15 percent share in the CD-SEM market.

The company has two reticle inspection lines: the Orbot RT-82000 and the ARIS-I. Reticles are the quartz plates that are used to transfer circuit patterns to wafers. Undetected reticle defects are particularly costly since they are reproduced over and over in chips.

PDC also offers patterned wafer defect detection systems that inspect wafers after circuits are imprinted, as they move between process. The company's WF 73X systems use combinations of laser beams and darkfield and brightfield detectors to illuminate and compare a chip to a perfect example as it passes in the production process.

Thermal Process and Implant (TPI) Product Business Group

The TPI business group is responsible for three broad product lines that are used to deposit and alter material on wafers. The group is organized into technological divisions: the Thermal Processing and Epi divisions, and the Implant division.

In thermal processing, high temperatures are used to deposit materials on wafers and manipulate wafer properties. The thermal processing division offers three technologies, including RTP, LPCVD, and capacitor solutions. In the RTP (rapid thermal processing) market, the company is the leading producer with a 57 percent market share.

Applied markets its RTP equipment under the XE*plus* Centura brand. LPCVD products, which use high temperatures to deposit polysilicon, include Polycide xZ Centura for integrated tungsten and polysilicon deposition, the Poly Centura for stand-alone poly, the DCS xZ chamber for tungsten, and the HT Silicon Nitride Centura for nitride. DRAM capacitor processing is addressed with the newly introduced Tanox Centura for tantalum oxide development and Hemispherical Silicon Grain Polysilicon formation.

The Epi division sells equipment that deposits epitaxial silicon on wafers. Epitaxial CVD systems were the company's first products and Applied's early reputation was built on their success. Today, Applied has a leading share with 57 percent of this market. Their products include Epi Centura and Precision 7700 Epi. The Implant division makes and markets equipment that shoots dopant ions at wafers, implanting them to different depths in the wafer surface. In later thermal processes, these dopants are activated. Applied is second in the ion implant market with a 31 percent share.

The Implant division offers four ion implanters: the xR80S, xR120S, xR200S and xR LEAP. They are mainly differentiated by the their energy ranges and they can process 220–235 wafers per hour.

Income statement

Year	Revenue ($m)	Net income ($m)	Net profit margin	Employees
1999	4,859.1	746.7	15.4%	12,755
1998	4,041.7	230.9	5.7%	12,060
1997	4,074.3	498.5	12.2%	13,924
1996	4,144.8	599.6	14.5%	11,403
1995	3,061.9	454.1	14.8%	10,537
1994	1,659.8	220.7	13.3%	6,497
1993	1,080.0	99.7	9.2%	4,739
1992	751.4	39.5	5.3%	3,909
1991	638.6	26.2	4.1%	3,543
1990	567.1	34.1	6.0%	3,281

Stock history

Year	Stock price ($) FY High	FY Low	FY Close	P/E High	Low	Per share ($) Earns	Div.	Book value
1999	45.09	16.09	44.91	47	17	0.95	0.00	5.67
1998	20.06	10.78	17.34	67	36	0.30	0.00	4.24
1997	27.09	6.47	16.69	41	10	0.66	0.00	4.01
1996	13.88	5.44	6.61	17	7	0.82	0.00	3.29
1995	14.97	4.63	12.53	23	7	0.64	0.00	2.49
1994	6.81	3.66	6.50	21	11	0.33	0.00	1.44
1993	5.00	1.83	3.94	31	11	0.16	0.00	0.93
1992	1.91	0.70	1.84	27	10	0.07	0.00	0.76
1991	1.19	0.52	0.76	24	10	0.05	0.00	0.60
1990	1.27	0.54	0.55	18	8	0.07	0.00	0.56

1999 year-end financials

Debt ratio	11.9%
Return on equity	20.0%
Cash ($m)	823.3
Current ratio	3.03
Long-term debt ($m)	584.4
Shares outstanding (m)	765.3
Dividend yield	0.0%
Dividend payout	0.0%
Market value ($m)	34,371.1

Financial data provided by Hoover's Online (www.hoovers.com) and Media General Financial Services, Inc.

Applied Materials contacts

Applied Materials, Inc.   Phone: 800–882–0373
3050 Bowers Avenue   Fax: 408–748–9943
Santa Clara, CA 95054, USA   URL: www.appliedmaterials.com

CEO: James Morgan   CFO: Joseph Bronson   HR: Seitaro Ishii

Bertelsmann AG –
Gütersloh, Germany

Executive snapshot

"Under the prevailing conditions, whoever wants to secure his future and the jobs of his employees must combine forces," says Bertelsmann chairman and CEO Thomas Middelhoff.

And that, in a nutshell, is exactly how the privately held media giant is preparing for the 21st century.

Bertelsmann backdrop

The Bertelsmann story, its growth in the worldwide media markets of books, newspapers, radio, television, and new electronic media, really builds in the post-World War II period, but the company's roots are much deeper.

An entrepreneurial hymn

On July 1, 1835, printer Carl Bertelsmann establishes the C. Bertelsmann publishing house with a printing shop in Gütersloh. His first bestseller is titled *Theomele*. It is a Protestant hymnal. He also publishes general educational books and edits two newspapers.

Future focus

Bertelsmann, the media giant

In most businesses, new technology replaces old technologies. The automobile replaced the horse and buggy. The internal combustion engine replaced the steam engine. The jet plane replaced the piston-engine plane.

The media business is different, no question about it. A new medium does not replace an old medium. The new medium supplements the old medium and develops its own market. Newspapers didn't replace books. Magazines didn't replace newspapers. Radio didn't replace magazines. Television didn't replace radio. And the Internet didn't replace anything.

Bertelsmann is into all of these media. A lack of focus? On the surface, sure. But maybe not. Maybe the essence of Bertelsmann is not media at all, but news and ideas and concepts. Maybe Bertelsmann is focused not on media, but on content.

Ideas transcend borders. What makes Bertelsmann a media giant is the global nature of its business. Seventy-two percent of its business is outside Germany, a figure that is likely to increase substantially in the future.

What moves the world is not products and services, but ideas. Look at the worldwide impact of such ideas as Christianity, free enterprise and democracy. The company that controls a major segment of the market for the dissemination of ideas is in a powerful position.

Nor is there any question that ideas flow freely between media. Note the number of non-fiction books written by reporters and ex-reporters of such publications as the *New York Times* and the *Wall Street Journal*. And note, too, the number of magazine articles that have been expanded into books.

Talent, too, moves from one medium to another. From radio to television to motion pictures. Not only on-air talent, but producers and writers, too. The world of ideas recognizes no artificial barriers between media.

Bertelsmann, however, has one barrier that might prove to be an obstacle in the future. All of its many ventures are highly decentralized. In the short term, this might be an advantage. Decentralization can provide better management and improved earnings. On the other hand, a decentralized company can easily miss the next turn in the technological road. It's too easy for the individual units of a decentralized company to look at developing technology and say, "That's not within our span of operations."

Fortunately, Bertelsmann seems to have found the knack of jumping on new ideas in spite of the way the company is organized. For example, it has created three major ventures in the Internet field. One each, with America Online, Lycos and Barnesandnoble.com. Whether the company can keep up with the Internet medium remains to be seen. But so far it seems to be ahead of the pack.

After Bertelsmann, his son Heinrich takes the reins. The publishing company now employs 14 people and Heinrich expands into literature, producing the works of authors such as Lord Byron and the Brothers Grimm, and into history, philosophy, and linguistics texts. He also continues his father's work with newspapers, founding the *Konservativer Volksfreund* in 1862, which lasts for 30 years.

By the time of Heinrich's death in 1887, the company employs 70 people. His son-in-law Johannes Mohn assumes the management of the company. Mohn reorients the firm back toward theological texts and company growth slows. In 1921, the company employs 85 people.

Heinrich Mohn is the fourth generation to head the family enterprise. He reanimates the company by expanding into popular fiction and attracting the mass market reading audience in the 1920s. An imaginative sales manager, Fritz Wixforth uses innovative marketing and advertising techniques, such as window displays, multi-novel sets, novelty packs, and competitions, to promote the books and by 1939 and on the eve of the company's greatest crisis, the publishing house has grown to 400 employees.

World War II leaves Bertelsmann in ruins. As a member of the Confessional Church, that part of the Protestant Church which openly opposed Hitler, Heinrich Mohn had opposed the Nazi Party and in 1933, printed the "Tecklenburger Bekenntnis" (Tecklenburg Confession), which called upon the church to offer resistance to the totalitarian state. An embarrassment to the government, Fritz Wixforth and other Bertelsmann employees are arrested by the Nazis and imprisoned. Shortly afterwards, the C. Bertelsmann publishing house is closed by the Nazis. The company's buildings are destroyed in British bombing raids on the city of Gütersloh. And by the end of the war, the only surviving assets are printing presses.

An empire built on book clubs

It falls to Reinhard Mohn, the fifth generation of family leaders, to rebuild the publishing house. It is Mohn, who fought in the Afrika Korps under Rommel and spent three years as a prisoner of war in the United States, who shapes the Bertelsmann of today.

While in America, Mohn is introduced to the book club concept and on his return home, he presides over the founding of the Bertelsmann Lesering, Germany's first book club. The success of the then-new direct distribution method is one of the company's greatest triumphs. After six months the "Lesering" already has 52,000 members, and 100,000 within the year.

The creation of a large direct sales market in the book club enables Bertelsmann to produce and successfully sell new products and it establishes its own encyclopedia. Among the best known German brands, Bertelsmann encyclopedias are sold direct to customers as *Grosse Bertelsmann Lexikothek* and through the book retail trade as *Bertelsmann Lexikon Verlag.*

A record club joins the book club in 1956 and, soon after, Bertelsmann establishes its own record company. The Ariola label becomes one of the most successful in Germany. In 1958, the company's Sonopress subsidiary starts pressing records. In the next 40 years, it follows technological advances from the LP to the cassette tape to today's CD and DVD.

Bertelsmann makes the first tentative steps toward international status in the 1960s by expanding its book club network. It founds "Círculo de Lectores" a book club in Spain. In 1966, the company acquires a stake in the Austrian book club, Donauland, and in 1970, Loisirs is formed in France. Book clubs in Portugal, the UK, Italy, Canada and the Netherlands follow.

Expanding into a global media giant

In the 1970s, taking its cue from the growth of conglomerates, the company expands into new media industries. Bertelsmann takes over the Berlin film production company, Ufa. Very rapidly, the newly emerging television market is exploited as an important business field for Ufa Productions. With the acquisition of a 25 percent stake in Gruner

+ Jahr, a well-known German printing and publishing house that produces *Stern*, *Brigitte* and *Capital*, Bertelsmann jumps into the magazine business. In 1973, the company raises its investment, building a majority   stake.

At the same time, the company continues to consolidate its power in the book world. It acquires the Goldmann publishing house, which is now Germany's leading paperback publisher, and the Spanish publishing company Plaza y Janés in Barcelona. The company also begins an expansion into the US media markets that is still making headlines today. It acquires the world's largest paperback publisher, Bantam Books, and the US record label, Arista.

In the 1980s, Bertelsmann and Gruner + Jahr merge their activities in the area of the electronic media into Ufa Film- und Fernseh-GmbH in Hamburg. Ufa in turn acquires a 40 percent stake in the first private German language television station, RTLplus, which grows to become Europe's largest advertising-financed television channel.

In 1986, in the US, the RCA label and the Doubleday publishing house join the Bertelsmann fold. Within a year, the company consolidates, merging its US publishers into the Bantam Doubleday Dell Publishing Group and the worldwide music business into the Bertelsmann Music Group (BMG).

With the fall of the Berlin Wall, Bertelsmann expands its existing operations into Eastern and Central Europe. In 1990, Gruner + Jahr acquires a stake in *Népszabadság*, Hungary's leading daily newspaper. In 1991, a majority shareholding is acquired in the Dresdner Druck- und Verlagshaus and in 1992, the Berliner Verlag is taken over.

In the early 1990s, the company launches "Premiere," a German pioneer in pay TV in which the company owns a 37.5 percent stake. By 1997, it boasts some 1.5 million subscribers.

Bringing the Internet to Europe

With the advent of the Internet, Bertelsmann enters the multimedia age. In co-operation with America Online, the European online service AOL is formed which, after only 16 months, has 500,000 subscribers in Germany, France and the UK alone. Bertelsmann also acquires PixelPark, the leading German multimedia agency. This multimedia drive is rounded off by the involvement of the company in the area of technical Internet services: In 1996 Bertelsmann establishes the companies Telemedia and mediaWays.

In January 1997, Bertelsmann merges Ufa Film und Fernseh-GmbH with Compagnie Luxembourgeoise de Télédiffusion (CLT) which has been involved in private broadcasting since 1931. This move creates the largest television company in Europe with radio and television stations in Germany, France, the Benelux countries, the UK, Sweden and the Czech Republic.

A premiere of a different kind is taking place on the other side of the globe in the same month: after many years of preparatory work Bertelsmann opens the first book club for China in Shanghai. At the official start, the club already has 15,000 members.

On July 1, 1998, Bertelsmann AG completes its acquisition of Random House, Inc. Combined with Bertelsmann's long-held Bantam Doubleday Dell publishing division and with their affiliated companies in Canada, the UK, Australia, New Zealand, and South Africa, the purchase creates a new worldwide English-language trade book publishing company.

As the race for market leadership continues, in the last months of 1998, the company makes news by purchasing a 50 percent stake in US online book retailer Barnesandnoble.com, making an investment in NuvoMedia's Rocket Book (electronic books), and purchasing a majority stake in Springer.

In 1999, Reinhard Mohn transfers his controlling stake in the private company to Bertelsmann Verwaltungsgesellschaft, an administrative shell run by company executives and the Mohn family.

In early 2000, the company reorganizes its online activities. It sells its half-interest in AOL Europe to partner America Online and spins off Lycos Europe, its joint venture with Lycos. The company also announces it will take bol.com, its online book e-tailer, public.

Bertelsmann close-up

The small town of Gütersloh in northern Germany is a far cry from the great corporate centers of the world. In 1835, Carl Bertelsmann started a small print shop here and although his business, Bertelsmann AG, which is still headquartered in the town, may not seem to have strayed far from its beginnings, nothing is further from the truth. Today, Bertelsmann AG is the world's fourth largest media company. It owns over 600 companies and employs 64,937 people in 54 countries. In fiscal 1999, annual sales were DM 26 billion. Seventy-two percent of its revenues are generated outside of Germany.

The company tends to grow via acquisitions, mergers, and joint ventures, and it is hard to beat at its chosen strategy. Recently, it has made much news as it pursues market leadership with high-profile acquisitions in book publishing. These deals led at least one observer to characterize the company's strategy as "blitzkrieg." The description, however, does not take into account the willingness of the sellers, nor Bertelsmann's rare ability to make its media empire pay.

The privately held company has six major business groups. Ranked by revenue generation, they are: Bertelsmann Book AG, BMG Entertainment, CLT-UFA, Gruner + Jahr, Bertelsmann Arvato AG, and Multimedia. The business operations include book clubs, literary and scientific publishing companies, daily newspapers, consumer magazines, trade journals, music and film companies, radio and television stations, online services, printing shops and service companies as well as other technical firms.

Bertelsmann Book AG

Books are Bertelsmann's heritage. Publishing was its first business and, in 1998, Bertelsmann Book AG reclaimed its role as the company's largest group. The book group grossed DM 8.3 billion in 1999 and the mid-1998 acquisition of Random House, a $1.22 billion US publisher, has pushed it to the top of the global publishing industry.

The group's book and music clubs accounted for roughly 53 percent of revenues; book publishing 42 percent; professional information 5 percent. With the purchase of Random House, Bertelsmann has become the world's largest English-language publisher.

Bertelsmann's book clubs, the initial engine of its post-war growth, boast a membership of more than 25 million subscribers worldwide. In North America, Doubleday Direct, Inc. is the largest direct-marketing consumer book club group, with over 4.5 million members. The group includes the Doubleday Book Club, Crossings and Crossing For Kids, Audio Books Direct, and other specialty clubs, such as Mystery Guild and the Science Fiction Book Club.

There are Doubleday Book & Music Clubs in Australia and New Zealand. Newer clubs in the east European countries of Poland, Hungary and the Czech Republic claim memberships totaling more than 1.8 million. There is even a club in China: the Shanghai Bertelsmann Book Club, launched in partnership in January 1997 with Shanghai Science and Technical Publishers, has more than 170,000 members.

In Europe, the France Loisirs Group, a joint venture with Havas Edition, serves about five million members in France, Belgium, Canada, and Switzerland. The Bertelsmann Club operates in Germany; in Austria, it's the Donauland Club. In England, the group runs Book Club Associates, a joint venture with Reed Elsevier UK and in the Netherlands, the ECI voor Boeken en Platen B.V. enjoys a high level of membership. Membership in the Circulo de Lectores in Spain is more than 1.5 million – it is one of the strongest European book clubs. Mondolibri, a joint venture with the Mondadori Group, operates in Italy.

In book publishing, the group has such a controlling grip on the market that it draws flack for the editorial power it *might* wield over the intellectual content of the book world. In the US, Random House has been merged into the Bantam Doubleday Dell Publishing Group creating the world's largest publisher. In the UK, Transworld Publishers UK was merged with Random House UK to create a similarly substantial market giant.

On the continent, the group includes publishers such as Goldmann, C. Bertelsmann, Knaus, Blanvalet, Siedler, and the Karl Blessing company. Lexikon Verlag produces and direct markets large encyclopedic and reference works.

In addition to trade publishing, the group includes a cartography division with a portfolio ranging from world maps to national and international street maps, rambling maps and guidebooks. Professional publishing groups include a bevy of businesses in the areas of science/economics, medicine, transportation, and construction and environment. The group doubled the size of its professional information arm with the purchase of 82 percent of scientific publisher Springer, announced in late November, 1998.

BMG Entertainment AG

BMG Entertainment is one of the largest music companies in the world. In 1999, the group enjoyed record revenues of DM8.1 billion. Its operations include more than 200 active music labels in over 50 countries, as well as home video, interactive entertainment, direct marketing, music publishing, merchandising, and compact disc and cassette manufacturing businesses.

Headquartered in New York City's Times Square, BMG's worldwide operations are organized into four separate divisions: BMG Entertainment North America; BMG Entertainment International; BMG Entertainment TV/Film Europe and BMG Entertainment Storage Media.

BMG's share of the international music market is an impressive 14 percent. Its international division boasts the top domestic market share in nine major countries around the world including Brazil, Germany, Italy and Spain. Blame them for the "Marcarena" craze, which sold some 14 million copies. Major geographical units include: the Germany/Switzerland/Austria (GSA) region, the company's stronghold; the Latin region, where it is the only music company to have offices in every Spanish-speaking and Portuguese-speaking country (excluding Cuba); the UK and Ireland; and the former Eastern Bloc countries, such as Poland where BMG is the market leader.

In Entertainment North America, the company's labels include RCA Records, Arista Records, and the Windham Hill Group. The division has enjoyed record growth in an almost flat market. Driven by the success of artists such as Toni Braxton, Kenny G, the Dave Matthews Band, Alan Jackson, and Clint Black, it recorded sales gains of over 100 percent in 1998.

In addition to other businesses, the North American group operates BMG Direct, the world's largest music club and has established niche music clubs such as Sound and Spirit serving the rapidly growing Christian music genre, and the BMG Jazz Club.

BMG Entertainment Storage Media is home to Sonopress, a leading manufacturer of compact discs, CD-ROMs, DVDs and cassettes, producing more than 600 million units annually in eight countries. Sonopress is the world's second largest CD manufacturing group, with a daily production capacity of more than 2.5 million units.

CLT-UFA

In 1997, Bertelsmann's UFA broadcasting unit merged with the Luxembourg CLT creating Europe's largest commercial broadcasting network, with annual sales of more than DM 6.4 billion. (Bertelsmann and CLT's parent company, Audiofina, each have an equal ownership share and management responsibility in the new company.) CLT-UFA's major businesses are television and radio production and broadcasting.

The group dominates commercial television in Europe, operating 22 TV channels in nine European countries and accounting for 85 percent of the group's sales. Almost two-thirds of that revenue comes from Germany, which is Europe's largest market. Its crown jewel is RTL, in which CLT-UFA has an 89 percent stake, leads viewer ratings and is Germany's major made-for-TV film and television series producer. Its advertising share is roughly 30 percent of the entire market.

In France, CLT-UFA is represented by channel M6 with a viewer share of 13.4 percent and a market share of 17.9 percent. The group has a stake in TMC (Télé Monte Carlo), with more than 3.7 million viewers in France, Monaco, and Switzerland and its Holland Media Group (HMG) claims 58 percent of Dutch advertising revenue and a 36 percent share of the country's viewers. In Belgium, CLT-UFA broadcasts through the RTL TVI and Club RTL channels which earn a 69.4 percent share of the advertising market and a 26.5 percent share of the audience, and RTL's Télé Lëtzebuerg which has a 60 percent audience share. The group is also expanding with new stations in the UK and Eastern Europe.

In commercial radio, the group is the largest in Europe and third largest in the world with 18 stations in eight countries. RTL has been the top French radio station for the past 15 years. Talk Radio in the UK, Klassik Radio as well as 104.6 RTL, Berliner Rundfunk, Radio NRW and Antenne Bayern operate in Germany. CLT-UFA is also the market leader in Belgium, Luxembourg and the UK, and is expanding in Scandinavia and Eastern Europe.

Gruner + Jahr

With 1999 annual revenues of DM 5.4 billion, Gruner + Jahr (G+J) is

Bertelsmann's periodical publishing group. It is one of Europe's largest printing and publishing houses with 80 magazines and 9 newspapers worldwide. Its major businesses are magazines, newspapers, electronic media, and printing.

The flagship magazine of the group's German properties is *Stern*, Europe's largest weekly current affairs magazine. Other large circulation properties include *Brigitte*, a women's magazine with a paid circulation of 900,000 copies sold and a readership of 3.5 million; *Flora*, Europe's second largest gardening magazine; and *Stern* spin-offs *Art* and *Geo*. *Konr@d*. *Tip*, published in Berlin, is Germany's largest city magazine and the bi-weekly programming guide *TV Today* sports a circulation of 1.1 million.

Among 40-odd US magazines are well-known names such as *McCalls*, *Parents*, *Family Circle*, and *Fitness*, purchased from The New York Times Company in the mid-90s. Prisma Presse in France includes *Capital*, Europe's best-selling business title. Other magazine divisions are located in Spain, Poland and Italy, with new publications on the presses in China and Russia.

The group's daily newspapers are particularly strong in Berlin, where *Berliner Zeitung* is the largest paper and the tabloid *Berliner Kurier* is the third largest. The *Sächsische Zeitung* is the leading daily in Dresden. The group also owns papers in Hungary and Slovakia.

Gruner + Jahr is well advanced in Germany's cyberworld. In addition to the large and popular sites maintained by its periodicals, the group is firmly established in online portals and search engines. *Fireball*, a joint venture project of G+J Electronic Media Service GmbH with the Technical University of Berlin and Alta Vista in Palo Alto (USA), is the largest search engine for German language Internet content worldwide. It also set up *Paperball*, a meta-search engine that searches through the current online editions of more than 70 German-language daily newspapers and can create personal newspapers for users.

Gruner + Jahr owns and operates a number of printing plants. A new newspaper printing plant with a rotary illustration press for the *Sächsische Zeitung* began production in Dresden in the fall of 1997. In the US, Brown Printing Company includes plants in California and Kentucky.

Bertelsmann Arvato AG

Bertelsmann Arvato AG is Europe's largest media service company with a total of 18 printing and services companies in Western Europe, Poland, Russia, Columbia, and the US. Organized into three broad groups, printing and technical companies, services, and special printing, this group contributed DM3.8 billion to Bertelsmann's 1999 revenues.

A lion's share of the group's revenue comes from its worldwide printing operations. In the US, Offset Paperback Manufacturers is the country's leading paperback manufacturer producing over a million books per day, 40 percent of the market. Berryville Graphics produces 70 million hardcovers per year. And both companies, along with Dynamic Graphic Finishing, are poised to profit from the merger with Random House.

In Germany, Elsnerdruck ranks as one of the continent's largest paperback producers and Mohndruck, located in Gütersloh and boasting perhaps the most advanced printing technology in the world, would certainly make Carl Bertelsmann proud. The group's printing operations in Columbia and Portugal lead in their markets.

The companies comprising Bertelsmann Distribution Services include fulfillment and distribution services for publishing and entertainment companies, a direct marketing operation, customer loyalty reward programs, the eps Electronic Printing Service, call centers, and financial and industrial information services.

Established distribution businesses throughout Europe are being joined by new distribution and customer care center businesses in the US. In early 1998, a book distribution center was opened as a joint venture in partnership with Terra Verlag in Russia and the group is expanding in Poland.

Bertelsmann Multimedia

The Multimedia group is Bertelsmann's cutting edge and it is becoming obvious that the company is serious about its position in the emerging online industries. It has organized the group into three main businesses: New Media, mediaSystems, and E-Commerce. Its 1999 revenues hit DM 1.4 billion.

New Media's services are driven by the group's joint venture with America Online. AOL Bertelsmann Online has divisions in Germany, the UK, France, Ireland and five other countries, with more than 2.7 million subscribers. The group holds a 50 percent stake in the operation.

The group is also creating online content in a variety of areas. In the medical field it owns "bs medic," in recreation, "Sports 1" and the "Game Channel," search portals in partnership with Lycos, and news and travel services. AdOn Online Marketing is selling online marketing and advertising. To develop multimedia content, Bertelsmann also operates production centers, such as T1 New Media.

Bertelsmann mediaSystems covers the corporate market for Internet services with Pixelpark, Germany's leading multimedia consulting firm, and systems provider Telemedia. It is also in the process of creating cyberspace itself. In 1996, mediaWays, formed an alliance with the debis Systemhaus unit of Daimler–Benz and started to build what is now the second largest TCP/IP network in Germany.

Major e-commerce activities include a 50 percent stake in US online bookseller barnesandnoble.com. The group's own bol.com is a major European bookselling venture that has quickly opened sites in Germany, the UK, Netherlands, Spain, Switzerland, and, in partnership with Havas, in France.

Income statement

Year	Revenue ($m)	Net income ($m)	Net profit margin	Employees
1999	14,164.8	495.8	3.5%	64,937
1998	12,701.5	620.7	4.9%	57,807
1997	12,859.7	584.6	4.5%	57,173
1996	14,126.2	593.8	4.2%	57,996
1995	14,888.8	591.8	4.0%	57,397
1994	11,589.3	477.9	4.1%	51,767
1993	10,049.8	387.5	3.9%	50,437
1992	10,469.2	373.4	3.6%	48,781
1991	7,984.9	297.7	3.7%	45,110
1990	7,992.0	306.2	3.8%	43,509

1998 year-end financials

Debt ratio	12.9%
Return on equity	–
Cash ($m)	229.6
Current ratio	–
Long-term debt ($m)	378.4

Financial data provided by Hoover's Online (www.hoovers.com) and Media General Financial Services, Inc.

Bertelsmann contacts

Bertelsmann AG
Carl-Bertelsmann-Strasse 270
Postfach 111
D-33311 Gütersloh, Germany

Phone: +49.52 41.80–0
Fax: +49.52 41.7 51 66
URL: www.bertelsmann.de

CEO: Thomas Middelhoff   CFO: Sigfried Luther   HR: Gert Stuerzebecher

Cisco Systems, Inc. –
San Jose, California, USA

Executive snapshot

On a fast track, Cisco is setting the pace in the internetworking industry.

"Our objective is to be number one or number two in our markets and to have a 40–70 percent share in those markets," says Cisco CEO John Chambers. "To do that, we stay focused on customer needs, stick to our core competencies – partnering with others when we need to – and maintain a healthy paranoia."

Cisco backdrop

Cisco Systems is one of the *Future Focus* youngsters, literally a corporate teenager. Yet, the company has built a customer and revenue base that is the envy of many more mature competitors. The keys to its fast-track growth are the rapid rise of the Internet and an acquisition spree that keeps Cisco on the leading edge of technological change.

Talking across networks

It may be hard to imagine in today's world, but in the early 1980s, the Director of Computer Facilities for Stanford University's Department of Computer Science and the Director of Computer Facilities for

Future focus

The best route to success

The best, the easiest and often the only route to fame and fortune is to be the first company in a new category. That's exactly the strategy followed by Leonard Bosack and Sandy Lerner. In six years the husband-and-wife team turned an idea into $174 million. The category: routers.

But how do you find a new category? The answer to that one is easy, too. The best ideas, the most powerful ideas, the ideas that will last the longest and produce the most wealth are ideas that are born out of frustration.

- Edwin Land's 3-year-old daughter was frustrated because she couldn't see the photograph her father just took. Result: instant photography.
- Rosa Parks was frustrated because she couldn't sit in front of the bus. Result: desegregation in the South.
- Bosack and Lerner were frustrated because they couldn't send electronic messages to each other across the Stanford campus. Result: Cisco Systems, Inc., a company that in April 2000 was worth $480 billion on the stock market, a remarkable record for a 16-year-old company.

What frustrates you can make you wealthy if you listen to your frustrations and act on them with persistence and determination. You need persistence because most people just accept what life offers them. "That's the way it is."

(You want to make a fortune. Here's a thought. No industry frustrates as many people as the airline industry. Yet millions of passengers just accept those frustrations by shrugging their shoulders and saying, "That's just the way the airline industry is.")

Bosack's and Lerner's idea – to build a highly specialized computer that translates one network's protocol into another network's protocol – was turned down 76 times by venture capitalists. That's not surprising. Many hare-brained ideas get funded because they promise "pie in the sky" and the more outlandish, the better. The Skycar, a combination automobile/airplane. Home delivery of groceries via the Internet. The TV/PC. Where are the problems that these ideas are trying to solve?

Ideas that solve long-standing, existing problems are much harder to sell. The venture capitalist says: "But that's just the way things are. If there was a better way to do it, somebody would already be doing it." Don't be misled by the Cisco story. What works in business is not just being first. Being first is only the license you buy that gives you the first crack at category leadership.

What really works in business is not sales, not profits, not better products or services, not satisfied customers, although these things help. What really works in business is market domination. When you dominate a market, your future is almost guaranteed. A large percentage of customers just naturally gravitate to the leader. "Nobody got fired for buying from IBM."

Next to being first, the smartest thing Cisco did is their raft of acquisitions in the networking area. In the last seven years, Cisco made 40 acquisitions for which they paid over $17 billion, an astounding amount for a company doing only $12.1 billion in annual sales.

There's no question in our minds that Cisco would not be the same company today without those acquisitions. In the fast-moving networking business there is no way that Cisco could have kept up without buying the technology it needed.

In our consulting work, we are often asked by a client, "How do we successfully compete with Company B." Our first answer invariably is, "Can you buy them?" Any company that has something that can cause problems for your company has something that can benefit you.

Good things happen when you buy a competitor. It reduces your competition, increases your market share, increases your focus and increases your market domination. If the price is anything near reasonable, you can't go wrong buying market share.

Today Cisco Systems is almost twice as big as its nearest competition. That's market domination, the goal for any company that wants to have a successful 21st-century career.

Stanford's Graduate School of Business are unable to send each other electronic messages across campus. And they don't like it.

The problem: the school owns several independently developed computer networks that are incompatible. They cannot speak to each other and so, neither can their directors, former Stanford students and husband and wife Leonard Bosack and Sandy Lerner.

The solution: linking the networks through another computer that translates their messages and forwards them to the proper server, a fancy piece of work called a multiprotocol router. Bosack and Lerner are now able to trade messages.

As word spreads and demand grows for the "internetworking" capabilities of the router, Bosack and Lerner ask Stanford University to go into the router business with them. In 1984, after Stanford declines, the pair start their own business, which they incorporate using the name of a nearby town, Cisco.

For the first two years, Cisco is a home-based business. Funding the business with credit cards and mortgage money, Bosack and Lerner buy a used mainframe and start building routers in their garage.

In 1986, the fledgling company ships its first product, the AGS router and attends its first tradeshow. Its first customers, including Rutgers University and Hewlett Packard Labs, are colleagues and others who hear of the router over the fledgling Internet, which is still mainly a network of academic institutions and governmental agencies. In that year, Cisco doubles its headcount to four employees and expands ... into just about every room in its owners' home.

In short order, Cisco is earning $100,000 and more per month, all without a sales staff or a marketing plan. In 1987, the company moves out of the house and into offices in Menlo Park, California headquarters.

From hat-in-hand to cashing out

Cash-starved, Bosack and Lerner start pitching the company to venture capitalists. They are turned down 76 times. Late in 1987, however, they make their 77th pitch, this time to Don Valentine, founder of Sequoia Capital, a Silicon Valley firm that has already backed Apple Computer and 3Com. In December, Lerner and Bosack give Sequoia an ownership stake, the controlling position in the company, and the mandate to build a professional management team. In return, Sequoia gives the company $2.3 million. Cisco now boasts ten employees and year-end revenues hit $1.5 million.

In 1988, Valentine recruits John Morgridge as CEO. Morgridge, the former CEO of a laptop computer company, gets off to a fast start.

He creates the systems that Cisco will need to grow and expands the staff to 48 employees by year-end.

Morgridge's relationship with Sandy Lerner is not as smooth. But conflict among the company's leaders does not slow Cisco's growth. During 1989, the company signs its first OEM agreement and the workforce more than triples to 174. As the Internet era starts to explode, there is not a serious competitor in sight. Revenues hit $28 million and less than 18 months after Morgridge signs on, the company prepares to go public.

In 1990, the World Wide Web is established and on February 20, Cisco launches its initial public offering. In just over two years, Sequoia Capital's $2.3 million stake in the company is worth $65 million and Don Valentine is Chairman of the Board.

Lerner and Bosack's two-thirds share makes them rich, but does not give them control of the fast-growing company. In August, a group of the company's executives tell Valentine that either Sandy Lerner must go or they will resign *en masse*. Valentine fires Lerner on August 28 and Bosack resigns the next day. The consolation prize: the pair sell their shares in Cisco for $174 million.

Again, the internal conflict has no effect on the company's growth. Sales of just over 5000 routers push the year's revenues to $69.8 million and generate a net profit of $1.4 million. The workforce expands to 248 employees.

In 1991, Morgridge hires John Chambers away from Wang. Chambers starts his Cisco tenure as an executive vice president, with the understanding that he will eventually ascend to the CEO spot. Cisco's hot growth streak continues as revenues hit $183 million and net profits explode to $43 million. The workforce doubles to 500 employees.

The company makes its first international steps with the opening of Nihon Cisco, a Japanese subsidiary, in 1992. It also expands into internetwork management software with the first release of CiscoWorks. Cisco also faces the first major threats to its position as the pre-eminent linker of networks. Competitors are starting to sell their own routers and more significantly, new technology in areas such as switching threatens the growth of the router market itself. High-speed switches do not replace routers, but they are a less expensive alternative to building network capacity.

Switching visions

By the end of 1992, the router business is growing as fast as the Web. Revenues hit $382 million and net profit is a very healthy $82 million. But Cisco's customers are also buying other internetworking products, such as switches and hubs, and not from Cisco – the company does not sell them.

In 1993, Cisco makes a critical strategic decision: it decides to follow the market and expand beyond routers by reframing itself as a supplier of end-to-end networking solutions. Knowing that it doesn't have the time or expertise to address the entire market internally, the management team decides to buy it.

In September, the company makes its first acquisition, paying $89 million for Crescendo Communications and obtaining a company that sells about $10 million of workgroup hub products per year in return. Three months later, it expands into the WAN (wide area network) market in a joint development partnership with Cascade Communications, in which Cisco buys a minority stake.

The router business continues to surge and Cisco's lifetime production total hits 124,000 by year-end. The company opens new subsidiaries in Hong Kong and Mexico. The workforce swells above 1400 generating $714 million in revenues and $176 million in net profits.

In 1994, Cisco continues expanding its product lines with three more acquisitions. The $91 million purchase of Newport Systems brings remote access products. Another $320 million buys Kalpana Inc., the leading maker of Ethernet switches, and LightStream Corporation to jumpstart the company's expansion into LAN (local area network) switches.

Cisco also makes its first forays into online business in 1994, mainly in the hope of finding effective ways to deal with its unrelenting growth. Cisco Connection Online (CCO) first uses the Internet to streamline sales of Cisco-imprinted coffee mugs, shirts, and technical brochures. Sales of the ancillary products explode.

A second excursion is launched by the heavily overworked and chronically understaffed Technical Assistance Center. The creation of a Web-based troubleshooting site creates instant relief for the support staff and is popular with customers who can now get quick answers to minor problems anytime they need them.

In 1994, John Morgridge reaches a personal milestone as Cisco becomes a $1 billion company. In January 1995, he celebrates by accepting a position as the company's chairman. John Chambers takes over as president and the CEO. Revenues for the year hit $1.3 billion; net profit is $323 million. The company moves to new digs in San Jose, CA and now employs 2200 people.

Sticking to the plan

Chambers begins his leadership tenure by sticking to the well-proven plan. Acquisitions continue apace. The purchase of Combinet, Inc. for $144 million and Internet Junction for $5.5 million add remote access software and hardware. Grand Junction brings Fast Ethernet and Ethernet switches in a $350 million deal, and Network Translation, Inc. adds network management and security products. The company also takes four minority stakes in companies developing complementary products and technologies.

In 1995, Cisco continues building its online infrastructure. It takes aim squarely at its complicated ordering process, which a buyer from Sprint, one of Cisco's major customers, calls a "disaster." Ordering the company's complex and custom-built products from thick print catalogs results in frequent pricing errors. And, with thousands of possible configurations, errors in product specifications are common. Fully 40 percent of orders have to be returned to customers for correction before they can be processed, wasting the time and effort of both buyer and seller, and delaying sales.

CCO starts small: first, it gives customers online access to order status and then, online pricing is introduced. In March 1996, with the help of software from Calico Technologies, the company launches Cisco Marketplace.

Marketplace includes full product documentation on over 12,000 parts and, even better, customers can use the service 24 hours per day, 7 days per week. It eliminates order configuration errors by simply rejecting specifications that are unworkable and suggesting the correct options. It eliminates pricing errors by pricing the orders automatically with latest information.

The online service is an instant hit with customers. In the first seven months of operation, Cisco books $125 million in online orders. CCO also automatically handles 50,000 order status checks and over 60,000 product enquiries each month, saving the company hundreds of millions of dollars in service costs.

Fiscal 1995 ends with $2.23 billion in revenues and $456 million in net income. Cisco employs over 3800 people.

Having attained his sea legs with little trouble, Chambers picks up the pace in 1996. He engineers seven acquisitions adding access servers, new security products, Gigabit Ethernet and Token Ring switches, SNA solutions, and Netsys software to Cisco's product lines.

Dwarfing all of the others combined is the July 1996 purchase of neighbor StrataCom, Inc., for $4.5 billion – at the time, the second largest deal ever made in Silicon Valley and 72 times StrataCom's 1995 earnings. The StrataCom acquisition makes Cisco a major player in the ATM switching market, which is developing faster than the company had anticipated.

Shareholders can hardly complain about the spending. On a split-adjusted basis, Cisco stock has risen from 56 cents per share at the IPO to $57 per share on the day of the StrataCom deal.

The company sells its 1000,000th router in fiscal 1996. International sales account for 48 percent of its $4.09 billion in revenues and net income hits $913 million. The company has just under 8800 employees.

Setting the pace

Cisco enters 1997 as the undisputed leader of the networking industry. Its sales are almost twice that of its nearest competitor and its profit margins, which rival Microsoft's, are the highest in its industry. The company backs off the acquisition pace only slightly, making six minority equity investments and purchasing six more companies. LightSpeed International, Inc., Ardent Communications, and Dagaz keep Cisco on the edge of converging voice, video and data technologies. Canada's Keystone Systems adds expertise in the emerging SONET transport technology. Global Internet Software Group contributes turnkey security software for the small and medium business segment, and Telesend adds depth to the company's WAN access products.

Web-based sales via CCO almost double every quarter, starting at $81 million in the first quarter. Online orders total $837 million by year-end, almost $70 million each month.

As the leading player in the industry, Cisco begins using its position to create strategic alliances that further solidify its influence. It joins forces with Hewlett-Packard to create network-ready PCs and with telecom equipment maker Alcatel to provide networking solutions to telecommunications companies.

Cisco also signs pacts with Microsoft and Intel, hoping to stretch the dominance of "Wintel" into "Wintelco." And it forms an alliance with MCI that earns Cisco a slot as a prime contractor on a $3 billion project to rebuild the US Postal Service computer network.

Revenues grow 57 percent to $6.4 billion in fiscal 1997, earning Cisco the 332nd spot on the *Fortune 500*. Ranked in the top five of the 500 in return on revenues and return on assets, Cisco profits break the billion-dollar mark for the first time at $1.04 billion. The company now employs 10,700 people.

In 1998, international sales fall slightly, reflecting poor economic conditions in Asia. But Cisco continues its global expansion, adding new subsidiaries in China, Croatia, Denmark, Finland, Hungary, Norway, Puerto Rico, Romania, Saudi Arabia, and Slovakia. Chambers continues to pursue marketplace leadership via acquisition. In addition to two minority investment stakes, Cisco purchases eight companies – the most in a single year.

The company continues preparing for the convergence of voice, data, and video by acquiring IP (Internet Protocol) telephony expertise, wireless technology, and programmable switches from companies such as Summa Four, Clarity Wireless, and Selsius Systems. It expands its depth in SONET with routers from PipeLinks, Inc., and its DSL offerings with NetSpeed, Inc. Cisco adds Dell to its portfolio of alliances when it agrees to create network-ready PCs with the direct marketer. It signs a pact with US West to provide its customers with high-speed Cisco modems.

Following in the footsteps of other great brand builders, Cisco emerges from the high-tech shadows in late 1998 and announces a $60 million worldwide ad campaign designed to bring its name to consumers everywhere. Like Intel, Cisco plans to label the computers and other equipment containing its networking products.

By year-end 1998, after three years under John Chamber's leadership, Cisco's stock price has grown almost 800 percent and the company's market value breaks the $100 billion mark.

In early 1999, the company announces three more acquisitions, all aimed at expanding its share of the emerging IP telephony markets. It acquires telephone equipment from Sentient Networks and Fibex Systems. And, in a $2 billion deal, Cisco buys GeoTel and its call-routing telecommunications software. In March 1999, the company launches plans to create a new $1 billion facility on 400 acres in San Jose. It will eventually house over 20,000 employees. Later in the year, Cisco invests $1.5 billion in a 20 percent stake in KPMG's consulting business and, in its largest acquisition ever, Cisco buys fiber-optic equipment maker Cerent for $7 billion.

The pace continues in 2000 as Cisco snaps up Pirelli's fiber-optic telephone equipment business for over $2 billion, and then spends another $1.6 billion for Aironet Wireless Communications and SightPath. Cisco's high-flying common stock makes it the world's most valuable company, with a greater market cap than General Electric and Microsoft, in March 2000.

Cisco close-up

Those observers who have tracked the emergence and rapid growth of the Internet will not be surprised by the equally steep growth trajectory of Cisco Systems. The Internet is enabled by the ability of networks to communicate with each other and, happily for Cisco, the company has spent its first 16 years firmly focused on the products that make that communication possible.

Cisco is currently the leader in the hotly contested Internet equipment market and all of its eggs are in one basket: the hardware and software that links computer networks. Its stock was one of the favorites of the 1990s boom and the company boasts a market capitalization of over $480 billion. Around 80 percent of the world's Internet traffic runs through Cisco equipment and in fiscal 1999, that added up to $12.15 billion in annual revenue.

With over 225 sales and support offices in 75 countries, Cisco has already created the infrastructure it needs to support a global operation.

Currently, international sales and export sales, mainly in Europe, Asia-Pacific and Canada, account for just under half of the company's revenues.

The company conducts business around the world through a series of over 50 operating and sales subsidiaries. It maintains three headquarters: San Jose, California, which houses corporate headquarters and the operational base for the Americas; Paris, which covers European operations; and Tokyo, for Asian operations. Staffing the company's operations are around 21,000 employees. This includes 10,900 people in operations, 1500 in finance and administration, and 8600 in sales and marketing.

Cisco takes a multi-channel approach to marketing and sales. The company's 7200 employee-strong direct sales force, distributors, value-added resellers, service providers, and system integrators are all used to bring its products to market.

Cisco's most lucrative and largest-volume channel is its Web site. Launched in 1997, www.cisco.com is one of the leading online stores and it accounted for roughly $9.6 billion of 1999 revenues, or fully 80 percent of revenues.

Like many companies in the computer hardware and software industries, Cisco has organized its operations around its customers. There are three major customer groups in the networking industry: service providers; enterprise; and small and medium businesses. In each, Cisco is either first or second in market share. In June 1998, the company added a fourth emerging group to the mix, consumers.

As voice, data, and video transmissions converge, Cisco's service-provider customers include companies that specialize in Internet access, wireless and traditional telephone companies, and cable companies. Including companies such as US West, Cox Communications, and Convergent Communications, service providers contribute about 30 percent of Cisco's revenue.

Enterprise customers include large organizations, such as the US Post Office, Charles Schwab and Company, and PeopleSoft. This group needs end-to-end solutions that span multiple locations and connect smaller, unrelated networks. Enterprise customers account for about 50 percent of the company's revenues.

The company's small/medium business customers require equipment for internal networks and connections to the Internet, suppliers, and customers. The lower-priced access and switching products targeted at these businesses are among Cisco's fastest growing segments. The needs of these customers are largely serviced by Cisco resellers and account for about 20 percent of revenues.

Cisco's newest customer group is consumers themselves. The company is making and marketing the equipment needed to create computer networks in the home and connect them to external networks and service providers.

Cisco was founded on the strength of a single product, but its growth has been driven by its ability to remain on the leading edge of the ever-expanding and changing vision of exactly what end-to-end networking means. This has resulted in a planning cycle that is based on Internet years, a time period that CEO John Chambers likens to one-seventh of a calendar year.

As new technologies and environmental change impact Cisco's markets, the company quickly crafts a response from one of four options:

- internal efforts;
- joint development projects with outside companies;
- adding an outside company's product to its offerings; or
- purchasing all or part of an outside company for the needed resources.

In the last seven years, the last option has played a huge role in Cisco's growth. The company has made over 40 acquisitions – over $17 billion worth – since its first in 1993, each adding to the breadth of its product offerings. These product lines now support all major networking technologies and standards, including Ethernet, Gigabit Ethernet, Token Ring, Asynchronous Transfer Mode switching, Synchronous Optical Network/ Synchronous Digit Hierarchy, Digital Subscriber Line, Dial, and converged data, voice and video technologies. Here are its major product lines.

Hardware

Routing products. Cisco's founders invented the multiprotocol router, which moves information between networks that speak different "languages." Routers are the backbone of connected networks and the infrastructure of the Internet. The company currently owns an 85 percent share of the router market.

The company offers a broad range of routers, starting with the Cisco 12000 Gigabit Switch Router series, the 7500 series, the 7200 series Universal Broadband Router, the 4500 and 4700 series, the 3810 and 3600 series, the 2600 series of Modular Access Routers, and the 2500, 1600, 1000, 800, 700, and 90 series product families. It also sells a wide variety of router accessories, including line cards, interface processors, port adapters, and network modules.

Access servers. Cisco's access server families give remote users the ability to access the Internet and organizational intranets. They are designed for a range of applications from high volume service providers to remote servers for small businesses.

The company's products include with the AccessPath LS3 and TS3 integrated systems, the AS5800, 5300, and 5200 Universal Access servers, and the 2500 series.

LAN switches. Switches increase the data packet capacity and efficiency of routers and, thus, communication between networks. Cisco owns a 35 percent share of the LAN switch market.

The company's most popular LAN switches are sold under the Catalyst name and include the 6000, 5000, and 4000 series. It also sells the token ring switches in the 3900 series, the 3000 series, and the 2900 series, as well as XL switches, micro switches, the WS-C1400 concentrator and the FastPAD product families.

Hubs. Cisco's hubs connect shared devices and network segments. The company sells 1500 series 10/100 Micro Hubs and the 100, 200, and 300 FastHub series.

WAN switches. Cisco's WAN switching solutions are used in high-demand networks through which integrated traffic, including voice, video, and data, is moving. WAN switches are offered in the MGX, IGX and BPX product lines. ATM products include the Lightstream 1010 switch, MGX concentrator, and Voice Network and Dial Access Switching Systems.

Internet service/security products. Cisco's Internet Service and Security Products are designed to enhance quality of service and network security. Service products include LocalDirector, Cache Engine, and DistributedDirector, which ensure timely access and eliminate redundant content between multiple servers. Security products include the IOS and PIX Firewall, to prevent unauthorized access; NetSonar, to create a secure environment for Internet commerce; and NetRanger, which terminates unauthorized activity.

Other products. Cisco also sells the products and accessories needed to create and link networks. These include cabling, transceivers, and power supplies.

Software

Cisco IOS software. Cisco Internetwork Operating System (IOS) is the software platform that controls all of the company's products and ties them together under a single standard. It also represents the company's bid to define and control the industry standard for networking products, in much the same way as Microsoft did with Windows. (IOS technologies are licensed to other companies, including competitors, for use in their products.)

The latest version of IOS is Release 12.0 and most Cisco products have at least some features of the platform built in. The software supports LAN and WAN protocols, helps optimize WAN services, and control access. IOS also allows centralized, integrated, and automated installation and management of products.

The Cisco IOS software platform provides network services and enables network applications. Foundational network services include connectivity, security, scalability, reliability, and management. Enabling network services support applications such as multimedia, quality of service, and voice.

Network management applications. CiscoWorks 2000 is a suite of standards-based applications that allows customers to manage their Cisco devices from a single console. It includes programs such as Resource Manager Essentials, CWSI Campus, CiscoView, and Internetwork Performance Monitor.

The Netsys Management suite is a family of network management tools used in troubleshooting, managing, and planning networks. It includes the Performance, Connectivity, and LAN Service Manager programs.

For IBM environments, where existing mainframe systems are linked to newer open networks, the company sells the CiscoWorks Blue suite. This includes Maps, SNA View, and Internetwork Status Monitor.

For Windows, Cisco created CiscoWorks Windows, Total Control Manager, Enterprise Accounting (a family of enterprise network management accounting and billing applications), and Netsys Baseliner.

Other software. The company offers additional management and access software. User Control Point allows the creation of individualized user services over a single network and WebClient supports remote access into mainframe systems. Product-based software includes the CiscoSecure suite for access servers and Catalyst switching software.

For the layperson, the upshot of this rather bewildering assortment of hardware and software is that from a single product line, Cisco has quickly made itself a one-stop shop for Internet plumbing supplies. Now, with the convergence of data and voice technologies, the company is preparing to compete with companies such as Lucent and Nortel in the $250 billion telecommunications equipment market.

Income statement

Year	Revenue ($m)	Net income ($m)	Net profit margin	Employees
1999	12,154.0	2,096.0	17.2%	21,000
1998	8,458.8	1,350.1	16.0%	15,000
1997	6,440.2	1,048.7	16.3%	11,000
1996	4,096.0	913.3	22.3%	8,782
1995	1,978.9	421.0	21.3%	4,086
1994	1,243.0	314.9	25.3%	2,443
1993	649.0	172.0	26.5%	1,451
1992	339.6	84.4	24.9%	882
1991	183.2	43.2	23.6%	505
1990	69.8	13.9	19.9%	254

Stock history

	Stock price ($)			P/E		Per share ($)		
Year	FY High	FY Low	FY Close	High	Low	Earns	Div.	Book value
1999	34.63	10.28	31.06	112	33	0.31	0.00	1.77
1998	17.43	7.58	15.97	83	36	0.21	0.00	1.14
1997	9.00	5.03	8.85	53	30	0.17	0.00	0.71
1996	6.58	2.85	5.76	41	18	0.16	0.00	0.48
1995	3.27	1.13	3.10	41	14	0.08	0.00	0.28
1994	2.27	1.04	1.17	38	17	0.06	0.00	0.18
1993	1.59	0.62	1.44	40	16	0.04	0.00	0.11
1992	0.75	0.26	0.74	38	13	0.02	0.00	0.06
1991	0.27	0.07	0.27	27	7	0.01	0.00	0.03
1990	0.11	0.04	0.09	11	4	0.01	0.00	0.02

1999 year-end financials

Debt ratio	0.0%
Return on equity	22.3%
Cash ($m)	827.0
Current ratio	1.54
Long-term debt ($m)	0.0
Shares outstanding (millions)	6,595.0
Dividend yield	0.0%
Dividend payout	0.0%
Market value ($m)	204,841.4

Financial data provided by Hoover's Online (www.hoovers.com) and Media General Financial Services, Inc.

Cisco contacts

Cisco Systems, Inc.   Phone: 408–526–4000
170 West Tasman Drive   Fax: 408–526–4100
San Jose, CA 95134, USA   URL: www.cisco.com

CEO: John Chambers   CFO: Larry Carter   HR: Barbara Beck

Dell Computer Corporation –

Round Rock, Texas, USA

Executive snapshot

The secret of the second largest computer systems company in the world
is simple.

"The success of Dell Computer is founded on the power of direct
connections with our customers," says company founder and CEO Michael
Dell.

Dell backdrop

The "Dell Story" has become an entrepreneurial legend that so inex-
tricably intertwines Michael Dell and the company he founded that
sometimes it is difficult to figure out which Dell is being discussed.

Birth of a salesman

It starts in 1983, when the 18-year-old Dell is enrolled as a freshman
in the premed program at the University of Texas in Austin. He, as the
story goes, is not very interested in the medical profession, but he
does like computers. Late 1983 finds him buying up remaindered IBM
PCs from local retailers, upgrading them in his room, and selling them
to anyone who will buy them, students, small businesses, etc.

Future focus

Direct from Dell

If it weren't true, you would think the Dell story reads like a dime novel. College kid takes on the world's most powerful company and in a dozen years builds the world's second largest computer brand. And, in the process, makes millionaires out of literally thousands of investors.

But it's not a novel. It's real life and there's nothing novel about the Dell story at all. It's the way business normally works. Anyone that starts a company, runs a company, or works for a company should study Dell to learn what makes the business world go round. What can you learn from Dell?

1 Start early. The personal computer revolution in the business field started in August 1981 with the introduction of the IBM PC. How many managers asked themselves back in 1981, "Should we go into the personal computer business in competition with IBM?"

Not too many. You had to be a college student, premed at that, with only the thought of making a few extra bucks, to jump into the computer business.

What was possible in 1983 is not possible today. And may not have been possible in 1985 or 1987 or 1989. Who knows, except earlier is better.

2 Narrow the focus. Over the past two decades, there have been several hundred brands of personal computers. How many were sold only by phone? None, that I know of.

Why not? Because conventional wisdom said that IBM must know what they're doing. And they use computer retailers and a direct sales force to sell their PCs. So we have to do the same.

Fortunately for Michael Dell, he was too young and too inexperienced to know what the conventional wisdom was. He just knew that he had no chance of selling an unknown brand assembled by a bunch of college students to retail outlets. They preferred selling IBMs, Compaqs and Macintoshes.

Dell was lucky in other ways. No sooner had his company become successful than it did what all successful companies do. It branched out. The first branch was a direct sales force put together to call on corporate customers. Lucky for Dell, that branch bombed. The second branch was into the retail field. Lucky for Dell, that branch also bombed. Now Dell was back to its core strategy: direct sales to corporate customers. Unfortunately it can't leave well enough alone. The latest branching out at Dell is into the consumer marketplace. Maybe it will get lucky again.

3 Companies create markets. Markets don't create opportunities for companies. What was the market for direct sales of personal computers before Dell? Very small. No one thought that it was an efficient way to sell PCs. Since Dell became a big deal, many other companies have jumped into direct selling, including brand leader Compaq.

What is the market for direct sales of television sets, automobiles, pianos? Very small. Does that mean that these products could not be sold in this fashion? Not necessarily. It only means that no one has tried to do so in a powerful way. Companies create markets. Markets don't just arise out of nowhere.

4 Successful companies go "whole hog." If the only strategic decision Dell ever made were to sell computers direct, the company would have never become the powerhouse that it is. The brilliance of the Dell strategy is taking the direct-selling concept to the next level.

When you buy a computer at retail, you generally want to take the box home. Selling by phone is different. You don't need to deliver instantly. You have a couple of days to build the computer from scratch. The customer benefits from Dell's ability to tailor its products. (It's what we once called "The personalized personal computer.") Dell customer service representatives deftly present a wide range of choices. Do you want more memory (or less)? Do you want a modem and what speed? Do you want a CD, a floppy drive, a Zip drive? What software do you want us to load on your machine? The choices are endless.

You can't get a tailor-made personal computer at retail. This is the essence of Dell's strategy. Helping Dell, of course, is the increasing complexity of personal computers. As long as there are hundreds of viable options, and as long as Dell maintains its focus on its direct-sales distribution method, the company should continue to be an economic power for decades to come.

Dell's freshman year is not yet over when he decides he can make a living selling computers and at the end of the school year, he informs his unhappy parents of his plan. A compromise is reached: Michael will run his business over the summer vacation. If it is not a profitable endeavor, he will return to school.

In the summer of 1984, in his first month, Dell sells $180,000 worth of PCs and the medical profession loses a future colleague. By 1985, the young tycoon abandons upgrading older PCs and starts assembling his own brand featuring an 8-megahertz Intel 8088 processor. Dell buys components, assembles them to order, and sells them directly to customers at a 15 percent discount to established brands. Demand is strong and the business is self-funding. A year later, Dell Computer has 250 employees and the company introduces an Intel-based 286 model that is as good as any other machine on the market.

Going global ... and public

In June 1987, the company makes its first foray beyond the US when it opens a subsidiary sales office in the United Kingdom. It begins to build its strength in service and becomes the first PC company to offer next day, on-site product service. Just three years after Dell's formal start, the company's incoming call rate reaches almost 1700 per day, driving sales over $100 million.

In October 1987, in the wake of the US stock market crash, the company completes a private placement through Goldman Sachs. In June 1988, the company goes public, raising $30 million in the initial public offering. The company employs 650 people and records sales of $159 million.

In 1990, the company opens its first manufacturing center outside the US in Limerick, Ireland. It serves European, Middle Eastern, and African markets. The new decade also ushers in a learning period for the company as it tries to build its own components. Dell also makes its first move into the consumer market, striking deals with computer and office supply chain stores. The moves cause inventories and costs to rise. The firm records a 64 percent drop in profits on increased sales.

The company introduces its first notebook PC in 1991 and the service that becomes known as DellPlus. It offers free installation of applications software as a standard service option, using patented technology to install items from network cards to customers' proprietary, in-house applications as part of the manufacturing process. Sales jump to $890 million that year.

In 1992, Dell more than doubles its revenues – revenue hits the $2 billion mark. It is included for the first time among the *Fortune 500*. Dell introduces the product line that will become its workhorse, the Dimension PC.

The company is one of the top five PC makers worldwide by 1993. It expands into Asia and the Pacific with sales subsidiaries in Australia and Japan. Revenues approach $3 billion for the fiscal year.

Heads spin in a fast recovery

Fast expansion, a lack of focus on its direct sale business model, and quality problems in its notebook line make 1994 a critical year in the young company's history. Michael Dell's reaction to the crisis, which causes a $36 million loss in net income, shows a maturity well beyond that of most 28-year-olds: he hires a senior management team designed to solve the company's problems and puts them to work.

Motorola's Mort Tofler, who understands the assembly business and the intricacies of international growth, takes over day-to-day operations. New hires from Apple Computer's successful PowerBook notebook line right Dell's quality problems and Dell introduces the Latitude line, which remains one of the highest quality machines on the market. The company quits the retail market, putting all of its efforts back into direct sales. Within the year, the company is back on track and Michael Dell is crowned a comeback king by the media.

In 1995, $1000 invested in Dell's initial offering is worth over $11,000. Dell starts the construction of an Asia-Pacific manufacturing center in Penang, Malaysia, which will generate its products for the region.

Direct sales reign supreme

The 238,000 square foot Penang manufacturing center comes online in 1996 and the company opens what may be the primary engine for its future growth, the Dell online store at www.dell.com. The company also expands into the fast-growing network server market with its PowerEdge line. The fiscal year's revenues break over $5 billion and earn Dell a spot in the Standard & Poor's 500 stock index.

In 1997, the company ships its 10,000,000th computer system and the $1000 invested in the initial offering is worth almost $120,000. Dell continues its push beyond the stand-alone personal computer and enters the $15 billion workstation market with the Precision line.

In August 1997, Dell takes a lesson from the automotive industry and introduces leasing plans for its products. It forms Dell Financial Services L.P. (DFS), a joint venture with Newcourt Credit Group, an asset-based financier with $23 billion in owned and managed assets, operating in 24 countries. DFS provides services ranging from simple hardware leases to corporate technology finance agreements that include software, extra support, installation, and asset recovery services. Revenues for the fiscal year climb to $7.7 billion.

In 1998, a red-letter year in the company's history, the lucky investor who had the foresight to purchase and hold tight to $1000 of stock in Dell's initial offering owns a stake worth over $370,000. Michael Dell, at 33 years old, is the longest-tenured CEO in the industry and thanks to the stock market bonanza is, according to *Fortune*, the world's thirteenth richest person.

In June 1998, the company enters the $24 billion enterprise computing market with the introduction of the PowerVault product line. A little more than a year after introducing its leasing program, in November 1998, Dell Financial Services tops $1 billion in lease originations. It boasts over 81,000 lease agreements covering 400,000 assets and over half of Dell's top 20 corporate customers are using the program.

Continued expansion, in and outside of the US, is a clear pattern. In March 1998, Dell begins development of a new, 570-acre manufacturing campus in Austin, Texas with the construction of a manufacturing facility for servers and workstations. The 300,000-square-foot facility will employ 1200 when fully staffed.

In August 1998, the company announces plans for a new manufacturing and customer center in Eldorado do Sul, Brazil that opens in 1999. From this plant, the company manufactures and sells its products to customers in Brazil, Argentina, Uruguay, Paraguay and Chile.

At the same time, the company begins direct sales and technical-support operations in nine major metropolitan areas of China, including Beijing, Shanghai, Guangzhou and Xiamen. As part of Dell's direct operations in China, toll-free sales and technical-support telephone numbers are established to provide immediate local-language assistance to customers. The company provides service to the Chinese market through a new 135,000-square-foot integrated sales and manufacturing facility and customer call center in the southern coastal city of Xiamen in Fujian Province.

Sales via the Internet reach $10 million per day in 1998 and the company receives two million visits each week to the 44 country-specific stores at www.dell.com. Dell is the biggest online seller of computers. It addresses the number one concern of online shoppers, transaction security, covering the $50 liability typically not covered by lenders should a customer's credit-card numbers be stolen over the Internet.

In 1998, the company begins a $70 million advertising campaign designed to build name and brand recognition. For the fiscal year, it records almost $1 billion in net income on $12.3 billion in sales.

In 1999, Dell makes the first acquisition in its history. The company buys network equipment maker, ConvergeNet Technologies, in a $340 million deal. Dell also expands its product offerings into the low-end of the PC market with their first computer priced under $1000, and into the wireless market with pagers.

In fiscal 2000 and beyond, the siren call of the Internet lures the company into Internet services. The company expands its Internet presence with the launch of www.gigabuys.com, which combined with the DellWare program, is an online source for more than 30,000 computer-related products. Dell also announces a series of programs providing Internet infrastructure services including Service Provider Direct, Dell Expert Services, PowerApp web server appliances, and Dell Ventures for Internet-based investments.

Dell close-up

In the late 1990s, tracking Dell Computer Corporation has been like trying to follow a speeding bullet with the naked eye. At best, the observer can examine stop-action photographs and marvel at the computer company's growth trajectory. By way of illustration, examine the sales generated on www.dell.com, the company's Web site, since July 1996 when it debuted. Eighteen months later, at the end of FY 98, the company reported $4 million in *daily* sales. Sounds good, yes? By fiscal 2000, daily sales rose to $40 million per day, accounting for roughly 50 percent of revenues. Dell's total sales were $25.2 billion in fiscal 2000.

Between 1995 and 1999, the company grew at 53 percent annually and profits increased 89 percent annually. In 18 consecutive quarters, the company has reported record revenues in what has become a commodity-type market where margins are very tight, price-cutting the norm, and competing products usually feature few differences. It is a long way from company founder Michael Dell selling computers from his dorm room.

Headquartered in Round Rock, Texas, not far from Austin where Michael Dell started the company in that University of Texas dormitory in 1984, Dell Computer Corporation is the world's leading direct computer systems company. In the US, it is the leading supplier of PCs to business customers, government agencies, educational institutions and consumers, and controls nearly a third of the market. The company employs over 36,500 people worldwide.

Geographic markets

Dell's main revenue base continues to be the US, but it is expanding fast globally. The company operates sales offices in 33 countries around the world and sells its products and services in more than 170 countries and territories. Its Web site contains over 80 country-specific online stores.

Texas is home to Dell Americas, the regional business unit for the US, Canada and Latin America. Dell Americas contributes 71 percent of the company's revenue, or $17.9 billion. Its market position is number one in the US and it employs 24,300 people. Operating subsidiaries are located in Ontario, Canada, Santiago, Chile, Monterrey and Mexico City, Mexico, Bogota, Colombia and Eldorado do Sul, Brazil.

Dell maintains three regional headquarters for its major geographical markets. Dell Europe, which covers Europe, the Middle East and Africa, is headquartered in Bracknell, UK. The region contributes 22 percent of revenues, $5.6 billion in fiscal 2000. It is number two in the market and employs 9100. Subsidiaries are located in 15 European countries, South Africa, and the United Arab Emirates.

Dell Asia is based in Hong Kong and serves the Asia-Pacific region, and Dell Japan covers the Japanese market from Kawasaki. The region accounts for 7 percent of the company's revenues, or $1.1 billion in fiscal 2000. It is number seven in the Asia-Pacific market; in Japan, the company is also number seven. Total employees in the two regions is 3100 people. Subsidiaries are located in Australia, China, India, Malaysia, New Zealand, Singapore, Taiwan, Thailand, and South Korea.

There are six manufacturing centers. In Austin and Nashville in the US, and Eldorado do Sul, Brazil for the Americas, in Limerick, Ireland for Europe, the Middle East and Africa, in Penang for Asia-Pacific and Japan, and in Xiamen, China for the mainland. Each makes the company's full line of products.

Products and services

Understanding the company's product line is simple. It sells personal computer systems directly to its customers, nearly two-thirds of whom are large corporations, government agencies, and educational institutions. Dell also serves medium and small businesses and is currently making a concerted effort to capture a substantial share of the home-PC market.

The products include a full range from personal computers aimed at small business and home use to enterprise-level PC-based network servers and workstations. Each unit is manufactured to order based on a customer purchase. The company's products are highly regarded for their quality as well as price to performance ratio. In 1998, the company earned more than 325 product and service awards from technology publications around the world.

The Dimension desktop PC line is designed for small-business and home users. The OptiPlex line is aimed at corporate and institutional customers who need networked systems.

Two lines of notebook PCs cover the market. The high performance Latitude line is designed for large corporate, government and education customers, and addresses total cost of ownership, network connectivity and broad operating-system support. The less sophisticated, more economical Inspiron machines are targeted at individuals or small to medium-sized businesses.

Dell Precision workstations run more complex applications, such as CAD programs, digital content creation, software development, and economic modeling. They are ranked first in sales worldwide. PowerEdge Network Servers are the fastest-growing brand in the category since their introduction in September 1996. Dell is second in the US server market, fourth worldwide.

The PowerVault line was introduced in June 1998 and extends the company's reach into enterprise systems. These products include SCSI-based storage subsystems, tape backup systems, storage management software, and enterprise-level, scalable disk subsystems.

Dell supplements its computers with a wide range of value-added services including factory integration of proprietary hardware and software, leasing and installation, warranty coverage, and end-user support. The company offers extensive on-site servicing through partnerships with companies such as Wang Global and Unisys. Counting these partners, it claims a service force of over 25,000 worldwide.

The DellWare program completes the package by making available over 30,000 hardware, software, and peripheral products from other companies in the industry.

Income Statement

Year	Revenue ($m)	Net income ($m)	Net profit margin	Employees
1999	18,243.0	1,460.0	8.0%	24,400
1998	12,327.0	944.0	7.7%	16,000
1997	7,759.0	518.0	6.7%	10,350
1996	5,296.0	272.0	5.1%	8,400
1995	3,475.3	149.2	4.3%	6,400
1994	2,873.2	(35.9)	–	5,980
1993	2,013.9	101.6	5.0%	4,650
1992	889.9	50.9	5.7%	2,970
1991	546.2	27.2	5.0%	2,050
1990	388.6	5.1	1.3%	1,500

Stock history

	Stock price ($)			P/E		Per share ($)		
Year	FY High	FY Low	FY Close	High	Low	Earns	Div.	Book value
1999	50.19	12.61	50.00	95	24	0.53	0.00	0.91
1998	12.98	3.74	12.43	41	12	0.32	0.00	0.50
1997	4.52	0.84	4.13	25	5	0.17	0.00	0.29
1996	1.54	0.62	0.86	17	7	0.09	0.00	0.33
1995	0.75	0.30	0.67	15	6	0.05	0.00	0.26
1994	0.77	0.22	0.34	–	–	(0.02)	0.00	0.19
1993	0.78	0.23	0.72	16	5	0.05	0.00	0.16
1992	0.38	0.21	0.33	13	7	0.03	0.00	0.12
1991	0.24	0.05	0.24	12	2	0.02	0.00	0.06
1990	0.10	0.05	0.05	10	5	0.01	0.00	0.04

1999 year-end financials

Debt ratio	18.1%
Return on equity	80.8%
Cash ($m)	520.0
Current ratio	1.72
Long-term debt ($m)	512.0
Shares outstanding (millions)	2,543.0
Dividend yield	0.0%
Dividend payout	
Market value ($m)	127,150.0

Financial data provided by Hoover's Online (www.hoovers.com) and Media General Financial Services, Inc.

Dell contacts

Dell Computer Corporation   Phone: 512–338–4400
One Dell Way   Fax: 512–728–3653
Round Rock, TX 78682, USA   URL: www.dell.com

CEO: Michael Dell   CFO: James Schneider   HR: Thomas Green

Telefonaktiebolaget LM Ericsson

– Stockholm, Sweden

Executive snapshot

Convergence remains the driving concept in today's telecommunications industry and LM Ericsson installed a new leader and a new organizational structure to cope with the coming changes.

"Above all, we have to increase the tempo and quality of what we are doing. Tempo and speed are becoming increasingly important in intensified international competition, especially within our industry; telecommunications and IT," says LM Ericsson chairman and CEO Lars Ramqvist.

Ericsson backdrop

LM Ericsson has come full circle. Founded in the opportunity and chaos of the communications revolution of the late 19th century, the company is faced with many of the same challenges almost exactly a century later – this time as a major player in a huge industry, instead of a single entrepreneur in a rented kitchen.

LM Ericsson, the man

Lars Magnus Ericsson is 21 years old when he finally reaches Stockholm, but he has already come a long way. The young man is 11 when his father dies in 1857, a farm boy in the Varmland province in central

Future focus

Selling outside the box

The nine-dot puzzle has become a cliche of management theorists. (Connect the dots with four straight lines without the pen leaving the paper.) It can't be done without getting outside the box. The lesson: think outside the box. Easier said than done. There seems to be an invisible barrier that keeps every human being inside a "barless" jail. Leaving the box is not an option.

So, too, with companies. There seems to be a box around the border that serves to keep a company focused on its own country. Leaving the country is not an option. We often see this in our consulting work. "Why don't you go global?" "Huh. We, ah ... we need to, ah ... increase our market share ..." (Or profits ... or technological skills.) There's always a reason why a company does not want to leave the country box.

Ericsson is an unusual company. Just five years after the company was founded, it secured its first international order. This would not be unusual today, but Ericsson was founded in 1876. By 1900 the company was selling its equipment around the world, in China, Australia, New Zealand and South Africa. More than anything else, in our opinion, this relentless drive to become a global company is responsible for Ericsson's continuing success. In some businesses it may be possible to remain a domestic-only player, but not in any business built around a technology.

Today's technology leaders are all global players, from Microsoft to Cisco to Oracle to IBM. You can't be a technological leader if your marketing efforts terminate at the border. Companies in smaller countries seem to suffer from a double dose of inferiority. First they are small in comparison with the larger companies around the world. Second, their country is small in comparison with larger countries.

Sweden is a small country. So why was Ericsson able to accomplish what much larger companies could not? Our experience suggests that some cultures seem possessed by the desire to carry their ideas and concepts to the far corners of the world. A corporate missionary zeal, if you will. While in other countries, that missionary zeal is missing.

Today you have no choice. It's the law of the jungle. Eat or be eaten. If you don't take your products and services to the far corners of the world, companies in those far corners will take their products into your country and take away your business, by virtue of their larger size, reputation and accumulated corporate knowledge. Today, Ericsson is the most global of the telecommunication companies with operations in some 140 countries.

The success of Ericsson has another aspect. Ericsson elected to focus on a communications product. If you want to build a company that will live for 100 years or more, you can't go wrong when you select some aspect of human communications. A significant percentage of the enormous fortunes that have been built in the past 100 years have been built around communications empires. Newspapers, magazines, television, telephone, cable, TV, and, of course, the Internet. People do not want to live isolated lives as hermits. They want to know what is happening to the rest of the human race. Communications technologies seem to have an unlimited potential.

Take Ericsson, for example. Here is a company founded two years before General Electric. Yet we predict that Ericsson will have a bright future while General Electric's star will begin to fade. The difference does not lie in the skill or experience of the managers of each corporation. Rather the difference is purely in the nature of the businesses the two companies have elected to pursue. Nothing ensures a long and prosperous life more than picking the right business to focus on.

Like most companies, Ericsson has made its share of mistakes along the way. The company launched and sold off units making such products as radios, television sets, electric meters and electric cattle fences. It even made a large investment in the "automated office," or office of the future, which never went anywhere.

You could also fault Ericsson for operating in both halves of the telecom business: handsets and systems. In theory, of course, the company might be better off focusing on one side of the business or another. (Like Nokia, which is the world's largest maker of mobile phones.) But there is some rationale for being in both businesses. What you learn in one half can be helpful in the other half. Only time will tell who has the better strategy, Ericsson or Nokia.

One thing is certain. Both companies are more focused (and consequently in better shape) than their American competitor Motorola. In addition to telecom products, Motorola is into computers, microprocessors and, of course, made a disastrous investment in the Iridium satellite system.

Sweden, where he is the last son living at home with his mother and two younger sisters.

Leaving school at 14, he works as a farm laborer, as a worker in an ore drilling crew, and as a construction laborer on the railroad. Drawn to the mechanical trades and anxious to earn a better living, he saves enough to apprentice himself to a metal smith and a machinist.

By 1867, Ericsson is ready for a world of larger opportunity and comes to Stockholm. After a week's work to prove himself, the young man obtains a job at the Oller & Company Telegraph Factory. His salary is five krona per week, an amount he recalls later as "sufficient for my needs, so that I thankfully saw life much brighter than ever before and felt then the first breath of the joy of life in my heart."

Oller is the first telegraph equipment maker in Sweden, and Ericsson works in the emerging industry for six years, learning to manufacture the products. In his time off he studies drafting, and learns to speak German and English. In 1873, the company founder, impressed with Ericsson's industriousness, recommends him for the first of two grants from the Swedish government.

Ericsson travels to Germany where he works at a number of firms, learning new methods for making telegraph equipment, instruments and indicators. He brings his new-found knowledge home to Stockholm, but puts it to work at Oller for only a few short months.

In April 1876, the 30-year old Ericsson opens a telegraph equipment repair shop in a rented kitchen at 15 Drottninggatan in Stockholm. Investor Maria Stromberg lends him 1000 krona to capitalize the company and Ericsson buys a pedal lathe and hires a 12-year-old assistant. A few weeks later, former Oller colleague Carl Andersson joins Ericsson with another 1000 krona and becomes a partner in the newly established LM Ericsson & Company. Work comes fast and the repair shop moves to larger digs.

Armed with the knowledge he gains from repairing broken equipment, Ericsson soon begins producing new equipment with improved designs. In 1877, he creates a dial telegraph instrument for use in railway systems and a fire telegraph system for small communities. Quality in design and construction become hallmarks of the new company's products. By year-end, the company employs four more workers.

In 1878, the entrepreneur marries Hilda Simonsson, who soon proves as enterprising as her husband. She takes on the job of winding of electromagnetic reels with silk-insulated copper wire and, rumor has it, even takes the reels to bed at night, winding herself to sleep.

LM Ericsson, the telephone maker

In 1877 and 1878, the rush to telephony set off by Bell's invention begins to reach Sweden. At Ericsson, foreign-made phones show up for repair. Unsurprisingly, the boss soon comes to the conclusion that he can make better telephones than these, and he does.

In November 1878, Ericsson sells its first phones in pairs. They are "magnet telephones with signal trumpet" that sell for a hefty 55 krona per pair. The company sells 22 pairs by year-end and, in 1879 sells 74 more of the luxury items. Ericsson grows to 10 employees, counting the owners.

In 1880, Bell's telephone company begins constructing telephone networks in Stockholm, Gothenburg, Malmo, Sundsvall and Soderhamn, and Ericsson gets an early taste of Ma Bell's monopolistic power. The US company uses its own equipment and does not plan to share the market with another ... no matter how good his equipment.

Luckily, there are Swedes who want a piece of this new business and one such entrepreneur bids on a system in the city of Gavle. He wins the bid with the help of Ericsson equipment, which the purchasing agents find better designed and made than Bell's. That same year, Ericsson wins a telephone equipment order from Bergen, Norway. It is the first international order for the 5-year-old company.

In 1882, Henrik Cedergren secures Ericsson's future when he begins planning the country's first economical telephone service. Envisioning a telephone in every Swedish home, Cedergren forms Stockholms Allmanna Telefonaktiebolag (SAT) and contracts with Ericsson for the system's equipment.

Ericsson not only provides 1000 telephones and 22 switchboards, it also creates the first "multiple desk" in Europe and automatic connecting switchboards that enable SAT to undercut Bell's subscription rates by half. By year-end, SAT has 785 subscribers and Ericsson is building a factory at Tulegatan to house its fast-growing operations.

In 1884, the company moves into the new facility with almost 100 employees. In 1885, Ericsson releases the first mass-produced telephone handset incorporating receiver and speaker in one unit. By 1886, SAT is a resounding success with over 3000 subscribers, almost twice Bell's total, all using Ericsson equipment. In 1888, the 20,000th telephone leaves Ericsson's factory floor. The company also becomes the impetus for, and primary customer of, Sieverts Kabelverk, the first Swedish covered-copper cable company.

By the end of the decade, Ericsson employs 153 people and the company is already expanding its new factory. Revenues hit SKr500,000. In 1891, Ericsson gains a competitor when Swedish telephone operator Telegrafveret starts buying up local operators and then decides to manufacture its own equipment.

Ericsson responds by building its export business. In 1893, it makes its first sale to the Dutch. The company also creates the first desk telephone with handset and launches it internationally. The popular phone, which helps push annual production above 10,000 for the first time, becomes the company's trademark.

In 1896, Ericsson creates Aktiebolaget LM Ericsson & Co., a new corporation that takes the place of Ericsson & Company. It is capitalized at one million krona and its founder owns all the shares, except for a small number distributed to Carl Anderson, now the company's works manager, and 31 other key employees.

In the late 1890s, Ericsson begins to withdraw from the business. In 1900, he resigns the presidency and in 1901, he resigns as chairman, keeping a seat on the board. Then, in 1903 at age 57, Ericsson sells off his shares and returns to a life of farming – albeit under very different circumstances than he had left 40 years before – on his estate outside Stockholm.

Building an international customer base

The 1890s bring Ericsson's first concerted moves toward an international organization. As domestic competition grows (SAT starts its own equipment unit in 1896), the company starts to look to new growth markets. The export business expands quickly. By 1900, Ericsson is selling equipment in China, Australia, New Zealand, and South Africa. It supplies the British military with field telephones during the Boer War. At the end of the century, the company boasts annual revenues of SKr4 million and 90 percent is attributable to exports.

In 1897, Ericsson begins assembling phones at a factory in St. Petersburg, Russia. In 1899, it expands that operation to include manufacturing. The move proves prescient when, in 1901, SAT wins long-term contracts to operate telephone companies in Russia and Poland. Realizing he cannot supply the equipment needs of an international operation and that Ericsson is already in position to serve the markets, Cedergren sells the SAT manufacturing operation to Ericsson for a stock stake and the company again becomes SAT's chief supplier.

In 1902, Ericsson opens its first office in New York City and opens a factory in Buffalo, NY in 1904. In 1905, the telecom company joins SAT and Swedish industrialist Marcus Wallenberg in a consortium to operate the Mexican telephone system. In 1907, the network in Mexico comes online and Ericsson's annual phone production exceeds 82,000 units. For the first time, Ericsson is a telephone operating company.

In 1908, the company wins a contract to modernize Bangkok's phone system and in 1909, when Henrik Cedergren dies, Ericsson forms a Mexican subsidiary that controls the telephone service in that nation. In the second decade of the new century, expansion continues with new manufacturing subsidiaries in France, Hungary, Great Britain and Austria. World War I impacts the export business around the world and with the Russian Revolution in 1917, the company loses its operations in that country.

Nevertheless, the global demand for telecom remains very strong and in 1918, SAT is merged into Ericsson. As a result, Ericsson's revenues continue to rise through a catastrophic decade, from SKr9 million in 1913 to SKr14 million in 1920.In early 1920s, the company expands into the Netherlands and wins a 50-year concession for telephone operations in southern Italy and Sicily.

The Match King and hard times

In December 1926, at age 81, Lars Magnus Ericsson passes away and a run of hard times begins that almost destroys the company he founded 50 years before. The instrument of Ericsson's downfall is Ivar Krueger, the Match King.

Kreuger makes his first fortune in construction in the late 1910s and as the roaring twenties dawn, he buys control of Swedish Match AB and declares his ambition to control the production and sale of matches worldwide. He proceeds to make his vision a reality, making loans to governments in return for exclusive match concessions and building a complex web involving controlling stakes in hundreds of companies.

A favored son in the investment community, Kreuger is providing investment returns of 30 percent and is billed as the world's most eligible bachelor. In the second half of the 1920s, the Match King starts to diversity and one of his favored investments is Ericsson. He buys stakes in 1926 and again in 1927. By 1930, Kreuger actually controls the company.

Unhappily, Kreuger's empire is a house of cards and he is involved in a wide gamut of dishonest activities – bribery, forged bonds, and inflated sales between his companies. The 1929 crash and ensuing depression squeezes Krueger and, in 1931, to raise cash he sells his stake in Ericsson to Sosthenes Behn's rival telecom company ITT. The deal is made and Kreuger pockets the $11 million in cash, but it is too late. Kreuger commits suicide in March 1932. Then, audits find that Kreuger looted the company's cash reserves replacing the money with French telephone bonds. Ericsson is bankrupt *and* in the hands of a foreign competitor in the midst of a global depression.

It takes all three of Sweden's major banks and foreign banks to revive Ericsson. ITT's interest is reduced, but it retains a stake and a place on the board. The company is forced to reduce its workforce, reorganize, and suspend dividend payments.

By 1937, Ericsson is starting to see the light at the end of tunnel. It is rebuilding cash reserves and in 1938, even begins some long postponed investments in its plants. And then, the light goes out as the world descends into World War II.

During the war, Ericsson works for the Swedish government. Its exports are largely suspended with 80 percent of revenues generated domestically. The company makes telephones, aviation instruments, machine guns, and ammunition, and given the trials of the previous years, actually regains a measure of stability.

Expansion and diversification

The post-war boom generates record demand for telecom equipment and Ericsson's fortunes improve along with it. In 1947, the company expands its manufacturing capacity, building new Swedish plants in Soderhamn, Karlskrona, and Katrineholm. That same year, the company receives a SKr20 million payment for its operations in Poland, now nationalized.

In 1950, Ericsson delivers the first automatic exchange based on crossbar switches. The world's first automatic international call is made using the company's equipment. In 1951, Ericsson buys a controlling stake in US-based North Electric Company of Ohio for $1.7 million. In 1952, the company celebrates the making of its five millionth telephone.

In 1954, its radio subsidiary, Svenska Radioaktiebolaget, enters the fast-developing market for televisions. By 1957, the company is turning TV sets into record-setting revenue figures. The company's export sales make a steady recovery in the 1950s and its Latin American business is particularly strong. Until 1958 that is, when Mexico nationalizes its phone system, taking over the company's operations.

In 1960, the last chapter in the company's run-in with the Match King is written when ITT also gets bitten by the diversification bug and decides to sell its stake in the company. A Swedish consortium led by Marcus Wallenberg, Jr buys the shares from ITT.

The 1960s bring a series of business unit trades that makes Ericsson look more like a business broker than a telecom company. It buys ands sells units making electric cattle fences, radios, TVs, electric meters, and its stake in North Electric. Telecom equipment remains the company's stock in trade and by 1971, Ericsson has sold it millionth crossbar switch. But the company is behind in the race for innovative technology and it knows it.

Ericsson renews its development efforts in the early 1970s and in 1975 regains its edge with the introduction of AXE, a computer-controlled exchange. AXE is Ericsson's most successful product ever and remains its major platform 25 years later. The exchange wins every major telecom contract for two years after its introduction. Bjorn Svedberg, who headed the development project, becomes Ericsson's CEO in 1978.

Unhappily, the lesson in focus does not sink in. In 1980, Ericsson is seduced by the idea of the automated office. It buys a controlling stake in Datasaab, a struggling Swedish computer maker, and teams up with US partner ARCO to meet the anticipated demand.

The market never materializes and Ericsson's profits plunge. By 1985, the company has sold only 3000 units. In 1988, the entire business is dumped at a bargain basement price on Finnish competitor Nokia.

Focus, finally

Ericsson takes a good look around after it leaves the office systems business and it sees what has always been its greatest competency – telephone equipment. By 1985, its AXE digital exchanges are already in use in 63 countries and in 22 mobile systems, an area where demand is steadily growing.

In the mid-1980s, the company wins major contracts with NTT (Japan's phone company), British Telecom, and the French government. Just a few years into the mobile era, Ericsson has a 45 percent share of the world market for mobile systems and in 1989, annual revenues hit SKr39.5 billion.

In 1990, Lars Ramqvist takes over as CEO and the company starts a joyride that that will lead it from SKr45 billion in revenues in that year to 1999s SKr215.4 billion. The key is the company's long standing globalism. In 1994, Ericsson becomes the leading supplier of mobile systems in China with a $400 million equipment deal. In 1995, Ericsson is selling mobile phones in 15 new markets, including India, Vietnam, and countries in Latin America and the Middle East.

By 1996, AXE is the world's best-selling telephone system, with a total of 118 million lines installed or on order in 117 countries, and Ericsson's cellular systems serve 54 million subscribers in 92 countries. Annual revenues drive past the SKr100 billion mark to SKr124.2 billion.

In 1997, 75 million subscribers are connecting through Ericsson systems and the company boasts operations in more than 130 countries. Revenues set yet another record at SKr167 billion, but change is in the air. Convergence is now the name of the game and new Internet technologies are shaking up the industry. Ericsson knows it must adjust to emerging markets.

It starts its move at the peak of its success. In 1998, the company sets another sales record and names Sven-Christer Nilsson as CEO.

Nilsson studies the company and the market for a few months and restructures around customer segments and converging technologies.

The AXE platform is extended with the launch of AXE Open Architecture, which prepares the systems for multimedia traffic. In May 1998, Nilsson goes on the prowl for acquisitions, planning to buy the new technologies he needs.

That same year, Ericsson acquires California-based router and remote access product maker Advanced Computer Communications for SKr2.3 billion. The company also purchases stakes in Mariposa Technology with its ATM-based access products for voice and data transmission, and Juniper, for that company's gigabit router.

The new technologies are selling as fast as Ericsson can buy them. In 1998, the company wins contracts with Dishner in India and Sonera in Finland for remote access systems. In January 1999, British Telecom buys AXE-based systems to deliver combined telephone and datacom services.

Ericsson's restructuring takes effect January 1, 1999, and the company announces it will reduce its workforce by 11,000 employees over two years. The same month, it releases its smallest phone ever, the T28 dual band mobile phone with voice control, automatic world clock, and new battery technology.

In April, the company introduces Mobile Advantage, a wireless office system that connects over public networks. It advertises the solution as "one-phone, one-number accessibility anywhere, anytime." Also in April, Ericsson acquires US-based Torrent Networking Technologies, a supplier of high-capacity aggregation routers, which will be added to Ericsson's carrier-class networking portfolio. The company also acquires California-based TouchWave Inc. for its enterprise IP-technology solutions, which will be added to its PBX systems.

Unfortunately, Sven-Christer Nilsson moves too slowly to refocus Ericsson and he is ousted in a management shake-up in mid-1999. Chairman Lars Ramqvist takes over the CEO position and picks up the restructuring pace. He cuts 15,000 jobs and as the new year begins, sells off Energy Systems power subsidiary to Emerson Electric for $725 million.

In 1999, Ericsson agrees to accept CDMA as the industry standard for wireless communications. It licenses the technology for Qualcomm and buys that company's wireless CDMA infrastructure

operations. Continuing the move toward convergence, Ericsson purchases router maker Torrent Networking Technologies, Touchwave
(an Internet telephony company), and signs a deal for Internet software with Microsoft.

Ericsson close-up

In 1998, telecommunications giant LM Ericsson declared the dawning of the "New Telecoms World." This is a place where mobile communications rule the day, and Internet and telephone networks merge
into a single platform. It is also a world where Ericsson intends to be
among the industry leaders.

The 125-year-old Swedish company has some strong advantages in
the race to the new world. It is big – Ericsson employs 103,000 people
and generated 1999 net sales of SKr215.4 billion. It is global – the
company has been an international player for over 100 years. And it is
established – the company owns the best-selling systems in mobile
telephony and enjoys the largest customer base in the industry.

Of course, any and all of those strengths could also prove to be
shortcomings in a fast-changing environment where new technology
and aggressive competitors can turn the market on its head overnight.
In fact, the company's momentum has slowed and 1999 was a year of
transition with all the attendant costs that usually implies.

The company is acting quickly to reposition itself. Ericsson's investments in technological innovation are on the increase. Of its
100,000 employees, roughly 22,000 in 25 countries are in R&D. It
spent SKr33 billion on R&D in 1999.

The company established a new centralized corporate function for
technology. It will coordinate Ericsson's research and development
and deal with standards, patents, and strategic partnerships. Currently,
it is focused on IP-telephony, wireless data communications, and third-
generation mobile systems.

Ericsson also fundamentally revamped its management team, which
is now led by chairman Lars Ramqvist. Ramqvist has accelarated a
sweeping reorganization in the company's structure that started on
January 1, 1999.

Business segments

Like many companies in the computer and networking industries, Ericsson restructured around customer segments. There are three: network operators and service providers; consumer products (mainly mobile phones); and enterprise solutions. These segments are further organized into major product groups.

Network operators and service providers (NO/SP)
The NO/SP business units create, manufacture, and market the systems that control telecom and data networks. Ericsson employs 64,695 people in these businesses and it is the company's most lucrative, generating SKr149.9 billion in 1999, equal to 69 percent of total sales.

Ericsson systems are based on the company's 25-year-old AXE line, a digital exchange system for wireline and mobile networks and the world's most successful telecommunications system. The AXE platform for Ericsson's mobile telecommunications systems is installed in more than 100 countries, with over 350 network operators. Over 30 percent of the world's mobile telephone users are connected to the company's systems. NO/SP is the company's most profitable segment and it is the world leader in the wireless telephony systems market. One of the segment's goals is to transfer that leading position into the wireless datacom systems market.

The segment is composed of a series of product-based units: GSM, TDMA, and PDC Systems, WCDMA, Wireline Systems, Datacom and IP Services, Transmission Solutions, Professional Services and New and Special Business Operations.

- *GSM Systems.* GSM is the world's most accepted mobile standard and is the dominant standard in Europe. Ericsson is the market leader with 130 systems in 65 countries boasting over 50 million subscribers.
- *TDMA Systems.* TDMA is the digital standard currently used widely in the Americas and parts of Asia. Over 18 million subscribers in more than 35 countries are connected to the company's TDMA systems.
- *PDC Systems.* PDC, the world's second-largest digital standard for mobile systems, is based on TDMA technology and is used in Japan.

Ericsson is the system supplier to six mobile telephone operators in Japan.

- *WCDMA Systems.* The WCDMA standard is the basis for the new third generation of mobile systems that offer IP (Internet Protocol) in addition to telecom services. Ericsson delivered several of the world's first WCDMA experimental systems in Japan in 1998. Ericsson is also participating in experimental systems with operators in Germany, the UK, Italy, and Sweden.
- *Datacom and IP Services.* The Datacom and IP Services unit is spearheading Ericsson's charge into the new, and extremely competitive, Internet-based telephone markets. The unit has gotten closer to customers in this market by setting up shop in the US in Boston and is building market share for its ATM switches designed to transmit both data and telephone traffic over wide area networks.
- *Wireline Systems.* Ericsson's wireline systems are used to manage over 140 million fixed lines for more than 350 customers in 130 countries.
- *Transmission Solutions.* This unit is the home of Ericsson's transport networks for wireline and mobile networks. Just over 100 customers in 80 countries have chosen Ericsson for these digital SDH and fiber optic WDM-based products. Transmission Solutions also includes Mini-Link, a line of wireless microwave links for mobile telephone networks' antennas that handle long-distance traffic in wireless and wireline networks.
- *Professional Services.* This new unit is focused on the market for the operation, maintenance, and management of network systems. Its services include business and network planning, installation and upgrades, and training and support.
- *New and Special Business Operations.* This cutting-edge unit is designed to stay ahead of emerging markets with new ventures. Currently it is exploring areas such as wireless Internet, private radio over cellular, satellite communication, and e-commerce.

Consumer

"Make yourself heard" is the theme of Ericsson's global ad campaign aimed at building brand awareness and phone sales. The company is the world's third largest manufacturer of mobile telephones, but its goal is to move up at least one rank.

Of the 160 million mobile phones estimated to have been sold worldwide in 1998, Ericsson sold just over 24 million. Sales in the segment, which also included pagers and satellite phones, reached SKr46.4 billion in 1999, 21 percent of Ericsson's total revenues. More than 16,400 employees are working in these businesses.

The company may lag compared to arch-rival, and *Future Focus* companion, Nokia, but in 1998 and 1999, it still introduced 40 new mobile phone products. Foremost among them are the SH 888, I 888 World and S 868 mobile telephones, dual-band instruments which increase service reliability by connecting the caller on whichever is the least busy of two networks at any given moment. The I 888 World phone, which can be used in 120 countries, and the SH 888 also include built-in infrared ports, allowing local wireless connections to computers.

Also noteworthy is the T28, the thinnest GSM telephone on the market. The phone is equipped with the latest technology and has a number of features, such as voice-controlled dialing and answering, a world clock and the capability of operating with two telephone numbers.

Ericsson also makes mobile phones for Globalstar, the US operator of a low-level satellite network. The phones will work either via Globalstar or as GSM instruments.

At the end of 1998, Ericsson left the personal pager business. The business, which will probably disappear altogether as mobile phone capabilities grow and prices drop, was liquidated and the employees transferred to the mobile telephones unit.

Enterprise solutions

Ericsson's Enterprise Solutions segment is cobbled together from parts of its old Mobile Systems, Infocom Systems, and Ericsson Data businesses. The segment provides communications solutions for businesses and other organizations worldwide and employs 9615 people. In 1999, net sales amounted to SKr17.3 billion or eight percent of the company's total sales.

There are three business units in the segment: Enterprise Systems; Wireless Office Solutions; and Business Consulting. Ericsson is the market leader in the wireless voice market and second in the wireless office segment.

- *Enterprise Systems.* This unit is home to Ericsson's private branch exchange business and is active in the newly emerging Voice over IP (VoIP) and computer telephony segments. Its traditional PBX systems are being augmented with gateway products that allow users to connect their PBXs over the Internet and provide a full range of voice over data offerings for wide area network access. Among the products are call center solutions, modems, frame relay, ATM, router and remote access solutions.
- *Wireless Office Solutions.* This unit offers premises-based wireless solutions that includes the integration of cordless technology into Ericsson PBX platforms, wireless radio, and intranet systems, such GSM on the net, where LAN-connected GSM base stations provide access to next-generation VoIP networking and services.
- *Business Consulting*: This newly formed unit includes a 2700-employee consulting practice aimed at creating networked solutions for enterprises. It is a dedicated professional services business that includes skills in IT, network management and outsourcing, integration and e-commerce.

Other businesses
- *Defense Systems.* Defense Systems is the military arm of Ericsson Microwave Systems. It manufactures land, sea, and airborne radar systems.
- *Cables.* Ericsson Cables manufactures and markets copper and fiber optic cable, power cable, and network products. Copper cable accounts for the largest percentage of sales, and the unit is experiencing strong growth in its fiber optic submarine cables. Ericsson Cable Contracting is a new subsidiary that engineers and constructs optofiber cable networks. The Power Cable unit makes high-voltage lines.
- *Microelectronics.* Ericsson Microelectronics had sales of SKr8.6 billion in 1999. The unit develops and manufactures components, such as power transistors and ATM chips, for telecommunications systems and mobile telephones.

Regional markets

Ericsson is the most global company in the telecom industry. It operates in 140 countries. Further, 95 percent of its sales are generated and over half of its employees live and work outside of Sweden.

Given its global nature, Ericsson has also reorganized along geographic lines. The company is using this structure to decentralize its chain of command and cut reaction time. Toward that end, executives are moving out of the Stockholm headquarters and into regional headquarters that are closer to customers.

The new market headquarters for Europe, the Middle East and Africa is London; North America is in Richardson, Texas; Asia-Pacific is in Hong Kong; and Latin America is in Miami.

Europe, the Middle East and Africa

Ericsson's sales in Europe, the Middle East and Africa hit SKr115 billion – or 53 percent of total revenues – in 1999. Roughly 40 percent of those sales are generated in Western Europe, which accounts for 41 percent of Ericsson's net sales. The company has operations in about 100 of the 120 countries in the region.

Ericsson is the leader in mobile systems in Western Europe, with a market share of about 45 percent. In 1998, it won about half of all new contracts for mobile systems in that area and there are over 100 million mobile phone subscribers connected to Ericsson systems.

The UK is the company's largest market in the area; it is Ericsson's third largest market. Italy is the second largest market followed its home nation, Sweden, where the company enjoys a 30 percent market share. Ericsson also supplies all the GSM operators in Spain and Holland.

Ericsson has operations in 25 of the 28 countries in Central and Eastern Europe, where sales are growing with developing infrastructures. The company operates in all countries in the Middle East, where its largest markets are Israel, United Arab Emirates, Lebanon, and Saudi Arabia. Finally, Ericsson is at work in 20 of Africa's 55 countries, where South Africa and Egypt are the largest markets.

Asia-Pacific

Even in the face of a widespread economic downturn in Asia, the company's business in the area has slipped only slightly. The nations of the Asia-Pacific contribute 20 percent of Ericsson's revenues at SKr44.9 billion in 1999.

The major reason for this fortunate performance is the company's commanding position in China. The company is represented throughout the country and has created eight joint-venture companies, five of which have production facilities, with Chinese companies – an investment pattern that gives Ericsson favored status with the government.

In China, Ericsson holds more than a 40 percent share of the market for mobile systems. It is currently supplying the equipment for the country's first ATM-based data network.

Japan is Ericsson's second largest market in Asia-Pacific. PDC-based mobile systems account for 98 percent of Ericsson's sales in the island nation. Australia is the third largest market in Asia-Pacific and Taiwan is fourth.

The impact of the economic turbulence of late did hurt revenues in Southeast Asia, particularly in Singapore, Indonesia, Thailand and Malaysia. In 1998, sales declined in this area, which account for less than five percent of Ericsson's sales in the Asia-Pacific market.

Latin America
Comprising Central and South America, and the Caribbean nations, this region generates 14 percent of Ericsson's annual revenues or SKr30.2 billion in 1999. Ericsson is the leading telecommunications supplier in Latin America, with a market share for wireline and mobile telecommunications systems of 40 percent. (TDMA is the standard in mobile systems.)

The region is Ericsson's fastest growing largely because of the trend toward privatization in the telecom sector, particularly in Brazil, Mexico, Chile, and Argentina. Brazil is the company's fourth largest market worldwide, and it generates almost half of the region's revenues. Further, future growth seems sure since only four percent of the population is subscribed to mobile services.

Mexico, Argentina and Chile account for about one-third of Ericsson's net sales in Latin America. Ericsson has 2500 employees in Mexico. Argentina is buying TDMA networks and Chile is the first country in Latin America to install GSM systems, supplied by Ericsson.

North America
North America represents the smallest portion of Ericsson's global revenues,

but the US is its single largest market. The US and Canada generated sales of SKr25.1 billion, or 11 percent of Ericsson's revenues, in 1999. Mobile systems and mobile phones are major products sold in this area, accounting for 87 percent of sales. Ericsson's largest customers in the US are AirTouch, AT&T Wireless, BellSouth, and MCI WorldCom. In Canada, Microcell and Rogers Cantel are major customers.

In mobile systems, the US is the predominant user of TDMA-based digital systems and Ericsson holds a 39 percent share of that market, a close second to Lucent Technologies. Ericsson is the market leader for GSM systems with a 52 percent share.

Income statement

Year	Revenue ($m)	Net income ($m)	Net profit margin	Employees
1998	22,759.6	1,609.3	7.1%	103,667
1997	21,219.1	1,510.5	7.1%	100,774
1996	18,290.8	1,033.1	5.6%	93,949
1995	14,902.3	813.1	5.5%	84,513
1994	11,341.8	531.1	4.7%	76,144
1993	7,622.2	340.2	4.5%	69,597
1992	6,643.9	67.7	1.0%	66,232
1991	8,274.8	160.1	1.9%	71,247
1990	8,289.3	612.4	7.4%	70,238
1989	6,367.4	296.7	4.7%	69,229

Stock history

Year	Stock price ($) FY High	FY Low	FY Close	P/E High	Low	Per share ($) Earns	Div.	Book value
1998	34.00	15.00	23.94	41	18	0.82	0.00	3.99
1997	25.31	14.31	18.66	29	17	0.86	0.00	3.42
1996	15.88	8.69	15.09	30	16	0.53	0.11	3.06
1995	13.13	6.72	9.75	29	15	0.45	0.08	2.67
1994	7.95	4.98	6.89	21	13	0.37	0.11	1.80
1993	7.53	2.92	5.05	40	15	0.19	0.00	1.47
1992	3.41	2.23	3.31	85	56	0.04	0.07	1.42
1991	5.00	1.92	2.41	56	21	0.09	0.06	1.74
1990	5.95	3.23	4.03	19	10	0.32	0.05	1.71
1989	3.60	1.47	3.59	15	6	0.24	0.04	1.02

1998 year-end financials

Debt ratio	16.7%
Return on equity	22.3%
Cash ($m)	2,250.0
Current ratio	1.88
Long-term debt ($m)	1,556.0
Shares outstanding (millions)	1,951.4
Dividend yield	0.0%
Dividend payout	0.0%
Market value ($m)	46,715.4

Financial data provided by Hoover's Online (www.hoovers.com) and Media General Financial Services, Inc.

Ericsson contacts

Telefonaktiebolaget LM Ericsson   Phone: +46–8–719–0000
Telefonplan   Fax: +46–8–184–085
SE-126 25 Stockholm, Sweden   URL: www.ericsson.com

CEO: Lars Ramqvist   CFO: Sten Fornell   HR: Britt Reigo

Glaxo Wellcome plc –
Greenford, Middlesex, UK

Executive snapshot

Among the corporate giants that rule the pharmaceuticals industry, there is only one critical competency: the ability to create and produce breakthrough, proprietary drugs.

   "We remain on track to achieve our goal of bringing three significant medicines to the market a year from the year 2000 onwards." – Sir Richard Sykes, chairman of Glaxo Wellcome plc.

Glaxo Wellcome backdrop

The discovery of a new drug is not unlike prospecting for a rich vein of gold. There is a huge upfront investment in time and energy with a highly uncertain outcome. But in both cases, when the find is made, the stream of profits is immediate and correspondingly rewarding. It is an analogy that Joseph Edward Nathan would have appreciated.

Gold fever vs. asthma

Joseph Nathan, the 18-year-old son of a London wholesale tailor, certainly isn't thinking about pharmaceuticals in August 1853, when he steps on board the *William Ackers* and begins his passage to Australia. He is dreaming of gold, recently discovered near Melbourne.

Future focus

Welcome to Glaxo

The pharmaceutical business is a high-technology business with an unusual twist. The most successful companies in the pharmaceutical field are also the luckiest. To find a blockbuster drug, you have to be lucky. Out of literally billions of possible chemical combinations, only a few will turn out to have useful pharmaceutical properties.

So then, how do you get lucky? The obvious approach is to have the largest research & development staff that will find the largest number of potentially useful drugs. And if you have the largest number of compounds in field trials, you are likely to find more winners than your competitors. Glaxo Wellcome has had more than its share of pharmaceutical winners. From Zantac, the first £1 billion drug, to Zovirax to Zofran to Zinnat. Seven of the world's top 50 prescription drugs are owned Glaxo.

Glaxo is not a young company. It was founded as a trading company in New Zealand more than 140 years ago. You can live a long corporate life, but not without change. To make the successful transition from trading to pharmaceutical obviously required many changes along the way. Glaxo made a number of key decisions that characterize successful companies everywhere.

1   An investment in the future. In 1919, the company set up one of the world's first research and development operations. Today Glaxo has more than 10,000 employees involved in its R&D efforts, spending more than £1 billion annually.
2   A dedication to branding. In 1905, the company marketed dried milk under the Defiance brand name. (The following year the product was renamed "Glaxo.") In 1923, the company marketed its first pharmaceutical product, a vitamin D concentrate called "Ostelin."
3   A dedication to globalization. In 1876, the company first opened an office in London and then gradually expanded the business. By 1931 Glaxo products were sold in 12 countries from China to Cuba.
4   A dedication to change. From a diversified trading company headquartered in New Zealand, Glaxo Wellcome metamorphosed into the

world's largest pharmaceutical company. Throughout its history, Glaxo periodically refocused itself by selling off businesses, including trading, wholesaling, food, surgical supplies, veterinary products. Sacrifice is a key ingredient in the long-term success of any company.

In 1995, Glaxo merged with Wellcome to become the world's largest pharmaceutical company. As large as Glaxo Wellcome is, the company accounts for only 4.6 percent of the world's pharmaceutical business. Forecast: you can expect to see more such mergers in Glaxo's future.

Size and focus are the keys to success. They seem contradictory, but they're not. You want to be the big fish in a small pond. When you are the leader in your field, you attract the best people. Who doesn't want to work for a company like Microsoft or Coca-Cola or Glaxo Wellcome?

When you are the leader in your field, you attract the best products. Smaller companies that develop promising drugs naturally gravitate to leaders like Glaxo for co-marketing arrangements or other joint selling agreements.

When you are the leader in your field, you attract the best suppliers. Given a choice, what company doesn't want to sell its products or services to the leader in the field?

Whoever said it's harder to stay on top once you get there than it is to get there in the first place doesn't know much about wrestling or corporate strategy. Leadership is the single, most important goal for any company. The manifold benefits of leadership for companies like Glaxo Wellcome are likely to last for many decades to come.

Nathan arrives in Melbourne four months later, but never makes it to the gold fields. An asthmatic, he is advised that he may not have the physical strength needed to mine gold. Besides, there is a fortune to be made selling supplies to the miners themselves.

A natural entrepreneur, Nathan heeds the advice and, backed by local businessmen, he sets up shop in Melbourne, a boom town that triples in size with the gold strike. He remains in Melbourne until December 1857, when newly married he enters a partnership with a brother-in-law in Wellington, New Zealand.

In Wellington, the partners run an import business that sells a wide range of goods from England to the local population. But the pair are not well matched. In 1873, Nathan, by now a family man with 11 children, starts Glaxo's first incarnation; a trading business named Joseph Nathan & Company.

In 1876, the company opens its first office in England, and in the 1880s, as refrigerated shipping becomes available, Nathan transforms the company from importer to exporter. He is instrumental in the development of railways and port facilities, and charters ships to transport New Zealand meats to England. He also begins bringing his sons into the business.

In the early 1890s, as shipping expands and competition emerges, Nathan moves into wool, and when that is not sufficiently successful, into butter. Soon, the company owns a chain of 17 creameries.

In 1893, Nathan's wife dies of cancer and he begins spending ever longer periods conducting business from London. By 1899, after three years of negotiations with his seven sons, Joseph Nathan & Company becomes a London-based limited liability company with a capitalization of £127,000.

Glaxo for bonnie babies

In 1903, the Nathans begin to realize the potential of dried powdered milk as a use for the surplus skimmed milk produced at the company's New Zealand creameries and butteries. And, in November, they enter into a complicated business arrangement that gives them the rights to a patented American method of producing dried milk, the Just-Hatmaker process.

After several missteps and convoluted legal actions, in January 1905 the family forms the Imperial Dried Milk Company. It is fully owned by Joseph Nathan and four of his sons. They market its product under the unappetizing name of Defiance Dried Milk and seem to believe it will replace liquid milk altogether. It is an unrealistic goal at best, and the proof lies in the product's very poor initial sales.

The Nathans, however, are nothing if not practical and in 1906, they rename the product, Glaxo Baby Food (after the name Lacto is rejected by Great Britain's Trade Marks Office). Glaxo is repositioned as a safer alternative to whole milk for babies.

Youngest son Alec Nathan is recalled from New Zealand to run the "Glaxo Department." He relaunches the product in 1908, with a short-lived newspaper ad campaign calling the powered milk, "The Food that Builds Bonnie Babies." He also establishes the "Glaxo Baby Book" to give advice to new mothers, and hires a registered nurse to answer correspondence.

Alec's efforts are not immediately rewarded and when Joseph Nathan passes away at age 77 in 1912 and second son Louis Nathan takes over leadership of the family business, Glaxo is still contributing only a small portion of the company's revenues. In 1913, the company goes public to raise cash and begins developing a network of sales agents in India, Canada, and South America, but the onset of World War I stifles both efforts. The war signals a major change of fortune for Alec Nathan and Glaxo. Powdered milk is in great demand with military and civil authorities, and in late 1914 the company is contracting with outside sources to fill its orders. Sales of Glaxo explode from £50,000 in 1913 to £550,000 in 1918.

In 1916, the Glaxo department outgrows its space and moves to larger offices; in 1917, new quarters are built in England and three new production factories are opened in New Zealand.

Baby steps into pharmaceuticals

The end of World War I is the end of Glaxo's almost effortless expansion. In 1919, sales drop ten percent to £495,000 and Alec Nathan begins a major drive to increase the quality and consistency of Glaxo. In 1919, he hires a chemist and pharmacist named Harry Jephcott and ensconces him in a windowless London warehouse – the first Glaxo laboratory. Another of the Nathan brothers, Maurice, calls it, "Alec's bloody folly."

Jephcott, and the small staff he hires, create the company's first standardized quality control and do raise quality levels. But the Nathan brothers do not anticipate or react quickly enough to the post-war slump in demand. As supplies rise and demand falls, the company cuts prices to stimulate sales. In 1921, sales of Glaxo are £1.5 million, but profits a mere £7700. At the same time, Nathan & Company is encountering financial difficulties of its own and the brothers begin a battle over control of the business that will last for decades.

In 1923, on a trip to the US, Jephcott learns of and purchases the rights to a process for extracting Vitamin D from cod liver oil. By 1924, Nathan & Company is marketing the extract to doctors as Ostelin Vitamin D, the first standardized vitamin concentrate in England and Glaxo's first pharmaceutical product. The vitamin extract is also added to Glaxo Baby Food, creating Sunshine Glaxo, designed to promote skeletal growth in children.

The new products set the agenda for future developments, but do little to quell the familial infighting, which has by now become a running battle between the New Zealand operations run by Fred Nathan and the English operations run by Alec Nathan. Fred wants the company to remain a diversified trading business; Alec needs more resources to develop the Glaxo Department. Hints to the final outcome occur in 1927, when Alec replaces Louis as chairman of Nathan & Company and in 1929, when Jephcott, who is now GM of Glaxo, is appointed to the board.

In 1929, Jephcott adopts a new irradiation process that produces the parent substance of Vitamin D, ergosterol, a more potent and less pungent substitute for fish oil extract. The company applies it to create a new product, Ostermilk, which quickly replaces the Glaxo brand name in the marketplace. In 1931, Ostelin, a pure form of the vitamin, is released as a liquid and tablet in a variety of doses.

Early globalization efforts continue in the 1920s, again mainly through the appointment of sales representatives in countries such as Italy and Greece. By 1931, Glaxo vitamins are sold in 12 countries from China to Cuba.

In 1932, Farex, a new cereal food fortified with vitamins, is introduced, as are a range of Vitamin A-based products, including Adexolin in capsule, liquid and emulsion, Ostomalt, and Maltoline.

In 1935, Nathan & Company turns the Glaxo department into Glaxo Laboratories Ltd, a wholly owned subsidiary. In 1936, the new company moves into an impressive, newly constructed headquarters, including labs, offices, and production facilities, in Greenford, located a few miles west of London. Growth is steady for the remainder of the decade and in 1939, the company's sales of pharmaceuticals outstrip food product sales. In that year, Glaxo employs 600 people in Greenford. Its annual revenue is £1.1 million; net profit is £230,000. And then war breaks out.

Penicillin and the ascension of Harry Jephcott

Corporate biographers Richard Davenport-Hines and Judy Slinn call World War II "the hinge of [Glaxo's] fortunes," and so it is. The British government awards the company contracts for powdered milk and eggs, orange juice, and even medicated soap. Sales of Farex and Ostermilk register huge gains (300 percent for the latter product), and vitamin sales also take off.

Even more significantly, in 1941, Glaxo becomes a charter member of The Therapeutic Research Corporation (TRC). TRC is a joint venture among Britain's major pharmaceutical companies designed to stimulate research and maximize production for the war effort. It exposes Glaxo to a wide range of new research and technologies, and as Davenport-Hines and Slinn say, draws the company into "the centre of the British pharmaceutical industry."

It is through TRC that Glaxo first becomes involved with the production of penicillin, a vital antibiotic for combating wound infections. At the time, penicillin is grown from mold and cannot be mass-produced. In 1942 Glaxo opens a small plant in Aylesbury, to grow and extract penicillin. It quickly expands into three other plants and by 1944, Glaxo is supplying 80 percent of the country's penicillin.

Glaxo escapes World War II largely unscathed. International operations are disrupted and its most notable domestic incident is a direct bomb strike on the Greenford factory that destroys the food blending operation and part of the analytical laboratory. Nevertheless, in 1945 the company's sales exceed £2.5 million for the first time and profits hit £512,000.

With the war's conclusion, Alec Nathan retires and ends the unbroken succession of the family leadership. Newly-knighted Harry Jephcott becomes chairman of Joseph Nathan & Company and quickly reveals himself a decisive and capable leader.

Jephcott first secures the company's hold on the penicillin market by licensing a new fermentation method allowing mass production from American companies Merck and Squibb. Second, he signs a development pact with Merck for additional products. And, third, he agrees with Squibb not to compete with each other in British and North American markets.

In January 1947, Jephcott sells off Nathan food businesses and trading firms in New Zealand. Glaxo Labs absorbs Nathan & Company and is listed as a public company on the London Stock Exchange. "Glaxo baby swallows parent," declares one newspaper headline. Jephcott also rebuilds the board of directors with his own appointees.

The company flings itself into the drug business and, before the end of the decade, is marketing a host of new drugs. The products include: a combined vaccine to protect against whooping cough and diphtheria; Crystapen, an advanced form of penicillin; streptomycin, for the treatment of tuberculosis; a penicillin-based veterinary antibiotic; and the isolation and commercial development of vitamin B12. In 1949, the company synthesizes L-thyroxine for the treatment for hypothyroidism and, in 1950, it releases its first cortisone steroid treatments.

By 1950, sales reach £5.9 million and net profits £1.23 million.

Growing global

In the late 1940s and continuing through the 1950s, Glaxo builds and imposes control on an international network of subsidiaries. It is a slow and not entirely wholehearted process that grows through a combination of direct investment and acquisition.

After the war, Glaxo re-establishes links with its existing prewar operations in countries such as Italy and Greece. In the late 1940s, the company begins creating new subsidiaries, first adding operations in Uruguay, Pakistan, South Africa, and Canada, and then expanding mainly in the Commonwealth.

By 1957, Glaxo products are represented in 70 countries and the company has nine international headquarters with manufacturing capabilities. The 1958 acquisition of Allen & Hanburys Ltd, with roots stretching back to 1715, adds operations in South Africa, Canada, and Australia. The 1961 acquisition of Evans Medical brings Glaxo a foothold in France, in addition to operations in other countries.

By that year, Glaxo is large enough to merit a reorganization. Glaxo Group Ltd is created as the new London-based parent company that will manage global operations and Glaxo Laboratories is turned into the Group's UK subsidiary. In 1963, Harry Jephcott retires and Alan Wilson assumes the role of chairman.

Product development continues at a steady pace throughout the 1950s and 1960s. Glaxo releases a wide variety of corticosteroid products aimed at treating rheumatoid arthritis, dermatological inflammations, and respiratory allergies. It also begins producing and selling bulk steroids.

The company creates a series of vaccines to fight diseases such as tetanus and influenza. And, in 1956, it releases Britain's first freeze-dried BCG vaccine designed to protect children against tuberculosis. Major product releases continue with: Betnovate, a steroid skin disease treatment in 1963; Ceparin, Glaxo's first injectable cephalosporin antibiotic in 1964; Ventolin for asthma in 1966; and in 1969, Glaxo's first oral cephalosporin, Ceporex.

By 1970, the Glaxo Group is a £160 million company with a diversity of business interests. It operates around the world, making and selling over-the-counter pharmaceutical drugs, vaccines, animal health products, laboratory chemicals, surgical equipment, hospital furniture, farm and garden chemicals, milk products, baby and invalid foods, and prescription-only medicines.

Imposing focus and the big payoff

In late 1971, the Glaxo story almost comes to a premature ending. UK-based Beecham Group makes an unfriendly bid to take control of the company and Glaxo counters with a proposal for a merger with a second UK company, Boots. Happily for Glaxo, the English Monopolies Commission reviews Beecham's proposed combination and rejects it as detrimental to competition.

The close call prompts Glaxo to restructure once more and now Glaxo Holdings Ltd is formed as the Group's new parent company. In 1973, Austin Bide replaces Alan Wilson and the company begins to sharpen its focus on prescription (ethical) medicines and divest its many other businesses. Over the next decade, it begins selling off its unrelated divisions, including the Wholesaling, Surgical Products, Veterinary, Foods and Generic divisions.

The proceeds are invested in the prescription drug business to strengthen its position in global markets and boost R&D. Glaxo builds its position in Japan by buying into and building its existing agency,

Shin Nihon. The company continues its expansion into Europe, building market share in France and Germany in particular.

In 1978, Glaxo makes a belated entry into the US, the world's largest market representing about 30 percent of the global market, when it acquires Florida-based Meyer Laboratories and its well-developed sales force. In 1980, Meyer Labs is transformed into Glaxo, Inc.

The R&D efforts in the1970s set the stage for the fast-track growth of the next decade. Led by Dr David Jack, Glaxo focuses its research on discovering chemicals capable of causing specific reactions in the human body. In 1972, Becotide, an oral medication for asthma is released and in 1975, Beconase for rhinitis conditions is launched. Trandate, for hypertension, arrives in 1977 and one year later, the company ships Zinacef, a broad-spectrum injectable antibiotic.

The most important work, however, is being pursued in the company's Ware research center. In 1972, teams there are searching for an effective treatment for peptic ulcers, a disease affecting over 10 percent of the world's population. Beecham, now SmithKline Beecham, beats Glaxo to the punch with Tagamet, launched in 1977. But that same year, David Jack and the Glaxo teams find a more effective solution based on the compound ranitidine.

By 1980 Glaxo's sales hit £618 million, of which roughly 25 percent are generated domestically. The company has wholly owned subsidiaries in 70 countries and is represented by agencies in 100 others.

Beginning in late 1981, after cutting the typical drug development process time in half through the use of concurrent testing, Glaxo launches Zantac, an anti-ulcer medication based on ranitidine, worldwide.

Destined to become the world's top selling medicine by the end of the 1980s, Zantac is Glaxo's greatest triumph. By 1983, Zantac alone is generating almost £100 million in revenues. By 1985, it exceeds £400 million, and by 1988, it becomes the first drug to sell over £1 billion in a single year. In the late 1980s, Zantac is contributing 50 percent of Glaxo's revenues.

By 1990, the company, now led by former financial director Paul Girolami, has annual revenues of £3.17 billion and profits of just over £1 billion. The company employs over 31,000 people worldwide and is the second largest ethical pharmaceutical company in the world.

The run for global leadership

After a decade of exponential growth, Glaxo is forced to look forward to the pending loss of patent protection on the drug that contributes almost half of its annual revenues. To address the problem, it turns to R&D, releasing many of the drugs that will help maintain its momentum through the end of the millenium. In 1990, Glaxo releases Flixonase and Serevent for the treatment of rhinitis and asthma, and Zofran, an anti-nausea treatment for cancer patients. In 1991, it launches three more drugs: Cutivate for skin diseases; Imigran for migraines; and Lacipil for high blood pressure. In 1993, Flixotide for bronchial conditions is released.

As Zantac's patents begin to expire in 1994, company revenues hit £5.6 billion. Chairman Paul Girolami retires and head of Glaxo Group Research Richard Sykes is appointed to lead the charge into the post-Zantac world. In January 1995, Sykes does just that when he launches a successful takeover bid for UK-based Wellcome plc, a long-time competitor founded in 1880. By May 1995, the companies formally merge and in September, Glaxo Wellcome plc is introduced worldwide. The new giant is the world's largest pharmaceutical company, a £7.6 billion business with a wide variety of products.

The combined products and R&D help the company weather the loss of Zantac's exclusivity with a minimum of pain. Revenues actually rise in 1996 to a record high of £8.3 billion, but remain slightly lower in 1997 and 1998 – just below £8 billion.

In 1998, the company goes back on the acquisition trail when it attempts unsuccessfully to merge with SmithKline Beecham. It does, however, successfully become Poland's largest pharmaceutical company with the acquisition of Polfa Poznan.

In 1999, Glaxo makes a few adjustments to its product lines. It sells several anesthesia products, including Ultiva, to Abbott Laboratories and discontinues the Wellferon hepatitis treatment. When seven patients die while taking Raxar, it also is discontinued.

The company threatens to leave the UK after almost 80 years when the National Health Service refuses to include its anti-flu inhalant Relenza under its coverage because of the cost. Glaxo also cuts 3400 jobs in an effort to reduce costs.

In January 2000, Glaxo's board announces that it has voted for a merger of equals with SmithKline Beecham. The merged firm, Glaxo SmithKline, will be a £15 billion pharmaceutical company.

Glaxo Wellcome close-up

In the prescription drug business, the final few years of the 20th century culminated in a heated battle to occupy the very pinnacle of the industry – and Glaxo Wellcome plc wants that top spot. To get it, the company has undertaken mega-mergers, overcome patent expirations on Zantac – the world's best-selling prescription medication – and sunk billions into R&D.

The results: Glaxo has run a breakneck race for the leadership in prescription drugs, earned £8.49 billion in annual revenues in 1999, and assembled the most extensive global network in the industry.

Glaxo Welcome is a global pharmaceutical conglomerate in the business of creating, manufacturing, and marketing prescription and over-the-counter (OTC) medicines. Headquartered in the UK, it owns operating companies in 57 countries, manufactures its products in 33 countries, and sells them in 150 countries. The company maintains a worldwide workforce of 55,000 employees.

R&D is the lifeblood of the pharmaceuticals industry and Glaxo has accelerated that process. Since 1995, it has maintained an R&D budget of over £1.1 billion per year. Major labs and research sites are located in Stevenage, Greenford, and Ware in the UK; North Carolina and California in the USA; Tsukuba Science City, Japan; Verona, Italy; Les Ulis, France; Madrid, Spain; and Mississauga, Canada. And, the company staffs its product development efforts with 10,000 people worldwide.

A revamped development process has the company's new product pipeline filled with over 60 projects in varying stages of completion. Twenty of them are introduced in 1998. Glaxo has adopted a concurrent process that utilizes early evaluation and cross-functional authority to identify and speed the transformation of research into products. It maintains three "Discovery Centers" (UK/Japan/France, USA, and Italy/Spain). Their work is organized into six Therapeutic Research Teams, each with a focus on one broad market area: gastroenterology,

HIV and opportunistic infections, hospital and critical care, infectious diseases, neurology, and respiratory.

Manufacturing is conducted worldwide using a two-tier system. The highly proprietary active ingredients in Glaxo drugs are made by its International Actives Supply (IAS) network. IAS has three major sites in the UK and one in Singapore. There are also smaller IAS plants in India, Bangladesh, Egypt and Spain.

Active ingredients are passed on to second-tier formulation facilities. This network of "Product Supply" plants manufactures finished drugs using the active ingredients, other chemicals and packaging.

Glaxo's customers vary based on the national practices and regulations of the countries in which it operates. Its main customers are wholesale distributors and hospitals. In some countries, direct sales are made to pharmacies and health maintenance organizations (HMOs). The company uses a direct sales force to market and support its customers.

Glaxo also co-markets select products in joint ventures with other companies in the industry. Recently ended, its largest joint venture was with US-based Warner-Lambert Company. Under the agreement, the companies created OTC versions of major Glaxo prescription products. In 1998, sales of the OTC remedies hit £136 million. Using the expertise gained in the venture, Glaxo now plans to pursue future "switch" opportunities on its own.

In the US, Glaxo reaches its ultimate customers, individual consumers, with direct advertising. The consumer-direct ads influence patients to request specific products from their doctors. In most other markets, this advertising is illegal or strictly limited.

Even as a leading drug maker with revenues approaching £9 billion, Glaxo enjoys plenty of room for growth in the global market for pharmaceuticals, which is estimated at £181 billion. With only a 4.6 percent portion of the pie, Glaxo Wellcome is well positioned to expand its global market share.

In geographic terms, the company's largest market is North America (the US and Canada), which contributes 45 percent of annual revenues – or £3.77 billion – in 1999. The US is Glaxo's single largest market, contributing 42 percent of sales at £3.55 billion. Major product groups in North America are respiratory drugs, where Glaxo had 82 percent of the prescription smoking cessation market by November 1998, drugs for the treatment of depression and migraines, and HIV drugs.

Europe, Africa, and the Middle East follow with 38 percent of revenues, or £3.14 billion. Glaxo enjoys strong national positions in the UK, France, and Italy. The 1998 acquisition of Poland's Polfa Poznan S.A. added £52 million to sales and enhanced the company's position in Eastern Europe. Respiratory drugs are a major growth engine in this region.

The remaining 18 percent is split roughly equally between Asia-Pacific, Japan, and Latin America with £604 million, £566 million, and £402 million respectively. In Asia-Pacific, economic downturns have slowed growth in markets, such as Indonesia, Malaysia and Thailand. India is Glaxo's largest regional market, followed by Australia. In Japan, sales slowed because of price reductions and healthcare reforms that have increased patient co-payments. In Latin America, Brazil is Glaxo's largest market, with 38 percent of the region's sales. Together they account for just over 50 percent of the region's sales. Mexico is the second largest market.

Products

Glaxo Wellcome currently makes close to 50 major products in nine therapeutic areas. Among these are seven drugs – Zantac, Imigran, Zovirax, Serevent, Zofran, Flixotide, and Zinnat – that are ranked among the world's top 50 prescription medications. The following are the company's major groups and products.

Respiratory
Respiratory medications are Glaxo's largest segment by revenue. Sales reached £2.46 billion in 1999 and represent 29 percent of total revenues. Glaxo owns four of the top six ranking products in the global anti-asthma market and its market share is 30 percent. The major growth engines in this segment are asthma and hayfever medications – Serevent, Flixotide/Flovent and Flixonase/Flonase – all introduced since 1990.

Serevent is an extended-relief bronchodilator. Its 1999 sales hit £569 million and represent seven percent of corporate revenues.

Glaxo's leading seller is Flixotide, an inhaled steroid for bronchitis and bronchial asthma. It is sold in the US as Flovent, where it is the market leader, and was introduced in Japan in December 1998 as Flutide. Flixotide's 1999 sales also hit £666 million.

Flixonase is an intra-nasal hayfever medication, which is sold in the US as Flonase. Flonase is the leading product in this category in the US, with a 28 percent market share. It contributes four percent of Glaxo's revenues with sales of £333 million.

Zyban, introduced in 1997, is a fast-growth, smoking cessation drug, which is leading the US prescription market in this area with a 33 percent share. In 1999, Zyban hit £72 million in sales, and is now available in Canada and Europe.

The newest respiratory product is Seretide, a new asthma combination product containing Serevent and Flixotide in one inhaler. Its 1999 sales reached £58 million.

More mature drugs in this area are: Ventolin, a temporary relief beta$_2$ agonist for asthma; Becotide and Beclovent, inhaled steroids for bronchial asthma and chronic bronchitis; and Beconase, an intra-nasal preparation for hayfever. All are declining in sales, having been replaced by newer Glaxo products and/or increased competition from generics because of expired patents.

Viral infections

Anti-viral medications contribute 19 percent of Glaxo's revenues or £1.63 billion in 1999. It is an area in flux, as new products are rapidly replacing more mature drugs. This area includes medications aimed at diseases such as herpes, HIV/AIDS, hepatitis, chicken pox, malaria, and influenza. The company is the leader in the US market for anti-AIDS/HIV drugs, with a 66 percent share.

Zovirax, for the treatment of herpes infections, contributed five percent of revenues or £412 million in 1999. Sales of the drug are declining due to patent expiry.

A newer anti-herpes medication, Valtrex, is rapidly replacing Zovirax in the company's product lines. In 1999, it contributed two percent of sales or £177 million.

In the fast growing HIV products, the newly released Combivir, a combination of two older medications (Retrovir and Epivir) was launched in late 1997 and 1998 in the US, Europe, Canada, Latin America, and Asia. In 1999, it contributed five percent of revenues with sales of £454 million.

Epivir with £325 million in sales, is declining because of the conversion to Combivir. Retrovir sales, at £86 million, are also in decline for the same reason.

Glaxo also released Ziagen, a new reverse transcriptase inhibitor for HIV treatment and Agenerase, a protease inhibitor, in late in 1998 and 1999. Together they produced £114 million in sales.

The area also features: Lamivudine, to treat chronic hepatitis B; Wellvone and Mepron, for pneumonia; Malarone, for malaria; and Relenza, for influenza.

Central nervous system (CNS) disorders

Glaxo's CNS medication portfolio contributes 16 percent of the company's revenues with total sales of £1.31 billion in 1999. It includes drugs for the treatment of migraines, epilepsy, and depression.

Imigran, sold in the US as Imitrex, is a receptor agonist designed to treat migraine and cluster headaches. Available in tablet, nasal spray, and suppository forms, it is Glaxo's second best-selling drug, contributing eight percent of revenues with sales of £653 million. It is the market leader in the US.

For all of Imigran's success, Glaxo released a new migraine product, Naramig (Amerge in the US) with a stronger receptor agonist in March 1998. It sold £63 million by year-end 1999.

Lamictal is Glaxo's treatment for severe epilepsy. Its 1999 sales of £223 million were highly respectable in a mature market.

Wellbutrin is a popular anti-depressant available only in the US. Made in tablet or sustained release forms, it contributed four percent to corporate revenues with 1999 sales of £353 million.

Bacterial infections

Glaxo makes a range of antibiotics for the treatment of bacterial infections. Sales of these products hit £836 million in 1999, contributing 10 percent of annual revenues. There are four products in this area.

Glaxo's best seller here is Zinnat (Ceftin in the US), an oral antibiotic used for common infections of the lower respiratory tract. Its 1999 sales were £420 million, contributing five percent of annual sales.

Fortum (Fortaz in the US) and Zinacef are injectable antibiotics used in hospitals. Fortum is for severe infections, Zinacef for surgical infections. Sales of both are declining year-to-year, but nevertheless contributed £313 million in 1999.

Gastrointestinal

Still the home of Glaxo's greatest product triumph, sales of gastrointestinal medications were £647 million in 1999 – eight percent of total revenues. Sales declines in this area have begun to flatten, but will probably continue in the near term. The products are used in the treatment of ulcers.

Almost all of the sales are attributable to Zantac, which even after patent expiry continues to be the market leader for the treatment of peptic ulcers and other gastric acid-related disorders. Zantac, which for many years contributed 40 percent of Glaxo's total revenue, contributed £400 million to revenue in 1999.

Oncology

Sales of oncology medications were £521 million in 1999, or six percent of total revenue. The drugs in this group are used in the treatment of cancers.

Zofran, a drug used to combat the nausea caused by cancer treatments, leads the anti-emetic market with a share of 38 percent. It is the first 5-HT$_3$ antagonist to be released worldwide and is available in both oral and injectable forms. Its 1999 sales were £416 million.

Also in this area is Navelbine, a cytotoxic for lung and breast cancers. Its sales were £43 million in 1999.

Cardiovascular

Glaxo's sales of cardiovascular drugs were £253 million in 1999 and they contributed three percent of the company's revenues. These products include five drugs: Lanoxin, to control cardiac arrhythmia; Flolan, a blood clot inhibitor; and Lacipil, Trandate, and Pritor, all used to treat hypertension.

Dermatologicals

Glaxo's sales of dermatological products hit £254 million in 1999, or three percent of total revenues. There are three major products in this area: Betnovate, Cutivate, and Dermovate, anti-inflammatory steroid products for the treatment of eczema and psoriasis.

Anesthesia

Anesthesia products contributed sales of £97 million, or roughly one percent of total revenues, in 1999. There are five drugs in this group, mostly neuromuscular blocking agents that are used as muscle relaxants in surgery. They are Tracrium, Nimbex, Nuormax, Ultiva, and Tracrium.

Others
A few non-categorized products added £470 million to Glaxo's sales in 1999. These are: Zyloric, for the treatment of gout; Imuran, an immunosuppressant used to help suppress rejection in organ transplants; and Exosuf, for the treatment of neonatal respiratory distress. Also included in this are sales of OTC products developed in joint ventures, and local products sold in individual markets.

Income statement

Year	Revenue ($m)	Net income ($m)	Net profit margin	Employees
1999	13,718.1	2,926.2	21.3%	–
1998	13,247.8	3,046.8	23.0%	54,350
1997	13,180.6	3,055.6	23.2%	53,068
1996	14,284.0	3,419.9	23.9%	53,808
1995	15,850.4	3,691.4	23.3%	65,702
1994	10,319.6	1,655.1	16.0%	47,189
1993	8,730.0	2,011.2	23.0%	–
1992	7,353.1	1,800.2	24.5%	–
1991	7,796.7	1,966.3	25.2%	–
1990	5,516.7	1,481.1	26.8%	–

Stock history

	Stock price ($)			P/E		Per share ($)		
Year	FY High	FY Low	FY Close	High	Low	Earns	Div.	Book value
1999	76.19	48.06	55.88	47	30	1.61	1.29	2.79
1998	69.69	47.13	69.50	41	28	1.70	0.00	2.47
1997	48.50	29.88	47.88	28	17	1.72	0.00	1.70
1996	34.38	22.25	31.75	18	11	1.94	0.98	1.18
1995	28.38	18.75	28.13	123	82	0.23	0.00	1.21
1994	25.50	16.63	24.38	–	–	1.05	0.94	413.55
1993	22.00	14.75	16.63	–	–	1.32	0.75	5,105.20
1992	30.25	16.25	16.88	–	–	1.19	0.62	4,473.60
1991	35.25	20.19	25.38	–	–	1.31	1.03	4,517.44
1990	22.13	12.94	20.25	–	–	0.99	0.50	3,474.12

1999 year-end financials

Debt ratio	28.6%
Return on equity	61.2%
Cash ($m)	350.6
Current ratio	1.16
Long-term debt ($m)	2,035.9
Shares outstanding (millions)	1,820.4
Dividend yield	2.3%
Dividend payout	80.1%
Market value ($m)	101,724.1

Financial data provided by Hoover's Online (www.hoovers.com) and Media General Financial Services, Inc.

Glaxo Wellcome contacts

Glaxo Wellcome plc
Glaxo Wellcome House
Berkeley Avenue
Greenford
Middlesex UB6 0NN, UK

Phone: 0207 493 4060
Fax: 0207 408 0228
URL: www.glaxowellcome.co.uk

CEO: Robert Ingram   CFO: John Coombe   HR: Tony Mehew

Heineken NV – Amsterdam, The Netherlands

Executive snapshot

"Heineken plans to continue along the path it took many years ago," states Heineken CEO Karel Vuursteen. "[It is] a twin-track strategy which, based on our assessment of the market and our experience, moves us in one country to devote ourselves to capturing a leading position in the market and in another, a leading position within the premium segment."

The result has been creation of the world's second largest brewer and, in almost every case, a spot among the market leaders in the 170 countries in which it competes.

Heineken backdrop

In 1592, William Shakespeare is the toast of the Avon theater district, China's Ming Dynasty is trembling before the Mongol horde, and the New World is still brand spanking new. That year in Amsterdam, Weijntgen Elberts, the widow of a brewer, buys a home in the center of the city. Soon, in a shed at the rear of the property, she starts brewing beer. Elberts names her shed-based brewery De Hooiberg ... The Haystack.

Elberts and later brew masters, apparently know how to make good beer, because 270-odd years later, in 1864, when The Haystack attracts the attention of Gerard Adriaan Heineken, it is the largest of the region's breweries. Heineken, a 22-year-old would-be brewer, convinces his mother to back him and buys De Hooiberg for 48,000 guilders.

Future focus

The power of perception

Why does one product become a leader while another product withers by the wayside? Conventional wisdom says that success has to do with quality. The better product lives and flourishes while the inferior one dies.

Conventional wisdom is almost always wrong. If not, then everyone would be rich and famous.

What accounts for the rise of Heineken to become the world's second largest brewing company? (Anheuser-Busch is the largest.) Conventional wisdom suggests that it's the quality of the beer. But numerous "blind" taste tests show that the average beer drinker cannot tell the difference between Heineken, Beck's, Carlsberg and other European-style lager beers.

If not taste, then what? It should be obvious that the beer drinker chooses between brands not on taste itself, but on the perception of taste. And there is a lot of evidence that suggests that beer drinkers in most countries of the world believe that Heineken does indeed taste better than other brands, especially less-expensive brands.

There is an enormous difference between taste and the perception of taste. (As one wag pointed out, it's like the difference between lightning and the lightning bug.) Yet most people refuse to see any difference between the two. "If I think it tastes better, it does taste better."

Corporate strategies that fail to see the difference between the two are doomed to failure, too. Improving the quality (or the taste) of a product is the conventional way for a company to increase its market share. Sometimes it works, sometimes it doesn't. When it works, it is usually because the company has also improved its perception of quality. (Sometimes accidentally.)

Why not reverse the process? Why not focus on improving the perception of quality? If you can do that, then your company will become successful regardless of the absolute quality of the product or service. (It's nice to do both, but first things first.)

How do you improve the perception of quality? That's no secret either. You improve the perception of quality by being the leader. Why is that? Everybody knows that the better product or service will win in the marketplace so they assume that the leading brand must be the better product.

But how do you get to be the leader? And this is the most important aspect of any business today. You have to be first. Coca-Cola was the first cola and thus was automatically the leader. As time went on, other cola brands were introduced: Pepsi-Cola, Royal Crown cola, etc. But Coca-Cola, by virtue of being first, was the leader and people assumed it must be better because "everybody knows that the better product wins in the marketplace."

Heineken was first. It's as simple as that. Heineken was the first high-priced imported beer in most countries of the world. (Today Heineken is sold in 170 countries.) Like many successful global companies, Heineken started its exporting career very early. The first market was France in the late 1870s. From there the company expanded to the rest of Europe, South America, Asia and Africa.

Whether by accident or not, the company treated globalization as the most important aspect of their strategy, not the nature of the local operations. So they bought, set up joint ventures, built breweries, licensed the brand, whatever it took to globalize. In 1933, the year Prohibition ended, Heineken was the first imported beer to re-enter the US market. Today America is Heineken's largest export market.

Whether by accident or not, Heineken also benefited from its brand name. When you think of beer, what country comes to mind? It's not Holland, it's Germany. It's no accident that the most successful beer brands in America have been German in origin. Budweiser, Busch, Michelob, Miller, Pabst, Schlitz, etc.

To most people, Heineken sounds like a German beer. Beck's, on the other hand, is an English name. The name alone is one reason that Heineken outsells Beck's in America by a wide margin. If you want to build a global brand, you need a name that works well in most of the countries around the world. Heineken is an almost perfect name. It's unique, distinctive and most important of all, suggests the country that is best known for beer.

One reason we are bullish on the future prospects of Heineken is the fact that the company has less than 7 percent of the world's beer market. (Coca-Cola has 70 percent of the world's cola market.) The company has the inside track on a race with a long way to go. Keeping its current strategy should result in a gradually increasing market share.

What mistakes has Heineken made? For one thing, it has far too many brands. Cutting back on some of its 70 brands would increase profits and make the company stronger. Second, it should devote far more attention to its basic Heineken brand, starting with a worldwide marketing campaign in the pattern of Coca-Cola.

Nonetheless, a company that makes one brilliant move can also make a lot of mistakes and still not harm its future prospects. Microsoft, Intel and many other powerful, worldwide companies have also strayed from the straight and narrow from time to time without hurting their long-term prospects.

Heineken belongs in this category.

The new owner is no slouch when it comes to business. Within four years, he has built enough demand that a new brewery is needed in the local Amsterdam market. Nor is Heineken content to rest on his brew's laurels. In 1869, he literally turns the operation on its head when he abandons top fermentation brewing for the Bavarian technique of bottom fermentation.

Fits and starts of an international brand

On January 11, 1873, Heineken's brewery is incorporated and issues stock under the name Heineken's Bierbrouwerij Maatschappij NV. Gerald Heineken, the principal shareholder, is president. That year, 17,000 hectoliters of beer are brewed and sold under the Heineken name. The company moves quickly to expand nationally and begins construction on a new brewery in Rotterdam that comes online in 1874.

In the second half of the decade, Heineken takes its first steps toward globalization. The results are mixed. The company begins exporting its beer to France with good results. But the leasing of a Belgian brewery, Brasserie Bavaro Belge, in 1878 is not as successful and in 1880, the lease along with a purchase option is allowed to expire.

By 1880, Heineken has expanded it sales almost 400 percent since becoming a public company. It brews and sells 64,000 hectoliters that year. Product quality and technological excellence, two recurring themes throughout the company's history, are the highlights of the decade. Newly invented mechanical cooling systems replace the use of naturally-formed ice in the breweries in Amsterdam and Rotterdam by 1883.

In 1886, the company's A-yeast strain, which is still used today, is perfected in Rotterdam. This work is rewarded in 1889, when Heineken beer is awarded a gold medal of honor at the World Exhibition in Paris.

Gerard Heineken dies on March 18, 1893 and with his passing the first era in Heineken's history ends. For the rest of the century and into World War I, the company remains closely held by the Heineken family, but is run, quite capably, by outsiders. In 1900, beer sales hit 200,000 hectoliters.

In 1914, on the eve of World War I, beer sales grow to 300,000 hectoliters. That same year, another Heineken – Gerald's son, Henry Pierre – emerges among the leaders of the company. He first takes a place on the executive board of the company and three years later, in 1917, he assumes the top leadership position as the company's chairman.

It is Henry Heineken who first explores the US market for the company's beer. After the war ends in 1918, he books passage to New York and during the voyage meets Leo Van Munching. Van Munching, the ship's bartender, impresses Heineken with his knowledge of beer and, by the end of the journey, has secured a position as the US representative for Heineken beer. Unhappily, the new market has barely been addressed when, in 1920, the US adopts the Eighteenth Amendment banning the sale of alcohol throughout the country. Heineken's US expansion comes to an abrupt halt.

The company's technological growth continues unabated and by 1921, Heineken reports a profit of two million guilders (NLG). In 1925, a new brewery in Rotterdam is opened. In 1927, the royal family of The Netherlands recognizes the company's rich legacy and bright future when it grants the brewer the right to use Prince Hendrik's coat of arms and the family's royal coat of arms along with the title of Royal Purveyor on its products.

As the high-flying twenties nosedive into the depressing thirties, Heineken is selling 571,000 hectoliters of beer in kegs annually. In 1929 and 1930, the company installs its first bottling lines in the Rotterdam brewery, expanding its internal capabilities beyond kegs for the first time and gaining greater control over the quality of its bottled beers.

The company also establishes The Netherlands' first training program for brewing professionals. In conjunction with the coursework, a pilot brewery for testing new production methods, products, and employee training is opened in Rotterdam.

Even in the face of worldwide depression, the brewer expands internationally. In 1931, Heineken establishes Malayan Breweries Ltd, a jointly held brewery formed with Fraser & Neave in Singapore.

As Prohibition ends in the US, Heineken is the first imported beer to re-enter the market. Leo Van Munching leaves Holland with his family and 50 cases of Heineken, and sets up shop in New York in 1933. Van Munching, as described in his grandson Philip's book, *Beer Blast*, is "a workaholic with an ego the size of Manhattan" and establishes a firm foothold for the Dutch brewery in New York City despite the tight economy of the time.

By 1937, the company has laid the foundations for an international brand, but has not yet reaped the rewards. The profit for the year is NLG1.5 million, a 25 percent decline from 1921, but still a respectable showing given the economic hardships of the 1930s.

Closed by force of arms

The work of Heineken and Van Munching in New York comes to its first crescendo in 1939. Understanding the marketing value of full-scale participation in the 1939 World Fair in New York, Henry Heineken himself serves as a member of the event's organizing committee.

Thousands of US beer lovers get their first introduction to the imported brew at the company's pavilion, "Heineken on the Zuyderzee." Heineken sells 10,000 hectoliters of its brew during the heavily attended affair and Van Munching gets much of the credit, earning his appointment as the sole US importer for the beer.

The World Fair triumph pales as the aggression of Germany's Nazi party spills over Europe's national borders. Heineken prepares for war by forming The Foundation of the Central Brewery, which ensures that the balance of power among Dutch brewers will remain intact through the conflict. The company is also listed on the Amsterdam stock exchange for the first time.

In 1940, Henry Heineken steps down from the executive board, but remains active as a member of the company's supervisory council. Barely six months later, in May 1940, the Netherlands is overrun by the Germans and Heineken shipments are cut off for the remainder of World War II.

Ever enterprising, Leo Van Munching keeps Heineken flowing in the US by importing beer from the company's brewery on Java. This route works until the Japanese enter the war and capture most of the Asia-Pacific region. In 1942, with the war at its peak, the third generation of the Heineken family, the founder's grandson Alfred, enters the business.

The end of the war in 1945 marks the start a slow recovery for the company. Grain shortages after the war cause the Dutch government to prohibit beer exports until August 1946. By 1950, net profit has risen to NLG2.6 million. But that amount is earned on only 400,000 hectoliters of beer, less than the company was producing 30 years earlier.

One unforeseen benefit of the war years is the exposure of tens of thousands of American soldiers to European beers. When the GIs return home, many bring back a taste for Heineken. Alfred Heineken follows the American forces home. In the post-war years, he works with Van Munching in the US. He studies marketing and advertising, and assists in the early growth of the Van Munching distribution system. He returns to corporate headquarters in 1948 and, in 1953, takes a leadership role in the company.

Building a global brewing network

Heineken expands via construction at existing and new facilities as well as acquisitions throughout the remaining years of the decade. In 1953, Heineken's historical roots get even deeper when the brewer purchases the De Sleutel brewery in Dordrecht. Founded in 1433, De Sleutel is the oldest continuing business in the Netherlands.

The company continues to expand its domestic capacity. In 1954, the capacity at the Amsterdam and Rotterdam breweries is increased and a new brewery is begun in 's-Hertogenbosch. In 1958 the new brewery opens and, with the demand for Heineken beer swelling beyond all expectations, the company starts expanding the new plant one year later.

In the late 1950s and early 1960s Heineken embarks on a series of international acquisitions that form the nucleus of the present-day company. By 1960, the Dutch brewer partially or fully owns 28 breweries.

In Europe the company purchases Three Horseshoes Brewery in the Netherlands and Belgium's Albert Maltings and Brasseries Leopold breweries. It also buys a share of Italian brewer Mobiliare Industriale Cisalpina.

Its African holdings increase substantially. The company owns the Kumasi Brewery in Ghana, Nigerian Breweries in Lagos, and Bralima, which boasts operations in Zaire, Ruanda Burundi, and French Equatorial Africa. The company also owns Nova Empresa de Cerveja in Angola, Bouteillerie de Léopoldville in Zaire, and Egypt's Crown Brewery in Alexandria and Brewery Les Pyramides in Cairo.

In Asia, Malayan Breweries now operates plants in Singapore, New Zealand, and New Guinea. In South America, the company owns Cerveceria Heineken de Venezuela. By 1960, this adds up to sales of 3.8 million hectoliters, including the record sale of one million units in the US. The company's net profit hits NLG8 million. In 1961 Malayan Breweries opens a new plant in Kuala Lumpur, and Heineken accumulates a 75 percent share in Netherlands-based Koloniale Brouwerijen, along with its breweries in Africa and Asia. In October that same year, the company enters a strategic alliance with the UK's Whitbread & Co. Ltd. A third brewery is opened in Nigeria in 1962.

The rapid expansion also brings a few less-than-stellar investments. Political upheaval in Indonesia forces plant closings and the company sells off its brewing operation in Venezuela after years of losses. The new owners, however, continue to produce Heineken at the plant.

The 1960s bring technological advances as the traditional wooden beer keg disappears in 1961 and is replaced by today's metal keg. In 1963, the company forms a subsidiary named Heineken Technisch Beheer. It includes the corporate research laboratory, the pilot brewery, purchasing operations, engineering and training under one roof.

The Heineken Foundation is also established in 1963. Its initial purpose is to stimulate scientific research in biochemistry and includes the administration of the Dr HP Heineken Prize, a NLG35,000 grant awarded for excellence in that discipline. The first prize is awarded in 1964 on the 100th anniversary of the purchase of the first Heineken brewery.

In 1965, for the first time, a Heineken brewery produces over one million hectoliters in a single year and, in 1967, capacity is boosted once more with the installation of the company's first automated filling line for draught beer.

The crowning achievement of the decade is Heineken's 1968 acquisition of a major competitor, Netherlands' Amstel Brouwerij. The Amstel takeover brings along with it a worldwide chain of breweries including Surinam's Surinaamse Brouwerij, Curacao's Antilliaanse Brouwerij, the Jordan Brewery Co. Ltd and Lebanon's Brasserie et Malterie Almaza in the Middle East, the Athenian Brewery in Greece and the Brasserie de Madagascar. Heineken also purchases soft drinks producer Vrumona in the Netherlands.

By 1970, Heineken is producing 11.3 million hectoliters of beer per year and net profit has ballooned to NLG46.6 million.

The world under license

The Amstel acquisition also introduces Heineken to licensing – a third method of globalization for its expansionist toolkit. Within a year of the merger Heineken begins licensing territorial rights to brew beer, under the company name, on a large scale.

In 1969, the UK's Whitbread & Co. Ltd starts brewing Heineken in a new brewery near London. Brewers in Sierra Leone and Trinidad begin producing Heineken in 1972 and Jamaica is licensed in 1973. The company continues its expansion on all other fronts as well. In 1970, Ibecor S.A. is formed to manage an increased stake in the African operations of Belgium's Interbrew SA. In 1972, Heineken purchases a majority stake in France's third-largest brewer – Albra. A year later, the company starts a new brewery in St Lucia and brings a new brewery online in Jakarta.

Domestic growth includes the completion of renovations at the 's-Hertogenbosch brewery, which now boasts a 3.8 million hectoliter production capacity – a quantity that matches the company's entire production just a decade earlier, and ground is broken for a new brewery in Zoeterwoude, which will replace the outdated Rotterdam plant. Two more Dutch brewers, Bokma and Coebergh, are also brought into the Heineken family. In 1971, Alfred Heineken becomes the third generation to lead the company as chairman of the executive board. That same year, his father Henry Heineken passes away.

In the mid-1970s, the licensing strategy continues as the rights to produce Heineken in Norway and Sweden are sold, as well as licenses to produce the brew in St Lucia, Tahiti, and Haiti. In 1974, in a joint venture with Whitbread, Heineken purchases a majority stake in Italy's Birra Dreher. That same year Heineken purchases 40 percent of Trinidad's National Brewing Company Ltd. In 1975, new breweries in Greece and Martinique come online.

Licensing continues through the end of the decade as licenses are granted in Ireland in 1978 and Italy in 1979. In the early 1980s, territorial licenses are added in France, Morocco, Greece, South Korea, and in Japan, under the auspices of the Kirin Brewery.

By 1980, Heineken has good reason to celebrate the work of the past decade – the company has more than doubled its size. Annual sales of beer are now 25.9 million hectoliters; net profit is NLG83.1 million.

Intensifying the brew

In the 1980s, Heineken shapes its global brewing network. Minority investments that are performing well are bolstered to increase profits, regional organizations are strengthened to build market share, and operations are rationalized and consolidated to build productivity.

The effort really begins in 1979, when the company increases its partial stakes in Italy's Birra Dreher and France's Albra into full ownership positions. Albra becomes Heineken France SA. In Italy, Moretti Sud is purchased and merged with Dreher.

In 1981, establishment of the company's second and third corporate brands quietly takes shape. The Amstel brand jumps the Atlantic when Amstel Brewery Canada Ltd is established through the acquisition of Henninger's brewery in Ontario. In 1982, Heineken purchases the remaining shares of Murphy Brewery Ireland Ltd, making it a fully-owned subsidiary.

In the European market, the company bolsters its commanding position with the purchase of Brouwerij de Ridder in Maastricht that same year. The French market is effectively captured when that government approves the 1984 merger of Heineken France with Union de Brasseries and Brasserie Pelforth. The new brewing giant operates under the name Sogebra and Heineken owns a controlling stake of 51 percent. At the same time, the company purchases a one-third interest in Spain's market leader El Aguila, which within a year grows to a controlling 51 percent stake. And in 1985, Athenian Breweries is strengthened with the purchase of Breweries of Greece SA.

In the Caribbean and South America, Heineken continues building its network in the early 1980s with a 15 percent stake in Quilmes International, a brewer based in Bermuda with operations in Argentina, Uruguay, and Paraguay, and a 60 percent interest in the Bahamas' Commonwealth Breweries Ltd. Minority interests are also purchased in Brasserie Internationale d'Haïti and Cerveceria Bohemia in the Dominican Republic, which is quickly followed with a joint venture by Heineken and Bohemia, named Cerveceria Nacional Dominicana.

Heineken roughly doubles its investment stakes in African brewers in the first half of the 1980s. In addition, in 1985, it purchases a one-third share in Cameroon's Internationale Brasserie SA, Cameroon and in 1986, it acquires 51 percent of Brasseries de Bourbon in Reunion.

The second half of the decade brings more of the same. In 1986, Beverages Investment Pte. Ltd is established in Singapore. It is a joint venture between Heineken and Fraser & Neave, and it includes the company's holdings in Malayan Breweries Ltd. In 1989, Malayan Breweries becomes Guinness Anchor Berhad when it is merged with Guinness Malaysia.

Italy's Dreher beefs up once again with 20 percent stakes in Societá Internationale Birraria and Nuova Birra Messina, and in 1988, it purchases the remaining shares in both operations. The subsidiary also increases its interest in Sarde Produzione Agricole Industriale to full ownership. In 1988, Heineken locks up France when it buys the remaining 49 percent of Sogebra. The brewer also makes an early stab at the Chinese market in 1988. That year, it's Asia Pacific Breweries invests in a joint venture in the Mila Brewery in Shanghai.

The decade ends with the retirement of the third generation of Heineken family ownership. Alfred Heineken resigns from the executive board having reached the company's mandatory retirement age. He leaves behind a global industry leader: in 1990 sales of beer are 53.5 million hectoliters and net profit is NLG366 million – four times 1980's results.

Anywhere there are beer drinkers

In the last decade of the 20th century, Heineken focuses on the last large beer markets as yet untapped by the brewer. In 1991, Heineken gets its first direct toehold on the huge US beer market when it pulls its exclusive importer in the US, Van Munching & Company, into the corporate family. It purchases the operation from Leo Van Munching, Jr, the son of the founder. Over the previous decades, Van Munching, Jr has established a nationwide distribution system and has built Heineken into the leading imported brew in the nation – it is outselling its nearest competitor by two to one when Heineken takes over.

The company also extends its grasp on the Asia-Pacific market through its operating company, Asia Pacific Breweries (APB). In 1991, APB, in a joint venture with Brierly Investments Ltd, takes a majority stake in New Zealand's Dominion Breweries. In 1993, APB doubles its stake in Dominion, which owns a 42 percent share of the domestic market.

APB is particularly active in Southeast Asia. In 1991, the company starts construction on a brewery in Ho Chi Min City, Vietnam. It holds a 60 percent stake in the project. In 1993, the new brewery begins producing Tiger beer for the local market and one year later, starts turning out Heineken beer. In 1995, APB receives permission for a second brewery near Hanoi City in northern Vietnam. It holds a 42.5 percent stake in Hatay Brewery Limited.

In 1993, APB moves into Thailand with a stake in a new brewery outside of Bangkok, which will produce Heineken beer for the Thai market. And in 1994, its starts construction on a new joint venture brewery in Cambodia. The Cambodia Brewery Limited will produce Tiger and ABC Stout.

The new markets are sometimes politically unstable and in 1994, APB begins a joint venture brewery with the Union of Myanmar Holdings Ltd (UMEHL) that the company is forced to abandon less than two years later.

"Since then the public opinion and issues surrounding this market have changed to a degree that could have an adverse effect on our brand and corporate reputation" announces Heineken CEO Karel Vuursteen in 1996. "Heineken has a heritage of good corporate citizenship in many markets around the globe."

APB continues moving into China with a one-third stake in the Fujian Brewery in 1993. In 1994, it begins work on a second jointly-owned brewery, this time on Hainan Island. The company also opens sales offices in Guangzhou and Shanghai.

As the markets stabilize in Eastern Europe, Heineken is quick to enter the former Communist Bloc. In 1991, it purchases a 50.3 percent interest in the Hungarian brewery Komáromi Sörgyár RT, which produces Amstel in Hungary. In 1994, it purchases full ownership of the company.

In 1994, Heineken enters Poland with 24.9 percent stake in brewer Zywiec. Zywiec leads the premium segment of the Polish beer market. By 1998, the stake has increased to 50 percent.

In 1994, through Brewinvest, a joint venture of Heineken's Athenian Brewery, the company acquires 80 percent of state-owned Zagorka Brewery in Bulgaria. Zagorka is the country's leading beer with a 20 percent market share. In 1998, Brewinvest acquires a 60.2 percent interest in Bulgaria's Ariana Brewery. Heineken also acquires a 66 percent stake in Slovakia's largest brewer, Zlaty Bazant, and in 1997, adds a 49 percent interest in Slovakia's Karsay brewery.

Heineken does not ignore its traditional European stronghold in the 1990s. In 1993, it begins importing Heineken beer into Germany for the first time. Previously the German market was closed by legislation prohibiting the use of preservatives in beer.

Heineken also builds its share of the Swiss beer market with the purchase of a 52 percent stake in Haldengut, the parent of Calanda Haldengut, the second largest brewer in that country. In 1994, Heineken makes a tender offer for the outstanding shares of Brauerei Haldengut and Calanda Bräu.

Dreher is renamed Heineken Italia in 1993, and early in 1994 it acquires Interbrew Italia, which controls a five percent share of the Italian market. One year later, the operating subsidiary acquires Birra Moretti, Italy's third largest brewery. Heineken Italia now controls a 38 percent market share in Italy.

In France, Sogebra builds market share with the purchase of a 54 percent stake in the Fischer Group, the fourth largest brewer in that country. Sogebra follows that purchase with a public tender offer giving it full ownership. The operating company also acquires Société Adelshoffen and 66 percent of Groupe Saint-Arnould, consolidating its position even further.

In Africa, Heineken builds its investment share when Unilever sells its brewery stakes. Heineken increases its share of Nigerian Breweries to 28 percent and its stake in Ghana's Kumasi Brewery to 50.1 percent. In 1997, it adds a 90 percent interest in ABC Brewery in Accra to its portfolio. In 1998, however, tragedy strikes when 36 employees are killed in a terrorist attack in Rwanda.

At year-end 1998, Heineken is the second largest brewer in the world. Production is just under 80 million hectoliters and net profit is NLG981 million.

Heineken continues its global expansion via acquisition in 1998 with the purchase of a stake in Pivara Skopje, the largest brewer in the former Yugoslav republic of Macedonia. In 1999, it buys 18 percent of Israel's leading brewer, Tempo, the maker of Goldstar and Maccabee beer. In January 2000, Heineken buys an 88 percent stake in Spanish brewer Cruzcampo.

Heineken close-up

Heineken NV and its worldwide network of affiliate breweries sold over 90.9 million hectoliters of beer in 1999. For the non-brewers in the audience, that means that beer drinkers around the globe are consuming something in the order of 56,000 glasses of Heineken beer *per minute*. And, that translates into NLG15.7 billion in the 1999 annual revenue.

Amsterdam-based Heineken is the largest brewer in Europe and the world's second largest beer company. As the most globally diverse brewer, the company sells its products in 170 countries and owns more than 110 breweries in over 50 countries. These operations are supported by the efforts of approximately 36,700 employees worldwide. In addition to owning over 70 beer brands worldwide, Heineken brews three major global brands: Heineken, Amstel, and Murphy's.

Heineken, in the familiar green bottle, is the leading beer in Europe and is available in 170 countries – more than any other beer. With 20.4 million hectoliters sold in 1999, it accounts for roughly 22 percent of the brewer's total revenue. The company's first beer, at the turn of the century it celebrated its 127th anniversary.

As befitting a lead brand, there is a strong marketing effort supporting Heineken. The logo from the Heineken label is much in evidence at tennis events including the US Open, the Davis Cup, and the Australian Open, as well as many less prominent matches. In rugby, the Heineken Cup is in its sixth year and includes several dozen European teams.

In music, the company sponsors the Red Star Concert in the US and Heineken Music Horizons in Hong Kong. Even James Bond, the famous British secret agent 007, recommends Heineken. In 1997, the beer was featured in the Bond film, *Tomorrow Never Dies* and a new "007" can was launched to capitalize on the promotion. The entertainment extends to the Internet, where the brand's website (http://www.heineken.nl) targets consumers with games, contests, and news.

The company's Amstel brand, acquired in 1968, contributes about nine percent of annual revenues. In 1999, that meant 7.9 million hectoliters of beer. Amstel is sold in 90 countries and is the fourth best-selling international beer brand.

Amstel sponsorships include soccer's UEFA Champions League in Europe, the Africa Cup of Nations (the continent's most prestigious soccer event), and the Asian Cup. It supports the cycling world championship, as well as the Amstel Gold Race in the Netherlands. The brand also has its own website (http://www.amstel.nl).

The Ireland-based Murphy's brands represent Heineken's third widely distributed corporate brand. Murphy's specialty brews, led by its Irish Stout, are sold in 65 countries and account for less than one percent of the company's sales.

The Murphy's Irish Pub marketing concept has been successfully building the brand's value, and the Murphy's Irish Open golf tournament has proven a high-profile venue.

Heineken's vision of beer as a global business is long established. The company has been exporting its beer from Amsterdam since 1876 and by the 1950s, fully half of its production was destined for export markets. A corporate strategy of globalization has been aggressively pursued for the past four decades.

The reasoning is clear: the worldwide beer market is currently estimated at something in excess of 1.2 billion hectoliters annually and in that light, even the largest brewers remain small fish happily swimming in a big pond. However, the traditional market strongholds in the US and Europe, while still large and valuable, are mature and growing only slowly. Tapping into new growth markets – today's include Asia-Pacific and China, Latin America, Africa, and Eastern Europe – is critical for future success.

Tastes in beer, however, vary significantly among peoples and regions. Simply exporting a single brand or two is not enough. Hence, Heineken's focus is on growth via the acquisition of regional brewers, which it manages as a loose federation.

The Heineken global network

Europe

Heineken operates the largest breweries in Europe. Overall, the Heineken brand is Europe's leading beer, and Amstel is also a leader among the top beer brands. Sales in this region account for fully 72 percent of Heineken's revenue, and 45.4 million hectoliters of beer.

In The Netherlands, the Heineken and Amstel beers are best-sellers. Other major company-owned brands include Vos and Bierbrouwerij. The brewer also maintains a position in the Dutch soft drink and mineral water markets, selling Pepsi-Cola, SiSi, and 7Up brands.

In France, the company purchased majority shares in the fourth and fifth largest brewers, the Fischer Group and Groupe Saint-Arnould, in the mid-1990s. The Heineken brand is the leader in the premium segment of the market. Desperados, Kingston, and Adelscott brands star in the specialty segment. Amstel is the leader in the keg beer segment.

In Spain, the Dutch brewer distributes its brands through El Aguila, a brewer in which Heineken holds a 71 percent share, and Cruzcampo. The Heineken brand is the leader in premium beers, followed by the Aguila-Amstel brand and Murphy's Irish Stout.

Heineken Italia includes ownership of Birra Moretti, Italy's third largest brewer and a leading beer brand in that country.

In Greece, the company's Athenian Brewery is the country's market leader. Amstel is the nation's leading beer brand and the Heineken brand leads in the premium segment. Ioli mineral water is also a leading brand.

In Ireland, the fully-owned Murphy Brewery Ltd is the home of fast-growing Murphy's Irish Stout. Heineken is the country's leading lager beer and Amstel, which was first launched in 1996 in the home consumption market, is increasing its share. In the UK, Heineken Export and Cold Filtered beers and locally produced Amstel are sold.

Heineken owns 91 percent of Switzerland's Calanda Haldengut AG. It brews leading regional brands, Calanda BraY and Haldengut. Amstel and Heineken are sold here, as well as the French brands, Desperados, Kingston and Adelscott.

In Eastern Europe, Heinken owns Slovakia's largest brewery, Zlaty Bazant, and Malterie Karsay. It also controls 75 percent of Poland's largest brewer, Zywiec, and Bulgaria's Zagorka and Ariana breweries. Heineken has a production contract with Czech brewer Pilsner Urquell for the Gambrinus brand. The Heineken brand is exported to Kazakhstan, the Ukraine, and Russia, and Amstel is sold in seven countries in the region.

The Americas

The US is Heineken's largest export market and the company maintains operating companies, participating interests, and licensing agreements there. Heineken is the second largest import in the US, after the Corona brand. Amstel Light is the largest import in the light beer market. The company also sells Amstel Bier, Amstel 1870 lager, Murphy's Irish Stout, and Murphy's Irish Amber in the US.

Heineken is the leading imported beer brand in the Caribbean. The company owns the Commonwealth Brewery, which produces Kalik and Kalik Light beer in the Bahamas, the Windward & Leeward Brewery in St Lucia, the Surinaamse Brouwerij and its Parbo beer brand in Surinam, the Brasserie Lorraine in Martinique, and the Antilliaanse Brouwerij in Curacao. Heineken is also sold in Puerto Rico, the company's largest export market in the Caribbean, and the Dominican Republic, where the brand is brewed locally.

In Central and South America, the company has a minority interest in Cervejarias Kaiser of Brazil and a licensing partnership with

Argentina's Quilmes brewery. Sales in this region add up to 9.6 million hectoliters.

Africa

Heineken's holdings in Africa are extensive, and recently at risk because of the political unrest on that continent. In 1998, tragedy struck when 36 Heineken employees were killed in a terrorist attack in Rwanda. In Brazzaville, the company's soft drink factory was destroyed and its brewery closed. In Sierra Leone, a brewery had to be closed due to civil unrest.

Nevertheless, the company remains committed to its operations on the continent, which account for 8.4 million hectoliters. These include full and partial ownership in: the Bramila brewery in the Democratic Republic of Congo (formerly Zaire); a brewery and soft drink factory in Burundi; the Rwandan operations noted above and the Primus brand; Brasserie de Bourbon in Reunion; the Nocal and EKA breweries in Angola; the ABC and Kumasi breweries in Ghana; and the Nigerian breweries. In South Africa, Amstel beer is brewed under license and is sold in kegs and bottles. To develop and train employees, Heineken also operates central training schools in the Democratic Republic of Congo and Nigeria.

Asia-Pacific

The Asia-Pacific region is estimated to be a high-growth market for beer in the near term. In 1999 it accounted for 7.4 million hectoliters. Heineken operates via joint ventures, fully owned subsidiaries, licensing partners, and exports.

Accounting for half of the beer consumption in the region, China is a much prized market. Heineken sells the Heineken, Tiger, Amstel, and Anchor brands in China. It maintains breweries in Shanghai, Fuzhou, and on Hainan Island.

In Singapore, the company operates a brewery and also sells several specialty beers including the Anchor Ice and Baron brands. New Zealand's DB Group produces DB Export Gold, Heineken, and Amstel. On Papua New Guinea, SP Holding operates a brewery and a soft drinks factory.

The Vietnam Brewery produces Tiger and Heineken beers, leaders in the premium beer market, and the Bivina brand. The company also operates in Cambodia and Thailand, where locally brewed Heineken also leads the premium segment.

In Indonesia, Heineken's largest fully owned operating company, Multi Bintang, sells the Bintang brand and Guinness, which is produced under license. On East Java, a new brewery has recently opened in Sampang Agung and the company also owns a plant on New Caledonia. On Tahiti, Heineken is brewed locally under license.

Income statement

Year	Revenue ($m)	Net income ($m)	Net profit margin	Employees
1998	7,360.8	522.2	7.1%	33,511
1997	6,668.0	375.7	5.6%	32,421
1996	7,052.5	379.2	5.4%	31,682
1995	6,492.1	413.1	6.4%	27,379
1994	5,750.7	381.7	6.6%	26,197
1993	4,646.7	266.5	5.7%	23,997
1992	4,918.3	254.6	5.2%	25,320
1991	5,077.7	239.4	4.7%	27,502
1990	4,860.9	216.7	4.5%	28,908
1989	4,097.5	170.3	4.2%	29,127

1998 year-end financials

Debt ratio	18.5%
Return on equity	—
Cash ($m)	1,055.5
Current ratio	1.49
Long-term debt ($m)	612.9

Financial data provided by Hoover's Online (www.hoovers.com) and Media General Financial Services, Inc.

Heineken contacts

Heineken NV
Tweede Weteringplantsoen 21
1017 ZD Amsterdam
The Netherlands

Phone: +31–20–523–92–39
Fax: +31–20–626–35–03
URL: www.heinekencorp.nl

CEO: Karel Vuursteen   CFO: David Hazelwood   HR: R. Bart De Jonge

HSBC Holdings plc –

London, UK

Executive snapshot

Being one of the world's largest banks is not good enough for HSBC, which is currently running third in a close field. Its primary goal is simple: "Our vision is to become the world's leading financial services company," says John Bond, chairman, HSBC Holdings.

HSBC backdrop

The development of HSBC echoes the growing connection between the East and the West. Founded only 20 years after the British established the Hong Kong colony, the bank has played an important role in the development of China and seems destined to share in the future potential of the world's largest market.

Acing the competition

Thomas Sutherland is leaving Bombay on a P&O (Peninsular and Oriental) steamer when he hears the news: Hong Kong is finally going to get a local bank. The newly forming Bank of China will be headquartered

Future focus

Riding the global horse

Banking used to be a local business. An individual or company doing business in one city or town just naturally gravitated to one of the local banks. Why would you do business with a bank that didn't know you or your community and wasn't aware of your good name and reputation? It made sense for a bank to concentrate on a single community.

There still is a market for a local bank. But there is also a much bigger market for the bank that can operate around the world. This is especially true in the business side of banking. As business goes global, so does banking. In spite of different regulations, different currencies and other difficulties, banks have been following their customers around the world.

In this regard, the banking industry is in the process of mimicking two other business services: advertising and accounting. In virtually all the largest business centers, the leading advertising agency is a global company. So, too, with accounting. The Big Five accounting firms dominate the business on a worldwide basis.

What happened in advertising and accounting will happen in banking. It is just going to take longer. But like most situations in business, there is a significant advantage to being the first player in the category. In the banking business, HSBC did it first.

Not only has HSBC been around for more than 135 years, but has also been playing the global game almost from its inception. In its first year the bank had 17 agents spread throughout the Far East, with agents being replaced by branches in the next few years. By the turn of the century, the bank had branches in Europe and North America.

HSBC is the first foreign bank to open in Hamburg and Lyons and the second to open a branch in New York City.

Acquisitions have also played a role in the global expansion of HSBC. In 1959, the bank purchased The Mercantile Bank with operations in India. In 1960, HSBC bought the British Bank of the Middle East. In 1980, HSBC bought a stake in New York's Marine Midland Bank and eventually acquired the rest of the bank. In 1990, the bank bought Lloyds Bank Canada. In 1992, HSBC acquired Midland Bank in the UK.

Today HSBC has more than 5000 offices in 80 countries. Of particular note is the bank's strong perception in the trade. The *Banker* magazine has called HSBC "the world's strongest bank." *Euromoney* magazine called HSBC "the best bank in Asia" and *Forbes* magazine rated HSBC second in its list of "Super 50" global companies. Truly HSBC is a global banking powerhouse.

Unfortunately over the years HSBC acquired a number of companies outside the banking field, including stakes in Cathy Pacific Airways, the *South China Morning Post* newspaper and shipping firms. Recently HSBC realized its mistake and sold off most of these investments.

One category of investments that HSBC did keep, however, was its seven insurance companies that operate in 27 countries. They represent, only eight percent of the bank's profits. We would strongly suggest that HSBC divest these companies and invest the proceeds in additional banking operations.

Only time will tell, but we are even more critical of another banking/insurance conglomerate, Citibank Group. Formed by the merger of Citicorp and Travelers, the Group intends to mine the synergies between insurance and banking. Fool's gold is what they will mine, in our opinion.

Too bad. What HSBC has accomplished in the business arena, Citibank was attempting to accomplish in consumer banking. (In the long run, Citibank will pay a high price for its lack of focus.)

HSBC is by far the leading global business bank. This is a powerful position, especially since business is rapidly going global. It is not going to be easy for HSBC's competitors to catch up. It takes a while to build the facilities, the organization and the culture to do business on the worldwide scale of HSBC.

There is one major flaw in HSBC's strategy. It's the name itself. Unlike other "initial" companies, HSBC doesn't stand for anything. GE stands for General Electric and most customers know that. IBM stands for International Business Machines. But what does HSBC stand for? Originally HSBC stood for "Hongkong & Shanghai Banking Company." HSBC is a global bank and needs a global name.

Sooner or later it will have one. Our guess is that 90 percent or more of the company's 135,000 employees know that HSBC is a bad name and will pressure management to make a change before competition has a chance to catch up. If HSBC was a consumer product, the brand would be in deep trouble. But as a business bank, the HSBC brand is so far ahead that it will be decades before serious global competition arises. HSBC has time to correct its name problem.

in Hong Kong, but it will be controlled by investors in Bombay and they will surely take a lion's share of its profits.

It is 1864 and by the time the steamer completes its run to Hong Kong in late July, Sutherland decides that if there is going to be a local bank, it should be owned and controlled by hometown interests. In fact, he is going to beat Bank of China to the punch and spearhead the venture himself.

Thirty-year-old Sutherland is no financier. He is the Hong Kong superintendent for P&O, a shipping line. His qualifications to launch a bank, according to Frank H.H. King's authoritative studies into HSBC's history, seem to be based on the fact that he had recently read a 20-year-old magazine article on the principles of Scottish banking.

Improbable as this sounds, Sutherland disembarks at Hong Kong, and less than a week later releases a prospectus for a new bank, the Hongkong and Shanghai Banking Company, Ltd. (HongkongBank). The prospectus lists the leading merchants, the *taipans* of Hong Kong, as members of the provisional committee. But Sutherland appears to have played a little fast and loose with their names; at least one did not agree to participate, but is nonetheless named.

In any case, HongkongBank is roundly supported, particularly in light of the plans for Bank of China. Between August 1864 and March 1865, the provisional committee, comprised of 14 businessmen of various nationalities, meets 23 times. They authorize the release of 20,000 HK$250 shares in the bank, with a limit on ownership of 500 shares. Half of the share price is to be paid on issue, so the bank will initially be capitalized to the tune of HK$2.5 million.

In September, the first employee is hired, accountant John Grigor, and soon after, Victor Kresser is appointed as the manager of operations in Hong Kong. In October, 1 Queen's Road in Victoria is rented as the bank's first home. In November, experienced banker David McLean is hired to man a Shanghai office. In the same month, the shares are offered; the issue is quickly oversubscribed.

What about Bank of China? In late October 1864, its representative, Neale Porter, arrives in Hong Kong to sell shares and appoint directors. He can't get a nibble. Porter is enterprising and he soon suggests HongkongBank merge with Bank of China. He is rejected. He tries to promote a merger again in early 1865 and is again refused. Bank of China never obtains a charter and in October 1866, it disappears for good.

Survival of the newest

HongkongBank officially opens for business on March 3, 1965. In April, McLean opens the Shanghai branch. In July, a London agency is established. During this period, a full-fledged financial crisis has developed. Several of the bank's directors' businesses are bankrupted and by the end of 1866, fully half the banks in Hong Kong at the start of the downturn are no longer in operation. HongkongBank, on the other hand, weathers the storm with little problem – it is simply not fully invested yet.

The bank quickly expands using a network of agents, mainly merchants already established in certain regions. By the beginning of 1866, the bank has 17 agents spread throughout the Far East and further locations such as Paris, San Francisco, and Valparaiso, Chile. Within the next few years, most are replaced with formal bank branches. Also in 1866, HongkongBank extends its first loan to the Hong Kong government. The loan is for HK$100,000 at eight percent annual interest for six months. The bank's first loans to Chinese governments are extended in 1867 and 1868. By decade's end, the bank has assets of HK$38 million and HK$367,000 in net earnings.

In the early 1870s, several less-than-stellar loans catch up with HongkongBank. The worst of them, made by Victor Kresser, are in the sugar industry. By 1873, the bank is in so deep, it is forced to become involved with the operations of the companies or lose its capital. At the same time, currency and trading losses in London hit the bank. By 1874, reserves have dropped precipitously from HK$1 million to HK$100,000, and shareholder dividends are omitted.

The only saving grace is a loan to China, the so-called Foochow Loan. The Foochow Loan is underwritten with bonds, which generate HK$125,000 to the bank on issuance. That amount effectively doubles the bank's profits for the first half of 1875 and leads to its recovery. It also leads to a management shake-up and a period of reorganization. After one false start, the shake-up in management brings Thomas Jackson to the helm of the bank. A career banker, Jackson is first hired by HongkongBank in 1866. In 1876, he is manager of the Shanghai branch when he gets the nod as chief manager.

"Lucky" Jackson and Asian expansion

Jackson serves three terms as chief manager. Each time, just after he "retires," the bank's fortunes fade and he is called back to revive them. His timing leads to the nickname "Lucky" Jackson.

The defining trend of his quarter-century of leadership is a long-term 61 percent fall in the value of silver. Jackson deals with the 25-year slide in silver by operating on a double standard. In Hong Kong, the bank's reserves are kept in silver; in England, they are in gold. This strategy allows the bank to minimize exchange losses. Other Eastern banks are not so lucky and as they fall, HongkongBank solicits the business of their former customers. The result is an extended period of growth that more than doubles the bank's branches and agencies between 1876 and 1902.

During Jackson's tenure, HongkongBank creates an international branch network with strong coverage in China and Asia. By 1900, it has offices in northern China, Thailand, the Philippines, Singapore, Burma, Ceylon, Malaysia, and Vietnam. Further abroad, it is the first foreign bank to open offices in Hamburg and Lyons, and the second to open a branch in New York.

In 1882, the bank's performance allows it to raise another HK$2.5 million in capital via a share offering. The successful placement makes it one of the largest banks in the world. In 1890, it raises another HK$2.5 million bringing the total capitalization to HK$10 million.

Jackson retires in 1902. He leaves HongkongBank as the unchallenged leader in the East. For the six-month period ending June 1902, the bank records HK$271 million in assets and net earnings of HK$2.1 million.

HongkongBank extends its influence in the years before World War I. Its leading position in the East makes it China's choice to represent Great Britain in the China Consortium, a multinational group of banks that pools resources to finance infrastructure development in that country. The bank also leads finance efforts in Japan, Thailand, and the Philippines.

The war brings a period of internal, as well as external, conflict. The staff are multinational and now must deal with the fact that many of their home countries are enemies. German directors on the board are forced to resign and ultimately, German employees are expelled from China.

The bank itself, headquartered far from the major warfare, weathers the conflict with little hardship. And the price of silver soars in that period. In 1919, assets hit HK$432 million and net earnings reach HK$7.4 million.

Asia in conflict

In the first years following the war, HongkongBank anticipates a return to normalcy. The firm expands its existing operations in China, the Philippines, and Thailand. It even establishes a branch in Russia, a short-lived venture that folds with the Russian Revolution.

The China Consortium is revived, without Germany, and the bank resumes its lead role. The country, plagued with political factions and minor conflict, reunites in 1928 under the Nationalist forces. The bank thrives and, in 1930, it rises over HK$1 billion in assets for the first time. Net earnings reach HK$20 million. And then comes the prolonged slide into World War II.

In the early 1930s, Japan grows increasingly militaristic and China is its main target. The worldwide depression impacts the bank's performance, which remains flat to down throughout the decade. Silver, which recovered during World War I and peaked in 1920, resumes its long slide.

Management, now led by Vandeleur Grayburn, cuts internal costs. In the face of silver's fall, Grayburn also slowly moves the bank's reserves into gold. HongkongBank, doing business throughout Asia, tries to accommodate the increasing combativeness of Japan. As the situation worsens, Grayburn begins preparing for war. He arranges a succession plan; Arthur Morse in London will lead the bank if Hong Kong is cut off. Grayburn also secures the bank's reserves, moving them to England.

In 1941, the chief manager's worries are realized as Japan launches a series of largely unopposed attacks throughout the Pacific. On Christmas Day 1941, Hong Kong surrenders. The Japanese take control of the bank. Morse becomes acting chief manager and operations continue in London, but with Europe and Asia at war, its operations are restricted mainly to the US and India. The bank essentially remains suspended in time through the war.

It is the bank's employees that suffer the real hardship. Over half the eastern staff are imprisoned by the Japanese. Some are executed; others die from lack of care in captivity. Vandeleur Grayburn perishes in 1943 in a POW camp.

With the war's end in 1945, the company reopens its branches and resumes business. In 1946, headquarters is moved back to Hong Kong. In the first full year after the war, assets jump to HK$2 billion and net earnings of HK$9.6 million are recorded.

The peace is short lived. In 1947, Mao's Communists and Chiang Kai-shek's Nationalists wage a civil war for control of China. By 1949, the Communists are victorious. By the mid-1950s, except for a branch in Shanghai, HongkongBank is pushed off Mainland China. With Chinese operations severely restricted and Hong Kong increasingly vulnerable to the whims of the Communist regime, management soon realizes that the bank needs to expand its geographic base.

Beyond Asia

Starting in the second half of the 1950s, the bank's strategy turns toward acquisition and geographic expansion. The bank creates its first subsidiary in 1955, in the US, with the formation of HongkongBank of California (HBC). In 1959, the bank purchases The Mercantile Bank, with operations in India, and in 1960, British Bank of the Middle East (BritishBank) which operates in the nations of the Persian Gulf. The acquisitions grow HongkongBank's assets by almost 70 percent and turn it into a *de facto* holding company, although it takes some time to reorganize effectively.

Hong Kong remains the major source of the company's profit and it does not neglect its home base. In 1960, it expands into mortgage and small business finance with another subsidiary, Wayfoong Finance. And, in 1965, after local competitor Hang Seng Bank suffers a run, HongkongBank buys a 61.5 percent interest to help stabilize the economy. It is a fine investment in what will eventually become Hong Kong's second largest bank.

The expansion efforts lose focus in the 1970s. The bank purchases investment banking and insurance firms. And then, as assets continue an unbroken advance, it takes stakes in Cathy Pacific Airways, the

South China Morning Post newspaper, and shipping companies. In an unusual turn of events, the increased diversification is successful because of the rapidly expanding local economy. By 1979, the bank holds assets of over HK$125 billion and group profits exceed HK$1 billion for the first time.

In the 1980s, the future of Hong Kong becomes a critical issue for the bank. The uncertainty spurs geographic expansion. Expansion gets a second push in 1985, when the world learns that the bank's hometown will be returned to China in 1997.

The bank first tackles North America, selling off its California subsidiary for a stake in New York's Marine Midland Bank in 1980. In 1983, it buys 51 percent of US-based treasury securities dealer Carroll McEntee & McGinley, and in 1987, builds its stake in Marine Midland Bank to full ownership.

Operations in Canada are established in 1981 with the founding of Hongkong Bank of Canada. Most of the assets of the Bank of British Columbia are added in 1986 and Lloyds Bank Canada is acquired in 1990.

Building a British stronghold

The UK's 1985 agreement to leave Hong Kong when its lease with China expires in 1997 fundamentally alters the bank's future. The bank begins building a new asset base in the UK. In the 1980s, it acquires London securities dealer James Capel & Co., merchant bank Anthony Gibbs, and takes a run at the Royal Bank Group of Scotland. In 1992, it leaps to the forefront of British banking with the acquisition of Midland Bank.

In 1993, Hong Kong's local bank leaves for London. A holding company, HSBC Holdings, is formed to administer the network of companies, and headquarters is established in London.

The late 1990s also bring a new focus to the company's wide-ranging operations. Investments unrelated to finance are sold, including Cathay Pacific Airways. HSBC reinvests the capital in building the reach of its banking. It expands in Malaysia, incorporating existing branches into Hongkong Bank Malaysia Berhad. HSBC also returns to

China as that country opens to foreign business. A Beijing branch is opened, as is a Hang Seng branch in Guangzhou.

In 1995, a joint venture in the US, Wells Fargo HSBC Trade Bank is formed. In the 1990s, South American operations become a focus. Banco HSBC Bamerindus is established in Brazil, the Roberts Group in Argentina is acquired and a 19.9 percent interest in Mexico's Grupo Financiero Serfin is purchased. In 1999, Midland Bank acquires a 70 percent share of Malta's Mid-Med Bank and opens talks with the Korean government to acquire a controlling stake in the Seoul Bank.

The Korean negotiations are unsuccessful. HSBC does buy Republic New York and Safra Republic Holdings, in a $9.5 billion deal.

In 2000, HSBC agrees to buy Credit Commercial de France, making it a leading player in that nation. It also makes announces two new forays onto the Internet: one with Chueng Kong Holdings and one with Merrill Lynch.

HSBC close-up

Money, and the profit to be earned by correctly managing its ebb and flow, is the business of UK-based HSBC Holdings. The banking giant's abilities in that regard are beginning to earn it accolades such as "world's strongest bank" from *The Banker* magazine and "best bank in Asia" from *Euromoney*. In 1998, *Forbes* rated HSBC second in its "Super 50" global companies.

Why all the attention? HSBC, at the ripe old age of 135 years, is the parent company of a worldwide network of financial institutions. Over its many decades it has grown from Hong Kong's hometown bank, where it was headquartered until 1993, to over 5000 offices in 80 countries and territories, located in the Asia-Pacific region, Europe, the Americas, the Middle East, and Africa. HSBC serves over 20 million personal banking customers worldwide.

Strongly anchored in commercial banking, HSBC's more than 135,000 employees provide a wide range of financial services. These include: personal, corporate, investment, and private banking; trade services; cash management; treasury and capital markets services; insurance; consumer and business finance; pension and investment fund management; trustee services; and securities and custody services.

HSBC is strongly positioned in Asia; it is arguably the most powerful banker in the region. Today, with most of those nations struggling through a recession, that's not much of a selling point. But, over the long-term, solid positions in China, Southeast Asia, and the rest of the Pacific Rim seem destined to prosper.

Asia's economic troubles have impacted HSBC's performance, but not as much as one might expect. Over the past several decades, the company has also built strongholds in the UK and the US, spreading its business risk via geographic diversity.

The company's geographic balance is a strategic goal. It purposely balances its earnings, deriving half from the mature markets of OECD (Organization for Economic Co-operation and Development) countries and half from the world's emerging markets. This global outlook is reflected in the company's continuing efforts to build a worldwide brand. All of the group's companies are in the process of adding "HSBC" to their names and all are adopting the hexagonal logo.

In 1999, HSBC's assets under management continued to grow, hitting US$569 billion. Operating profits also grew in 1999, to just over US$9.7 billion. Net profits settled at US$5.4 billion. HSBC delivered 17.5 percent growth for the year. The company targets 20 percent annual growth for shareholders and it usually hits its goal; US$100 invested in HSBC stock at the beginning of 1974 would have grown to over US$11,000 by the end of 1998.

The holding company accounts for its major operations by country. These are divided into three categories: large business nations, those with over 1 million customers; major business nations, those with over 200,000 customers; and a catch-all called international businesses, which includes smaller banks and other businesses distributed throughout the world.

Large business nations

HSBC controls four large nation-based groups. These operate in the UK, the Hong Kong SAR (Special Administrative Region) and Mainland China, Brazil and the US.

United Kingdom

The UK operations are anchored by HSBC Bank, formerly Midland Bank, one of the principal clearing banks. Headquartered in London, the bank serves a personal customer base of over 5.5 million and an additional 500,000 business customers. Midland maintains a network of 1700 branches in the UK and offices in 28 countries and territories, principally in continental Europe and Latin America.

A decade ago, HSBC established the UK's first stand-alone, 24-hour, person-to-person telephone banking service named First Direct. It is still adding over 100,000 new check accounts a year and at year-end 1999 boasted over one million customers. In 1998, First Direct rolled out a PC banking service, which was extended to all customers in 1999. HSBC is also extending its non-traditional banking outlets by opening more branches at Wm. Morrison Supermarkets plc.

The UK banking operations generated the largest share of HSBC's profits in 1999. Operating profit rose to US$2.7 billion and net profit to US$1.85 billion.

Hong Kong SAR and Mainland China

The Hongkong and Shanghai Bank (more commonly known as HongkongBank) is the founding member of the HSBC group and its anchor in the Asia-Pacific region. Headquartered in Hong Kong, it is the SAR's leading commercial bank. HongkongBank operates a network of 220 branches that serves 75 percent of the territory's adult population. Throughout Asia-Pacific, the bank and its subsidiaries maintain another 170 offices in 20 countries and territories. World-wide, the firm has over 3000 offices in 71 countries.

On Mainland China, the bank has eight branches, one sub-branch, and three representative offices. These include locations in Wuhan, Chongqing, Shenzhen, and Beijing.

HongkongBank is a central bank and, as such, issues currency, controls foreign exchange, and regulates Hong Kong's money supply. It offers commercial banking, asset management, investment banking, finance, securities trading, insurance, property development and management, and even ship brokering services.

HSBC's founding bank also owns a 62.1 percent equity interest in Hang Seng Bank, which in turn has 46 branches in the Hong Kong SAR, making it is the second largest local bank. Hang Seng Bank has additional branches in Singapore and China.

Hang Seng recently opened Hong Kong's first automated securities phone-trading service and first automated mobile phone messaging service for securities customers. HongkongBank and Hang Seng Bank offer interbank fund transfers on their automated teller machine (ATM) networks.

Formerly HSBC's largest source of profit, the economic turmoil in Asia has impacted performance in this business. Net profit was US$2.3 billion in 1999.

United States

"Superior customer service, every time" is the catchphrase for the new five-year strategic plan for HSBC Americas, Inc. The group is currently uniting under the HSBC name and building market share via acquisition. It is anchored in the US by HSBC Bank, USA (formerly Marine Midland Bank). HSBC Bank, USA is operating in New York State with 380 banking locations statewide. Headquartered in Buffalo, the bank serves over two million personal customers and 120,000 commercial customers.

HSBC Holdings owns a 20 percent stake in San Francisco-based Wells Fargo HSBC Trade Bank. The Trade Bank provides trade finance and international banking services in the western US through offices in five states and Wells Fargo's 32 regional commercial banking offices in ten more states.

The group recently acquired First Commercial Bank of Philadelphia, which serves that area's Asian communities, and Republic New York Corporation, which controls the Republic National Bank of New York and will add a million new customers to the group. The addition gives HSBC Americas the third largest branch network in New York. The Republic New York acquisition also includes Safra Republic Holdings, an international private banking business. Safra doubles HSBC's international private banking business.

In 1999, HSBC Americas' net profit was US$466 million.

Brazil

Banco HSBC Bamerindus was established in Brazil in 1997. Headquartered in Curitiba, it operates a network of 1900 branches and sub-branches, the second largest banking network in Brazil.

HSBC Bamerindus has begun opening premier branches, a new level of service in Brazil. In 1998, it launched two new business units: Auto Finance and Real Estate. Auto Finance, which provides personal car loans, is operating in 15 cities. The Real Estate unit provides development loans and related services to corporate customers. HSBC Bamerindus also offers investment funds. It has US$3.8 billion under management and a customer base of 216,000 clients.

In its first full year, HSBC's Brazilian operations generated net profit of US$165 million, or four percent of HSBC's total. In 1999, Latin American operations contributed US$178 million in profit.

Major business nations
There are seven major business nations or regions in the HSBC universe. Five of these (Argentina, Canada, Malaysia, Saudi Arabia, and the Middle East) are served by dedicated anchor banks. The remaining two, India and Singapore, are served by group banks headquartered in other areas.

In Canada, Hongkong Bank of Canada is the largest foreign-owned bank and the seventh largest in the country. Headquartered in Vancouver, it has 140 branches across Canada and two in the western US. The bank recently acquired National Westminster Bank of Canada. It is also building its investment businesses with the recent acquisitions of Moss, Lawson Holdings Limited, a retail broker, and Gordon Capital Corporation, an institutional investment dealer. Group-owned HSBC InvestDirect Canada is the first Internet-based discount brokerage business in Canada.

In Argentina, Buenos Aires-based Banco Roberts was acquired in 1997. It is one of the nation's largest privately owned banks, with 60 branches throughout the country. HSBC is installing new systems and standards and is consolidating the bank's product and client base.

In Malaysia, HSBC Bank Malaysia Berhad is the largest foreign-owned bank and the fifth largest bank in the country. It has 36 branches. In the face of economic uncertainties, the bank is restricting credit and loans, and is concentrating instead on non-interest income and non-credit risk business.

In Saudi Arabia, HSBC owns a 40 percent stake in The Saudi British Bank, which has 75 branches and ladies' sections with an office in

London. It maintains an import and export finance business run under the name SABB Trade Services and is broadening its product lines to include accounts designed for women and students, and Islamic loans and trade funds. The bank also owns an ATM network of 124 machines.

Other nations in the Middle East are served by HSBC subsidiary BritishBank of the Middle East. BritishBank is the largest international bank in the Middle East, with 31 branches located in the United Arab Emirates, Oman, Bahrain, Qatar, Jordan, Lebanon and the Palestinian Autonomous Area, including an offshore banking unit in Bahrain. The bank also has branches in Mumbai and Trivandrum, India, and Baku, Azerbaijan, as well as private banking operations in London and Geneva.

BritishBank is in the process of building a network of service centers that will centralize processing and administrative functions in the region. New headquarters buildings are being constructed in Doha, Qatar, and Beirut, Lebanon.

India is served by 31 HSBC branches, primarily operated by BritishBank and HongkongBank. In personal banking, loan demand is strong and the nation is also home to HSBC's third-largest credit card center in Asia, after Hong Kong and Taiwan. The new Central Services Center has been constructed in Mumbai, which centralized back-office operation for credit cards and custodian services, training and technical services staff, and network services management teams.

Singapore, with 30 HSBC branches, is struggling through financial turmoil. HSBC tightened its control with a new management structure and revised work processes and is maintaining a holding pattern in preparation for an eventual upturn. Operations have shifted away from loans and credit into the Singapore bond and derivatives market.

International businesses

HSBC labels as international businesses smaller full service and specialty banks, many in emerging markets, and those corporate and institutional banking service firms which regularly operate worldwide.

Group banks maintain branches in France, Italy, Spain, Belgium, Ireland and the Netherlands. They also operate in the Channel Islands, Turkey, and Greece.

HongkongBank of Australia has 16 branches on that continent. Personal banking was launched in Korea with the opening of the first branch in Seoul and new branches recently opened in Bangladesh, Sri Lanka, and Taiwan. In 1998, 100 percent-owned subsidiary in Kazakhstan, HSBC Bank Kazakhstan, was established.

HSBC has varying stakes in diverse group of smaller banks. In Germany, the group owns a 73 percent stake in investment banking firm HSBC Trinkaus & Burkhardt KgaA; in Switzerland, a 95 percent stake in private banker HSBC Guyerzeller Bank AG. HSBC holds 40 percent in the Egyptian British Bank, a 46 percent stake in British Arab Commercial Bank Limited, and a 21 percent share of The Cyprus Popular Bank Limited.

HSBC also operates international businesses with dedicated functions. These include: HSBC Financial Institutions, currently focused on cross-border Euro services; HSBC Investment Banking and Markets; HSBC Loan Syndication; HSBC Asset Management; HSBC Equator Bank plc, a trade finance business; and HSBC Private Equity.

Finally, HSBC operates seven insurance companies, which include underwriting, brokering, and agency activities in the life and general insurance sectors. These products are cross-marketed through the group's banks. HSBC insurance firms are operating in 27 countries and territories, and serve over 1.5 million customers.

Income statement

Year	Revenue ($m)	Net income ($m)	Net profit margin	Employees
1998	483,128.0	4,318.0	0.9%	–
1997	471,156.2	5,519.5	1.2%	132,969
1996	405,451.8	5,334.0	1.3%	109,298
1995	351,465.8	3,815.0	1.1%	109,093
1994	315,325.3	3,212.4	1.0%	–
1993	304,438.9	2,668.4	0.9%	–

1998 year-end financials

Equity as % of assets	5.7%
Return on assets	0.9%
Return on equity	–
Long-term debt ($m)	19,953.0

Financial data provided by Hoover's Online (www.hoovers.com) and Media General Financial Services, Inc.

HSBC contacts

HSBC Holdings plc
10 Lower Thames St.
London EC3R 6AE, UK

Phone: +44–207–260–0500
Fax: +44–207–260–0501
URL: www.hsbc.com

CEO: Keith Whitson   CFO: Douglas Flint   HR: J.C.S. Rankin

Intel Corporation –
Santa Clara, California, USA

Executive snapshot

"The operative word is focus," says Intel chairman Andrew Grove. "You have to put all your effort behind the one thing you do better than the other people in the business, and then not hedge your bets."

This intensity of focus has resulted in a corporate steamroller that not only dominates the processor chip industry, but also drives growth in the entire PC industry.

Intel backdrop

There is a memorable scene in the 1967 film *The Graduate* where a young, alienated Dustin Hoffman is collared at his graduation party and is given a one-word summation of the future economy. "Plastics," he is told. The advice turns out to be incorrect. The word should have been "semiconductors."

Two unhappy employees

In 1967, while Hoffman chases Ali McGraw up and down the California coast, Robert Noyce and Gordon Moore are becoming more and more dissatisfied with their jobs at Fairchild Semiconductor. Found-

Future focus

Creating a monopoly

With all the talk of free enterprise, competition and survival of the fittest, the harsh reality is that nothing is more effective in the world of business today than creating a monopoly. Not a monopoly that will get your company broken up by the antitrust laws in some countries, but a *de facto* monopoly that allows you to control the market on a worldwide basis.

Intel is a good example. With 80 percent of the world's microprocessor market, Intel dominates the category. For all practical purposes, Intel has a microprocessor monopoly.

The rewards of a *de facto* monopoly position are considerable. Over the past decade, Intel has enjoyed a net profit margin of 23.1 percent. Compare that with Advanced Micro Devices (AMD), the world's second largest microprocessor producer. In the past 10 years, AMD has (enjoyed?) a net profit margin of 5.7 percent. It's not a fair fight. Intel has roughly ten times the volume and four times the profit margins of the No. 2 company.

Actually, Intel's hefty profit margins act as an umbrella for AMD, Cyrix and the other companies in the microprocessor field. Intel could crush its competitors by lowering the price boom, but wisely chooses not to. Putting competition out of business would surely provoke a government antitrust suit. Restraint is an admirable attribute for a monopolist.

How do you create a monopoly? You have to do a number of things exceptionally well.

First, and most important, you have to be first. Your company has to be perceived as the inventor of the category, the first brand on the market. In 1971, Intel introduced the world's first microprocessor, the 4004, a 4-bit chip. The following year the company introduced the 8008, an 8-bit chip.

Second, you have to have patience. It wasn't until 1974 that someone actually built a computer using an Intel chip. (The MITS Altair 8080.) In the meantime, Intel got antsy. In 1972, it diversified into digital watches with the purchase of Microna for 70,000 shares of stock (worth $1,645,000 at the previous year's offering price.)

What seems to make sense in 1972 makes no sense today. Back then watches were a multi-billion dollar market and semiconductors were a multi-million dollar market. Ergo, let's get into watches. (If you try to run a company by the numbers, you'll run the company into the ground.)

Luckily Intel's watch business went nowhere and the company shut it down five years later. What if the reverse were true? What if the digital watch business had taken off? Intel today might be a moderately successful, diversified manufacturer of consumer products and semiconductors. Not nearly as powerful as Intel actually is today. Failure is not necessarily bad for you, especially if it helps you focus.

Third, you have to be prepared to narrow your focus. It wasn't until 1985 that Intel finally dropped its memory chip business to focus on microprocessors. This was a key decision that would have a long-lasting effect on Intel's fortunes. Andrew Grove, Intel's CEO, said: "I'd rather have all my eggs in one basket and spend my time worrying about whether that's the right basket than try to put one egg in every basket."

Focus works in the long run, but not necessarily in the short run. In 1986, revenues fell and Intel recorded a loss of $173 million and laid off almost 30 percent of its workforce.

Fourth, build a brand. You cannot dominate a market with an ingredient product like a microprocessor without building a brand in the ultimate buyer's mind. In 1991, Intel launched its "Intel Inside" campaign with an advertising budget of $20 million. But the key to the success of the campaign was the $125 million it spent on co-op advertising. It was these "third party" endorsements that made Intel a household name.

When you have a strong brand, you can withstand a lot of negative publicity. In 1994, Intel generated a wave of negative publicity when a bug was discovered in its Pentium chip forcing the company to take a $475 million charge against earnings.

Customers forget. And the brand bounces back. Every major airline in the world (with the exception of Qantas and Southwest) has had a fatal accident, yet brands like American, United, British Airways, Lufthansa, Swissair remain strong brands.

Fifth, support a strong research and development effort. Combining a narrow focus with a massive R&D program makes a company almost invincible. Intel's annual R&D budget is greater than AMD's annual sales. The company spends more than 10 percent of its sales on research & development and employs nearly 20 percent of its workforce in this area.

What doesn't make sense is the constant search for new markets to conquer. Intel should have learned the digital watch lesson, but it didn't. Over the years it has gotten into computer hardware, videophones, videoconferencing products and networking products. Most of these ventures are likely to go nowhere. And even if they do, they could cause Intel to become unfocused.

Rather than look for ways to get into other businesses, Intel might be better off to look at technologies that could make the silicon chip obsolete. Optical computers, for example.

ing members of the integrated circuit manufacturing company and highly respected engineers, the pair are reduced to managing the company without any real say in its direction.

So, with $2.5 million in venture capital raised in a single afternoon and a page and a half business plan, Noyce and Moore leave Fairchild, and in July 1968 incorporate under the name Intel, a shortened version of Integrated Electronics. They open shop in a 17,000 square foot building formerly occupied by Union Carbide and hire their first two employees; one is the director of operations, Moore's former Fairchild assistant, Andrew Grove.

Intel's first new product challenge is to find a way to replace the then-current core magnetic memory technology with memory on integrated circuits, or chips. They settle on two possible approaches: silicon gate MOS, which had been discovered in the Fairchild labs, and Schottky bipolar. Intel puts two engineering teams to work on the problem; the first to succeed in creating a working manufacturing process will be the technology Intel uses. The company finishes its first year with revenues of $2672.

In the spring of 1969, the bipolar team wins the race, producing Intel's first commercial product, the 3101 chip. Honeywell buys it for their newest computer and Intel is on its way. The MOS team conquers its challenge soon after and Honeywell also contracts for the first MOS memory chip. That year, Intel revenues total $566,000, mostly from the sale of its 3101 chip.

By the end of 1970, annual revenues rise to $4.2 million. Intel's first commercial success comes in the form of the 1103, the first dynamic random access memory (DRAM). The 1103, introduced in 1970, undercuts the pricing of magnetic memory and largely replaces it.

More significantly for Intel's future prosperity, in 1970, the company also takes a job to create eight logic chips for use by a Japanese company developing the Busicom calculator. Unable to find the time needed to design eight new chips, Ted Hoff, the Intel engineer in charge of the project, reworks the chip array. Hoff reduces the Busicom to four chips: two memory chips, an I/O device, and a chip that acts like a simple computer – the first ever CPU.

The calculator company buys the redesign, but demands price reductions. Intel agrees, as long as it retains the ownership of the chips and the right to market them to other manufacturers. And so, in November 1971, Intel introduces the world's first microprocessor, the 4004.

The 4004 chip does not set the world afire. It is a 4-bit chip and is capable of running 60,000 operations per second, but it is slow compared to the state-of-the-art, mainframe computing of the time. Further, the machine that CPUs will eventually power, the PC, does not yet exist. Instead, the early CPU is used in traffic lights, cash registers, and gas pumps.

Luckily, Intel does not need to depend on the 4004 for growth. Its memory chips are selling well and the 1103 is in use at 14 of the 18 leading mainframe makers. The chip is the world's largest-selling semiconductor device by the end of 1971. Intel also creates the first erasable programmable read-only memory chip or EPROM. The memory chips help drive 1971 revenues to $9.43 million.

In October 1971, the company raises $6.8 million in its initial public offering. Company founders Noyce and Moore retain 37 percent of the stock, a stake worth $20 million in the three-year-old company.

In 1972, Intel uses part of its newly acquired wealth to expand outside the US. To hold costs down, it moves chip assembly operations to new plants in Malaysia and the Philippines. Taken with the newly invented digital watch, the company takes an early stab at diversifying and ponies up 70,000 shares of stock to purchase Cupertino,

CA start-up Microna. Digital watches, thinks senior management, are the wave of the future and will account for one-third of all watch sales in less than a decade.

Intel introduces its next-generation processor in 1972. The new 8008 is twice as powerful as the 4004. The company supports the new CPU with its first development system, the $5000 Intellec 4. The tool helps engineers at OEMs design uses for the chip and, happily for Intel, also helps lock them into using Intel products. The company records revenues of $23.4 million for the year.

In 1973, revenues almost triple to $66.17 million and Intel spends freely, also tripling R&D expenditures and plowing money into labs and production facilities, including a third fabrication plant in Livermore, CA.

Catching the PC wave

The PC era dawns in 1974 with arrival of the Altair, the same computer kit that launches Microsoft in the software business. The Altair is powered by Intel's new 8080 processor and sells faster than it can be packaged, creating back orders for the Intel chip.

The growing demand for processors and memory also attracts competition. Companies such as Motorola, AMD, and Zilog jump into the processor business. Intel speeds up its development process and counters with new iterations of its own, starting work on the 16-bit 8086 in May 1976.

In late 1977, Intel learns an early lesson in focus and decides to jettison Microna and its digital watch business. The chipmaker does not have the skills needed to run a consumer business and the digital watch market is rapidly disappearing. It is a relatively inexpensive lesson, costing Intel just over $1 million in a year when revenues total over $280 million and income is $32 million.

In 1978, a little over two years after starting work on the 8086, Intel begins manufacturing the new chip. At the same time, the company institutes Operation Crush, an intensive sales push designed to give the company and its new chip a dominant position in the processor market by December 1980.

By 1979, the company records $400 million in revenues and holds 40 percent of the processor market. It has also released the 8088 processor, a hybrid chip that combines 16-bit power with less expensive 8-bit connectors.

In 1980, Operation Crush hauls in a sale that will prove pivotal to Intel's future. IBM wants the 8088 for a secret project that turns out to be its first personal computer, a runaway success that takes Intel along for a joyride.

In 1981, Intel revenues hit $789 million. Demand from IBM and its competitors drive demand for Intel's processors well beyond the company's capacity. In 1982, the company releases the 80286 processor, which becomes the brain in IBM's new PC AT and the *de facto* standard for the PC industry.

"In 1983 and the early part of 1984 we had a heated-up market. Everything we made was in short supply," remembers Andy Grove in his book, *Only the Paranoid Survive*. "People were pleading with us for more parts and we were booking orders further and further out in time to guarantee a supply. We were scrambling to build more capacity, starting factory construction at different locations and hiring people to ramp up our production volumes." By year-end 1984, Intel's revenues are $1.6 billion.

Thanks for the memories

While Intel is growing its processor business in leaps and bounds, its memory chip business is disappearing almost as quickly. In the late 1970s and early 1980s, Japanese memory chip makers including Fujitsu, Hitachi, and NEC undercut US companies by raising the yields of their manufacturing processes to as high as 80 percent vs. 50 percent in the US. On top of the price advantage, in 1980, Hewlett-Packard releases a study that shows that in terms of quality even the worst Japanese firms were better than the best US firms.

As the new decade opens, the Japanese also grab the technological lead, bringing 64k memory to market two years before US firms. Then, within six months of Intel's 64k introduction, the Japanese releases 256k memory chips.

In 1984, a record year in Intel's history, an all-out price war begins. DRAM prices fall 70 percent by the end of 1985. Intel leaves the DRAM market, which had contributed $41 million to the company coffers at its peak in 1978, altogether and the company's financial performance hits a wall.

In 1985 and 1986, Intel's delayed reaction to the memory war hits home and the chipmaker's growth stops for the first time. Revenues drop to just under $1.3 billion in 1986 and the company records a loss of $173 million. Excess capacity forces the closure of plants in Puerto Rico and Barbados, and the company lays off almost 30 percent of its workforce.

In contrast, spending on R&D continues to grow throughout the period and in 1985, it releases the 386 microprocessor. The 386 is a 32-bit chip that for the first time allows users to run multiple programs simultaneously. There are 275,000 transistors in the chip, over a 100 times more than 1971's 4004.

IBM is slow to switch to the 386. It rightly worries that it will negatively impact their minicomputer business. But, in late 1986, a young computer company named Compaq starts a rush on the chip when it uses the 386 in its new top-of-the-line machine.

By the end of the first quarter of 1987, Intel is coming out of its slump and Andy Grove takes over the CEO spot from founder Gordon Moore. By year-end, driven by high-profit 386 sales, revenues hit $1.9 billion. By the end of 1988, revenues climb to $2.876 billion and income jumps up over $450 million.

Intel sheds more of it memory business in 1989, when it leaves the market for EPROM and contracts simply to buy the chips labeled with the Intel name from Samsung. Intel concentrates instead on higher-margin flash memory.

The company also launches its first ever consumer advertising, a $4 million campaign designed to promote its less expensive 386 SX processor as an economical way to move to 32-bit processors. At the high end, Intel ships the 486 processor, the first with a built-in math coprocessor. Revenues increase to $3.1 billion.

"Intel Inside"

Advertising the 386 SX proves so successful that, in 1991, Intel launches the now ubiquitous "Intel Inside" campaign to build its brand name among consumers. The company spends $20 million on its own advertising and budgets another $125 million for a co-op campaign for computer makers that is based on their purchases from Intel. The "Intel Inside" campaign helps drive 1991 revenues up to $4.7 billion. In 1992, revenues climb again to $5.8 billion and net income exceeds $1 billion for the first time.

In 1993, Intel raises the processor bar again with the introduction of the Pentium. One hundred shares of Intel stock, purchased for $2350 at its IPO, is now worth $438,500.

By 1994, over 1200 computer makers, virtually every significant company in the industry, are participating in the "Intel Inside" program. Intel is the largest computer chipmaker in the world, recording over $11 billion in sales.

The Pentium is selling well and rapidly moving into full-scale production when Intel discovers a bug in the chip that causes errors in complex mathematical calculations. Finding that the error will occur very rarely, only once in every nine billion divisions, Intel does not announce the flaw.

In the fall of 1994, the rest of the world discovers the Pentium bug on its own. After weeks of damaging negative publicity and the refusal of major computer makers such as IBM to sell the chip, the company belatedly decides to recall the Pentium. Andy Grove tells *Inc.* his delayed response is "my biggest mistake." Intel takes a $475 million charge against earnings, but quickly regains its reputation with consumers.

In 1995, Intel introduces 0.35 micron manufacturing technology, which enables high-volume production of its new Pentium Pro processor. The Pentium Pro contains 5.5 million transistors and is designed for high-end PC computing. Sales of Pentium chips surpass the 486 family that same year, providing a majority of Intel's revenues. The company employs over 41,000 people and revenues hit $16.2 billion, with net income of $3.5 billion.

In 1996, Intel begins to extend its brands aggressively. New Pentiums operating at 150, 166, and 200 MHz are introduced, while older 120- and 133-MHz versions are used in entry-level PCs. Similar line extensions are made in the Pentium lines for notebook computers and the OverDrive line of processor upgrades.

Intel also expands its ProShare videoconferencing products, first introduced for business customers. Now, the brand is extended to home PC users with the introduction of the Intel Video Phone that allows people to see and hear each other over home phone lines. By year-end, the chipmaker employs over 48,500 people and breaks the $20 billion revenue mark.

In January 1997, Intel introduces the Pentium MMX, a processor designed to run media-rich applications and the Internet more efficiently. Soon after, the company adds MMX technology to its high-end Pentium Pro line, renaming it the Pentium II processor. The Pentium II packages 7.5 million-transistors in a single chip. For portable computing, the company creates the Intel Mobile Module, which plugs into a notebook's motherboard and improves performance. Not yet content, the company also unveils plans for its next-generation processor featuring 64-bit architecture. Scheduled to ship in 1999, the chip is named Merced.

In February, Intel expands its network product lines by acquiring Denmark's Case Technology. Case is an innovator in fast ethernet networking technology.

Intel's 0.25 micron manufacturing process comes online in the summer of 1997. It produces circuits that are 400 times smaller than a human hair. Intel is the first high-volume manufacturer to use the 0.25-micron process and, at the same time, sets to work developing its next-generation 0.18-micron technology. By the end of 1997, the Pentium II represents about 25 percent of Intel's microprocessor production and the company records revenues over $25 billion.

Intel continues to consolidate its dominant position in the semiconductor industry in 1998. In January, it acquires former competitor Chips & Technologies, Inc. for $17.50 per share and later in the year, it buys Digital's semiconductor operations for $625 million.

The company also attracts the unwelcome attention of the Federal Trade Commission (FTC), which in June sues Intel for unfairly withholding technical information from companies with which it has disputes. Intel does not deny the facts of the case, but maintains that

it is fully within its rights to refuse to divulge its intellectual properties whenever it pleases.

During 1998, Intel again expands its networking business with a
$6 per share merger with Shiva Corp. It also purchases iCat, an e-
commerce software company based in Seattle. Intel signs agreements
with Kodak and Polaroid to promote digital photography, using the
chipmaker's technologies.

Product development remains fast paced. The 333 MHz Pentium
II processor is introduced in January, followed by two new brands, the
high-end Xeon, and low-end Celeron family. The company also breaks
ground on the first 300 mm wafer fab, a $1.5 billion facility in Oregon
that will use 12 inch wafers, and a $50 million research center in China.

In June, Andy Grove resigns the CEO slot, but retains his position
as chairman. Craig Barrett becomes Intel's first new leader in over a
decade. Company revenues, impacted by slowed growth, remain flat
for the year.

In 1999, Intel settles its FTC case and eases some of its competitive tactics. But the FTC continues its inquiry.

Intel returns to its roots when it invests $100 million in memory
chip maker Samsung. But, under the direction of its new CEO, the
company also begins to diversify. It takes a growing position in networking products with the acquisition of Level One, Dialogic, IPivot,
and DSP Communications. Intel also buys a stake in World Online
International, a European Internet provider.

In the core chip business, 1999 brings the introduction of the
Camino chipset, supporting the use of RDRAM memory architecture.
The company also ships prototypes of its first 64-bit processor, Itanium,
formerly named Mercer.

The new century sees the release of Intel's first 1-gigahertz
Pentium. The company buys Denmark-based chipmaker GIGA and
continues its diversification with a new line of low-cost consumer PCs
designed for Internet use.

Intel close-up

"Faster, smaller, and less-expensive" is the battle cry at Intel Corporation, the world's leading producer of the silicon chips that provide

the command centers of computers and an increasingly vast array of other smart products. The Silicon Valley chipmaker is known worldwide for its willingness to cannibalize its own products by continually raising the performance levels in a market that it already dominates. In fiscal 1999, Intel held better than 86 percent of the microprocessor market.

Intel's founding vision was to design and manufacture silicon chips and it has not strayed far from that vision in the 30 years since its founding in 1968. The company's first products were memory chips and, in 1971, it made the world's first microprocessor, a creation that led directly to the desktop computer. Today, Intel supplies the computer industry with the chips, boards, systems and software that are the major components in PCs.

In fiscal 1999, Intel generated revenues of $29.3 billion and net income of $7.3 billion. Its sales are global: 43 percent of revenues come from the Americas, 27 percent from Europe, 23 percent from the Asia-Pacific region, and 7 percent from Japan.

Intel's major customers are original equipment manufacturers of computer systems and peripheral equipment. Intel also sells to PC end users, who buy chip upgrades and business communications and networking products through retail channels. Other customers include the makers of industrial, consumer, and telecommunications products.

The company employs almost 70,200 people in plants and sales offices worldwide. Intel's manufacturing plants total over 25 million square feet.

Wafer production, which includes microprocessor fabrication, assembly, and testing, is conducted inside the US at facilities in Arizona, Oregon, California, Massachusetts and New Mexico. Fabrication plants, or fabs, in Israel and Ireland supply additional microprocessor production.

Intel's component assembly and testing is performed at facilities in Malaysia, the Philippines, China, and Costa Rica. Microprocessor board-level products and systems are made in the US in Oregon, Washington and Puerto Rico, as well as in Ireland.

Intel's Architecture Research labs are located in Oregon. These labs employ about 450 scientists charged with creating new products and markets for the company. Major projects include economical video conferencing and Intel's "Anywhere in the Home" initiative, which is trying to create computerized homes.

Intel's products are licensed and sold through sales offices located near major concentrations of its customers. Sales and marketing offices are located in the US and over 30 other countries. In addition, there are operating subsidiaries in the UK, Hong Kong, Japan, and Brazil.

Intel is organized around product groups. The company's major products are microprocessors, chipsets, embedded processors and microcontrollers, flash memory, network and communications products, and video conferencing and digital imaging products.

Microprocessors

Microprocessor chips, also known as central processing units or CPUs, are the brains of a computer. They process data and control the devices inside and attached to PCs and other computers. They are also Intel's bread and butter, providing a lion's share of the company's revenues and gross margin.

Intel's CPUs are always getting smaller, faster and, in terms of their computing power per dollar, less expensive. By continually decreasing the size of the circuits etched into its silicon chips, the company crams an ever-greater number of transistors into each microprocessor, making them more powerful. It also places ever-greater numbers of microprocessors on each silicon wafer, raising yields and lowering prices. In 1999, Intel began using 0.18-micron process manufacturing technology, which enabled it to introduce even more powerful processors.

In an ongoing effort to maintain its dominant position, Intel has also rapidly expanded its 32-bit CPU product lines and is now developing the 64-bit Itanium family of processors. It offers a range of microprocessors designed specifically for different levels of computers. CPUs are available for separate market segments ranging from the under-$1000 PC to high-performance workstations and servers.

At the top of the line is the company's Pentium III Xeon microprocessor, which operates at 800 MHz. Xeon is made for demanding applications, such as dual processor workstations and network servers.

The company's Pentium III processor is next. Today, it is available at speeds up to 1 GHz. It is the workhorse found in many full-featured desktop computers. The Mobile Pentium III is essentially the same chip designed for notebook computers. It runs at 600 and 650 MHz.

For lower-priced and lower-powered PCs, Intel established a new brand, Celeron, in March 1998. The Celeron is based on the same architecture as the Pentium II processor and offers a cost-effective alternative for basic PC systems. The first Celeron ran at 333 MHz. In January 1999, Intel cut its prices on the line by about 25 percent in a bid to grab increased market share at the low end of the PC market. In January 2000, it added a 533 MHz Celeron and a mobile Celeron running up to 500 MHz.

Chipsets

Aimed at the OEM market, Intel's chipsets are special-purpose chips that work in tandem with a CPU to manage selected PC functions. They usually support and extend the logic functions, graphic, video and other capabilities of CPUs.

Intel's latest family of chipsets is the 440 and 450 AGP series, first introduced in 1997. These chips enhance visual computing, delivering improved 3-D imaging performance. They are designed to work with the company's major CPU families.

In January 1998, the company added depth to its chipset products with the acquisition of Chips and Technologies, Inc., a leading supplier of notebook graphics-accelerator chips. Soon after, Intel announced its 740 graphics accelerator. Today, the company is developing its 800 series.

Intel sells its chipsets individually or already assembled with CPUs on ready-to-run motherboards that OEM customers use as the main components for their PCs. Intel motherboards allow OEMs to speed time-to-market and focus on other areas of their product lines.

Embedded processors and microcontrollers

Embedded chips can be programmed to control specific functions in a wide variety of products. These are sold directly to the makers of products including point-of-sale terminals, telecommunications equipment, automobile engine and braking systems, hard disk drives, laser printers, input/output control modules, home appliances, factory automation control products and medical instrumentation.

Intel's embedded product lines include controller chips in MCS 296 and MCS 51 families. The company also manufactures a large number of embedded processors under the Strongarm brand name.

Flash memory products

Intel began producing innovative flash memory products with double the capacity of other chips on the market in late 1997. Flash memory chips are used to store user data and computer program code. They provide easily reprogrammable memory for computers, mobile phones and many other products and retain information when the power is turned off. The market for the chips is expected to double from $3 billion to $6 billion between 1998 and 2001.

In September 1997, the company introduced its first double-density flash memory products under the StrataFlash and Boot Block brands. The low-cost technology quickly expanded the market for the chips. Intel is also a key player in creating flash memory cards that can be used in notebook computers and as the "film" in digital cameras. The cards can be used repeatedly without loss of image and memory quality. Intel sells the cards under the FlashFile brand.

Networking and communications products

Intel's networking and communications products give it a growing stronghold in the huge equipment market for PCs connected in local area networks or LANs. These hardware and software products are sold to corporate network administrators, small businesses and individuals, through reseller, retail, and original equipment manufacturer channels.

These products include adapters for desktop, notebook, and server computers, switching and stackable hubs, print servers, routers, and switches. The company also sells the LANDesk software family that enables network managers to control and manage client PCs, provide centrally managed virus protection, and monitor and diagnose network equipment health.

In 1998, Intel further extended its product lines with the InBusiness family of networking products designed for small businesses. InBusiness offers a combination of hubs, switches, and Internet software products designed for small business customers.

Conferencing products

In seeking new markets and applications that require more powerful (and expensive) semiconductors, Intel has taken an active interest in the development of PC-based video conferencing and digital photography. The company's conferencing products, marketed under the ProShare and TeamStation brands, allow PC users to share documents and meet over ISDN or corporate LAN networks.

Developed in tandem with the video conferencing push is the Intel Create & Share camera pack. Aimed at the consumer market, the camera pack includes an Intel PC camera, hardware, and an integrated suite of communications and image-editing software.

In an ongoing effort to create continued demand, Intel also created a PC Camera Kit for manufacturers. The kit helps OEMs build their own PC cameras using Intel's products and includes Intel PC camera silicon, software, schematics, design documentation, and suggested manufacturing procedures.

Income statement

Year	Revenue ($m)	Net income ($m)	Net profit margin	Employees
1999	29,389.0	7,314.0	24.9%	70,200
1998	26,273.0	6,068.0	23.1%	64,500
1997	25,070.0	6,945.0	27.7%	63,700
1996	20,847.0	5,157.0	24.7%	48,500
1995	16,202.0	3,566.0	22.0%	41,600
1994	11,521.0	2,288.0	19.9%	32,600
1993	8,782.0	2,295.0	26.1%	29,500
1992	5,844.0	1,066.5	18.2%	25,800
1991	4,778.6	818.6	17.1%	24,600
1990	3,921.3	650.3	16.6%	23,900

Stock history

| | Stock price ($) | | | P/E | | Per share ($) | | |
Year	FY High	FY Low	FY Close	High	Low	Earns	Div.	Book value
1999	89.50	50.13	82.31	42	24	2.11	0.11	9.76
1998	63.09	32.83	59.28	36	19	1.73	0.07	7.05
1997	51.00	31.44	35.13	26	16	1.94	0.06	5.93
1996	35.38	12.45	32.73	24	9	1.45	0.05	5.14
1995	19.59	7.88	14.19	19	8	1.01	0.04	3.70
1994	9.19	6.34	7.98	14	10	0.66	0.03	2.80
1993	9.28	5.34	7.75	14	8	0.65	0.03	2.24
1992	5.72	2.91	5.44	18	9	0.31	0.01	1.63
1991	3.70	2.36	3.06	15	9	0.25	0.00	1.35
1990	3.25	1.75	2.41	16	9	0.20	0.00	1.12

1999 year-end financials

Debt ratio	2.9%
Return on equity	26.2%
Cash ($m)	3,695.0
Current ratio	2.51
Long-term debt ($m)	955.0
Shares outstanding (millions)	3,334.0
Dividend yield	0.1%
Dividend payout	5.2%
Market value ($m)	274,421.5

Financial data provided by Hoover's Online (www.hoovers.com) and Media General Financial Services, Inc.

Intel contacts

Intel Corporation
2200 Mission College Blvd
Santa Clara, CA 95052, USA

Phone: (408) 765–8080
Fax: (408) 765–6284
URL: www.intel.com

CEO: Craig Barrett   CFO: Andy Bryant   HR: Patricia Murray

Interface, Inc. –

Atlanta, Georgia, USA

Executive snapshot

Big, visionary goals sometimes seem outside the realm of possibility – at least, until someone achieves them.

"At Interface, we seek to become the first sustainable corporation in the world, and following that, the first restorative company," unabashedly declares Interface CEO Ray Anderson.

Interface backdrop

Sustainability is a compelling vision, but it is not Interface's first vision. The company's founding vision is based on a product, the free-lay carpet tile, which company founder Ray Anderson finds in the late 1960s while he is development director for Deering Milliken's floor covering division.

Falling in love

" … I fell in love with a new idea, which I saw for the first time in June 1969 in Kidderminster, England – carpet tiles, a new concept for covering an office floor," writes Anderson in his 1998 book, *Mid-Course*

Future focus

Interface with the floor

Interface is not just a carpet company. It's a carpet company with a focus
– modular carpet tiles. It's also a company that illustrates the principle:
"If you don't go global, somebody else will and then they will come into
your country and take your business away from you."

Interface illustrates the principle that there is opportunity everywhere even in a mature business like floor coverings if you keep your eyes
open and are willing to narrow your focus. Modular carpet tiles are a
European invention, but Interface is an American company founded by
Ray Anderson.

Veni. Vidi. Vici. Anderson came to the UK while he was working for
Milliken, a leading US textile company, where he saw modular carpeting
for the first time. Eventually Anderson set up the company that con-
quered the carpet tile market. Today Interface has a dominant 40 percent worldwide market share.

With annual sales in excess of $1 billion, manufacturing facilities
in nine countries and customers in more than 100 countries, Interface
is a good example of the modern, global corporation with a focus. The
company, however, still needs to work on its operations outside of the
US. Too high a percentage of its sales (69 percent) are in North
America.

One good focus leads to another. Starting with modular carpeting as
a product focus naturally leads Interface to concentrate its marketing
efforts on the corporate customers who account for the majority of the
carpet tile business. This narrow customer focus, on the other hand, allows Interface to expand into related businesses like the installation of
its carpet products and the manufacture and sale of the fabrics used to
cover the cubicle walls in open-plan office furniture systems, which are
the major markets for modular carpeting.

A narrow product focus leads to a narrow customer focus that sometimes needs to be expanded in order to keep out the competition. Interface, for example, also manufactures some traditional broadloom
carpeting. Why? Maybe the company needs the full line in order to handle

all the carpeting needs of the large corporate customers that represent the bulk of its business. Companies like Hewlett-Packard, Compaq and Mobil. And as more and more companies go global, Interface is in the right position to go global with them. (The shoe store that sells socks isn't branching out into the clothing business. It still has a shoe focus, but also sells socks as a convenience for its shoe customers.)

On the other hand, Interface, like most companies, could not resist the temptation to try to broaden its product line. In 1987, for example, the company shortened its name from Interface Flooring Systems to Interface, Inc. Then it assigned the old name to its carpeting division and launched a program under the theme "Diversify and Integrate Worldwide."

One result of this effort was the Specialty Products Group. At Interface, this group manufactures and sells flooring-related products such as raised-access flooring systems, adhesives, anti-microbial additives and other chemical compounds used in flooring. The Specialty Products Group accounts for five percent of sales.

Every industrial company that we know of has a specialty products group that accounts for some five percent of sales. "This is our future," claims company management. But the truth is that the specialty products groups of the world seldom make any money, always claim much more than five percent of management's time and seldom lead to any significant product advances.

The company of the future will have a narrow focus with all of its efforts devoted to one product or one market. Then when conditions change, the entire company will need to change. This can generally only be brought about by top management that is totally focused on the mainstream product. It seldom arises out of a development in the specialty products group. A singular company with a singular product is the wave of the future. Then when the future changes, the company should face that change as a unified entity.

Interface, as a company, should keep its eyes open for the next development in floor covering systems. Then jump on that development and pioneer the idea on a global basis in much the same way that it did with modular carpet tiles.

Correction. He brings home the idea and leads the development effort to create the new product for Milliken. By 1972, the company is the leader in carpet tile sales in the emerging US market.

That same year, Anderson begins his own entrepreneurial odyssey when he opens negotiations with Carpets International (CI), the UK's largest carpet company, with its own patented carpet tile design. In early 1973, Anderson leaves Milliken after CI agrees to a fifty-fifty joint venture to found a new company that will manufacture and sell its carpet tiles in the US under his leadership.

With $450,000 from private investors and almost all of Anderson's life savings in the pot, a manufacturing company and a sales company are incorporated under the Carpets International-Georgia, Inc. (CIGI) moniker in April 1973. Anderson is the CEO of the newly formed company and at year-end, the company records sales of $4000.

Anderson, however, is not a fan of slow growth and he has his sights set on market leadership. "It was an in-your-face-time," he writes. "Compete, compete, compete! Beat Milliken, beat Milliken!"

Building the market leader

Starting with ten empty acres in LaGrange, Georgia, within five years Anderson drives CIGI to almost $20 million in sales and net income of $1.1 million, putting the company on a fast track in what is usually thought of as a mature industry. In 1980, sales jump 50 percent to $30 million, net profits rise to $1.9 million. In 1981, the CIGI companies merge into a single entity, Interface Flooring Systems. Sales grow over 30 percent to $41 million with net income of $3.8 million.

In 1982, Interface makes its first move toward international expansion, purchasing Compact Carpets, Ltd., a Canadian broadloom maker, and two carpet tile makers in Northern Ireland.

In a textbook example of child outstripping parent, Interface loans CI $3.7 million to weather a business downturn and in return, obtains the rights to purchase 50.1 percent of the UK company. Anderson also buys in 20 percent of CI's share in the company, raising the American-owned stake in Interface to 60 percent.

That same year, Interface introduces carpeting treated with a patented anti-microbial agent named InterSept. InterSept, developed in partnership with a company named Chemmar Associates, inhibits the growth and spread of germs in carpeting, creating a significant potential for market expansion into the healthcare sectors. Sales for the year grow at a good clip to $57 million; net income rises to $4.6 million.

In 1983, Anderson takes Interface public. Interface purchases Carintusa, Inc., the exclusive importer of CI's woven broadloom, and several other carpet plants from the floundering company. The company also acquires KCI, Inc., a maker of fusion-bonded broadlooms and carpet tiles. Sales growth continues to $80 million and net income grows to $6 million.

Interface buys Chemmar Associates, and with it all rights to InterSept, in January 1984. It also consolidates its hold on the carpet tile market by purchasing all of CI's carpet tile operations for $8 million.

The company breaks the $100 million mark in annual revenues. But it stumbles on net income, which drops 20 percent on the year to $4.9 million, as infrastructure costs mount for the information, CAD, and distribution systems needed to serve the fast-growing company. However, the pause is only momentary and sets the stage for an unbroken record of growth that will extend into 1990.

In 1985, supported by its newly improved infrastructure, sales jump again to $123 million and net income recovers, growing to $8 million with the help of its 1982 convertible loan to CI. Interface turns the $3.7 million loan into a controlling stake in CI. After selling off its broadloom and carpet yarns operations, CI becomes a holding company named Debron Investments, Ltd. Debron has assets, including 25 percent of Interface's stock, of $50 million and no debt.

Sixteen months after Interface gains control of Debron, it uses the holding company's war chest to expand further into commercial interiors. In December 1986, Debron buys Guilford, Inc., the leading US maker of fabrics for office furniture systems and interiors. Two months later, Interface makes a successful tender offer for Debron's remaining shares, taking full control of both companies in the final move in a strategic coup that would impress Sun Tzu himself.

Also in December, Interface acquires chemical companies Rockland and React-Rite for just under $4 million in cash and stock. The companies broaden its capabilities in chemistry and bolster its InterSept brand products.

In 1987, reflecting its broader product lines, Interface Flooring Systems is shortened to Interface, Inc. The old name is assigned to the carpeting division. Rallying under its new battle cry – "Diversify and Integrate Worldwide" – and with the help of its new acquisitions, the company's sales almost double to $267 million while net income grows to $13.7 million.

Acquisition is still the name of the game and, in September 1988, the company purchases Heuga Holdings, a Dutch carpet tile maker. The deal brings together the two largest carpet tile companies in the world, virtually doubling Interface's operations and making it the world-wide leader in its core market. Better yet, Heuga brings with it greatly expanded global markets. Interface now records sales in 90 countries and an estimated 45 percent market share.

In the same transaction, the company acquires Pandel, Inc., a US maker of carpet backing and matting, further integrating its manufacturing capabilities. Year-end sales are just short of $400 million and net income jumps almost 47 percent to $20 million. Interface joins the *Fortune 500*.

In the next year, Interface reaps the rewards of its ability to serve global customers wherever they operate. Companies, such as Hewlett-Packard, Compaq, and Mobil, purchase Interface's products for installations around the world and sales grow quickly to $581 million in 1989, but the company's largest challenge to date looms just ahead.

Hitting the wall at a half-billion dollars

In the early 1990s, corporate growth via cost-cutting becomes the *stratégie du jour*. Cheered on by profit-hungry shareholders, massive worldwide downsizing becomes the order of the day. Less employees translates directly to less office space and less office space hits Interface where it hurts.

In 1990, growth only slows. Sales hit another record at $623 million, but income drops slightly to $23 million. The company is hit much harder the next year, when sales drop back to 1989 levels and net income plunges to just under $9 million. Anderson calls it "the most difficult economic climate since 1974, our start-up year, during which our very survival was at stake."

The company tries to cope with the downturn by earning a larger market share. It makes several smaller acquisitions, building its fabrics business with the acquisition of Stevens Linen and entering the raised-access flooring market with a purchase from France's Servoplan S.A. It buys Bentley Mills, re-entering into the broadloom business it had sold off earlier.

None of these business-as-usual strategies are able to revitalize the company. Sales remain essentially flat in 1992 and 1993 at around the $600 million mark. Net income recovers only slightly, remaining in the $13 million range in both years.

In late 1993, Anderson takes aggressive action to break through the barriers to growth. Turnaround pro Charles Eitel is hired to lead the US carpet tile business and Brian DeMoura takes over the fabrics group. As 1994 dawns, the management team turns its attention inward. Eitel summarizes the effort in *Management Review* magazine:

"The operation had become too complex. Quality was off, morale was bad, and sales were lagging. Within a year, we simplified production, empowered people to make decisions and instituted a massive waste reduction program that was totally employee-driven."

A host of award-winning new products are added to the internal improvements and Interface pops through its revenue bottleneck. By year-end, revenues hit $725 million and net income starts to climb again, hitting $16.5 million. Anderson is exuberant. "What an amazing year!" starts his annual message to shareholders.

A spear through the heart

Although it isn't yet obvious, Interface gains much more than sales growth in 1994. Through a personal epiphany, Ray Anderson discovers a new vision of business that will eventually affect the entire company. Asked to deliver a speech to employees on the company's environmental vision, Anderson realizes that aside from a policy of full compliance to the law, he has no environmental vision. His search for something to say leads him to Paul Hawken's seminal book on sustainable commerce, *The Ecology of Commerce.*

Not halfway through the book, Anderson for the first time sees Interface's place on the planet. It is, he realizes, a business based on non-renewable energy and materials making products that, even when discarded, will last forever in landfills. "Hawken's message was a spear in my chest that is still there," says Interface's CEO.

Anderson's speech turns out to be a climactic event in Interface history. In short, he proposes a radical new vision for the company: "Interface, the first name in industrial ecology, worldwide, through substance, not words."

In late 1994, the company embraces Anderson's challenge. It institutes an industrial ecology initiative called EcoSense and an employee-driven waste reduction program called QUEST. By year-end 1995, QUEST targets $70 million in annual savings from its war on waste and captures almost $10 million of that total. Sales grow to $800 million as net income grows more slowly to just over $16.8 million.

The reduction of waste, however, is only one small part of Interface's new vision of sustainability. It also leads the company to question its entire business model and it begins to see its relationships with customers as life-long and cyclical, and not merely ending with the sale of the product.

In 1996, Interface acquires 15 commercial floor covering contractors in the US and creates Re:Source Americas. This division, which encompasses 79 owned and allied dealerships, is the service arm that will build expanded customer relationships and manage the company's products throughout their life cycles. It also purchases Renovisions, Inc., a nationwide installation services firm based in Georgia that has pioneered a new method of carpet replacement in existing spaces.

By year-end, Interface breaks the billion-dollar mark for the first time and net income hits a record $26.4 million. Helping the results is another $15 million in savings from the QUEST initiative. In 1997, Interface continues to grow Re:Source, which now has 93 owned or affiliated dealers in the US and is expanding into Australia via the acquisition of Carpet Solutions. QUEST savings hit $50 million.

In June, Interface builds its fabrics group with the acquisition of the UK's Camborne Holdings Ltd, Europe's largest supplier of seating fabrics. The company also introduces its Terratex line of panel fabrics, which are made from 100 percent recycled polyester.

In December, the floor covering business expands with the $50 million acquisition of the European carpet businesses of UK's Readicut International plc. Interface plans to sell off certain businesses and retain Firth Carpets Ltd, a manufacturer of high-quality woven and tufted carpet primarily for the contract markets, and a 40 percent interest in Vebe Floorcoverings BV, a manufacturer of needlepunch carpet. Annual revenues grow to $1.13 billion and net income increases to $37.5 million.

In 1998, Interface responds to a sluggish market with its first ever restructuring. The company quickly consolidates operations and reduces employee head count by 280 people worldwide at a cost of $25 million. The company expands its raised-access flooring business in July, when it acquires Atlantic Access Flooring, Inc. and its line of steel panel raised-access flooring systems. With the acquisition of Atlantic, Interface now owns the broadest line of raised-access flooring systems in the industry. At year-end, annual revenues hit $1.28 billion and net income impacted by the restructuring falls to $29.8 million.

In 1999, Interface opens a new factory in Shanghai, China and in keeping with its environmental goals, it converts its City of Industry, California-based carpet plant to solar energy.

Interface also introduces a new flooring product that is branded Solenium. Made from a new specialized fiber, it combines the life and durability of flooring products, such as hardwoods or linoleum, with styling and comfort of carpet. It requires one-third less energy and material to make and is 100% recyclable.

Interface close up

"Carpet by itself isn't worth much" seems an unusual statement to read in the annual report of a billion-dollar carpet company. But then, Interface, Inc. is not the usual carpet company. Interface is in the process of radically transforming itself and, if successful, perhaps its entire industry.

Just over a quarter-century old, Interface was built on modular carpet, which is produced in tiles and short rolls and is used in commercial and institutional settings. The company is the world's leading provider of these products, as well as the largest producer of contract commercial carpet.

Interface also makes traditional broadloom carpeting and is the leading US manufacturer of the fabrics used in modular office systems. Raised-access flooring systems, anti-microbial additives, and adhesives used in making and installing its carpet and fabrics products round out the company's product lines.

With annual revenues of $1.22 billion, just off the high water mark in its history, Interface is growing its global markets. The company already sells its products to customers located in more than 100 countries, with North American sales accounting for 69 percent of revenues, the UK and Europe for 26 percent, and Asia-Pacific for 5 percent. Interface is currently expanding its ventures in China and Southeast Asia, South America, and Central and Eastern Europe.

Interface employs about 7250 people worldwide. About 6150 of these jobs are manufacturing and administrative positions. The rest are in the company's 1100-member direct marketing and sales force, the largest in the commercial floor covering industry.

Interface manufactures its products in the US, Canada, the UK, Ireland, the Netherlands, Thailand, Canada, and Australia. It maintains marketing offices in 95 locations in 39 countries and distribution facilities in 40 locations in six countries.

Interface is organized into four units: three product-based business groups and a research and development organization. These are the Floorcoverings, Interior Fabrics, Specialty Products, and Interface Research Corporation. In 1997, the company formed a new venture, an experiential training business named "one world learning" that provides internal training and sells its services to other companies.

Floorcoverings Group

The Floorcoverings Group is the home of Interface's carpeting lines and a substantial percentage of its annual sales. The group includes modular and broadloom carpet manufacturing operations, and a fast-developing, fully owned dealer and service network for carpet installation and maintenance. In 1999, floor covering sales hit $974 million.

Interface was founded to sell modular carpet tiles, a product developed in the UK. Typically used in commercial and institutional settings, the company's modular carpet is sold under the Interface and Heuga brand names. With a 40 percent market share, Interface is the leading maker of modular carpet tiles and roll goods.

Modular carpet tiles, usually made in squares of 50 centimeters, are installed without adhesive or fasteners using the company's patented GLASBAC technology. Modular carpet is also available in two-meter rolls that are often combined with tiles to create special design effects. Interface's modular products are sold either in standard styles or custom-made to client specifications.

The installed cost of modular carpets is generally higher than broadloom carpet. But these products are easily removed and replaced, so office partitions and furniture systems can be rearranged without removing, replacing or repairing the entire floor. They also provide access to sub-floor wiring and utilities without major damage. And tiles can be rotated between high-traffic and low-traffic areas and only worn tiles need be replaced. Thus, cost over the life of the product can be substantially reduced.

Interface's leading share in modular carpets has not stopped it from building a position in the traditional broadloom carpet market. Broadloom products are usually tufted carpets made in 12-foot rolls. The company participates in the high end of that market, making broadlooms aimed at interior designers, architects, and other carpeting specifiers.

The company's broadloom makers include Prince Street, known for multi-dimensional textured carpets, and Bentley Mills, which is known for its use of color. These brands were rated number two and three, respectively, for carpet design in the US in a 1998 industry survey of interior designers. The company also owns Firth Carpets, the UK's leading commercial broadloom manufacturer, and a 40 percent interest in Holland's Vebe Floorcoverings, one of the largest needle-punch carpet producers in Europe.

In addition to its carpet businesses, the Floorcoverings Group includes a growing collection of carpet-related services designed to enable the company to offer a "total interior solutions" approach to serving its customers around the world. These include:

- Re:Source Americas, a network of 97 fully owned and affiliated commercial floor covering dealers located in the major metropolitan areas of the US. This network enables the company to offer its customers installation and servicing throughout the life of its products.
- Renovisions, a US installation services firm that utilizes patented lifting equipment and specialty tools to lift office equipment and modular workstations in place, permitting the economical replacement of existing carpet with little disruption to the customer's business.
- Facilities Resource Group, a Chicago, Illinois-based provider of furniture installation and related services that is being expanded throughout the US market.
- Image, a carpet maintenance system that uses the company's specialty cleaning chemical products.
- Pandel, Inc., a producer of vinyl carpet tile backing and specialty mat and foam products.

Interior Fabrics Group

Interface's Interior Fabrics Group is the home of its commercial fabrics businesses. Its major product is the fabrics that are used to cover cubicle walls in open-plan office furniture systems. The group also makes fabrics for commercial upholstery, cubicle curtains, wall coverings, ceiling fabrics, and window treatments. Fabric sales totaled $197.1 million in 1999, contributing 16 percent of the company's annual revenues.

About half of the company's fabric sales are made to OEMs in the office systems industry and the group's direct sales force maintains accounts with virtually all of the major office furniture manufacturers. Interface has a 57 percent share of the panel fabric market. Fabrics are also sold to the makers of wall coverings, vertical blinds, cubicle curtains, acoustical wallboards, ceiling tiles, residential furniture, and contract jobbers.

The company's fabrics are available both in standard colors and designs (that are also coordinated with its carpeting lines) and custom made. The fabrics are made from synthetic materials, wool blends, and starting in 1997, 100 percent recycled polyester sold under the company's Terratex label. They are sold under the Guilford of Maine, Stevens Linen, Toltec, Intek, and Camborne brand names.

The Fabrics Group maintains a design studio in Massachusetts and marketing and distribution facilities are located in Canada and Hong Kong. Along with sales offices in New Jersey, Michigan, and the UK, its products are brought to market by sales reps in Japan, Hong Kong, Singapore, Korea, and South Africa. Manufacturing facilities are located in Maine, Massachusetts, Michigan, North Carolina, and West Yorkshire in the UK.

Specialty Products Group

Interface's Specialty Products Group is the home of two companies that make flooring-related products, such as raised-access flooring systems, adhesives, anti-microbial additives, and other chemical compounds used in flooring. The group contributes $57.1 million to the company's annual revenues.

The Rockland React-Rite business unit manufactures and markets chemical products, including InterSept. InterSept is a proprietary anti-microbial applied to the company's carpet products to keep them germ-free, an important quality for customers in the healthcare sector. The chemical is also licensed for non-competitive use in products such as paint, vinyl wall coverings, ceiling tiles, and air filters.

Rockland React-Rite manufactures a line of adhesives for carpet installation, and carpet cleaning solutions and maintenance chemicals, which are marketed by the Floorcovering Group as the Image maintenance system. The company's other products include: Protekt, a soil and stain retardant treatment; waterproof sheathing for fiber optic cables; accelerators, used to speed rubber curing; and Fatigue Fighter, an impact-absorbing flooring material.

Interface Architectural Resources, Inc. produces and markets the raised-access flooring systems used in information and high-tech settings. Its products include: Intercell, a low-profile cable management flooring system used in renovations; and Interstitial Systems, a flooring that allows separate, pressurized and climate-controlled airflow for the electrical and telecommunications cables.

Interface Architectural Resources markets Tec-Cor and Tec-Crete, which combine the tensile strength of steel and the compressive strength of concrete to create a uniform and sound-absorbent panel. Both products were acquired in the 1997 purchase of C-Tec, Inc., then the second largest manufacturer of raised-access flooring systems in the US.

As the company's business groups illustrate, Interface's focus has expanded in recent years to include a greater share of the textiles used in the typical commercial interior. It is actively building its global market share and is growing its ability to mass customize its products. But the company's most compelling feature is its transformational vision of environmental sustainability.

Petroleum-based materials make up almost 90 percent of cost of the raw materials in Interface's products. As a major player in a petroleum-dependent industry, Interface recently launched a pioneering journey to reduce its need for petroleum to zero. Nil.

Along the way, the company plans to eliminate completely the waste and harmful emissions created through its operations. It is working toward closed-loop manufacturing processes that will create new carpet from the recycled remains of worn-out products and that will use only renewable energy to drive those processes. The company is even addressing the transport of its products to the marketplace. For example, it is cutting packaging weights and moving closer to customers in order to create the most resource-efficient transport available.

Interface's ultimate goal is more ambitious still. It plans eventually to move beyond sustainable commerce into restorative commerce. It wants to run a business that leaves the earth healthier and more resource-rich at the end of each day. And show other companies how to do the same.

Doing well by doing good, is how CEO Ray Anderson characterizes the effort and it appears to have galvanized the company he founded in 1973. Interface estimates it has saved over $124 million in costs since it began its drive in earnest in 1995. During that same period, sales nearly doubled.

Income statement

Year	Revenue ($m)	Net income ($m)	Net profit margin	Employees
1999	1,228.2	23.5	1.9%	7,250
1998	1,281.1	29.8	2.3%	7,500
1997	1,135.3	37.5	3.3%	7,300
1996	1,002.1	26.4	2.6%	6,000
1995	802.1	16.8	2.1%	4,850
1994	725.3	16.5	2.3%	4,660
1993	625.1	13.8	2.2%	4,425
1992	594.1	12.3	2.1%	3,735
1991	581.8	8.9	1.5%	3,888
1990	623.5	23.6	3.8%	4,350

Stock history

Year	Stock price ($) FY High	FY Low	FY Close	P/E High	Low	Per share ($) Earns	Div.	Book value
1999	11.75	4.00	5.75	26	9	0.45	0.18	7.52
1998	22.88	8.25	9.28	41	15	0.56	0.12	7.60
1997	15.81	9.25	14.50	21	12	0.77	0.14	6.55
1996	10.25	5.81	10.06	17	10	0.60	0.13	6.23
1995	9.00	5.81	8.50	18	12	0.41	0.12	6.95
1994	8.50	4.88	6.19	21	12	0.41	0.12	6.57
1993	7.75	4.88	7.63	20	13	0.38	0.12	5.96
1992	8.25	4.81	6.19	23	13	0.36	0.12	5.40
1991	7.13	3.94	5.94	27	15	0.26	0.12	5.77
1990	9.88	3.38	4.88	16	5	0.62	0.12	5.77

1999 year-end financials

Debt ratio	50.7%
Return on equity	6.0%
Cash ($m)	2.5
Current ratio	2.06
Long-term debt ($m)	400.1
Shares outstanding (millions)	51.7
Dividend yield	3.1%
Dividend payout	40.0%
Market value ($m)	297.4

Financial data provided by Hoover's Online (www.hoovers.com) and Media General Financial Services, Inc.

Interface contacts

Interface, Inc.   Phone: 770–437–6800
2859 Paces Ferry Road, Suite 2000 Fax: 770–437–6809
Atlanta, GA 30339, USA   URL: www.ifsia.com

CEO: Ray C. Anderson   CFO: Daniel T. Hendrix   HR: Rodney Fuller

Microsoft Corporation –

Redmond, Washington, USA

Executive snapshot

"When we get up in the morning, what we're thinking about is software that's reliable, software that has a natural interface, and all the feedback we're getting from customers about where they want our software to go," says Bill Gates, founder and chairman of Microsoft. "That is our total focus as a company."

Microsoft is no longer as focused as Gates suggests, but its abilities as a software producer and aggressive competitor are undisputed.

Microsoft backdrop

Without the benefit of 20/20 hindsight, the Altair 8080 on the cover of the January 1975 issue of *Popular Electronics* looks exactly like what it is, a box full of indicator lights and toggle switches that does not do much, except keep the home hobbyist soldering to his heart's content. Paul Allen and Bill Gates, however, see much more in the Altair, which is billed as "the world's first minicomputer kit" and features an Intel 8080 chip. To them, the era of the PC, with all its attendant rewards, has just been announced.

Future focus

Creating a monopoly, part 2

With more than 90 percent of the personal computer operating system business, Microsoft has a *de facto* monopoly. Microsoft is also a prime example of an important business concept: if you can do one thing right, you can do a hundred things wrong and still be an enormously successful company.

The one thing Microsoft did right is to be first. Microsoft created the operating system for the world's first personal computer, the MITS Altair 8080. It was this coup that gave the company the opportunity to provide the operating system software for the IBM PC, the first 16-bit personal computer. IBM provided legitimacy to the personal computer and companies rushed to install them. Microsoft rode the rapid growth of the PC to become "the most powerful company in the opening stages of the 21st century."

Size isn't synonymous with power. With annual revenues of $19.7 billion, Microsoft is number 84 on the *Fortune 500* list. In other words, there are 83 American companies larger than Microsoft, but none more powerful in the sense that they control their markets and their destinies. Nor are any more profitable. Its net profit margin of 31 percent makes Microsoft the most profitable large company in America and perhaps the world. (The median company on the Fortune 500 list has a net profit margin of just 4.4 percent.)

What has Microsoft done wrong? The company has made several dozen cable, telecom and Internet investments that have little to do with Microsoft's core business. They include a $5 billion investment in AT&T, $1 billion in Comcast, $600 million in Nextel, $400 million in Canada's Rogers Cable. And these are just the tip of the iceberg. Microsoft tentacles reach into cable set-top boxes with the $425 million purchase of WebTV and its joint cable venture with NBC (MSNBC.) The company also operates MSN, an Internet online service. Microsoft is prepared to invest an additional $1 billion to earn a leadership position in this business.

This host of extracurricular activities obviously unfocuses the company and provides a distraction to Microsoft management. It doesn't matter. If you do one thing right, you can do a hundred things wrong and still come out on top.

Microsoft's future rides on the success of Windows 2000, an all-in-one operating system that runs well on everything from a notebook computer to the equivalent of a mainframe. According to one Microsoft veteran, Windows 2000 is "central to everything we are doing."

Windows 2000 has often been described in semi-apocalyptic terms, the most complex engineering project in history. With more than 30 million lines of code, and developed with the full-time help of nearly 4000 programmers, Windows 2000 is not a project for the faint of heart.

Will Windows 2000 be successful? That's asking the wrong question. Of course, Windows 2000 will be successful. The customer has no other choice.

The right question to ask is whether or not Microsoft would have been better off in the long run to develop a multiple-product strategy. That is, to introduce a number of different operating systems designed for different applications. One for personal computers, one for workstations, etc.

Monopolists always make the same mistake. There's no incentive for a monopolist to develop multiple products because they face no competition. "One size fits all" is their general ego-driven approach. After all, they know what's best for the industry.

Henry Ford was the Bill Gates of the automobile industry. With the introduction of the Model T in 1908, Ford began his personal program to dominate the car business. By concentrating on one model and steadily reducing prices, Henry Ford developed a virtual monopoly. By 1920, 60 percent of all the vehicles on American roads were Fords.

It wasn't until 1927 that Ford discontinued the Model T. Meanwhile General Motors was building a multiple product/multiple brand strategy that swiftly overtook Ford to establish GM as the leading US automobile manufacturer for the next six decades.

Will a similar fate overtake Microsoft? No one can predict the future, but we think not. In Henry Ford's day, there were literally hundreds of car companies. Today there are just a handful of operating systems on the market. Macintosh, Unix and Linux being the most prominent.

Where the competition is weak, the monopolist reigns supreme.

Get the sale, make the product

Allen and Gates have fooled with computers since their student days at Seattle's Lakeside School. In January 1975, Gates is a student at Harvard and Allen works nearby at Honeywell. The pair decides to create the software that will put the Altair to work and, in what will become a familiar theme at Microsoft, they call the machine's owner, Ed Roberts, telling him that they already have the product ready for the machine. Roberts agrees to see their program and the fledgling entrepreneurs immediately start using BASIC code to create it.

In February 1975, Allen brings their version of BASIC to New Mexico and demonstrates it to Roberts. The two programmers sell their first license to MITS, Roberts' company. Allen joins the firm as director of software. In April, MITS announces the software and by July, the program is shipping. Late that year, the program is released on floppy disk. In the same period, the name Micro-Soft is coined to describe the Gates-Allen collaboration and a 60/40 split is established. Gates get the 60 percent share.

In 1976, the 20-year-old Gates starts the first campaign to protect his software against piracy with a broadside in *Computer Notes* and in his opening address at the First Annual World Altair Computer Convention. BASIC, mainly because of the dearth of competing products, is becoming the standard programming language for minicomputers. New customers, such as NCR and General Electric, are licensing the BASIC software.

By July, the company starts to come together. Gates and Allen have a small group of programmers refining and enhancing BASIC to sell to computer makers. In November, Paul Allen resigns from MITS to work full time in the enterprise and the trade name Microsoft is registered with the Office of the Secretary of the State of New Mexico.

In January 1977, Bill Gates drops out of Harvard and a new partnership agreement between Allen and Gates is officially executed. Now, Gates gets 64 percent of Microsoft's profits. In July, the new company ships Microsoft FORTRAN, its second language product.

Microsoft earns $180,000 on its license with MITS, the ceiling of its royalty agreement, and attempts to dissolve the contract legally. At the same time MITS is sold to Pertec, which attempts to enforce the license. In November 1977, Microsoft wins the dispute and regains the full rights to BASIC. Microsoft, which records just over $380,000 in sales for the year, is on its own.

In 1978, Microsoft has 13 employees and total sales exceed $1 million for the first time. It ships its third product Microsoft CO-BOL-80. The company also creates ASCII Microsoft with Kazuhiko Nishi, the publisher of a Japanese computer magazine. It is the company's first international sales venture.

In 1979, the company moves from New Mexico to Bellevue, Washington. Intel releases the 8086 generation of chips and Microsoft remakes BASIC for the 16-bit processor. The company forms Vector Microsoft in Belgium and starts selling in the European market. It also forms a consumer products division that is charged with jumping into the rapidly emerging applications industry. The year's sales total over $4 million, mostly from its licensing of BASIC.

PC brain control

Microsoft enters the market for operating systems for the first time in 1980. It licenses the right to use AT&T's UNIX operating system and releases it as XENIX, an operating system for PCs. That same year, the company's consumer products group creates its first hardware product, the Z-80 SoftCard. The plug-in allows Apple II owners to run programs designed for the 8080/Z-80 computers and it sells 25,000 units by year-end. In 1981, Microsoft incorporates and sells a five percent stake to Technology Venture Investments for $1 million. Annual revenues grow to $16 million.

That year, the company makes two deals that will prove to be among the best in its history. First, it contracts with IBM to provide the operating system for the computer maker's first PC, a late entry into the fast-growing market. The deal is by now standard: IBM can license the software, but Microsoft retains ownership.

The second deal is with Seattle Computer, a small motherboard manufacturer, which has developed an 8086 operating system called 86-QDOS (quick and dirty operating system). Without telling Seattle whom it is working for, Microsoft licenses QDOS and reworks it for the new IBM PC. Then, two weeks before IBM releases its computer, Microsoft buys QDOS outright, paying Seattle $50,000. It proves a bargain. IBM's machine with Microsoft DOS goes on to set the standard for PCs worldwide.

In 1982, Microsoft forms its international division. Over the next few years, wholly owned subsidiaries are established in Italy, Sweden, Australia, Canada, Japan, and Mexico.

The company releases its first productivity application, a spreadsheet called Multiplan. Throughout the year, work proceeds in secret on a new program called Interface Manager. It will eventually be renamed Windows. Revenues more than double to $34 million and over 200 people now work at the software company.

In 1983, Paul Allen resigns from the day-to-day operations at Microsoft after he is diagnosed with Hodgkin's Disease. (The treatments successfully drive the disease into remission.) The company introduces the Microsoft Mouse, a then-new product, as well as the first version of Microsoft Word.

It's a Windows world

In November, in response to competitors' advances, Microsoft rushes to unveil Windows. Gates announces that the software will be running on 80 percent of IBM-compatible computers by the end of 1984, but it will not even ship until November 1985. The employee headcount reaches 450.

In 1984, the company ships Microsoft BASIC and Microsoft Multiplan with the introduction of Apple Computer's Macintosh. IBM chooses Microsoft XENIX and MS-DOS for its new-generation PC, the 286 IBM PC AT. The Microsoft Press is launched with two titles, and the company's new spreadsheet software Microsoft Excel ships in November.

In 1985, Microsoft finally ships its first version of Windows. At ten years old, the company has sales of $140 million for the fiscal year and employs over 1000 people. The company opens its first manufacturing plant outside the US in Ireland. It is a duplication and distribution center that supplies the European market.

Microsoft moves to its current Redmond, Washington-based campus in 1986. By year-end, the staff has grown to almost 1500 employees.

The company goes public in March, raising $61 million on the IPO. Gates owns 45 percent of the stock, worth about $350 million.

In 1987, the company moves into high gear. It announces Microsoft Operating System/2 (OS/2), which has been jointly developed with IBM, and Windows 2.0. On the applications front, it acquires Forethought, Inc., a software company that owns PowerPoint, a leading presentation application, and is the exclusive distributor of FileMaker Plus, a top-selling database for Macintosh. Microsoft also ships its first CD-ROM application, Microsoft Bookshelf. Microsoft stock soars and within one year of the IPO, Bill Gates is a billionaire.

In 1988, Microsoft and Ashton-Tate jointly develop Microsoft SQL Server, a database server software product for local area networks (LANs). The company expands into a new 245,000 square foot manufacturing and distribution site in Canyon Park, outside Seattle.

In 1989, the company steps up its commitment to multimedia CD-ROM with the formation of the multimedia division. MS-DOS 4.01 becomes the first Microsoft product designed specifically for the Soviet market.

Microsoft ships Windows 3.0 in May 1990 and the company records sales of over $1 billion, the first PC software company to break that mark in a single year. By year-end, over $200 million worth of MS-DOS has been sold since its introduction. It runs on over 80 million PCs worldwide.

Microsoft Windows 3.1 ships in 1992. The new version finally realizes the full potential of the windows-interface and over one million advance orders are placed worldwide. The company's stock has risen 1200 percent since the IPO; $10,000 worth of stock at the opening is now worth $300,000. It is estimated that 2000 Microsoft employees have become stock-option millionaires. Bill Gates, Paul Allen and senior exec Steve Ballmer are all billionaires.

Microsoft continues to expand its Windows franchise. In 1992, Windows for Workgroups 3.1 ships along with a beta version of Windows NT. Microsoft Access Database for Windows ships in the Fall and in January 1993, Microsoft Word celebrates its tenth anniversary with ten million sold. Revenues hit $2.3 billion and employee headcount approaches 11,500.

Microsoft Encarta, the first multimedia encyclopedia, ships in 1993, along with five new multimedia titles including Microsoft Dinosaurs and the 1993 edition of Bookshelf. MS-DOS 6.0, the last major stand-alone revision of the operating system, also ships and, boosted by version 3.1, the number of licensed users of Windows reaches 25 million.

The Windows world gets bigger

In 1994, the company announces it is working on a major revision called Windows 95. It is a fully integrated 32-bit operating system replacing Windows 3.11, Windows for Workgroups 3.11, and MS-DOS. The now familiar "Where Do You Want To Go Today" is launched with a $100 million global advertising campaign to build Microsoft's brand name.

Microsoft Windows 95 launches worldwide in August 1995. More than one million copies of Microsoft Windows 95 are sold at retail stores during the first four days in North America. Seven million sell by year-end. The company announces Microsoft Bob for Windows, a suite of programs for home users that fails as spectacularly as Windows 95 succeeds. The company also ships Internet Explorer, a free browser that competes head-to-head with industry leader Netscape.

MSN, the company's online service, is launched and over 500,000 members subscribe in the first 3 months. The company attempts to acquire Intuit, Inc., a leader in finance software for individuals and small businesses, but the US Justice Department threatens to contest the deal on antitrust grounds and it is abandoned. Employee headcount reaches 17,800 and revenues approach $6 billion.

In 1996, the Interactive Media group is formed and Vermeer Technology is acquired. Vermeer's FrontPage, a tool for creating and managing Web pages and sites, becomes the cornerstone of a full range of tools for Internet publishing. Microsoft Excel is the leading spreadsheet, with more than 30 million users worldwide.

In the online world, Microsoft's magazine venture, *Slate*, debuts. As does MSNBC, the news, talk, and information network from NBC News and Microsoft. MSNBC starts with 14 hours of programming per day.

In 1997, Office 97, the latest version of the leading productivity suite, and Internet Explorer 4.0 ship. Microsoft acquires WebTV Networks for $425 million in stock and cash. WebTV owns a complete system that provides consumers access to the Internet via television. The company leverages the deal with a $1 billion investment in Comcast, the US's fourth largest cable television operator.

Microsoft also makes a $150 million investment in an old rival, Apple Computers. In return, Apple signs up for future versions of Microsoft Office, Internet Explorer, and other Microsoft tools for the Macintosh and the bundling of Internet Explorer with the Mac OS. Revenues continue to hit new records, totaling over $11 billion for the year.

Windows 98 launches with a notable lack of critical acclaim in 1998, but still quickly sells 10 million copies via licensing and retail outlets. The beta version of Office 2000 also ships. The company releases the Visual Studio 6.0 development system, a complete suite for building scalable enterprise solutions.

MSN gets a much-needed facelift and local MSN portals are announced for 24 additional countries and regions. The online network includes several leading services, including MSNBC news, MSN CarPoint, Hotmail and the MSN Gaming Zone. Search engines AltaVista, Lycos, Infoseek, and Snap pay Microsoft a total of $60 million to be listed on MSN for one year.

Internet Explorer 4.0 conquers the browser market, overtaking Netscape's Navigator for the first time. The company is not able to celebrate the event fully, because its aggressive push into the emerging Internet market causes the US Justice Department to bring the company to trial. Fiscal 1998 revenues hit $14.4 billion.

In 1999, Microsoft buys a minority stake in AT&T for $5 billion and acquires Visio, a drawing software maker, for $1.3 billion. It also takes Expedia public, selling off a portion of its ownership in the IPO.

Pressure continues to build as the Justice Department builds a strong case against the software giant. In January 2000, Gates names Steve Ballmer as the new CEO. Soon after, the company is judged guilty of violating anti-trust laws. The prosecution recommends the company be broken up and as this book goes to press, the ultimate resolution of the case remains under consideration.

The threat of legal sanctions spurs the company's diversification efforts. Among many actions are the formation of Avanade, a joint venture with Andersen Consulting to develop large-scale Windows e-commerce applications and the founding of a new company, HomeAdvisor, which will enter the online mortgage market.

Microsoft close-up

If there is one main theme that runs through the economic history of the last quarter of the 20th century, it is the emergence, rise, and domination of the personal computer. Dell became a *Future Focus* company by focusing on PCs themselves and Intel made the list by focusing on the PC's most critical component. Now, Microsoft Corporation earns its spot by focusing on the software that makes the machine work for its owners.

"The revolution is here and it is soft," proclaimed the cofounder of Microsoft William "Bill" Gates III 20 years ago, and he was right. Today, Gates' baby is the world's leading software company. At year-end 1999, the company earned $19.7 billion in annual revenues, had no significant debt, and maintained a huge cash position of $17.2 billion. It employed 31,396 people. Ranked number 84 on the *Fortune 500* list, Microsoft has made Gates, who owns about a 15 percent stake in the company, one of the world's richest human beings.

From its first home in an Albuquerque, New Mexico strip mall, Microsoft has expanded worldwide. Stretching from its expansive corporate headquarters in the US, Microsoft's tentacles reach out across the globe via more than 80 subsidiaries located in 59 countries. Roughly a third of the company's employees work outside the US and 52 percent of the company's 1999 revenues came from international sales.

The company sells over 300 products and technologies, including many of the leading products in the major software categories. Among its software lines are operating systems for PCs, server applications for networks, various desktop applications, interactive media programs, and Internet platform and development tools. Microsoft also operates online, provides media services, and sells books and peripheral equipment.

Microsoft's organizational structure has expanded along with its revenue growth. From the original two-man shop, it has evolved into an unusual mixture of product-based and function-based divisions. There are five main business groups.

The Platforms and Applications Group

The Platforms and Applications Group creates, builds, and maintains the product lines that most people associate with the Microsoft brand name. Home to roughly 12,000 employees, this group embodies the company's core competency, writing software programs.

Platforms and Applications is the main revenue generator for the company and is organized into three divisions: Personal and Business Systems, Applications and Internet Client, and Consumer Platforms.

The Personal and Business Systems Division

This is the home of Microsoft Windows, Windows NT, and the Microsoft BackOffice product families. Depending on one's opinion, and everyone has one about Microsoft, this is the source of the company's strength in – or stranglehold on – the software industry. Windows products dominate the PC world with a market share of over 90 percent. Over 40% of the company's annual revenues, $8.5 billion in fiscal 1999, stem from these operating platforms.

Window's operating system software, like MS-DOS before it, simply allows people to communicate with their computers. Operating systems perform a variety of tasks, such as managing memory use, scheduling applications, accessing files, and managing information and communication flow inside the computer.

Microsoft's main desktop platform products are Windows 95, Windows 98, Windows 2000 and Windows NT Workstation. Released in August 1995, Windows 95 combined MS-DOS and Windows operating systems for the first time. Windows 98 became available at the end of fiscal 1998 and Windows 2000 in mid-2000. Windows NT, the operating platform Microsoft developed for more demanding business systems, was upgraded to version 4.0 in fiscal 1997 and the Windows 2000 version was released in early 2000.

The company also offers a full line of business systems products for computer networks including client/server, Internet, and intranet environments. Named the Microsoft BackOffice product family, they include Windows NT Server, Exchange Server, SQL Server, and a new platform for commercial Internet services called Normandy. Normandy – the invasion allusion is surely no coincidence – combines the Windows NT Server with the Internet Information Server and is aimed at Internet service providers.

The Applications and Internet Client Division

This is the home of software programs that cover the whole gamut of PC use. The group is responsible for enough product categories that it is subdivided into five areas of responsibility: the Desktop Applications Division, Internet Client and Collaboration Division, Tools Division, Web Authoring Product Unit, and Developer Relations.

Applications and Internet Client is the company's largest revenue generator. In fiscal 1999, the group brought over $8.82 billion into the company coffers.

The Desktop Applications Division makes 'productivity software' products. The best of these are sold in an applications package, or suite, labeled Microsoft Office. Office 95, which was released in fiscal 1996, has over 23 million users worldwide. Office 97 was released in fiscal 1997 and Office 2000 in 1999.

Available in three editions, Standard, Professional, and Small Business, Office combines Microsoft's best-selling programs: the word processor Word, the Excel spreadsheet program, and the PowerPoint presentation graphics program. More expensive versions add in the Access database program and Outlook, a personal organizer/messaging program. Office is available for every major platform, including the 32-bit and 16-bit versions of Windows and Apple's Macintosh operating system.

By the way, Word and Excel both own around an 80 percent market share in their categories. As a whole, the company controls about 27 percent of the total productivity applications market.

The Internet Client and Collaboration Division is the home of Microsoft's bid for Internet supremacy. Its primary product is the controversial Internet Explorer, which is distributed free and, in 1998, became the leading browser on the market when it surpassed Netscape's Navigator. It is Microsoft's aggressive strategy with Internet Explorer that renewed the wrath of the US Justice Department and led to the ongoing government antitrust action against the company.

The last three divisions, Tools, Web Authoring Products, and Developer Relations, are aimed at developing and maintaining the large base of independent software developers, corporate developers, and webmasters that continually add their own efforts to the list of Microsoft-based applications.

Consumer Platforms Division

This group is responsible for extending the Microsoft name beyond the PC and into the emerging markets for software that will run in electronic consumer goods. As yet, the division does not generate significant revenues. However, as the semiconductor moves into a wide variety of products beyond computers, it appears that large software markets will follow.

This group's flagship program is Windows CE, a scalable operating system that is designed to help users control non-PC devices. Windows CE is a compact version of Windows that is finding its way into everything from interactive televisions to hand-held personal assistants. Its largest application is its use in handheld personal electronic devices, such as the Palm PC.

Consumer Platforms is the home base of the products and technologies that are used in multimedia businesses, such as WebTV, and new joint development projects with other companies in the telecommunications, television and entertainment industries.

The Interactive Media Group

Microsoft has made two major strategic turns since its inception. The first was an ill-fated commitment to CD-ROM technology in the early 1990s and the second was its recent full-fledged adoption of Internet fever. The Interactive Media Group is mostly a grab bag of ventures outside the company's core competency that have grown from those decisions. In 1999, the group was composed of three divisions: Interactive Media, Desktop Finance, and Consumer Input Devices.

The Interactive Media Division

This division, the major unit of the group, is home to a diverse product portfolio that ranges from The Microsoft Network to MSNBC to the company's catalog of educational, informational and entertainment CD-ROM titles.

The Entertainment Business Unit makes entertainment and educational CD-ROM titles. Its major products for children include Scholastic's The Magic School Bus series, Creative Writer, and 3D Movie Maker. It also creates games for PCs, such as the best-selling Flight Simulator, Monster Truck Madness racing simulation and sports titles, including Microsoft Golf, Microsoft Soccer, and NBA Full Court Press. Microsoft holds about a five percent market share in the entertainment category and about two percent in education.

The Information Business Unit develops reference software and services. This is the home of Microsoft's Encarta multimedia encyclopedia and the Automap travel planning and mapping product line. This group also produces popular titles and services such as the Cinemania movie guide, the Bookshelf reference library, and Expedia, a Web-based travel service launched in October 1996. The company controls about 20 percent of the reference market.

In the online markets, Interactive Media is responsible for three major channels. There is MSNBC, the 24-hour news, talk and information service cable network and a news and information Internet service launched in partnership with NBC News in 1996. MSN, The Microsoft Network is one of the largest online services, but still a distant competitor of AOL. And finally, *Slate*, an interactive magazine of politics, culture, and public policy that recently switched to a paid subscription base.

The Desktop Finance Division (DFD)
DFD is Microsoft's bid to gain a foothold in the world of online banking. It is based on the personal finance product Microsoft Money that computerizes household finances and offers access to the online home-banking services of 17 US banks.

Microsoft Hardware
This business unit is responsible for the company's input peripherals. Its major products are the Microsoft Mouse, keyboards, and game devices.

The Sales and Support Group

With over 15,186 employees, Sales and Support is a functional group that brings the company's products and services to its customers around the globe. It is the company's second largest group and its main structure in the US is four units that target customers by size. These sales and support groups are aimed at enterprise (large business) customers, organization (mid-sized and small business) customers, education customers, and end-users.

The sales organization maintains geographically structured units that sell specifically to Europe, the Far East, the Middle East, Africa, Southeast Asia, the South Pacific, India, Brazil, and South America. There are also separate units for original equipment manufacturers and public networks, such as online services and cable operators.

Support functions were given greater priority, along with an additional $200 million in budget, in fiscal 1999. At the core of this effort is Microsoft's customer feedback loop, which is designed to collect, analyze and incorporate customer ideas and suggestions. Support engineers collect customer concerns and suggestions and relay them directly to product development teams. Microsoft has also created a Usability Lab, where customers are invited to work with new and existing products, so the company can learn about them from the user's perspective.

Sales and Support sells via three primary distribution channels: OEM licenses, organization licenses, and retail packaged products. Fees paid to the company by OEM channel licensees, such as computer maker Dell, reached $6.4 billion in 1999.

The Operations Group

This group is responsible for managing business operations and overall business planning. In other words, it is in charge of Microsoft's backroom. The unit employs 4120 in operations worldwide.

Run by COO Robert Herbold, Operations covers finance, manufacturing and distribution, information systems, human resources, public relations, procurement, corporate services, and real estate. For good measure, it is also responsible for the operations of the Microsoft

Press, a publisher with over 500 titles in print, and corporate marketing and advertising.

Microsoft Research

Headed up by Chief Technology Officer Nathan Myhrvold, Microsoft
Research was founded in 1991 and is the company's basic research
arm. The research group's primary focus is the development of computers that can see, hear, speak, learn, and think. It operates research
facilities in Redmond, Washington; San Francisco, California; Beijing,
China; and Cambridge, England.

Research employs over 350 scientists and engineers and it is growing – the group plans to employ 600 people by year-end 2000. The
group conducts research in technologies ranging from speech and visual recognition to decision theory, intentional programming, anima-
tion and 3-D graphics. In addition to the obvious field of computer
science, it pursues research in the areas of biology, mathematics, linguistics, and graphic arts.

Income statement

Year	Revenue ($m)	Net income ($m)	Net profit margin	Employees
1999	19,747.0	7,785.0	39.4%	31,396
1998	14,484.0	4,490.0	31.0%	27,055
1997	11,358.0	3,454.0	30.4%	22,232
1996	8,671.0	2,195.0	25.3%	20,561
1995	5,937.0	1,453.0	24.5%	17,801
1994	4,649.0	1,146.0	24.7%	15,257
1993	3,753.0	953.0	25.4%	14,430
1992	2,758.7	708.1	25.7%	11,542
1991	1,843.4	462.7	25.1%	8,226
1990	1,183.4	279.2	23.6%	5,635

Stock history

	Stock price ($)			P/E		Per share ($)		
Year	FY High	FY Low	FY Close	High	Low	Earns	Div.	Book value
1999	95.63	43.88	90.19	67	31	1.42	0.00	5.57
1998	54.28	29.50	54.19	65	35	0.84	0.00	3.35
1997	33.73	13.44	31.59	51	20	0.66	0.00	2.22
1996	15.73	9.98	15.02	37	23	0.43	0.00	1.45
1995	11.55	5.86	11.30	40	20	0.29	0.00	1.13
1994	6.83	4.40	6.44	28	18	0.24	0.00	0.98
1993	6.13	4.09	5.50	31	20	0.20	0.00	0.72
1992	5.55	2.52	4.38	35	16	0.16	0.00	0.50
1991	3.27	1.41	2.84	30	13	0.11	0.00	0.32
1990	2.19	0.72	2.11	31	10	0.07	0.00	0.22

1999 year-end financials

Debt ratio	0.0%
Return on equity	34.6%
Cash ($m)	4,975.0
Current ratio	2.32
Long-term debt ($m)	0.0
Shares outstanding (millions)	5,109.0
Dividend yield	0.0%
Dividend payout	0.0%
Market value ($m)	460,780.7

Financial data provided by Hoover's Online (www.hoovers.com) and Media General Financial Services, Inc.

Microsoft contacts

Microsoft Corporation   Phone: 425–882–8080
One Microsoft Way   Fax: 425–936–7329
Redmond, WA 98052–6399, USA   URL: www.microsoft.com

CEO: Steve Ballmer   CFO: John Connors   HR: Deborah Willingham

Nestlé SA –

Vevey, Switzerland

Executive snapshot

Balance – balance in products and balance in geographic markets are the keys to Nestlé's steady growth.

"Nestlé considers it very important to keep its activities and, even more, its risks evenly distributed." – Helmut Maucher, chairman, Nestlé SA.

Nestlé backdrop

From feeding infants to food products for the world, Nestlé has progressively expanded its brands since the early 1900s. Today, a walk through the local supermarket reveals shelf after shelf of the company's products.

Conscience and commerce

In the middle 1800s, the Industrial Revolution is generating undreamed-of wealth and a new leisure class. Yet, in Switzerland's working class, among the families powering the new factories, one in every five babies is dying before reaching its first birthday.

Future focus

Food for thought

It happens all the time. A diversified manufacturer of a number of different products decides to focus on one pioneering new product. The company discards everything except the pioneering new product and builds a dominant worldwide company.

In Nestlé's case, the company started out in Switzerland in 1857 as a manufacturer of liquid gases, carbonated beverages and commercial fertilizers. Then Henri Nestlé decided to develop a substitute for breast milk. By 1867, he came up with a pioneering new product which he called Farine Lactée.

Farine Lactée proved to be a big success so Nestlé's company dropped everything to focus on the breast-milk substitute. This was the critical decision in the formation of the world's largest food company.

Early on in the development of a new company there is nothing wrong with experimentation. That is, trying many different products, concepts, approaches. There comes a time, however, when a company must focus if it is ever going to amount to anything.

Once Henri Nestlé had his winning product, he took another step that is usually crucial in building a dominant company. He rapidly expanded. Within a few years after the introduction of Farine Lactée, the product was being sold in 16 different countries.

By 1900, Nestlé opened it first US factory and began a program of worldwide expansion, including the acquisition of a wide range of food products and companies. By 1920, the company owned 80 factories.

In 1938 the company introduced Nescafé, the world's first mass-produced instant coffee, a brand which would become Nestlé's most dominant product. (In some countries, Nescafé has as much as 70 percent of the coffee market.)

Today, Nestlé has more than 8000 food brands, including 52 products that might be considered global brands. They include, among others, Nescafé, Nestea, Buitoni, Mighty Dog, Friskies and After Eight.

Nestlé is also in the pharmaceutical business with two companies: Alcon Laboratories and Galderma. Alcon sells ophthalmology products in 170 countries. Galderma, a joint venture with L'Oréal, makes dermatological products sold to professionals. (Nestlé owns a 49 percent share of Gesparal, the holding company that controls L'Oréal, the world's largest beauty products company.)

As successful as Nestlé is, the question arises: is the company into too many different categories? The answer, in our opinion, is "yes and no."

Yes, Nestlé should probably divest its pharmaceutical operations and its investment in L'Oréal in order to focus on its dominant food operations. The company is obviously in no position to make major inroads against Glaxo Welcome, Merck and the other leading pharmaceutical companies.

In the food business, however, the answer is probably "no." In theory, of course, Nestlé has way too many food brands in way too many different categories. But in practice, the dynamics are different. Nestlé doesn't sell direct to consumers. It has to do business with "middlemen," primarily the supermarket chains.

Contrast Nestlé with Starbucks, a company that does sell its products directly to consumers. If Starbucks started to sell pasta in its coffee houses, the company would likely fall into serious trouble.

Nestlé, of course, does sell both Nescafé coffee and Buitoni pasta to its supermarket customers. When it comes to "middlemen" like the supermarket chains, might makes right.

The right approach to "middlemen" is from a position of strength. The most successful companies have a portfolio of strong brands. This gives the company enough leverage with the chains to secure satisfactory selling prices along with prominent display spaces.

Too many manufacturers view the "middlemen" as partners in their distribution channel. From manufacturer to distributer (or dealer or supermarket chain or retail store) to customer. But the "middlemen" are not on the manufacturer's side. They are on their own side. They view the manufacturer the way the Mafia views its protection clients, as an opportunity to extract the maximum amount of concessions.

Both sides may give lip service to the partnership concept. But each side keeps its own interests paramount. (And there's nothing wrong with that.) It's just that many manufacturers get so carried away with the partnership rhetoric that they overlook the essential dynamics of the situation.

Nestlé's collection of strong food brands is what gives the company leverage with its primary customers, the supermarket chains. As consolidation hits the supermarket industry, this leverage will become more and more important. The rise of discount operations like Wal-Mart and Kmart in the supermarket business will further increase the importance of this leverage.

Both Coca-Cola and Pepsi-Cola have learned this lesson. They have broadened their soft drink lines in order to gain greater leverage with the chains. In the US market, for example, Coca-Cola today has more than 40 percent of the total soft drink market with a future goal of reaching 50 percent. This would not be possible without multiple brands in several product categories.

With some 8000 brands, does Nestlé have too many brands on its plate? Probably. But there are signs that the company recognizes this fact and is in the process of converting its large number of local and regional brands into a smaller number of truly global brands. This is the future and if Nestlé executes this direction well there are plenty of reasons to believe that the company will remain the world's dominant food company.

With more and more women entering the workforce, the care of young children is a rising concern. Swiss businessman Henri Nestlé is moved and challenged by their plight. Nestlé has lived in Switzerland since 1843, when at the age of 30, he left his native Germany and established himself as a druggist in Vevey. By 1857, he has become prosperous enough to invest in the formation of a company that makes liquid gases, carbonated beverages, and commercial fertilizers.

Nestlé envisions a food for infants, a product that is affordable to all, and in the mid-1860s, begins looking for a product that can be used as a substitute for breast milk. By 1867, he has one; a thickened liquid containing powdered cow's milk, malted cereal, and sugar. Nestlé's new product is quickly put to the test, when a local doctor uses it as a last resort to save a 15-day old, prematurely born boy who is refusing his mother's milk and will soon die. The formula works and the baby survives.

The successful inventor immediately turns entrepreneur. Nestlé names his new product Farine Lactée and moves into mass production. It is packaged in tins branded with his family crest depicting a nest containing two baby birds being fed by their mother.

Farine Lactée is a popular product, but also a controversial one. In a foreshadowing of trials yet to come, some Swiss doctors and merchants object to the idea of a product that is meant to replace mother's milk and Nestlé's quasi-medical marketing claims.

Nestlé works hard to overcome these objections and he does, due in no small measure to the fact that his product is a nutritious source of food for babies. He also makes it clear that Farine Lactée is not meant to compete with mother's milk. "During the first months, the mother's milk will always be the most natural nutrient, and every mother able to do so should herself suckle her children," he writes in 1869.

By 1870, production of Farine Lactée is approaching 1000 tins per day. In the early years of the decade, Nestlé's milk food is being sold in 16 countries and demand triples to 3000 tins per day. Unable to keep up, the aging entrepreneur runs into a cash crunch as orders for his baby formula outgrow production capacity.

In 1874, at 61 years old, Henri Nestlé cashes out. He creates a joint stock company named Farine Lactée Henri Nestlé and sells the business to a group of Swiss investors led by Jules Monnerat, a Swiss politician and businessman, for one million Swiss francs. Monnerat is appointed chairman of the company.

Competition and global expansion

In the first years after Henri Nestlé's retirement, the newly formed company works hard to get its house in order. It organizes its manufacturing processes, builds capacity, and improves its quality efforts.

Its success soon proves a magnet to would-be competitors and in 1877, the Anglo-Swiss Condensed Milk Company throws its hat into the baby formula ring. Based in Cham, Switzerland, Anglo-Swiss is Europe's leading condensed milk maker. (It was founded in 1866, just one year before Nestlé, by two American brothers named Charles and George Page. The Pages located their company in Switzerland because of a ready supply of milk from the many dairy farms and the country's central location.)

Nestlé quickly counters by expanding into Anglo-Swiss's specialty. It launches a condensed milk product of its own. Anglo-Swiss offers to buy its competitor outright, and is firmly refused. In the process, a running rivalry develops between the companies. Anglo-Swiss is a formidable competitor, which by 1880 is producing 25 million cans of milk a year. Happily, however, the company is soon distracted by expansion plans in the US. This leaves its home markets less jealously guarded and Nestlé builds its market share in Europe.

Nestlé itself resists the temptation to expand its operations beyond Swiss borders for most of two decades. But as the century closes, the company begins to expand both its product lines and geographic operations.

In 1898, it makes it first acquisition, a Norwegian condensed milk company. In 1900, it opens its first US milk products factory, and then quickly establishes itself in the UK, Germany, and Spain.

In 1904, the company forms an alliance with the Swiss General Chocolate Company. (In 1875, Vevey resident and neighbor of Henri Nestlé, Daniel Peter first created milk chocolate. His new product grew into Swiss General, which now makes and sells the Peter and Kohler brands of chocolate.) Nestlé comes aboard to help the company distribute its products and, in the process, also gets the first Nestlé-branded chocolate products.

In 1905, Nestlé ends its rivalry with the Anglo-Swiss Milk Company by merging with the company. The new company is less than imaginatively named the Nestlé and Anglo-Swiss Milk Company. It boasts 19 factories, all in Europe except for one US plant.

In 1906, Nestlé circumvents increased import taxes in Australia by purchasing Cressbrook Dairy Company. Cressbrook gives the company a foothold in the East and a network for distribution soon follows with warehouses in Singapore, Hong Kong, and Bombay.

Boom, bust and boom again

The outbreak of World War I in 1914 disrupts Nestlé's operations in the warring nations and leads to shortages of the fresh milk it depends on for production. However, war also brings a huge increase in demand for the company's non-perishable milk and food products from both local customers and military authorities.

Between 1914 and 1918 the company's worldwide production doubles. It purchases stakes in US companies to keep up with the demand. The expansion continues through 1920, with additional purchases in Australia and its first factory in Brazil, the beginning of a series of operations in Latin America. By 1917, Nestlé owns 40 factories. By 1920, it owns 80 factories and positions in 12 more associated companies.

The post-war years also bring Nestlé's first fiscal crisis. Government contracts wind down with the war and customers who drank condensed and powdered milk during the war quickly switch back to fresh milk. The drop in demand for its milk products is compounded by rising prices for raw materials and deteriorating exchange rates. Nestlé is already bloated with debt from its fast run of expansion and in 1921, the company records its first ever annual loss, of SWF100 million.

The company quickly reorganizes with the help of Swiss banking expert Louis Dapples. Dapples consolidates operations, closing redundant factories worldwide, and reduces the company's outstanding debt from SWF293 million to SWF54.5 million in just two years. By 1923, the company is back on track.

Dapples also begins to expand the company's product lines. New investments are made in butter and cheese. Lactogen powdered milk is launched as well as a range of other dried milk products.

In 1929, Dapples gets Nestlé into chocolate in a big way when he merges the company with former ally Swiss General Chocolate (now named Peter, Cailler, Kohler, Chocolat Suisses SA). The merger adds 13 chocolate plants and makes Nestlé a leader in that industry.

In 1930, the Brazilian Coffee Institute asks Nestlé's help in developing uses for the nation's large coffee bean surplus. Perhaps, it reasons, a leading buyer of cocoa beans might also be interested in coffee beans. The company is interested, and it begins development work on powdered coffee products.

The company weathers the Depression era without major problems and even resumes its global expansion. It adds operations in Argentina, Chile, Mexico, and Cuba, and purchases additional businesses in Europe.

In 1936, Dapples reorganizes the growing company once more. This time, he creates a holding company for its many businesses, Nestlé & Anglo-Swiss Holding Company Ltd. In 1937, Dapples passes away and Edouard Miller is appointed chairman.

In 1938, the company's efforts in coffee yield Nescafé, the world's first mass-produced instant coffee and the company's first non-milk product. Nescafé is hardly established when Europe sinks into war once again.

World War II quickly engulfs the entire continent and isolates neutral Switzerland. To manage its far-flung empire, Nestlé sets up new headquarters in the US, transferring many of its key executives. Shortages and rising raw materials costs eat up company profits in the first years of the war. But the situation stabilizes and the company expands its operations in countries outside the conflict to maintain production.

As before, the sales of shelf-stable products boom with the conflict and Nescafé is a primary beneficiary. In 1943, the entire output of the Nescafé plant in the US, over 1 million cases, is purchased by the military. Military personnel worldwide get a taste for the product.

Revenues more than double over the war years and the company's exile in the US leads directly to the establishment of a major foothold in that country's markets. In 1946, Nestlé owns 107 factories on five continents and now operates in three major markets: milk products; chocolate; and beverages (or more specifically Nescafé). And its best years are just ahead.

Expanding into the post-war world

In 1947, Nestlé enters a major new segment of the food products industry – culinary products. It merges with Alimentana SA, the manufacturer of Maggi dehydrated seasonings and soups. (Another Swiss company, Alimentana's roots stretch back to 1882, when the Swiss Public Welfare Society commissioned a miller named Julius Maggi to create an easily prepared, non-perishable vegetable food product. Maggi responded with the first instant pea and bean soups.) The merger creates a new entity, the Nestlé Alimentana Company.

In 1950, the company bolsters its culinary lines with the acquisition of Britain's Crosse & Blackwell, a manufacturer of preserves and canned foods, such as soups and baked beans.

During the 1950s, Nestlé benefits from an explosion of demand around the world. The fastest growing groups are its two newest: beverages and culinary products. Sales of Nescafé triple in the 1950s and new products, such as Nestea, are added to its line. Sales also double. In 1960, the good times seem destined to continue forever and Nestlé is flush with cash. It spends the next 15 years building its market share and expanding its major product groups.

The culinary products group is transformed into a broader category labeled "prepared foods" as the company adds a bevy of brands to its portfolio. In 1963, Nestlé acquires an 80 percent stake in Swedish frozen food maker Findus. By 1969, Findus is a fully owned subsidiary. Nestlé also makes an initial investment in US-based Libby, McNeil & Libby and its canned foods, which by 1976 will grow to full ownership. In 1973, it crowns the group with the acquisition of US-based Stouffer Corp., a leader in frozen meals.

The company's beverages business grows just as quickly. In 1960s, its coffee business is extended when the process of freeze-drying is perfected. In 1966, freeze-dried Taster's Choice instant coffee is launched. Sales of Nescafé continue to rise steeply, growing fourfold between 1960 and 1974. The company also adds mineral waters to its beverage portfolio. It takes a stake in France's Vittel in 1968 and acquires US-based Deer Park, Canada's Allan Beverages, and Germany's Blaue Quelle by 1974.

In the milk products group, Nestlé adds ice cream with the founding of France-Glaces in 1960, and then stakes in Germany's Jopa and Spain's Delasa. In 1968, yogurts and desserts are acquired with the purchase of Chambourcy in France. In 1971, the company merges once again – this time, with Ursina-Franck, a Swiss company that brings more milk-based products and baby foods.

In the early 1970s, however, Nestlé's acquisitions binge begins to lose focus. California wineries and restaurant chains are added to the mix. And, then in 1974, the company leaves food and drink behind altogether with a 49 percent stake in cosmetics and haircare products giant L'Oréal.

Soon after the L'Oréal deal, world economics turn downward. The prices of raw materials, starting with oil, explode. Nestlé is squeezed as the price of coffee beans quadruples and cocoa triples.

The company responds to the losses by diversifying even further outside the food business. In 1977 it acquires Alcon Laboratories, Inc., a US manufacturer of pharmaceutical and ophthalmic products.

Group Chairman Pierre Liotard-Vogt tries hard to tie the whole bundle together, noting, "Today we find ourselves with a very wide range of activities, all of which have one thing in common: they all contribute to satisfying the requirements of the human body in various ways."

Boycott!

Nestlé's search for profits also drives it deeper into the world's developing nations. By the 1970s, the company has 81 factories in these countries and is increasing its marketing efforts proportionally. It is this trend that draws the company into a controversy that will stretch out over the next 25 years.

Mid-decade, the news breaks that in countries with high illiteracy rates, uneducated mothers are improperly using breast-milk substitutes to feed their babies. The results are horrific: tens of thousands of babies are malnourished and many are dying. The World Health Organization (WHO) points at the entire industry and specifically at Nestlé, with its new marketing emphasis in developing nations.

Unhappily and incomprehensibly, the industry and the company take a hard line. Its product are safe, Nestlé says, the dangers are overstated and the misuse is not its responsibility. It will not take action. The public, particularly in the US, is outraged. In 1977, a boycott of all the company's products is organized. Still, Nestlé will not change its marketing practices.

The boycott, and the company's intransigence, continue for *years*. By 1980, the activists are claiming to have cost the company millions in lost business and Nestlé is mired in controversy and stagnant sales. Finally, in 1981, a change in leadership breaks the impasse. New CEO

Helmut Maucher opens talks with WHO. By 1984, he agrees to market products meant for infants in accordance with the principles and aim of the WHO/UNICEF International Code of Marketing of Breastmilk Substitutes. The boycott is lifted after seven years.

Maucher does not stop there. After a good long look at the company's businesses, he begins a period of retrenchment. In his first few years, he sells off non-strategic and/or unprofitable brands and companies. He decentralizes the business, cuts costs, and reduces administrative staff.

Net profits rise from SWF683 million in 1980 to SWF1.4 billion in 1984. Liquid reserves double to SWF6 billion in the same period. Nestlé is financially sound and ready to go back to work.

Focusing on the major product groups

In 1984, Maucher begins to implement the next part of his strategy, building the width and breadth of the company's core product groups. In 1984, he buys Warner Cosmetics and adds it to Cosmair, Inc., under the management of L'Oréal.

Maucher's major move, however, is a US$3 billion takeover bid for US-based food giant Carnation. The deal is done in 1985 and Nestlé adds Carnation's milk and culinary products to its existing portfolios. It also gets a leading position in the pet foods business, which it keeps.

The company reaches out again in 1995. It buys Hills Brothers, Inc., the third largest coffee company in the US, and adds roasted coffee to its beverages portfolio.

In 1988, Nestlé looks to Europe in preparation for the coming of the EEC. It acquires the UK's Rowntree Mackintosh, the world's fourth largest manufacturer of chocolates and confectionery items, and Buitoni-Perugina, Italy's third largest food company. By 1989, Nestlé's annual sales hit SWF48 billion and the company employs 196,000 people worldwide.

In the 1990s, the selective expansion continues with corporate acquisitions, investment stakes, and brand purchases. In 1992, the company launches a hostile takeover of Perrier Vittel SA and wins its famous springs as well as leadership in the mineral water business.

In 1994, Nestlé buys Alpo pet food from Grand Met and Ortega-brand Mexican foods in 1995. In 1996, it acquires California fruit drink maker Koala Springs International. In November 1997, the mineral water group San Pellegrino is also added to beverage portfolio.

In 1998, Nestlé acquires two brands from Borden Brands International: Klim for milk powder worldwide and Cremora for non-dairy coffee creamer in Africa and the Middle East. It adds Spillers to the pet foods line, making the company the number two producer in the European pet food market.

A stellar decade is marred, however, by the continuing controversy over the marketing of baby food products in developing nations. Boycotts and demonstrations, this time centered mainly in the UK, reappear in the late 1980s and continue throughout the new decade. In 1999, The International Nestlé Boycott is in effect in 18 countries. The company says there are "no significant actions" against it.

In late 1998 and 1999, the company releases Nestlé Pure Life, bottled water marketed in developing nations. It sells its Findus frozen food brand and parts of its European frozen food business to EQT Scandinavia and forms a joint venture, Ice Cream Partners USA, by merging its ice cream unit with the non-retail US operations of Haagen-Dazs.

In December 1999, Nestle sells the Hills Bros and MJB coffee brands in the US to Sara Lee for an undisclosed sum. The deal includes the Chase & Sanborn unit. Two months later, in February 2000, the company buys the PowerBar brand.

Nestlé close-up

People eat and drink. Always have, always will. It's an escapable fact of life that Swiss food giant Nestlé depends on. Over the past 130-odd years, Nestlé has grown through innovation and acquisition into the world's largest food company and the largest industrial company in Switzerland. In 1999, Nestlé sold SWF74.6 billion worth of its products, generating a net profit of SWF4.7 billion.

Food and drink pour forth from the global company's 509 plants in over 80 countries. These are staffed by the company's 230,929 employees, one of the largest corporate workforces in the world.

Geographic sales of food and beverage products are well distributed. Europe, Nestlé's traditional stronghold, contributed 36.3 percent of 1999's revenues. The Americas accounted for 29.5 percent, and Asia-Pacific and Africa brought in 18.2 percent of total revenues.

Nestlé makes over 8500 products, sporting a collection of brand names that are common to pantries and kitchen cabinets worldwide. These include baby foods, milk and dairy products, breakfast cereals, desserts, ice creams, chocolate, prepared foods, beverages and mineral water and pet foods.

For all of its size, the company remains well focused: 95 percent of its sales are generated by foodstuffs and beverages. The strategy of the company is to be active in a number of profitable segments, without being overly exposed to downturns in any single area. Translated into action, this means that Nestlé's product lines are purposefully balanced in revenue production.

The company accounts for its products in five major segments. The three largest are: beverages, which account for 27.9 percent of sales; milk products at 26 percent; and prepared foods at 27 percent. Chocolate and candy contribute 13.7 percent and the remaining few points come from pharmaceutical products.

Beverages

Beverage sales at Nestlé reached SWF20 billion in 1999. These products include soluble, roasted and ground coffees; chocolate drinks; bottled water; and tea and fruit drinks.

Nestlé invented instant coffee and its Nescafé brand is the world leader in that category. Consumers drink over 3000 cups of Nescafé every second. The company also sells ready-to-drink Nescafé coffees, Taster's Choice, Ricoré, and Ricoffy soluble coffees.

Nestlé's chocolate and malt drinks are top ranked in their market segment. The most familiar brands are Nesquik/Nestlé Quik and Nescau, which are best sellers in Europe and the US. The Milo brand is sold in Latin America and Asia. The company is the world's leading seller of mineral and spring waters. In Europe, Nestlé owns brands such as Vittel, Contrex, Perrier, San Pellegrino, Levissima, Vera, and Fürst Bismarck. In the US, where it is also the leading seller of bottled water, the company's leading names are Arrowhead, Poland Spring, Zephyr Hills, Deer Park, and Ozarka.

In 1998, wholly owned Perrier Vittel SA launched Nestlé Pure Life, a purified water with added minerals. It is the first product that brings the Nestlé name to bottled water.

The beverages product group also includes: roasted coffees, including Dallmayr Prodomo, and Nespresso, an espresso coffee in capsules; fruit juices; and tea drinks, such as Nestea, in soluble and ready-to-drink forms.

Milk, nutrition, and ice-cream products

Nestlé's sells milk-based products in every conceivable form. Sales in this group hit SWF19.41 billion in 1999. It is the company's third largest group and the home of infant foods products, on which the business was founded, and a source of long-running conflict with health organizations and the general public.

A pioneer in the production of foods for babies and young children, Nestlé sells start-up and follow-up formulas, growing-up milks, cereals, and a variety of ready-to-eat and dehydrated foods. These are sold around the world under brands names such as Nan, Lactogen, Nesla, Nestum, and Cérélac.

The company also makes clinical nutrition products used under medical conditions for tube and oral feeding. The major products in this segment are Clinutren, Peptamen, and a powdered formula, sold under the Nutren brand.

The world leader in shelf-stable milks, Nestlé sells powdered, evaporated, and refrigerated milks. These are marketed under the Carnation, Milkmaid, and Nido names, among others. There are also coffee creamers in all forms, and milk drinks such as Fit'n Fresh – a fermented milk drink with fruit.

Ice cream is a growing product group that includes brands such as Frisco, Dairy Farm, Camy, and of course, Nestlé. The company is currently expanding its ice cream sales via impulse-oriented point-of-sale displays. It is filling those displays with products such as the Extrême Duo Cône, the first mass-produced two-scoop ice cream cone, and the

Mega line, which includes the new Mega Truffle, an ice cream stick combined with a chocolate truffle.

The company owns a wide variety of chilled dairy products, including yogurts, cheeses, desserts, and pasta sauces. Nestlé has been restructuring this portfolio, selling off some local products and building brands that are more global in appeal. Major products are sold under names such as LC1, Buitoni, Herta, and Chamyto.

The company's breakfast cereals are sold under the Nestlé name and are marketed outside of North America through a joint venture with General Mills named Cereal Partners Worldwide (CPW). CPW is active in 70 countries and its total market share is estimated at 19 percent, the second largest position.

Prepared dishes and cooking aids

The home of Stouffer's, Maggi, and Buitoni, this product group is Nestlé's second largest, and accounted for SWF20.1 billion in sales in 1999. It encompasses a huge selection of products that cover categories ranging from pasta to pet foods.

A leader in frozen prepared dishes, Nestlé owns two major brands, Stouffer's and Maggi. Stouffer's has a leading position in the US. In addition to its popular meals sold under the company name, it also markets lines such as Skillet Sensations and Lean Cuisine. Prepared and frozen dishes are sold in Europe and other regions under the Maggi and Crosse & Blackwell brands.

Nestlé sells soups, bouillons, sauces, and cooking preparations primarily under the Maggi name. A global business, Maggi products are adapted to the tastes, recipes, and ingredients of its local markets. For instance, it sells instant noodles in the Far East, a prepared dish of seasoned noodles called Nudelspass in Germany, a rice-based porridge in the Philippines, and Maggi Sofrito, a paste made of garlic, onion and aromatic herbs used in cooking, in Chile.

The prepared foods group sells Italian cuisine through the Buitoni brand. Buitoni makes refrigerated and shelf-stable pastas and sauces, pizzas, frozen dishes, and a range of other products. In Europe, the company sells delicatessen products and cold meats under the Herta brand. And, it also markets cold sauces and condiments under brands such as Thomy, Crosse & Blackwell, and Winiary.

Not quite as appetizing – for humans that is – is the company's stake in the US$25 billion pet food segment. The portfolio includes brands such as Friskies, Alpo, Mighty Dog, Fancy Feast, and Gourmet. Nestlé continues to build its position in the world pet food market via acquisition. It has recently added Spiller and its brands Felix and Fido to its European businesses, Jupiter and the Darling brand in Hungary and the Czech Republic, and formed a new joint venture in South Africa.

Chocolate and confectionery products

Nestlé is the world's leading manufacturer of chocolate and confectionery products. These range from chocolate tablets and bars, specialties and boxed chocolates, sugar confectioneries, and cookies. In 1999, the company sold SWF10.19 billion worth of these goodies.

The company owns international chocolate brands including Nestlé's, Crunch, KitKat, After Eight (the leading chocolate mint), and Baci. It also markets regional favorites such as Butterfinger, Baby Ruth, Charge, and Perugina.

Sugar confectionery products are sold under the Frutips and Polo brands. Cookie sales are concentrated in Latin America, where brands such as Sao Luiz, McKay, and La Rosa, are popular.

Other food businesses

The Foodservice Group supports Nestlé's products through the development of flavors and ingredients, and product sales to professional customers. The Food Ingredients Specialties (FIS) business develops, makes, and sells flavors and flavoring ingredients for internal use and for third parties.

Nestlé's Foodservice business serves professionals in the restaurant and hotel industries. The operation also adapts products to meet the unique needs of catering companies, fast-food chains, and airlines. In addition to products developed specifically for industry professionals, the division supplies the major Nestlé brands to this market sector. Major brand names include Chef, Davigel, Minor's, and Santa Rica.

Foodservice is also responsible for the development of product sales via automatic vending machines and beverage systems. Currently, the group is investing in building the number of vending machines bearing the Nescafé brand and selling hot and cold drinks.

Pharmaceuticals

This group is Nestlé's hedge against downturns in the food industry. It is comprised of two companies, Alcon Laboratories and Galderma. In 1999, sales of the group were SWF4.01 billion.

Texas-based Alcon Laboratories sells ophthalmology product in 170 countries and is a wholly owned subsidiary of Nestlé.

Alcon sells into three segments: eye surgery instruments and intraocular lenses and other products used during operations, sold under brands such as AcrySof, Legacy, and Accurus; ophthalmic drugs, including Tobradex, Betoptic, Patanol and Ciloxan; and, solutions for cleaning contact lenses, such as Opti-Free, Opti-One and Supra Clens.

Galderma, a joint venture with L'Oréal, makes dermatological products sold to professionals. This FF490 million company offers treatments including: Différine, a retinoid for the topical treatment of acne; Metrogel/Rozex, for rosacea; and Locéryl, for the treatment of nail fungus. The company sells products to support the treatments, such as Cetaphil, a range of cleansers and moisturizers, and Helioblock sunscreens.

L'Oréal SA

In keeping with its own dominance in the food products industry, Nestlé owns a 49 percent of Gesparal, the holding company that controls France's L'Oréal, the world's largest beauty products company. In 1998, L'Oréal's revenues totaled FF75.4 billion.

The company produces and markets makeup, perfume, and hair and skincare products. Its portfolio includes 500 brands for women and men including names such as Maybelline, Lancome, and Redken.

In addition to the joint venture Galderma, L'Oréal has a 19.5 percent stake in France's Sanofi-Synthelabo pharmaceutical group.

Income statement

Year	Revenue ($m)	Net income ($m)	Net profit margin	Employees
1998	52,168.3	3,120.0	6.0%	231,881
1997	47,883.2	2,739.7	5.7%	225,808
1996	45,091.3	2,535.2	5.6%	221,144
1995	48,933.6	2,527.9	5.2%	220,172
1994	43,478.7	2,483.7	5.7%	212,687
1993	38,620.1	1,939.5	5.0%	209,755
1992	37,138.0	1,838.5	5.0%	218,005
1991	37,081.2	1,814.2	4.9%	201,139
1990	36,310.9	1,779.2	4.9%	199,021
1989	31,172.0	1,565.2	5.0%	196,940

1998 year-end financials

Debt ratio	14.6%
Return on equity	—
Cash ($m)	3,623.9
Current ratio	1.18
Long-term debt ($m)	2,942.6

Financial data provided by Hoover's Online (www.hoovers.com) and Media General Financial Services, Inc.

Nestlé contacts

Nestlé SA
Avenue Nestlé 55
CH-1800, Vevey, Switzerland

Phone: 41–21–924–21–11
Fax: 41–21–924–28–13
URL: www.nestlé.com

CEO: Peter Brabeck-Letmathe   GM, Finance: Mario Corti
GM, Human Resources: Francisco Castaner

Nintendo Company, Ltd –
Kyoto, Japan

Executive snapshot

Nintendo Company, Ltd is a leader in the worldwide video games industry because it does not underestimate how hard it is to keep a child's attention.

"Bad [game] software in the marketplace won't sell, no matter what," says Nintendo president Hiroshi Yamauchi. "Even when you have good software, significant sales will last, in most cases, just three weeks or so."

Nintendo backdrop

Visualize the stereotypical video game producer. One gets a picture of a young company with attitude, nary a suit in sight, perhaps a skateboard ramp or two in the grounds. The Nintendo Company, at over 100 years old, hardly fits that profile. Yet, it has a long history of success in the games industry.

The house of cards

In 1889, in Japan's historic former capital Kyoto, Fusajiro Yamauchi begins making hanafuda cards, decks of Japanese playing cards used in a popular game where the images on the cards are matched for points.

Future focus

Playing the game at Nintendo

If you want to build a company with a secure future, it's not enough to have a narrow focus. You have to have a way to cope with technological change. Even better you have to have a way to create those technological changes yourself.

Nintendo started life as a manufacturer of playing cards. If Nintendo had kept its playing card focus, the company would have more than likely remained a bit player on the world scene.

But it wasn't diversification that paved the way for the company's success. Nintendo found that out in the sixties by foolish forays into taxicabs, love motels and instant rice. Nintendo had better luck with toys and indoor shooting galleries. But these products were only a warm-up for its break-through idea

When you study the histories of even the largest of companies, you generally find one crucial decision that played a major role in each company's success. Had this one decision not been made, it would be highly unlikely that the company would have ever achieved greatness. For Nintendo this decision was a licensing agreement with Magnavox in the early seventies. Thanks to Magnavox, Nintendo was in the electronic game business.

It was not a good time or a good market to be in. The market leader Atari, with its ill-conceived move into personal computers, had self-destructed. And the electronic game market itself, at least in the US, was in the doldrums.

What drives the electronic game business? Good games. So the market rises and falls depending on the creativity of the game designers. Nintendo's first big winner was *Donkey Kong*. This was followed by another enormous success, *Super Mario*.

The success of Nintendo illustrates the long-term power of a narrow focus. Compare Nintendo with Hasbro and Mattel, the two big American toy companies. Nintendo has a narrow focus (electronic games) while Hasbro and Mattel try to span the entire toy category.

In reality, toys are a child's version of an adult world. Toy guns, toy cars, toy building materials, toy people (dolls), etc. Anything an adult uses has its analogy in the toy world. This creates unlimited possibilities for toy products, but also creates a market that is much too broad for any one company. We expect toy companies like Hasbro and Mattel either to narrow their focuses or face extinction.

In its short electronic game history, Nintendo survived two major competitive challenges. In both cases, its narrow focus greatly contributed to the company's defensive abilities.

In 1989 Sega introduced the Genesis, the first 16-bit system, which featured greatly improved graphics. For a time, Sega outsold Nintendo. But the company responded with its own 16-bit system and thanks to its superior games Nintendo ultimately regained the upper hand.

History repeats itself. Currently Nintendo is in a bruising battle with the Sony PlayStation. Sony hit the market first with a 64-bit system, but Nintendo quickly followed with its own 64-bit machine.

Size doesn't matter. Focus does. In the long term, the larger company (Sony) is going to be no match in electronic games for the more focused company (Nintendo.) Look what happened to Magnavox, a major manufacturer of television sets, in the electronic game business. Sony is likely to follow the same path. As the electronic game business rises and then falls, someone at Sony is likely to say, "What are we doing in this lousy business?"

At Nintendo the answer to this same question is: "It may be a lousy business, but it's the only business we have."

Yamauchi, the great-grandfather of the current leader of the company, names his business Nintendo Koppai.

Gamblers discover that hanafuda is a good wagering game and the demand for the cards grows. Yamauchi expands Nintendo and takes on apprentices to make his cards, which are formed of hand-made paper and impressed with wood block prints. The small company opens two retail shops in Kyoto and Osaka.

In 1902, Yamauchi expands again, this time into Western-style playing cards, the first made in Japan. He plans to export the cards, but they become popular in Japan and Nintendo begins selling them in its own shops.

In 1907, the company establishes a distribution contract with Japan Tobacco and Salt Public Corp., a monopoly that begins selling Nintendo's cards in its nationwide chain of tobacco shops. Soon, Nintendo is the leading playing card manufacturer in Japan.

Fusajiro retires in 1929, turning the presidency and control of the company over to his son-in-law, Sekiryo Yamauchi. Sekiryo modernizes the company, renaming it Yamauchi Nintendo & Co., in 1933. Assembly-line manufacturing is introduced, as is a hierarchical structure of authority.

World War II causes an unexpected hiatus in growth as the Japanese government takes control of the economy. In 1947, after the war, Japan is "democratized" by the Occupation Forces. The country's great monopolies are broken up and small shops and family-owned businesses are encouraged. Sekiryo Yamauchi establishes a separate distribution company, Marufuku Co. Ltd, to sell Nintendo's cards to these new shops.

Learning the lesson of focus

In 1950 Sekiryo steps down, turning leadership of the company over to his grandson, Hiroshi Yamauchi. Hiroshi's first order of business is to consolidate his hold over the company. He absorbs the Nintendo manufacturing operation into the Marufuku distribution company, renaming the united entity Nintendo Playing Card Company, Ltd in 1951. Hiroshi fires his grandfather's management staff, as well as family members at work in the business. In 1952, he brings all operations under one roof.

In 1953, Nintendo's new leader turns his attention to products and introduces the first Japanese-made, mass-produced plastic-coated playing cards. In 1959, the company makes its first licensing agreement. It will make playing cards for children backed with cartoon characters. It is an auspicious move; the cartoon characters belong to the Walt Disney Company. Mickey Mouse is a hit and the company sells 600,000 decks in a year.

The 1960s bring on a bout of conglomerate fever and the company diversifies. Yamauchi drops the "playing cards" and gives the company its current name, Nintendo Company, Ltd. In 1962, he raises a war chest by going public and Nintendo's stock is listed on the Osaka and Kyoto Stock Exchanges.

The company buys a taxi company and opens a love-hotel (rooms are rented by the hour). It introduces a line of instant rice in single portions. In 1963, it starts manufacturing games in addition to playing cards. By 1969, all except the games are gone. Nintendo has learned a valuable lesson in focus and will henceforth concentrate on its strong suit, recreational games and toys. That year, the company expands the game department, forming an R&D unit and building a production plant in Uji City, outside Kyoto.

In 1970, Nintendo starts introducing toys into the Japanese market. The first, Ultra Hand, a hand that can grip objects, sells over a million units and generates about $6 million in revenues. The company extends the brand to include other toys, including Ultra Machine, a pitching machine that sells over two million units by 1973.

Nintendo also introduces the Beam Gun, a light-based toy target gun that "shoots" a solar-celled target. The Beam Gun sells over a million units in the early 1970s, generating about $30 million in revenue.

In 1973, the company applies the beam gun concept to skeet shooting, turning bowling alleys into indoor shooting galleries called Laser Clay Ranges. The idea is a hit and Nintendo expands on it, licensing the technology and adding images to the experience. Then the 1973 Oil Crisis drives the Japanese economy into recession and recreational spending dries up. With a large investment in the concept and nothing to replace it, the company is hard hit.

Out of crisis, into video games

The search for a new source of revenue leads Yamauchi to America where he discovers and licenses the right to build and sell an early electronic game system from Magnavox. It is Nintendo's first venture in what will become its most successful product line.

In 1977, in a joint venture with Mitsubishi Electric, Nintendo releases its *Color TV Game 6*, which plays variations on the simple video tennis game, *Pong*. The system sells one million units, as does its successor *Color TV Game 15*.

The company expands its video game success into the arcade market. In 1978, it starts designing coin-operated video games that utilize microcomputer technology. The company creates a slew of games with self-descriptive labels such as *Hellfire* and *Sheriff* and, in 1979, forms a separate operations division for the unit.

During the same period, Nintendo also creates the smallest computer games on the market using technology borrowed from the electronic calculator. The company's handheld *Game & Watch* combines a video game and a clock. It becomes a success and eventually 40 million are sold.

In 1980, a wholly owned subsidiary is formed in the US. Nintendo of America Inc. starts selling coin-operated video games into the world's largest games market. A year later, a young Nintendo game designer named Sigeru Miyamoto creates a new game so far outside the boundaries of the traditional shoot 'em up that, at first, no one is sure what to think of it. *Donkey Kong* becomes the hottest selling coin-operated machine in the industry. The American subsidiary sells over 60,000 units, grossing over $100 million in its second year in business.

Nintendo's Color TV games are by now badly outdated. New game systems featuring interchangeable cartridges are leading the market in the US and Japan, and Yamauchi decides to produce a system that will dominate the market. In 1983, he does.

The Famicom (short for Family Computer) system is introduced in early summer. It features greater game complexity and a substantially lower price than any competing system. In two months, a half million units are sold. Even after a costly defect that causes a recall, Famicom sales continue at a record pace to over two million units, and cartridge sales outpace that figure. Nintendo's market share in Japan exceeds 85 percent.

Global leadership through innovation

In 1985, the US version of Famicom is released as the Nintendo Entertainment System (NES). Nintendo literally rebuilds the US market, which has remained in the doldrums since its collapse in 1983. The system offers popular games such as *Duck Hunt* and *Super Mario Bros.* About 50,000 systems are sold the first year.

In 1986, Nintendo introduces the Famicom Disk Drive System with a modem in an effort to expand use of the system into a sort of early game-driven Internet in Japan. The unit sells 2 million pieces but never develops the user base needed to deliver services economically via the game boxes. In the US, NES reaches 3 million units sold.

Nintendo lays claim to over 90 percent of the Japanese video game market in 1987 and the company breaks out over $1 billion in revenues. NES is the best-selling toy in America and cartridge sales are booming. *The Legend of Zelda* becomes the first NES video game to exceed sales of one million units. *Dragon Quest*, introduced in February, sells over two million units.

By the end of 1988, the company has sales of $1.5 billion. Over 10 million Famicom's, 7 million NES systems, and 33 million game cartridges have been sold. The NES game library now stands at 65 titles.

In 1989, Nintendo of America capitalizes on its huge base of users and publishes the first issue of *Nintendo Power* magazine. Essentially an advertorial, the magazine sells over one million $15 subscriptions, making it the biggest children's magazine in the US. That same year, dedicated "World of Nintendo" sales displays are opened in US toy stores. Eventually over 10,000 stores sport the displays, which often encompass several aisles of Nintendo products.

Nintendo introduces an expanded version of *Game & Watch*, Game Boy, the first handheld game system with interchangeable games. The demand is tremendous: 200,000 are sold in two weeks in Japan; 40,000 are sold in the first day in the US and its entire 1.1 million unit shipment quickly sells out.

Competitive challenges

The company breaks over $2 billion in sales. Nintendo systems and games account for 23 percent of the total US toy business, and every one of the country's top 10 best-selling toys are Nintendo products. Then Sega, another Japanese video game company, launches Genesis, an innovative 16-bit system that ups the ante and successfully challenges Nintendo.

In 1990, Nintendo responds with the 16-bit Super Famicom. In Japan, *Dragon Quest 4* sells 1.3 million copies on its first day. The game retails for $75. There are over 70 licensees creating games for Nintendo and the system is in one of every three US households. Nintendo of America opens a state-of-the-art warehouse in Washington. It ships 600,000 units per day.

In 1991, the 16-bit Super Nintendo Entertainment System (Super NES), along with *Super Mario World*, is released in the US. Nintendo reaches $3.3 billion in revenues.

The battle for system leadership seesaws between Sega, Sony's PlayStation system, and Nintendo. Nintendo releases accessories and games in droves. In 1992, the Super NES Super Scope and Mario Paint with a mouse are released. A sequel, *The Legend of Zelda: A Link to the Past* is shipped. Combined Nintendo system sales reach 75 million. The Super FX Chip, enhanced technology for home video systems, comes in 1992. The first game using the Super FX Chip, *Star Fox*, releases in April. In 1994, Advanced Computer Modeling (ACM) graphics are incorporated into Nintendo games. In 1995, the one-billionth Game Boy game pack sells.

Net sales, however, are falling. From the 1993 peak, sales decline to $3.6 billion in 1994 and then, to $3.1 billion in 1995. They fall again to $2.6 billion in 1996, but that is the year Nintendo reconquers the market with its new generation 64-bit Nintendo 64 game system. The system goes on sale in Japan on June 23 and more than 500,000 systems sell the first day.

N64 wins the war

In September, Nintendo introduces the Game Boy pocket model, a sleeker, 30-percent smaller version of the handheld video game system. That same month, Nintendo 64 launches in America. The initial shipment of 350,000 units sells out in three days.

In the last quarter of 1996, Nintendo captures 50 percent of the entire 32/64-bit hardware market in the US, selling 1.74 million N64 machines. For the year, Nintendo earns 44 percent of all industry revenues, compared with 28 percent for Sony and 26 percent for Sega.

Also in 1996, the company introduces *Pokémon* (or *Pocket Monsters*) in Japan. In the next two years, the *Pokémon* game sells more than 8 million units and more than 100 million *Pokémon* characters sell through vending machines. A *Pokémon* animated television show is Japan's highest rated kids show and one million CDs featuring the theme song of the show are sold. The brand is extended to more than 1000 different products and *Pokémon*-related products become a $4 billion industry in Japan. Company revenues recover and, in 1997, total $3.1 billion.

New games for N64 are rapidly released. Among the bestsellers are *GoldenEye 007, Banjo-Kazooie, Major League Baseball*, and a new *Legend of Zelda* game that captivates the market in late 1998, drawing 500,000 advance deposits for the $69.95 game from anxious players. An exclusive, five-year license for *Star Wars* brand games is also signed.

The Game Boy system is updated and in November 1998, Game Boy Color, the first to generate full color games from the inside, is released. The new technology will simultaneously display 10, 32 or 56 colors of the player's choosing. *Pokémon* is also released in the US. The game sells 200,000 units in two weeks and in December, the Los Angeles Times reports, "retailers are selling out entire *Pokémon* shipments on the day the games arrive."

In 1999, Nintendo announces Dolphin, its next-generation game system run by a 400 MHz IBM PowerPC microprocessor and incorporating a Matsushita DVD player. The system is scheduled for release late in 2000. In the US, Pokemon mania rules, as Pokemon-brand games, cards, books, videos, television shows and toys sell without pause.

In early 2000, the company buys a 3% stake in convenience store operator Lawson to gain access to its online operations as a sales vehicle for video games. Nintendo also forms a joint venture with advertising agency Dentsu. Named ND Cube, it aims to develop game software for mobile phones and other portable appliances.

Nintendo close-up

Super Mario Bros, Donkey Kong, Game Boy, *Pokémon* … these things are the games of the well-off child between 5 and 17 years old. Used for a while and discarded, they seem inconsequential, until all their price tags are tallied. That tag comes to over $15 billion per year, the size of the worldwide video game market, and Nintendo Company Ltd owns over 25 percent of it.

Nintendo Co., Ltd, of Kyoto, Japan, is the world leader in the hotly contested video game industry. In fiscal 1999 that meant $4.8 billion in sales of game hardware and software, and $720 million in net income.

Well understanding the vagaries of the toy and game markets, the company maintains an exceptionally strong financial position. At fiscal year-end 1998, Nintendo's balance sheet showed $5.3 billion cash and cash equivalents, no debt, and total liabilities of 1.6 billion.

Nintendo's management team is as stable as its financial position. A family-owned, private company until going public in 1962, Nintendo is controlled by Hiroshi Yamauchi, who with family members holds around ten percent of the stock. Seventy-two years old, Yamauchi has been President of Nintendo since 1950. Its largest subsidiary, Nintendo of America, was founded and continues to be led by Yamauchi's son-in-law Minoru Arakawa.

The company has been headed by a member of the Yamauchi family since its inception in 1889. If Arakawa succeeds Yamauchi, as most observers believe will happen, the trend will continue at least one more generation.

Nintendo sells it products internationally and maintains distribution subsidiaries in the US, Canada, Spain, Australia, Germany, France, Hong Kong, and the Netherlands. The largest is Nintendo of America Inc., based in Redmond, Washington, which serves as headquarters for Nintendo's operations in the western hemisphere. More than 40 percent of American households own a Nintendo game system. The company also has stakes in a number of video game design companies, design alliances with others, and investments in educational programs for game designers.

Nintendo manufactures and markets hardware and software for home video game systems and portable, handheld systems. It holds a dominant marketing position, particularly in its two largest markets, the US and Japan. In Japan, the company boasts a market share of over 90 percent. In the US, it is the leading game system producer and game publisher in all predominant video game categories.

The company's product lines are based on two major system platforms.

The newest home game system is the Nintendo 64, a 64-bit next-generation machine designed in collaboration with Silicon Graphics, which was first introduced in 1996. The company sold more than 10 million units of Nintendo 64 hardware and more than 46 million pieces of Nintendo 64 software in fiscal 1998. Nintendo 64 hardware sales are supported by new, best-selling software titles, such *Star Fox 64*, *GoldenEye 007*, and *Diddy Kong Racing*. Each game sold over one million pieces in the US during fiscal 1998. *Super Mario 64* and *Super Mario Kart 64*, which were launched in fiscal 1997, also sold over one million units each in fiscal 1998. The installed base of Nintendo 64 systems is over 16 million worldwide.

Nintendo's second major platform is the Game Boy. The company sold 11 million units of Game Boy hardware and over 35 million units of Game Boy software in fiscal 1998. In the US, Game Boy dominates the handheld category with nearly 90 percent market share. Since the introduction of the Game Boy system in 1989, Nintendo has sold over 80 million hardware units, making it the biggest selling video system in history.

Income statement

Year	Revenue ($m)	Net income ($m)	Net profit margin	Employees
1999	4,806.0	720.5	15.0%	—
1998	4,015.4	629.0	15.7%	1,002
1997	3,378.3	528.9	15.7%	980
1996	3,302.0	558.2	16.9%	952
1995	4,802.8	481.3	10.0%	927
1994	4,726.1	512.4	10.8%	568
1993	5,681.0	771.0	13.6%	943
1992	4,405.0	655.0	14.9%	825
1991	3,463.0	489.0	14.1%	777
1990	1,522.0	209.0	13.7%	730

1999 year-end financials

Debt ratio	0.0%
Return on equity	—
Cash ($m)	5,361.3
Current ratio	4.28
Long-term debt ($m)	0.0

Financial data provided by Hoover's Online (www.hoovers.com) and Media General Financial Services, Inc.

Nintendo contacts

Nintendo Company, Ltd   Phone: +81–75–541–6111
60 Fukuine Kamitakamatsu-cho   Fax: +81–75–531–7996
Higashiyama-ku   URL: www.nintendo.co.jp
Kyoto 605–8660, Japan

CEO: Hiroshi Yamauchi   CFO: Hiroshi Yamauchi
HR: Yasuhiro Onishi

Nokia Corporation –
Helsinki, Finland

Executive snapshot

In the 1990s, Nokia Corporation sold off its traditional business groups and placed all of its chips on one bet.

"Our strategic intent, quite simply, is to achieve industry leadership in the most attractive global communications segments," says Jorma Ollila, president and CEO of Nokia. "What it means, to put it in a straightforward manner, is that our goal is not only to be among the top two companies in our chosen areas – our goal is to shape and define those areas."

Nokia backdrop

Nokia Corporation has deep roots in Finland's industrial heritage. It is the result of the merging of three successful companies that had little in common. Although its current businesses would surely astonish Nokia's three parents, they could hardly be anything less than completely proud of their offspring.

Three proud parents

It is a Finnish engineer named Fredrik Idestam who gives Nokia its name. While studying mining engineering in Germany in the early

Future focus

Nokia, the cellular celebrity

The world's largest seller of mobile phones is located where? In Finland, a country with a population of less than five million people?

How can this be? A $10 billion technological leader located in the frozen North, nestled again Russia on one side and the Arctic Circle on the other. Again the answer is focus. Any company that wants to be a world leader should study the Nokia story in great detail. It wasn't always so. At one point Nokia was a typical European conglomerate. Its products included paper, chemicals, rubber products, electronics, and machinery. For a short period of time Nokia was even in the computer business.

The turnaround started in the early 1990s. Nokia started dumping everything that wasn't related to its core mobile phone business. By 1995 the company had 90 percent of its business in cellular phones and the networks that link them.

Size doesn't matter. Focus does. Nokia's major competitors are Ericsson, a company twice its size and Motorola, a company three times its size. But neither Ericsson nor Motorola are focused the way Nokia is. What accounts for the company's success in competing with its larger competitors?

Let's start with perception. What's a Motorola? It could be a radio set, a pager, a satellite system, a computer chip, even a personal computer. The brand name Motorola doesn't mean anything precisely because it means everything.

What's a Nokia? A mobile or cellular phone. This singular identity is a powerful advantage in the marketing of Nokia products. Nokia is a brand that stands for something, the world's most popular cellular phone.

Then take management. How can you manage a company like Motorola, a company that's down to earth and into space. A company that makes microprocessors and personal computers. And once even tried to market mainframe computers. Management matters. It is possible to manage a diversified company like General Electric that markets a wide range of old-line industrial products. But when your conglomerate is

Motorola, a company that's on the leading edge of a variety of high-tech products, the management problem is impossible. No one mind can wrap itself around that wide a range of technologies.

At Nokia, management has only one technology to worry about. Wireless telecommunications.

And when you want to assess a company's future prospects, you need to ask yourself only one question, "Will the company's management make the right technological decisions in the future?" With Nokia, the answer is yes. With Motorola, you can only hope for the best.

Nokia is the world leader in cellular phones. Leadership itself is the most likely predictor of future success. Not sales, not profits, not even technological leadership. To the leader belongs the spoils. And one of the spoils of leadership is a company's ability to dominate a market. To set product parameters, pricing, terms, even distribution systems. If you want to compete with the leader, you have to play the game their way. Pepsi-Cola was forced to adopt Coca-Cola's bottling system, packaging standards, etc.

Nokia is beginning to use its product leadership to control the cellular phone marketplace. Nokia looks and acts like company that will live well into the 21st Century. And Nokia's strategy is as simple as one, two, three.

1 Narrow the focus.
2 Dominate a market with a future.
3 Control that market by using your leadership as a club.

1860s, Idestam is intrigued by the economic potential of a new machine that grinds wood into pulp for paper. He returns to Finland and, in 1865, sets up a mill using the machine on the Nokia River in the forests of south-western Finland. The mill becomes Nokia Corporation and grows to become a leading soft tissue manufacturer.

The river is a fine source of power and, in 1898, it attracts the attention of two executives of the Finnish Rubber Works. They open a plant to manufacture rubber galoshes on the bank of the river opposite the Nokia mill. During the following years, the company becomes

Finland's leading rubber producer making a wide variety of products from rubber boots and winter tires to balls and rubber bands.

In 1912, a third company opens, not on the Nokia, but in Helsinki. The Finnish Cable Works makes cables for the fast-growing power transmission industry, as well as telegraph and telephone networks.

In 1915, Nokia goes public and in 1922, the Finnish Rubber Works diversifies, buying a majority stake in Finnish Cable Works. Gradually, the shares of all three companies begin to accumulate into common ownership. Quietly, but relentlessly, all three companies grow.

During the 1960s, the Cable Works expands into electronics. In 1960, president Bjorn Westerlund founds an electronics department within the Finnish Cable Works, funding new product development with the revenues from more established business segments. It will eventually develop into the core business of today's company.

In 1962, the department begins work on radio-based telecommunication systems. In 1963, it develops and releases a radiotelephone, the precursor of the cellular phone. The phones are used on Professional Mobile Radio (PMR) systems and sell to the military, public utilities and emergency services organizations.

During the same period, Nokia has diversified into a host of new businesses. In 1962, it even becomes an early participant in the computer industry when it signs on as the Finnish agent for the French company Machines Bull.

A diversified Finnish giant

In 1967, encouraged by the government, Nokia, Finnish Rubber Works, and Finnish Cable Works merge, forming a new company under the Nokia name. The new company is a large, but highly diversified collection of businesses. Its major divisions include paper, chemicals, electronics, and machinery.

The president of the new company is Finnish Cable Works' president Westerlund. At the time, Nokia's electronics business is generating three percent of sales and employs about 450 people.

In 1969, Nokia is the first to introduce PCM, digitally based transmission equipment. Nokia's market share in wireline (or hardwired) and microwave transmission equipment starts a long period of growth.

The company supplies systems in the neighboring Soviet Union and Sweden to a variety of customers, including gas, oil, and railway companies.

All is not rosy, however. The 1973 Oil Crisis causes a drop in overall sales and profits as inflation and a growing trade deficit hurt the entire Finnish economy. The company is also negatively impacted by a recession in the Soviet Union. The USSR accounts for 39 percent of Nokia's exports.

Nokia responds to the economic turmoil of the period by increasing its focus on digital electronics and telecommunications and a period of expansion ensues. The company also begins developing phones and infrastructure products in preparation for the launch of the first Scandinavian NMT (Nordic Mobile Telephone) network.

In 1979, the company merges its radiophone division with a competing business developed by Salora, the region's largest color TV manufacturer. The jointly owned unit is named Mobira Oy and becomes the forerunner of today's Mobile Phones unit.

In 1981, the NMT network opens and Nokia buys a 51 percent stake in Finland's state-owned telecommunications company, renaming it Telenokia. In 1982, it buys a mobile phone company named Mobira and the Finnish Chemicals Corporation. That same year, it introduces the DX200, the first 100 percent digital telephone exchange in Europe.

In the next three years, the company takes a stake in Salora and buys Luxor, a Swedish electronics company. It earns a piece of the world markets by becoming an OEM serving companies such as IBM, Hitachi, Ericsson, and Northern Telecom.

In 1986, the company records sales of over $2 billion and net income of $111 million. It acquires a controlling stake in Finnish electrical wholesaler Sahkoliikkeiden. Nokia introduces a cellular mobile exchange and, soon after, the world's first NMT pocket phone, the Mobira Cityman 900.

By 1988, Nokia is Europe's third largest television manufacturer and with the purchase of Ericsson's data business, Nokia Data becomes the largest information technology company in Scandinavia. In 1989, it folds Mobira into Nokia Mobile Phones.

The early 1990s are difficult years. The worldwide economic recession and shrinking profits in its consumer electronics businesses hurt Nokia's performance. In 1990, gross sales of almost $6.1 billion yield only $95 million in net income. In 1991, sales drop almost 40 percent and the company loses $146 million.

Ollila focuses Nokia

Nokia responds to the challenge with an increased focus on its telecommunications businesses and begins to divest businesses outside that core. In 1991, a new standard in mobile telephony, GSM (Global System for Mobile communication) comes on line and Nokia is fully prepared with GSM-based equipment.

Just three years after buying Ericsson's data unit, the company sells Nokia Data, and leaves the computer industry. It expands further into telecommunications by buying their nearest competitor, UK mobile phone maker Technophone.

In May 1992, current President Jorma Ollila is appointed to head Nokia.

The company is the first to deliver a total GSM system including both phones and infrastructure and it introduces its first GSM portable phone, the Nokia 1011. In its last year of depressed finances, the company loses $78 million on $3.4 billion in revenues.

Nokia begins to benefit from the cellular boom in 1993. Revenues recover to over $4 billion and the company turns its biggest profit since 1988, $132 million. It purchases Tandy Corporation's mobile phone operations in the US and Korea.

In 1994, Nokia becomes the first European manufacturer to sell mobile phones in Japan. It also becomes the first to manufacture portable phones for all the major digital standards. The Nokia 2100, introduced that same year, is the world's smallest and lightest family of digital products. Total revenues rise to a record $6.3 billion and net income increases dramatically to $632 million.

Nokia's focus starts to pay off and the company sheds the rest of its businesses outside the communications core. In 1995, it sells the tire and cable machinery units. It also exits the color TV business. Revenues rise at record rates again to $8.4 billion, but net income, impacted by one-time charges, falls to $512 million.

Leading the race for mobile telecommunication

In 1996, Nokia releases a series of new phones including the world's first all-in-one communications handset. The Nokia 9000 Communicator is a wireless phone and a personal organizer. It also offers Internet access, e-mail, data and messaging services along with Internet access. It gets rave reviews as a leading-edge product and sells 100,000 units at $2000 each. The company also records 16 new network contracts, boosting its client list to 53 customers in 30 countries.

It increases its global manufacturing capabilities with new plants in China, Hungary, Sweden, and the UK. Net income recovers to $700 million, but total revenues remain relatively flat in a soft market.

In 1997, Nokia introduces Artus, a new wireless data product family that allows network operators to charge for Internet traffic in the same way as voice traffic. Continuing its expansion into Internet-related fields, in December 1997 it increases its data communication capabilities by acquiring California-based Ipsilon Networks Inc., an innovator in Internet Protocol technology.

By the end of the year, Nokia's global GSM infrastructure share has increased to almost 30 percent. It is the leading base station supplier in Europe and the leading worldwide network supplier of GSM systems.

Nokia Mobile Phones introduces a total of 31 new phone models and wireless data products for ten standards during 1997. The 6100 product family for GSM 900, 1800 and 1900 frequencies is announced, with release scheduled for February 1998. A new Nokia Communicator, with enhanced Internet browsing, e-mail access, fax transmission, and messaging features, ships.

The company's expertise in cellular is extended into the automotive industry. "Smart Traffic" products, such navigation and positioning tools, alarm systems, as well as other services, are investigated in partnership with major car companies.

During 1997, Nokia introduces a variety of new monitors, including 15, 17, 19 and 21 inch screen sizes and its first-flat screen display. Over half of the company's monitors are sold under the Nokia brand, the rest sell to PC manufacturers. Monitor sales expand into Central Europe and monitor production is increased in Hungary. The company's focus on telecommunications is reaching fruition. Revenue reaches a record $9.8 billion with net income over $1.1 billion.

By 1998, Nokia is beginning to exert control over the very development of the marketplace. In January, third-generation wireless standards are announced that are largely based on the company's proposals.

The new generation of networks, providing advanced wireless and multimedia services, will be implemented in the early years of this century, but Nokia is ahead of the game. In September 1998, the first successful trial call is made in Japan using new-generation technology from Nokia. In October, the company begins work on a trial third-generation system in China.

Mobile Phones continues its fast-paced new product schedule. In September, it builds on its analog cellular line with the Nokia 282 and releases a new Telecoil hearing aid accessory that for the first time extends digital telephony to the two million hearing aid users in North America. It also designs a handset specifically for the Chinese market. It displays and downloads Chinese characters as well as sends and receives faxes in Chinese. In December, it announces the making of its 100 millionth mobile phone, with production of mobile phones sometimes reaching 1 million per week.

Nokia fully acquires NE-Products, buying the remaining 30 percent from venture partner Elektrobit and folding it into the Mobile Phones group. NE-Products develops and manufactures wireless payphones.

The Telecommunications Group supplies the first high voice quality EFR network in India and in October in Germany, completes its fastest-ever network rollout. The company has installed 1000 base stations in ten months.

In 1999, Nokia wins major telecom supply contracts with Sprint, Brazil's Telefonica Celular, and DoCoMo, the wireless unit of Japan's NTT. The company also agrees to license its software to Hewlett-Packard and IBM for use in their servers. Nokia also releases phones that feature Internet access and continues to widen its lead as the world's top seller of mobile phones.

In early 2000, Nokia acquires Network Alchemy, a maker of secure network systems for processing online transactions. The company continues its work in establishing wireless standards. It agrees to partner with Ericsson and Motorola to develop an open standard for secure transactions over mobile devices.

Nokia close-up

As the portable cellphone becomes a ubiquitous personal possession of people around the world, Finland's Nokia Corporation grows ever more profitable. Nokia has been riding the trend toward mobile telephony since its inception and that focus paid off big in the last half decade of the 20th century.

Headquartered in Helsinki, this global telecommunications company is the world's leading supplier of mobile phones and the second largest supplier of the mobile and fixed networks through which the phones operate. Nokia also supplies products for fixed and wireless datacom, multimedia terminals, and computer monitors.

In 1999, Nokia recorded gross sales totaling EUR19.7 billion, earning EUR3.84 billion in net profits. It is listed on five European stock exchanges and on the New York Stock Exchange, under the symbol NOK.A. The company employs 55,260 people worldwide.

Nokia maintains manufacturing operations in ten countries on three continents. The company has a world-class R&D function with centers on fourth continents. Every third employee works in R&D.

Nokia mobile phones are sold in 130 countries. Its GSM technology has been sold to 87 network operators in 39 countries and its fixed network systems are in use in over 50 countries. In 1999, 53 percent of the company's sales originated from Europe, 22 percent came from the Asia-Pacific region, and 25 percent from the Americas. Its ten largest markets were the US, the UK, China, Germany, Italy, France, Australia, Brazil, the Netherlands, Finland and Denmark, representing 65 percent of the company's total sales.

The company is organized into the following five major operating groups by product.

Nokia Networks

The networks group develops and manufactures infrastructure equipment and systems for mobile and fixed networks. Nokia is the world's second largest supplier of GSM networks and a market leader in mobile data infrastructure. In addition, it is a significant supplier of advanced transmission and switching solutions.

Nokia Networks offers switching systems, access solutions, network management, and Internet protocol networking, as well as intelligent network solutions for telecom operators for both mobile and fixed networks. The global Customer Services network makes Nokia a full service house.

More simply, this group makes the equipment that forms the mysterious networks that connect your cellphone to the rest of the world.

Nokia Networks has research and development activities in Finland, Australia, Denmark, Germany, Hungary, Japan, Malaysia, Sweden, the UK and the US. Production is conducted in Finland, China, the UK and the US.

The group employs 23,718 people worldwide. In 1999, it generated net sales of EUR5.6 billion.

Nokia Mobile Phones

Nokia Mobile Phones is the world's largest mobile phone manufacturer. In 1999, Nokia's global market share for phones was 28 percent with 78.5 million phones sold. Nokia's handset product offerings cover all the major digital and analog standards in 130 countries worldwide. Nokia Mobile Phones released more than 18 new products in 1999, including a combined telephone and personal organizer offering Internet, e-mail, fax, and wireless imaging capabilities.

Nokia's handsets and accessories are manufactured in eight factories in seven countries: Finland, Brazil, China, Germany, Mexico, South Korea and the US. Product specification, marketing, and production are located and conducted on a regional basis in four areas: Europe, the Americas, Asia-Pacific, and Japan.

Nokia's development of new technologies and product families is a global effort. Research and development for cellular phones is conducted at 11 research centers in seven countries: Finland, Australia,

Denmark, Germany, Japan, the UK and the US. The group employs 23,775. In 1999, it generated net sales of EUR13.1 billion.

Nokia Communications Products

The communications products group maintains two major businesses:

Nokia Multimedia Network Terminals is a pioneer in digital satellite, cable and terrestrial network terminals for interactive multimedia applications. The business is driven by the growing use of broadband digital video, audio and data services, including television and interactive services.

Nokia Multimedia Network Terminals operates in a global market, and collaborates closely with program and content providers to offer consumers attractive products and services. Production is located in Sweden, with product development centers in Finland, Germany and Sweden. Sales offices are established in all the major markets in Europe as well as in Asia-Pacific and the Americas.

The second business is Nokia Industrial Electronics, which develops and manufactures computer and workstation monitors, including applications for professional desktop communication and new technology displays. Nokia is a leading professional computer and workstation display manufacturer in Europe. The company's displays are known for their picture quality, ergonomic design and user-friendliness.

Nokia Industrial Electronics also produces battery chargers for mobile phones, as well as other power supply applications for mobile communication. Nokia is strongly positioned in volume production of chargers, following the growth in the mobile phone market. Additionally, Nokia manufactures advanced RF filters and antennas for wireless communication. Nokia Industrial Electronics has production facilities in Finland, Hungary and Sweden, and R&D activities in Finland and Sweden.

Nokia Ventures Organization

Nokia Ventures Organization is designed to expand the company's business scope into promising new areas within communications solutions, products and services. It is currently seeking to exploit growth opportunities in the competitive arena emerging from the convergence of telecom and datacom. Nokia Venture Organization focuses first on new telecommunications and data communications solutions, as well as service and software businesses for multiple customer groups.

Nokia Ventures Organization includes three business units: Wireless Business Communications focuses on the development of new wireless solutions for corporate customers. Wireless Service Applications develops new solutions for the wireless environment, particularly in the area of healthcare. Wireless Software Solutions focuses on the development of software solutions based on the Wireless Application Protocol and other platforms.

To fuel future growth and to boost new product and business development, Nokia has also established a $100 million venture capital fund. Based in Silicon Valley, California, the fund focuses on new start-up businesses and technologies, and has global investment scope with special emphasis on innovation centers.

Nokia Research Center

Nokia Research Center is the corporate research unit and interacts closely with all Nokia business units. Its goal is to enhance the company's technological competitiveness. The center covers the full range of activities from exploration of new technologies and product/system concepts to their exploitation in actual product development in the business units.

To keep up to date with the latest technological developments and to influence them, the center maintains global contacts. It actively participates in various international R&D projects in cooperation with universities, research institutes and other telecommunications companies. Additionally, the center supports Nokia's active involvement in the work of global standards organizations to further develop and define standards in telecommunications.

Nokia Research Center's areas of technological interest are wireless and wireline telecommunications, audio-visual signal processing, software technology and electronics. Its main focuses include GSM enhancement, third-generation mobile technology, broadband communications, and multimedia.

Income statement

Year	Revenue ($m)	Net income ($m)	Net profit margin	Employees
1998	15,553.0	2,043.1	13.1%	44,543
1997	9,701.7	1,154.1	11.9%	36,647
1996	8,446.2	700.9	8.3%	31,723
1995	8,400.0	509.4	6.1%	31,948
1994	6,368.0	632.0	9.9%	28,600
1993	4,078.7	132.0	3.2%	25,800
1992	3,450.7	(78.4)	—	26,700
1991	3,731.8	(145.8)	—	29,167
1990	6,093.1	94.7	1.6%	37,336
1989	5,634.7	67.7	1.2%	41,326

Stock history

Year	Stock price ($) FY High	FY Low	FY Close	P/E High	Low	Per share ($) Earns	Div.	Book value
1998	15.68	4.16	15.05	37	10	0.46	0.00	1.23
1997	6.40	3.45	4.34	25	13	0.26	0.00	0.83
1996	3.70	1.95	3.60	23	12	0.16	0.04	0.71
1995	4.88	1.95	2.44	54	22	0.12	0.00	0.66
1994	—	—	—	—	—	—	—	—
1993	—	—	—	—	—	—	—	—
1992	—	—	—	—	—	—	—	—
1991	—	—	—	—	—	—	—	—
1990	—	—	—	—	—	—	—	—
1989	—	—	—	—	—	—	—	—

1998 year-end financials

Debt ratio	0.0%
Return on equity	39.5%
Cash ($m)	846.8
Current ratio	1.75
Long-term debt ($m)	0.0
Shares outstanding (millions)	4,844.8
Dividend yield	0.0%
Dividend payout	0.0%
Market value ($m)	72,913.8

Financial data provided by Hoover's Online (www.hoovers.com) and Media General Financial Services, Inc.

Nokia contacts

Nokia Corporation   Phone: +358–9–18–071
Keilalahdentie 4, PO Box 226   Fax: +358–9–65–2409
Espoo FIN-00045, Finland   URL: www.nokia.com

CEO: Jorma Ollila   CFO: Olli-Pekka Kallasvuo   HR: Hallstein Moerk

Nucor Corporation –
Charlotte, North Carolina, USA

Executive snapshot

In the steel business, where the winners and the losers are usually separated by only a few dollars in the cost of making a ton of steel, Nucor Corporation is unrelenting in its drive to become the leader in the industry.

"Our competitive strategy is to build manufacturing facilities economically, and to operate them efficiently. Period," declares Ken Iverson, Nucor chairman emeritus.

Nucor backdrop

From birth of the automobile to the dawning of the Nuclear Age, Nucor made everything from cars to radiation testers. The world's most efficient steel maker does not even enter the steel business until it is almost 60 years old.

Ransom Olds' comeback

Nucor starts its corporate existence as the Reo Motor Car Company. In August 1904, Ransom Eli Olds, who is as good a car designer as he is a bad businessman, forms Reo to produce cars and trucks in the fast-growing automotive sector. This is Olds' second car company. He has

Future focus

The road less traveled

It happens often. At a fork in the road, the company faces a choice. Do we take the road everybody else is taking, or do we take the road less traveled?

Nuclear Corporation of America faced that decision. After selling or liquidating all of its unprofitable businesses, the company was left with one profitable unit, its Vulcraft steel joist operation. (The standard focusing procedure.) The question was what to do next?

One of the advantages of narrowing the focus is to bring all of management's thinking to bear on a single problem. Fifty-five percent of the cost of joists is the bar steel used in its construction. One obvious way to reduce costs is to make your own steel.

Big Steel uses traditional smelting mills to make steel. But a traditional mill costs several hundred million dollars and, furthermore, how can you achieve a competitive advantage if you do it the same way as everybody else?

So Nuclear (now called Nucor) and its new president Ken Iverson decided to build a minimill which uses electric arc furnaces to melt scrap. It takes the road less traveled.

Would the minimill concept turn out to be a less expensive way to produce steel? Who really knew? Certainly the big steel producers, US Steel and Bethlehem, didn't think so.

You can do all the financial planning you want, but no one can predict the future. That's where strategy can play a crucial role in deciding which road to take.

If Nucor had taken the traditional road, it might have scored a few points, but it couldn't win big. Whatever advantages it might uncover would have been quickly copied by competition. You can't establish a competitive advantage in a commodity business by doing things the same way as your major competitors.

This is especially true in an old, established industry. In such an industry, your competitors have established strong relationships with the major customers. If you want to take business away from them, you must offer their customers some substantial advantage. And in a commodity business, virtually the only advantage you can offer is low price.

Nucor took a chance and scored big. Currently Nucor runs eight minimills with a ninth in the works. It is already the second largest steel producer in the US, trailing only USX-US Steel. Over the past five years, its net profit margin after taxes ranged from 6.4 to 7.9 percent. (This is higher than the average *Fortune 500* company achieved in those same years.) This is an astounding performance by a commodity company.

Compare Nucor with USX Corp, formerly US Steel, the world's largest steel company. While USX has much higher revenues than Nucor, its net profit margins have been averaging less than half of Nucor's. And make no mistake about it, revenues mean nothing without profits. What makes a powerful company is the bottom line, net profits after taxes. Without substantial net profits, a company has no future.

Many companies will face a similar "fork in the road" decision. One fork is marked "do it better." The other fork is marked "do it different."

When you take the "do it better" fork, you are betting that your company can do it better than everyone else. And maybe you can, at least in the short term. But in the long run, it is very difficult to come out substantially ahead of competition if you take a similar road to theirs.

Your only chance to win big is to take the fork marked "do it different." Maybe there is no clear-cut advantage in the do-it-different fork. So be it. It's the only road that offers your company an opportunity to come out on top.

Another company that faced a similar situation was Digital Equipment Corporation. Years ago, there were eight major computer manufacturers (IBM and the seven dwarfs.) When Digital decided to get into the computer business, it could have tried to do it better than the seven dwarfs. That is, market a mainframe line with significant advantages over the competition.

That would have been conventional thinking. Instead Digital decided to do it different and launched the first line of minicomputers. As a result, Digital Equipment Corporation became very successful, the second largest computer company in the world.

With its minimills, Nucor is on the road to do in steel what Digital Equipment did in computers.

already invented the Oldsmobile for the Olds Motor Works, but because he neglected to take an equity position in the start-up, has been squeezed out of that company. Olds' former employer even gets its founder's name and Ransom is forced to use his initials as the name of his new company.

By October that same year, Olds is driving a prototype of the company's first product, the Reo, a high-end touring car. By March 1905, the first batch of Reos rolls off the assembly line of the company's Lansing, Michigan factory.

Reo Motor Car Company is a hit and for the next 20 years, sells into the top end of the US automobile market. It also develops a line of trucks, the popular Reo Speedwagon.

The Great Depression of 1929 destroys the automobile market, particularly for luxury cars, and even though he is 70 years old and retired, Ransom Olds attempts to regain control of the company. He fails and in 1938, the company files for bankruptcy protection.

The company, now reorganized as Reo Motors, Inc., leaves the car market and attempts to diversify. It even introduces a line of lawn mowers, but never fully recovers from the Depression. In late 1954 and early 1955, it sells off all of its assets and distributes them to creditors and shareholders, leaving a $3 million tax loss on its books. That loss becomes the impetus for Nucor's second incarnation.

A nuclear conglomerate

To take advantage of the tax credit the loss generates, a group of stockholders takes control of the shell of Reo Motors and uses it to takeover a company named Nuclear Consultants, Inc. The entire company is renamed Nuclear Corporation of America. By the end of 1955, Nuclear Corp. goes public on the American Stock Exchange as the first traded stock in the nuclear industry.

Nuclear Corp. dabbles in nuclear testing devices and nuclear power projects, but mostly it spends its shareholder's money with little to show in return for the investment. Most notably, the company manufactures radiation sensors bearing the trade name of Nucor.

By 1960, the company has two major shareholders: investment banker Bear, Stearns and Company and Martin Marietta, the aerospace company. Looking for some kind of direction, they oust the current chairman and replace him with David Thomas. Thomas promptly forces the company's president to resign and takes on the day-to-day operation of the company himself.

Thomas' regime is not much better than the one he replaced. He sells a few companies, buys a few, and the way Ken Iverson, the man who shaped present-day Nucor, and others remember it, Thomas lives pretty well while he is doing it. He does do at least two things right: in 1962, he buys a steel joist maker named Vulcraft and he hires Ken Iverson to run the new unit. Without knowing it, he lays the foundations of Nucor.

The watershed year for Nuclear Corp. is 1965. Thomas has run the company up from $2 million in annual revenues to $20 million, but profits remain elusive and the company is perilously close to bankruptcy once again. By May, Thomas is forced to resign and by August, Ken Iverson is the president of Nuclear Corp.

"Apparently, managing the only profitable division in the company made me presidential material," writes Iverson in his book, *Plain Talk*. "Although I was just 39 years old, I wasn't too flattered. No one else wanted the job. It was mine by default."

Iverson sells or liquidates Nuclear's unprofitable businesses. By year-end, the company consists of one profitable business, the Vulcraft steel joist unit, and records over $2 million in losses on $22 million in sales.

Between 1955 and 1965, Nuclear loses money every year but two. In those two years, 1961 and 1963, it earns one cent per share. But, in 1966, under the leadership of Iverson, the whittled-down company starts earning a profit and has not stopped since. That year, corporate headquarters moves from Phoenix, Arizona to Charlotte, North Carolina to be near its joist operation, based in Florence, South Carolina.

Save money, make steel

Fifty-five percent of the cost in joists is bar steel and Iverson soon finds that price increases in the steel the company needs are squeezing its profits. He decides to "integrate backward." Nuclear will make its own bar steel.

Iverson persuades the board of directors he is right, but is unable to come up with the several hundred million dollars a traditional smelting mill costs. Instead, he comes up with a minimill concept, which will use electric arc furnaces to melt scrap (which is cheaper than iron ore) into the bar steel Vulcraft needs for its joists.

In 1968, with the help of a $6 million loan from the Wachovia Bank, Nuclear breaks ground for its minimill in Darlington, South Carolina. Iverson calls the project a "Bet-the-Company" risk. In July 1969, the mill comes on stream and a new era in the steel industry begins.

By 1970, the minimill produces more steel than Vulcraft needs and soon, Nuclear is selling steel to all comers, at prices that are well below those of Big Steel, the traditional integrated US steel makers. The company's profits start to grow. The company earns $1.1 million on $50 million in revenues in 1970, $2.7 million on $64 million in 1971, and $4.6 million on $83 million in 1972, when Nuclear Corporation of America takes a new name, Nucor Corporation.

In 1974, the company opens its second minimill in Norfolk, Nebraska. A third follows in 1975, and the original Darlington minimill is renovated in 1977. Nucor's net sales have surpassed $200 million and earnings exceed $12 million.

By 1980, Vulcraft is the leading joist maker in the US as Big Steel, unable to match Nucor's prices, abandons the market. The company expands into steel decking, also used in construction. That same year, Nucor Steel builds its fourth minimill in Plymouth, Utah. Nucor's annual revenues are approaching $500 million and profits are $45 million.

In 1985, the company opens Nucor Fastener, producing and selling bolts into a market that has been abandoned by the other US steel makers. The Saint Joe, Indiana plant is highly automated allowing Nucor to compete successfully against imports in the tight market. It is the only operating standard bolt factory in the country. Nucor revenues push past $750 million, earnings are $46 million.

By 1987, Nucor is the ninth largest steel maker in the US and will soon break $1 billion in annual revenues for the first time. Management decides it is time to enter the steel industry's largest single market, sheet steel.

Nucor makes its debut in the usual way, with an innovative plant that allows the company to cut costs by up to $75 per ton and price its steel well below the competition. It announces it will build the world's first continuous-cast flat rolled sheet steel mill in Crawfordsville, Indiana. It is the biggest challenge the company has ever undertaken and it requires that Nucor learn to cast steel continuously, a task that the industry has never before been able to accomplish.

In July 1988, the Blytheville, Arkansas beam mill melts its first heat of steel. By autumn, the plant is shipping finished I-beams.

In 1989, Crawfordsville mill begins continuously casting thin-slab sheet steel. Within the year, revenues rise to $1.4 billion and earnings to $75 million.

In 1992, Nucor opens its second sheet steel mill, located in Hickman, Arkansas. The plant has an annual capacity of one million tons. Scarcely two years later, its capacity is expanded to over two million tons. By 1993, revenues surpass $2 billion and earnings are $123 million.

In 1994, the company announces it next big innovation challenge with the establishment of the Nucor Iron Carbide plant in Trinidad. If the company can discover how to use iron carbide successfully in the steel making process, it can reduce the amount of scrap metal used to make steel by 20–50 percent. (Taken to its theoretical extremes, steel could be made with only iron carbide and oxygen.)

Big steel

By 1997, Nucor is Big Steel. It earns $294 million on almost $4.2 billion in sales. The company announces plans to construct a new mill in Berkeley County, South Carolina. The plant will produce wide-flange and bantam beams and have a capacity of 500,000 tons per year. Target completion is late 1998; estimated cost $150 million.

That same year, Nucor and Companhia Siderurgica Nacional, Latin America's largest steel maker, start exploring the feasibility of jointly constructing and operating a new steel mill in Brazil. The mill will produce hot-rolled, cold-rolled, and galvanized sheet steel.

Nucor also announces a major expansion to its Hickman, Arkansas sheet steel mill. It will add a cold rolling facility with 800,000 tons annual capacity; a galvanizing facility with 500,000 tons annual capacity; and associated pickling, oiling and annealing facilities.

In 1998, Nucor announces it will build its first steel plate plant, a $300 million minimill in Hertford County, North Carolina. Steel plate is used in the manufacture of rail cars, ships and barges, and refinery tanks. The one million ton capacity facility will bring the company's total production capacity to 12 million tons, bringing it within a million tons of its last Big Steel rival, the leading US steel producer, Pittsburgh-based USX-US Steel Group Inc.

Nucor also begins exploring the possibility of a thin-slab minimill in Coos Bay, Oregon. The sheet mill plant will be its first on the US West Coast, but development would not be complete until the early 2000s.

In December, the company announces that it is ending its investigation into a joint venture mill in Brazil. It cites the economic conditions in the US market and complications in Brazil.

In 1999, in the midst of flat sales, increased foreign competition, and lower earnings, Nucor is jolted by a management shake up. On January 1, 1999, F. Kenneth Iverson retires as Nucor's chairman. He is forced out by H. David Aycock and the board, according to media accounts.

Iverson's successor is CEO John Correnti, who lasts until June and then also resigns under pressure. Aycock, age 68 and previously retired, takes over as chairman and CEO, and appears to plan to keep the helm while he grooms a successor of his own choosing.

In early 2000, Nucor continues its quest for ever more efficient production. It partners with Australia's Broken Hill Proprietary Corporation and Japan's Ishikawajima-Harima Heavy Industries in a joint venture to license a new strip casting technology designed to be used in smaller, less expensive plants.

Nucor close-up

In 1965, Ken Iverson had just taken over the CEO spot at troubled Nuclear Corporation of America. He had one money-making division, a steel joist fabrication plant named Vulcraft, but it needed to reduce its dependence on purchased steel to increase its profitability. Iverson could not afford the huge blast furnaces and cost-intensive plants of traditional steel makers, so instead he decided to use an electric arc furnace to melt scrap metal for steel.

No one thought the idea had much merit, but Iverson pushed ahead anyway. In 1969, that first "minimill" came online and 30 years later, Nuclear Corp., now Nucor Corporation, is the second largest steel producer in the US and one of the world's lowest-cost steel manufacturers.

Nucor produced 10.3 million tons of steel in 1999, surpassing traditional market leaders such as Bethlehem Steel Corp. and LTV Steel Co. Inc., and hard on the trail of USX-US Steel. The company has literally reinvented the steel industry with the minimill concept, making steel by melting scrap metal in electric arc furnaces at a fraction of the cost and time of conventional steel making.

Nucor runs eight minimills with a ninth steel plate mill planned for the near future. It is 100 percent focused on making steel and steel products, such as steel-bearing components, metal buildings, cold-finished steel bars, hex bolts, and girders. Most of Nucor products are sold to service centers (or wholesalers) and end-product manufacturers. About 15 percent is sold to and used internally by the company's own fabricating divisions.

Nucor employs 7500 people and, with $547,762 in sales for each employee, it is highly productive. It operates using a highly decentralized management structure and is famous for its thrifty corporate culture. The company is headquartered on the first floor of a nondescript office building in Charlotte, North Carolina. It is staffed with less than 25 employees.

In 1999, revenues were $4.01 billion and generated net earning of $244 million. The company's total annual capacity is over 12 million tons and its operations are running at about 80 percent of capacity.

In addition to Nucor Steel, the minimill operator, the company runs eight businesses: Vulcraft, Nucor Cold Finish, Nucor-Yamato Steel Company, Nucor Fastener, Nucor Bearing Products, Nucor Building Systems, Nucor Grinding Balls, and Nucor Iron Carbide.

Nucor Steel

Nucor Steel's business is the manufacturing of steel. It produces bars, angles, light structural, sheet, and specialty steel products in seven minimills located in US states of South Carolina, Nebraska, Texas, Utah, Indiana, and Arkansas.

Nucor Steel's product line includes a wide range of coiled sheet, angles, straight-length and coiled rounds, channels, flats, forging billets and special small shapes. This is the steel used to make pipe, farm equipment, oil and gas equipment, mobile homes, transmission towers, bed frames, hand tools, automotive parts, highway signs, building construction, machinery and industrial equipment.

Four of the mills produce bar and light structural carbon and alloy steels. Their annual capacity is around three million tons. The three newest mills produce sheet steel. Ranging in age from 2 to 30 years old, all seven mills are among the most modern and efficient mills in the US.

Nucor-Yamato Steel Company

Nucor's eighth operating mill is a joint venture with Japanese steel maker Yamato Kogyo. Its revenues are about $900 million annually. It is Nucor's largest division and the company owns a 51 percent stake in the mill, which produces wide-flange steel beams, pilings, and other structural steel products using Yamato's continuous casting technology.

Originally constructed in 1993 and expanded 80 percent since then, the Blytheville, Arkansas plant has an annual capacity of over two million tons. Nucor-Yamato is one of the most productive structural mills in the world. It makes a ton of steel every seven-tenths of a man-hour.

Vulcraft

Acquired in 1962, when Nucor was still Nuclear Corp., Vulcraft has grown to become the largest US producer of steel joists, joist girders, and steel deck for building construction. Its 1999 annual sales of 616,000 tons of joists and girders represent about 40 percent of the US domestic market. It also sold 375,000 tons of steel decking.

The company's joists and joist girders are used in manufacturing buildings, retail stores, shopping centers, warehouses, schools, churches, hospitals and, to a lesser extent, in multi-story buildings, apartments and single-family dwellings. The steel decking is used in the same buildings in roofs and floors.

The cost of the steel represents about 45 percent of the joist sales dollar. Vulcraft gets 90 percent of its steel from Nucor Steel. Steel joists and joist girder sales are obtained by competitive bidding and Vulcraft submits quotes on between 80 and 90 percent of all projects using steel joists and joist girders.

The division has five plants, all close to Nucor Steel mills, in South Carolina, Nebraska, Alabama, Texas, and Indiana. Each plant has district sales offices located throughout its region.

Nucor Cold Finish

Nucor Cold Finish produces cold drawn and turned, ground and polished steel bars. The bars are made in carbon and alloy steels in rounds, hexagons, flats, and squares. Cold finished steel products are used extensively for shafting and machined precision parts.

The division has three facilities, in Nebraska, South Carolina, and Utah. Its total capacity is 350,000 tons per year. In 1999, it produced 243,000 tons mainly from steel produced at nearby Nucor Steel mills.

Nucor Fastener

Nucor Fastener produces standard steel hexhead cap screws, hex bolts, socket head cap screws, and structural bolts that are used in a broad range of markets, including automotive, machine tools, farm implements, construction, and military applications.

The division maintains two US facilities in Saint Joe, Indiana and Conway, Arkansas. Annual capacity is close to 115,000 tons.

Nucor Bearing Products, Inc.

Wilson, North Carolina-based Nucor Bearing produces and sells steel bearing components in heat-treated, fully machined, or as-forged condition. These are sold to companies in the bearing industry for inclusion in finished products such as automobiles, office equipment, electric motors, farm equipment and materials handling equipment.

The 177,000 square foot facility employs 180 people in a just-in-time operation that features low inventory levels and short lead times. To capitalize on its cost advantages in the marketplace, the facility is currently expanding and will increase its size to 250,000 square feet and its capacity by more than 250 percent.

Nucor Building Systems

Nucor Building Systems fabricates pre-engineered metal building systems with solid-web and open-web framing. These buildings range in size from less than 500 square feet to more than 1,000,000 square feet and are used in commercial, industrial, and institutional settings. The buildings are sold through a builder distribution network.

The division has two plants in the US. One is in Indiana; the other is in South Carolina. Together they have an annual capacity of about 100,000 tons, most of which is supplied by Nucor Steel.

Nucor Grinding Balls

Started in 1980, Nucor Grinding Balls is a specialty shop serving the mining industry. Mining companies use grinding balls in the processing of copper, iron, zinc, lead, gold, silver, and other ores. Based in Brigham City, Utah, the division is located close to its customers' operations in the US western states.

Nucor Iron Carbide, Inc.

The company's only international venture is the Nucor Iron Carbide facility in Trinidad, which opened in 1994. The plant produces iron carbide for use in the steel manufacturing process. In 1998, it produced about 200,000 tons of iron carbide, but operations have been suspended in search of a technological breakthrough in the production process. Nucor Iron Carbide is not profitable.

Income statement

Year	Revenue ($m)	Net income ($m)	Net profit margin	Employees
1999	4,009.3	244.6	6.1%	7,500
1998	4,151.2	263.7	6.4%	7,200
1997	4,184.5	294.5	7.0%	6,900
1996	3,647.0	248.2	6.8%	6,600
1995	3,462.0	274.5	7.9%	6,200
1994	2,975.6	226.6	7.6%	5,900
1993	2,253.7	123.5	5.5%	5,900
1992	1,619.2	79.2	4.9%	5,800
1991	1,465.5	64.7	4.4%	5,600
1990	1,481.6	75.1	5.1%	5,500

Stock history

Year	Stock price ($) FY High	FY Low	FY Close	P/E High	Low	Per share ($) Earns	Div.	Book value
1999	61.81	41.63	54.81	22	15	2.80	0.51	25.96
1998	60.63	35.25	43.25	20	12	3.00	0.46	23.73
1997	62.94	44.75	48.31	19	13	3.35	0.38	21.32
1996	63.88	45.13	51.00	23	16	2.83	0.31	18.33
1995	63.25	42.00	57.13	20	13	3.13	0.26	15.78
1994	72.00	48.75	55.38	28	19	2.60	0.18	12.85
1993	57.25	38.00	53.00	40	27	1.42	0.16	10.36
1992	39.94	20.94	39.19	43	23	0.92	0.14	9.04
1991	22.38	14.25	22.34	30	19	0.75	0.13	8.23
1990	20.44	12.06	15.50	23	14	0.88	0.12	7.70

1999 year-end financials

Debt ratio	14.7%
Return on equity	11.3%
Cash ($m)	572.2
Current ratio	2.90
Long-term debt ($m)	390.5
Shares outstanding (millions)	87.1
Dividend yield	0.9%
Dividend payout	18.2%
Market value ($m)	4,775.8

Financial data provided by Hoover's Online (www.hoovers.com) and Media General Financial Services, Inc.

Nucor contacts

Nucor Corporation   Phone: 704–366–7000
2100 Rexford Road   Fax: 704–362–4208
Charlotte, NC 28211, USA   URL: www.nucor.com

CEO: H. David Aycock   CFO: Terry Lisenby   HR: Jim Coblin

Quebecor, Inc. –
Montreal, Quebec, Canada

Executive snapshot

As new CEO Pierre Karl Peladeau takes the reins at Quebecor, the vertically integrated empire founded on a single community newspaper by his
father, he suggests the future "will see our different businesses working
more closely together to allow us to offer our customers the integrated
benefits of our publishing, printing, on-line and broadcasting services."

Quebecor backdrop

Opportunity is the operative word in Quebecor's history. Company
founder and CEO, until his death at age 72 in 1997, Pierre Peladeau
intuitively understood the competitive openings created by changes
in the business environment and acted quickly to grasp their full potential.

The newspaperman

Pierre Peladeau's mother cannot be pleased. Her son is fresh out of law
school and ready to sit for the Bar exam and now this. He fancies him-

Future focus

Building a Canadian house

If you had to pick one product that a Canadian company could use to build a worldwide empire, that product would have to be paper. Not only does Canada have the world's largest forest reserves, but also the country sits on top of the United States, the world's largest user of paper and newsprint products.

Quebecor has skillfully used its Canadian heritage to build a corporation that dominates many aspects of the paper industry, from the production of newsprint to the printing business to the publication of magazines and newspapers.

The history of Quebecor illustrates a number of important lessons for any would-be worldwide entrepreneur.

Start small. Like many other giant enterprises, Quebecor was started with a single entity, a neighborhood weekly newspaper that was losing money.

To be successful in the world today, you have to play with the cards you were dealt. Too many ambitious people would have said: "What possible giant corporation could I build with a small weekly newspaper?" And then they would have looked elsewhere.

Repeat success. After making his single newspaper profitable, Pierre Peladeau immediately repeated his success by starting four more local papers that duplicated the pattern of his first one.

This is a critical step to a successful career or a successful corporation. Keep doing the things that made you successful in the first place. This is not an easy pattern to follow. The grass is always greener on the other side of the corporate fence.

Seize the opportunity when it occurs. In the career of every hugely successful person, there seems to be a single occurrence that proves to be decisive. When Altair, the first personal computer, needed an operating system, Bill Gates quit Harvard to set up the world's first personal computer software company. When his computer assembly business started to take off, Michael Dell quit the University of Texas to focus on direct sales of personal computers.

When Montreal's largest French-language newspaper was shut down by a strike, Pierre Peladeau seized the opportunity to launch a new daily newspaper featuring the same editorial mix (sports, crime and girls) he had used in the weeklies. The new paper was called *Le Journal de Montreal*.

After the Montreal paper became successful, he repeated his success by starting *Le Journal de Quebec*.

Go public as soon as possible. If you want to build a giant corporation, you need to have a public corporation. It's a lot easier to buy companies with paper than it is to buy them with real money. It took Pierre Peladeau several years to find an underwriter for his stock issue, but he finally did so. This step provided the basis for an aggressive acquisition program.

Vertically integrate in low-technology areas. Vertical integration is always a good idea from a financial point of view. The problem is technology. If you integrate, you run the risk that your production facility can be made obsolete by innovations in technology.

Should a computer manufacturer integrate into microprocessors? Probably not. This is one of the reasons that companies like Silicon Graphics got into trouble. In a high-technology area, you need to narrow your focus to stay ahead of competition.

In Quebecor's case, vertical integration into printing, newsprint production and forest services was a good idea.

Go global. There are almost no reasons why any financially healthy company should not expand globally, using the same product or services and the same strategies.

This is exactly what Quebecor did. It bought printing and publishing companies in Mexico, India, France, the UK, Chile, Argentina, Norway, Sweden, Colombia and Spain.

Today Quebecor has a leading position in many parts of the world. It is:

- the largest printing company in the world;
- the second largest newspaper publisher in Canada; and
- the world's fourth largest newsprint producer.

Where Quebecor is missing the boat, in our opinion, is their recent expansion into television, multimedia and retailing. These operations have little to do with Quebecor's basic business. Further, for the most part, these operations are unprofitable.

self a newspaper magnate and not just any newspaper, but one that is in such dire financial straits that it has stopped publishing altogether.

Yet, like all great mothers, she supports him and in the process becomes the enabling force behind the founding of Quebecor. In 1950, Mme. Peladeau loans her son C$1500 and he buys a neighborhood weekly paper in Montreal, *Le Journal de Rosemont*, that is hovering on the brink of failure and has actually stopped printing.

The 25-year-old publisher starts his career as a jack-of-all-trades, writing, selling ads, and even distributing the newspaper himself. Peladeau finds he has a flair for promotion and one of his first attention-grabbing projects is a Miss Rosemont beauty contest, with an emphasis on the swimsuit competition.

The contest is a success (in fact, Miss Rosemont goes on to become Miss Canada) and Peladeau adopts the tabloid format. He revives his paper with a titillating mix of entertainment, sports, and crime news.

"At the end of the year, there was $134 in the cashbox," Peladeau tells a reporter from *Forces* magazine in 1997. "I was thrilled. I had won the battle and felt the rest would happen on its own."

Cash-strapped, but undaunted, Peladeau creates Les Publications Indépendantes to house his future empire. In the next four years, the publisher starts four more local weeklies in the image of the Rosemont paper.

In 1953, Peladeau's weeklies are produced by Montreal's sole French language printer. When the printer begins financing a competitor's paper, Peladeau realizes that unless he finds another alternative, his hard-earned cash will end up financing the competition.

The alternative presents itself in 1954, when newspaper *Le Canada* goes on the block. First, Peladeau unsuccessfully attempts to buy the paper itself. Then, he convinces the buyer to sell him the paper's printing presses. The new printing business is set up on Plessis Street in Montreal. It is the first printing facility of the newly formed Imprimerie Hebdo group.

During the second half of the 1950s, Peladeau continues to develop his small fiefdom. In the early 1960s, however, unhappy with the revenue potential generated by a hodgepodge of properties, he decides to refocus on a more popular format with centralized operations.

Peladeau sells off the neighborhood newspapers. He acquires and creates seven entertainment weeklies. He also divests his company's printing assets and centralizes the printing of all his new publications with the acquisition of Montreal Offset.

The strategy works. Soon the entertainment portfolio is generating 500,000 copies per week and Peladeau's companies hit C$1 million in annual revenues for the first time.

Moving up to the dailies

In 1964, when Montreal's largest French-language daily newspaper, *La Presse*, is shut down by a strike, the opportunistic entrepreneur strikes again. Peladeau realizes that it is the perfect time to launch a competing paper.

As company legend has it, within a week, the first edition of a new daily tabloid *Le Journal de Montréal* is off the presses and on the streets. It features the same mix of sensationalized news used in the earlier neighborhood weeklies – heavy on sports, crime, and pin-up girls; no editorials.

The strike lingers on for seven months and *Le Journal de Montréal* is quickly accepted by the news-hungry public. However, with the home-town favorite back on the newsstands, the *Journal*'s circulation crashes to 15,000 copies.

"During the first week *La Presse* got back to work after the strike, the circulation of *Le Journal de Montréal*, which had reached 80,000, began falling off," remembered Peladeau. "I called in my advisors and asked them what they thought. I had made a profit of $100,000 during the strike. They urged me to take the money and run to the bank." It is advice that Peladeau wholly ignores. He decides the new paper will live and begins a recovery program that will extend for four years and cost over C$600,000.

In 1965, faced with a distributor who is unwilling to offer Peladeau the aggressive support he needs to rebuild circulation, the publisher builds his own distribution company. In the space of a single day, he buys 50 trucks and strikes a deal with outlet owners. Messageries Dynamiques is born. In the same year, Quebecor is created as a centralized command post for the management of the printing, newspaper, and distribution businesses.

In 1967, while still battling to rebuild circulation at the Montreal daily, Peladeau launches *Le Journal de Québec*. In 1968, Peladeau centralizes financial control by transferring his various ownership stakes into Quebecor, Inc.

By 1969, *Le Journal de Montréal* returns to profitability and circulation stabilizes at 50,000. Quebecor also acquires the largest entertainment weekly in Quebec, *Echos Vedettes*.

Going public ... south of the border

In the early 1970s, Peladeau is ready to take Quebecor public, but cannot find an underwriter in Montreal's English-dominated financial community. In the meantime, the acquisitions continue as he builds the group's revenues and assets.

In 1971, Quebecor buys two Canadian printing companies, including Graphic Web in Ontario, the company's first printer outside of Quebec. The company also establishes a new printing unit Imprimerie Montréal-Magog, which is aimed at the US market. The newspapers are organized under the Publications Quebecor subsidiary.

With typical aplomb, Peladeau decides that if Montreal will not underwrite his company, perhaps New York might. And, in 1972, New York does.

In August, Quebecor becomes the first Canadian company to sell shares over-the-counter in the US before they are available in its home country. In November that year, the company is belatedly listed on the Montreal Exchange and in January 1973, Quebecor is accepted on the American Stock Exchange. By year-end 1972, Peladeau's mother's investment of C$1500 in a neighborhood weekly has grown into a company with C$30 million in annual revenue and profits of over C$1 million.

A full war chest puts Peladeau back on the acquisitions trail. During the next few years, Quebecor establishes its book publishing division and acquires Service de Musique Trans-Canada Ltd in the music distribution business. By the mid-70s, the company is one of the largest offset printers in Canada. Along the way, revenues rise to C$55 million and profits triple to C$3 million.

In 1977, Peladeau makes an unusual misstep when he attempts to crack the US newspaper market with a new daily in Philadelphia. The *Philadelphia Journal* brings the Quebecor's proven Canadian format to the US and in six months, the company builds a circulation of 100,000.

The existing paper, however, proves unwilling to share the market. It adopts changes to match the *Journal's* format and cuts advertising rates. Peladeau fights back for years, but to no avail. The *Journal* folds in 1980, leaving behind C$17 million in red ink.

The new decade also sees Quebecor in a new business. The company and Peladeau's daughter, Isabelle, enter magazine publishing with the launch of *Filles d'Aujourd'hui*.

Building the cash cows

In the 1980s, Quebecor's media ventures provide the company a high-profile in its hometown, but they are high-overhead, low-margin businesses, and Pierre Peladeau is thinking more and more about the bottom line. "The greatest goal of our business is profits," he declares in the company's annual report. "If we don't have profit, we don't have a business anymore."

In the mid-1980s, the CEO turns words into action by building the company's two international revenue generators, paper and printing, via an aggressive acquisition program. The first deal outside Canada is consummated in 1985, when Quebecor buys Michigan-based Pendell Printing, Inc. The magazine printer expands the company's capabilities in the US and serves as the impetus for the founding of Quebecor America, Inc.

In 1987, Peladeau hooks up with Robert Maxwell, head of the Mirror Newspaper Group, who is on a worldwide acquisitions spree. Together, they form Mircor, Inc. and for C$320 million buy a 54 percent stake in Donohue, Inc. Quebecor's 51 percent share gives it a controlling interest in the forest services company and gives its publishing and printing businesses a steady source for the paper and pulp products on which they depend.

In 1988, Peladeau spearheads another major acquisition when he purchases BCE Publitech, Inc, the printing operations of Bell Canada, for C$161 million and 21 percent share of Quebecor. The deal makes Quebecor Canada's largest commercial printer.

Donohue goes on the acquisition trail also, bringing in Canada's Gerard Saucier group with woodlands and three sawmills. That year, Quebecor breaks the C$1 billion mark in annual revenues.

Maxwell and Peladeau form something of a team. In 1988, they join forces to launch an ill-fated English-language paper, *The Daily News*, in Montreal.

In 1990, Quebecor buys Maxwell Graphics, Inc., with its 14 US printing businesses. Peladeau makes a fine deal, paying Maxwell US$510 million for the unit and establishing Quebecor Printing, Inc. (QPI), in which Maxwell takes a 25 percent stake for US$100 million.

By 1990, Peladeau has made no fewer than 64 acquisitions in a decade. He has driven revenues from under C$400 million to over C$2 billion in just five years, and turned Quebecor into a vertically integrated business.

Beyond North America

In 1991, the Maxwell connection comes undone when the Czech refugee turned British business tycoon drowns under mysterious circumstances. Shortly afterward, the news breaks that his empire is a house of cards, bankrupt and barely supported by the looting of its employees' pensions.

The collapse of Maxwell's enterprise is an opportunity for Quebecor, which promptly buys in his stake in QPI for US$5 million less than Maxwell paid three years before.

The early 1990s bring recession to the paper markets and Donohue spends the first half of the decade running a losing race. The losses keep Quebecor revenues flat to down and impact profits.

Printing subsidiary QPI has no such problems, however, and it embarks on what will be a decade-long expansion program. In 1991, it makes its first move outside North America with the cautious purchase of Mexican book printer Graficas Monte Alban, SA.

In 1992, QPI goes public and in 1993, it acquires book, magazine, and catalog publisher Arcata Corp. in the US and establishes a joint venture with the Tej Bandhu Group in India to build a telephone directory printing plant. The commercial printer enters Europe acquiring France's Groupe Fécomme. In 1994, it gobbles up the UK's HunterPrint Group plc, which prints weekend magazines and supplements for newspapers.

That same year, eldest son Erik convinces the aging CEO to venture into new media with the founding of Quebecor Multimedia Inc. "I told [Erik] we could climb aboard if he wanted," explains Peladeau in an interview, "and it was enough that he understood things. There is no need for the two of us."

In 1995, QPI goes back to France and purchases Group Jean Didier, the largest commercial printer in that country. That year, Quebecor recovers with a roar. Annual revenues hit C$5.5 billion and net income is C$186 million.

In 1996, Donohue joins the fray with the acquisition of QUNO Corporation, formerly the Chicago Tribune's Quebec and Ontario Paper Company. The C$1.1 billion purchase doubles Donohue's size.

Less successful is Peladeau's C$350 million bid to acquire Canada's chain of Sun papers being sold off by Roger's Corp. After a hard-hitting fight, where Peladeau is subjected to personal attacks in the media, the chain is bought out by the employees for C$445 million. "They won't be able to make it at $445 million," says Peladeau. "It's impossible. We can wait."

The year ends with C$6.2 billion in revenues and declining net income of C$146 million.

In 1997, Quebecor decides to try television and acquires a majority interest in TQS, Inc., the Télévision Quatre Saisons network. QPI moves into South America with the purchase of Editorial Antártica SA, Chile's second largest printer, and Argentina's Editorial Antártica SACIFE. It continues growing in the US market, purchasing Petty Co., a US$125 million specialty printer, and AmerSig Graphics, Inc., a catalog and magazine printer with annual revenues of US$210 million. In September 1997, QPI also buys the Franklin, Kentucky division of the Brown Printing Company.

The year ends in tragedy, however. In early December, Pierre Peladeau suffers a heart attack in his office. He slips into a coma and, fighter to the end, hangs on to life until December 24. He leaves behind a C$7 billion empire.

A well-oiled machine

Doubts about Quebecor's ability to survive the loss of its founder are quickly put to rest. Jean Neveu, a veteran executive, steps in as CEO and the company continues to expand its global reach.

In 1998, QPI's purchase of Tryckinvest i Norden AB (TINA), the largest commercial printer in the Nordic countries, makes it a pan-European printer. In South America, QPI purchases Asociación Editorial Stella, Peru's largest printer and a producer of books, magazines and directories, and Impreandes Presencia SA, one of Colombia's largest book printers.

In June, Donohue makes its second largest acquisition with the purchase of the newsprint division of Champion International Corporation. It makes the company the second largest newsprint producer in the US.

In the same month, the multimedia unit doubles the size of its Intellia consulting group when it merges with Socom, one of the largest Quebec graphic and interactive communications firms. It also becomes the first company to move into Montreal's new high-tech haven Cité du Multimédia.

The big news is made in December, when Quebecor finally captures the Sun newspaper chain, now operating as Sun Media Corp. Pierre Peladeau was right, they couldn't make it, but he surely would not be happy with the C$1 billion purchase price. The acquisition is completed in January 1999, and makes Quebecor owner of the only nationwide newspaper chain in Canada and the second largest newspaper publisher in the country.

In 1999, QPI becomes South America's largest printer with the purchase of Editorial Perfil, the largest publisher in Argentina. It also acquires the second largest printer in Spain, Cayfo, SA, and in its biggest acquisition to date, the company buys US-based printer World Color Press for US$2.7 billion. On February 15, Jean Neveu moves up to the company's chairmanship and Pierre Karl Peladeau, the founder's second son, becomes president and CEO of Quebecor.

Unhappily, the entire Peladeau family is not thrilled with the turn of events and its members file lawsuits against each other and the estate's executor in a battle for control of family assets, including the company.

In 2000, the company starts to move out of the forest products business when it announces it will sell off its controlling stake in Donohue to Abitibi-Consolidated. It also changes the name of its printing subsidiary to Quebecor World, Inc. to better reflect the global nature of the business. Early in the year, Quebecor makes a bid to expand it media businesses with a $4 billion offer for Quebec's largest cable firm, Le Groupe Videotron. The deal is rebuffed.

Quebecor close-up

From the trees in the forest to the news-stand, bookstore, and mailbox, Quebecor Inc. controls the flow of paper in a wide diversity of forms. Quebecor is the high-profile publisher of Canada's only national chain of newspapers, but the fine print reveals a deeper story: the engines that keep its presses turning are upstream from its publishing ventures. Forest products and commercial printing are the businesses that deliver the lion's share of the company's C$10.8 billion annual revenue.

Quebecor is one of Montreal's leading companies, and that city is where its late founder and architect, Pierre Peladeau, starred in the role of media mogul. Peladeau's huge entrepreneurial talent, his outspokenness and flair for controversy, and his battles with alcoholism and manic depression combined to make him a larger-than-life figure and a hometown favorite.

Quebecor is still controlled by the Peladeau family. Three of the founder's children are executives in the company. The youngest son, Pierre Karl Peladeau, took over as Quebecor's CEO in 1999.

The bulk of Quebecor's business and roughly 79 percent of its 1999 revenues are generated in Canada and the US. The company has made significant expansion moves in Europe, and has operations in South America and Asia also. Quebecor employs 60,000 people working in 15 countries.

On the 50th anniversary of its founding, Quebecor is a vertically integrated publishing company. It controls major businesses in three industry sectors: forest products, printing, and newspaper publishing.

Until 1999, the newspaper business was part of the company's communications subsidiary. That subsidiary has now split into three units: newspapers, multimedia, and what is left of the former communications company (a less-than-ideally focused basket of businesses including among other things, television stations, magazine and book publishing, and retail stores.)

Quebecor World, Inc.

Quebecor World, Inc. (QWI) is the world's largest commercial printer. QWI owns 160 printing facilities in 15 countries. It employs over 40,000 people worldwide.

In 1999, QWI's revenues rose to C$7.3 billion generating net income of C$703 million. Parent company Quebecor, Inc. receives 48.5 percent of the publicly held printer's earnings and controls 81 percent of the subsidiary's voting rights.

Geographically, the US is QWI's largest market, contributing just over C$4.3 billion in gross revenues. Canada is the company's second largest market with C$1.4 billion in revenues. QWI is aggressively expanding in Europe, with facilities in France, the UK, Spain, Sweden and Finland. In 1999, European revenues hit C$1.4 billion.

QWI is the largest commercial printer in South America with plants in Chile, Argentina, Peru, and Colombia, and intends to continue to expand in that market. Revenues in 1999 were C$144 million. The company also owns Tej-Quebecor Printing Ltd in India and Graficas Monte Alban in Mexico.

The company's main technologies are rotogravure and offset printing. It operates in seven market segments: magazines; advertising inserts and circulars; catalogs; books; direct mail and specialty printing; pre-press technologies; and CD-ROM production.

Magazine printing is QWI's largest business, accounting for roughly 30 percent of the group's revenues at C$2.17 billion. It is the printer of popular magazines, such as *Sports Illustrated*, *Fortune*, *Forbes Global*, *Le Figaro*, and *TV Guide*.

QWI magazine operations are high tech, offering advanced bindery technologies, mass customization ink jet addressing and messaging, and versioning. With *Money* magazine, for instance, the 2.4 million circulation is served by up to 3000 versions of each issue, each of which contains its own mix of editorial and advertising copy designed for different reader groups.

The production of advertising inserts and circulars was a C$1.54 billion business for QWI in 1999. Sears, JC Penney, and Radio Shack are among the company's customers in this segment. QWI is also the source of a good number of the direct marketing catalogs that jam mailboxes these days. Using many of the same technologies as used for magazines, the company printed C$1.1 billion worth of catalogs in 1999. Customers included major retailers, such as Office Depot and L.L. Bean.

Even with declines in demand, and hot competition, QWI manufactures over 300 million books annually. The company is the second largest book printer in the US, and in 1999 that added up to C$959 million in revenues. Customers include Random House, the American Management Association, and the Hearst Book Group.

In 1999, QWI also generated C$789 million in direct mail and specialty printing, C$397 million in pre-press services and CD-ROM sales, and C$348 million in directory printing for telephone companies in the US, the Caribbean, and India.

Donohue, Inc.

Moving further upstream, Quebecor's Donohue subsidiary is an integrated forest products company with operations in Canada and the US. Its woodlands operations are the source of raw timber, which is processed into dimension lumber and wood chips at the unit's sawmills. Wood from these operations and its recycling centers is sent to Donohue's paper and pulp mills.

In 1999, Donohue's revenues totaled C$2.48 billion with net earnings of C$212 million. Quebecor owns a 19.63 percent stake in Donohue and controls the company through a 63.22 percent share of its voting rights. Donohue owns 30-odd plants in North America and employs

8000 people. It operates in three core businesses: newsprint; market pulp; and lumber. It also owns paper recyclers and energy plants.

The largest Canadian lumber producer east of the Rocky Mountains, Donohue has 17 sawmills that turned out 1.2 billion board feet of pine in 1998 – close to its total capacity of 1.4 billion board feet. The wood chips that are byproducts of these operations are used in the company's pulp and paper mills.

Donohue owns three pulp mills in North America, which produced 393,000 metric tons in 1989. Current capacity is 581,000 tons. The pulp is used to make paper, newsprint, tissues, and paperboard.

The company is the world's fourth largest newsprint producer. Its seven newsprint and paper mills generated over two million metric tons of product in 1998; their full annual capacity is 2.4 million tons.

Donohue's raw material needs are also filled by its recycling operations, which consist of three facilities in Toronto, Canada and three in the US in Texas. In 1998, they produced over 450,000 tons of recycled paper, supplying 75 percent of the needs of the company's newsprint plants.

The forest products company owns a 60 percent stake in Canada's Manicouagan Power Company. Its hydroelectric plant provides the power for several of the company's Canadian mills.

In 2000, Quebecor announced the sale of its stake in Donohue to Abitibi-Consolidated.

Quebecor Communications, Inc.

In 1999, Quebecor Communications, Inc. (QCI) was the home of all of the company's downstream businesses – newspapers and magazine publishing, broadcast units, etc. These businesses are concentrated in Canada. And, despite contributing only C$247 million to Quebecor's total revenues, QCI receives a disproportionate amount of attention.

With the acquisition of Canadian newspaper company Sun Media, QCI was reorganized into three units and the subsidiary was stripped of it new media ventures and newspapers, leaving it with operations in broadcasting, retailing and distribution, and book and magazine publishing.

Broadcasting

Acquired in 1997, TQS, Inc. operates a general-interest French-language television network. TQS owns the television stations CFJP in Montreal and CFAP in Quebec City, as well as a relay transmitter in Rimouski. The network has also attracted three affiliates, including COGECO in Trois-Rivières, Sherbrooke, and Saguenay-Lac-Saint-Jean, Radio-Nord in Ottawa-Hull and Val-d'Or, and Télévision MBS, which operates a relay transmitter service in Rivière-du-Loup, Madawaska, Victoria, on the North Shore, in Carleton and at Baie-des-Chaleurs.

One of four French-language networks in Quebec, TQS reaches 97.5 percent of the broadcast area in the province. It is not profitable, but QCI targets a profit for the year 2001. Toward that end, it has positioned itself as the "black sheep of French-language television." TQS has taken aim at viewers between 18 and 49 years of age, with an irreverent mix of new shows, live broadcasts, premier movies, and a lengthened broadcast day.

Retailing and distribution

QCI owns Groupe Archambault, Quebec's leader in the retailing and distribution of CDs, books, news-stand publications, musical instruments, and sheet music. The company operates 12 Archambault superstores, four smaller Globe Musique stores, and a portfolio of distribution companies, including Distribution Select, Musicor/GAM, Musicor/GAM Video and Distribution Trans-Canada.

The Archambault stores offer customers 200,000 album titles, 100,000 book titles, 50,000 newspaper and magazine titles, 8000 video titles and more than 2000 multimedia titles, all under one roof. One location in the chain is the largest music, video, and bookstore in Canada. It is largest chain of record and CD stores in eastern Canada and the second-largest chain of French-language bookstores in Quebec.

The Distribution Select, Distribution Trans-Canada, Musicor/GAM and Musicor/GAM Video units distribute music and video products nationwide. Distribution Select and Musicor/GAM were the exclusive distributors of 26 of the 40 best-selling French-language albums in Quebec in 1998. At the end of 1999, Distribution Select was the largest independent distributor in Canada and Distribution Trans-Canada was the largest wholesaler in the record and video sector in Quebec.

Book and CD-ROM publishing
OCI's publishing unit is the largest publisher of French-language books in Quebec. Its principal market segments include general literature, textbooks, legal texts, and contract publishing. QCI also distributes books through Logidisque, which represents about 20 foreign publishers.

In 1998, QCI added CD-ROM publishing to its group when it acquired a 100 percent interest in Quebecor DIL Multimedia Inc., one of the largest distributors of French-language CD-ROMs in Canada, and a majority interest in St. Remy Multimedia Inc., which markets books and multimedia products in the US market.

Magazine publishing
QCI publishes a variety of magazines in several subject areas:

- women's magazines include *Femme Plus*, *Clin d'Oeil*, and *Filles d'Aujourd'hui*;
- interior design and home improvement magazines include *Les idées de ma maison*, *Décoration Chez-Soi* and *Rénovation-Bricolage*, as well as specialty seasonal magazines, such as *Cuisines et salles de bain*, *Portes et fenêtres*, *Piscines Terrasses et Jardins*, and *Le guide de la rénovation*; and
- entertainment weekly *Échos Vedettes*.

Sun Media Corporation
New Quebecor subsidiary Sun Media Corporation is the home to all the company's newspapers, making it the second largest publisher of daily newspapers in Canada and the only nationwide chain. Its papers include eight urban dailies, seven community dailies, 152 weekly papers and buyer's guides, and 19 other publications.

Sun has a presence in eight of the ten largest markets in the country and a 21.6 percent market share. The combined weekly circulation of the company's newspapers is over seven million copies. Its 1999 revenues were C$827 million.

Sun Media owns Canada's second and third largest dailies: *Le Journal de Montréal*, which is ranked first in Quebec with half of that market's classified advertising; and *The Toronto Sun*. Other leading daily papers include *Le Journal de Québec*, *The Winnipeg Sun*, *The Edmonton Sun*, *The*

Calgary Sun, *The Ottawa Sun*, *The Brockville Recorder and Times*, and the 150-year-old *London Free Press*.

Among Sun Media's 150-odd weeklies are newspapers in the Canadian provinces of Quebec, Manitoba, Alberta, Ontario, and Saskatchewan.

The subsidiary also owns a 29.9 percent share of Cable Pulse 24, a joint venture all-news cable station, broadcasting 24 hours a day in Toronto. Using an exclusive multi-screen system, CP24 pools the news resources of *The Toronto Sun* and regional television and radio companies.

Quebecor New Media, Inc.

The bailiwick of Quebecor's founder's eldest son, Erik Peladeau, Quebecor New Media, Inc. (QNMI) is home to the company's ventures online. Founded in 1994, the unit operated at a loss until 1999, when revenues hit C$25 million. Currently, its main businesses are Intellia, Inc. and newly acquired online service, Canoe.

Intellia Inc. is an Internet consulting firm with offices in Montreal, Toronto and Seattle. It offers an array of services including strategic consulting in interactive communications, the integration and development of transactional systems and databases, graphic and systems design, Web site hosting, and network installation.

Intellia clients include Nortel, Air Canada Vacations, and Canadian Tire. It has also developed classroom planning tools for US publisher Prentice Hall and multilingual instructional applications in 12 languages for Hewlett-Packard.

Canoe is a limited partnership originally formed by Sun Media (60 percent) and BCE Media Investments (40 percent). Canoe pursues two strategic objectives: the first is to provide a portal onto the World Wide Web and the second is the development of topical online sites.

These include: C-Health in health and wellbeing; JAM! Showbiz with the most exhaustive national film catalogue in Canada; SLAM! Sports which includes the official Canadian Web site of Major League Baseball; and the first online hockey subscription product in the country, SLAM! Hockey PLUS. Canoe also owns and operates financial site Canoe Money, the Trading Post online store, and a 75 percent stake in Autonet.Ca, the best-known online automobile service in Canada.

Income statement

Year	Revenue ($m)	Net income ($m)	Net profit margin	Employees
1998	5,485.6	112.4	2.0%	39,000
1997	4,905.6	100.2	2.0%	37,000
1996	4,562.8	107.1	2.3%	33,700
1995	4,069.6	136.9	3.4%	28,900
1994	2,834.2	63.2	2.2%	25,900
1993	2,324.3	56.4	2.4%	20,600
1992	1,994.3	68.7	3.4%	16,500
1991	2,051.8	16.0	0.8%	16,400
1990	2,098.1	67.2	3.2%	17,100
1989	1,515.9	16.0	1.1%	—

1998 year-end financials

Debt ratio	67.8%
Return on equity	—
Cash ($m)	89.1
Current ratio	1.32
Long-term debt ($m)	1,955.6

Financial data provided by Hoover's Online (www.hoovers.com) and Media General Financial Services, Inc.

Quebecor contacts

Quebecor, Inc.
612 Saint-Jacques Street
Montreal, Quebec
Canada H3C 4M8

Phone: (514) 877–9777
Fax: (514) 877–9757
URL: www.quebecor.com

CEO: Pierre Karl Péladeau   CFO: François R. Roy   HR: Julie Tremblay

Royal Dutch/Shell Group – The Hague, The Netherlands

Executive snapshot

In the 21st century, Royal Dutch/Shell believes its major product, crude oil, will be eclipsed as renewables take a leading role in energy production.

"Most people in the world still lack adequate access to convenient affordable energy. There is demand everywhere for cleaner energy. Meeting those demands offers commercial opportunities," says Mark Moody-Stuart, chairman, Royal Dutch/Shell group.

Shell backdrop

Two men create the foundation that grows to become the $100 billion Royal Dutch/Shell Group. They never meet and neither has anything in common with the other, except the entrepreneur's willingness to pursue a business opportunity, no matter what obstacles stand in the way.

The prospector and the trader

It is a love affair gone bad that drives Aeilko Jans Zijlker away from home and family in Groningen province of the northern Netherlands in 1860. The 20-year-old books passage for the Dutch East Indies and

Future focus

The case for diversity

An oil company lives or dies on its success in finding enough "black gold" to fill its tankers, refineries and gasoline stations. Royal Dutch/Shell has found more than its share, currently some 14 percent of the world's oil. Sooner or later every oil field will be depleted so the driving force of the company is "the discovery of new sources of supply."

Unlike more conventional businesses, there is a great deal of uncertainty in the oil business. Literally a company doesn't know where its next oil field will come from. In this environment, the managers who run companies like Royal Dutch/Shell need an exceptional dose of curiosity, open-mindedness, creativity and a willingness to take the huge risks needed to find new fields.

Could Royal Dutch/Shell's unusual organization account for its unusual success? I think so. Here is a corporation 60 percent owned by "Royal Dutch," a Netherlands company and 40 percent by "Shell," a UK company. Add to this a board of directors with no operating responsibilities and a chairmanship that rotates between the Netherlands and the UK and you have a most unusual company.

I think this may be the answer. Shell's unusual organization is the reason why the company is often called "the most cosmopolitan corporation in the world." Shell is a singular company with a singular mission run by a managerial group noted for its diversity. Shell managers literally consider themselves citizens of the world, a helpful mindset when the entire world is literally the happy hunting ground for oil.

Compare Shell with a typical Japanese company. Shell has 1700 operating companies in 140 different countries. Shell managers come from many different backgrounds and speak many different languages, although the company's working language is English. Shell is not a UK company or a Netherlands company. Royal Dutch/Shell is a world company.

A typical Japanese company, on the other hand, is still a Japanese company, no matter how many countries it operates in. Japanese managers will look alike, dress alike, think alike and act alike. There is strength in uniformity, of course, but maybe not in the oil business which is more entrepreneurial in nature.

If the US is a melting pot nation, and it is, then Royal Dutch/Shell is a melting pot company. Shell, in my opinion, exhibits some of the same traits that have made many American companies successful on the global scene.

Unlike some of its competitors, notably Exxon Corporation, Royal Dutch/Shell resisted the temptation to diversity and get into other lines of businesses. Exxon, on the other hand, burned through a billion dollars in an ill-fated attempt to get into the office equipment business.

"Exxon Office Systems?" Why would any customer in his right mind want to buy an expensive office system from an oil company?

Asked to explain his company's failure in office equipment, one Exxon executive said: "We did not understand the trivia of those businesses." (What the Exxon executive did not understand is the power of a focus. You can understand everything and still fail if your company lacks a focus.)

A word might also be said about Shell's vertical integration, from oil fields to gasoline stations. While vertical integration is neither good nor bad, in Shell's case I believe it makes sense.

In today's world, no company should be a commodity-only organization. To protect your future, you need a powerful brand.

Royal Dutch/Shell hasn't done badly as a brand builder. The Shell brand, by most measures, is the world's leading gasoline brand.

I also applaud Shell's decision to reduce its chemical businesses from 21 to 13. Perhaps it should reduce them even more. Like all companies, Shell is a big supplier of petroleum products to chemical companies. And it's always dangerous to compete with your customers. Better to stay out of the chemical product business altogether.

Solar power, forestry and other "renewable" energy sources, on the other hand, are areas where Shell should probably devote some of it resources. Oil experts have been predicting the eventual exhaustion of petroleum reserves for some time now. And that day may eventually come.

for the next 20 years, finds work, and presumably solace, on the tobacco plantations of Sumatra.

Until one day in 1880, when Zijlker, now a 40-year-old manager with the East Sumatra Tobacco Company, is caught in a severe rainstorm during a plantation inspection. Zijlker and the local overseer, take shelter for the night in a dark shed, where the overseer produces and lights a wooden torch that burns surprisingly brightly. It is impregnated with crude oil found floating on nearby streams and contains roughly 60 percent kerosene, a new cash crop that causes tobacco to fade from Zijlker's mind.

He acquires a concession to the land and tries without success to sell the rights to his unproven claim. There are no takers and for the next four years, Zijlker solicits the capital needed to develop the find himself.

On July 11, 1884, he becomes a wildcatter, drilling the first borehole on his north-eastern Sumatra claim. It takes almost a year to bring in the first minor gusher, at Telaga Tunggal, on June 15, 1885, but without any way to capture the crude oil and gas flowing from the well, it must be capped. It takes Zijlker until January 1888 to reopen the well, which six weeks later, is destroyed by fire.

In 1889, a dejected Zijlker is travelling back to Holland when he tells his story to Norbertus van den Berg, who is returning home to become Governor of the Netherlands Bank. Van den Berg takes up the torch and in 1890, with his influence and financial backing, the "Royal Dutch Company for the Exploitation of Petroleum Wells in the Netherlands East Indies" (Royal Dutch) is launched to develop Zijlker's claim.

Zijlker receives cash and 371 of the new company's 1300 shares, which he uses to pay his personal debts. Unhappily, he never sees the development of his oil concession. Zijlker dies suddenly, at age 50, on his journey back to Sumatra.

In that same year, Marcus Samuel, Jr tours the Caucasus searching for a competitive advantage. Samuel is the head of a successful English trading company founded in 1833 by his father. He has recently been offered the opportunity of his career: the rights to bring the valuable kerosene of the Caspian and Black Sea Petroleum Company (known by its Russian initials, Bnito) to Asian markets. One major problem stands in his way: the monopoly on the business enjoyed by John D. Rockefeller's Standard Oil Co.

In a burst of extraordinary and secret empire building, Samuel creates the world's first fleet of tankers to move the Russian kerosene more cost-effectively – Standard Oil's kerosene is shipped in tins. Further, he has the tankers designed so they are safe enough to move through the Suez Canal and cut 4000 miles off the trip – petroleum shipments are previously forbidden in the canal. Then he builds a network of storage and distribution facilities throughout Asia, so he can compete with Standard over the entire market.

In the summer of 1892, just two years later, the first ocean-going tanker, the SS *Murex* delivers its first cargo of kerosene from the Black Sea to Asia. By year-end 1893, ten more tankers are plying the sea lanes – all named after seashells, in honor of Samuel's father, who had started in business selling small boxes decorated with shells – and Standard Oil has a fully established competitor before they can make a move to stop it.

In that same year, the London-based kerosene shipping business is formalized as the Tank Syndicate, with Samuel, his brother, and the investors that financed the plan as members. By 1897, the business is Samuel's most profitable and he combines his oil interests, the fleet, and the distribution network into The "Shell" Transport and Trading Company.

In 1898, Shell records profits in its first year of trading of over £200,000. In 1899, profits grow to £366,000.

Movement toward merger

Royal Dutch does not get off to as fast a start as Shell. In fact, by 1891, the company is almost bankrupt and no oil is flowing in Sumatra. In late 1891, the company sends Jean Kessler to assess the situation in Sumatra. He finds an oil well, but no way to transport the oil to the refinery site, which is six miles away, and no refinery to process it, if it ever arrives.

Kessler saves the company. Within a few months, he creates a pipeline from well to refinery and builds stills and tanks, a tin factory for packing the oil, a saw-mill for cases, and other facilities, including barracks, workshops, a hospital, and even a small fort. He also imports experienced oil workers from the US.

On February 18, 1892, Kessler starts the pipeline flowing and Royal Dutch's first oil arrives at its new Pangkalan Brandan refinery. In April, the first cases of kerosene, sold under the name Crown Oil, come to market. Soon, the company is selling 20,000 cases of kerosene each month. But it does not begin making money until production increases to over 100,000 cases in 1895.

In 1896, Royal Dutch begins building its own tankers to bring oil to market. The proximity of the company's concessions to the Asian markets are an enviable advantage and, in 1897, Royal Dutch rejects takeover offers by Standard Oil *and* Shell.

Late that same year, the company almost perishes once more when seawater starts flowing from it oil wells. By July 1898, the company's stock is plummeting in Amsterdam and it doesn't recover until December 1899, when a new strike is finally made 80 miles to the north of its first strike.

By the turn of century, Royal Dutch is again on steady footing. In December 1900, the architect and driving force of the company Jean Kessler suffers a heart attack and dies at the age of 47. Henri Deterding is appointed interim managing director.

The first years of the 1900s are disastrous for Shell. The company is a growing global power, but starting in the fall of 1900, the price of oil collapses and a glut develops. All at once, the company's fortunes start to follow oil prices as civil unrest and industrial accidents disrupt production and distribution networks. Quietly, but quickly, Samuel begins to approach his competitors seeking a merger.

Both Royal Dutch and Standard Oil want Shell. But Standard Oil wants to purchase full ownership for $40 million and Royal Dutch appears content to accept a partnership of sorts. In late December 1901, Samuel rejects the US company and signs a draft agreement to create a new combination with Royal Dutch.

Over the next six years, Shell remains quasi-independent, but its financial condition continues to worsen and Royal Dutch, under Deterding's leadership, increases its control over the combined organizations. In January 1907, a complete merger of the operations, but not the shares, of the two companies is consummated. Royal Dutch, which owns a 60 percent share, and Shell Transport, which owns a 40 percent share, become holding companies. The world's second largest oil business, Royal Dutch/Shell Group, is formed.

"Nothing less than a genius"

Marcus Samuel is the group's chairman, but from the creation of Royal Dutch/Shell until just a few years before the outbreak of World War II, Henri Deterding controls operations and is the group's *de facto* leader and driving force.

Deterding solves Shell's financial woes within the year. In mid-1908, Samuel happily declares a substantial dividend and tells shareholders: "Your company for the first time in its history has no debts of any description outstanding – a matter upon which I heartily congratulate you ... In Mr. Deterding we have a gentleman who is nothing less than a genius."

Knowing that the key to success is a diverse network of producing interests, by 1915, Deterding purchases and develops production operations in Romania, Russia, Egypt, Venezuela, and Trinidad.

In 1910, Deterding visits the US and tries to build a more cooperative relationship with Standard Oil, but instead is dismissed with a $100 million buyout offer. Then, in 1911, the US government becomes Deterding's unlikely ally when it forces the breakup of Rockefeller's monopoly under the Sherman Antitrust Act.

Deterding plays into the development by buying a production foothold in the US. Shell acquires the American Gasoline Company and through it establishes a marketing arm for its gasoline from Sumatra in California. In 1912, the group buys a handful of small companies producing oil from a new strike in Oklahoma and combines them to form Roxana Petroleum.

In 1913, Shell buys its first producing wells in California. And, in 1915, this production along with the newly constructed Martinez refinery and pipeline become Shell of California.

In *The Prize*, Daniel Yergin's fine history of oil, the historian and consultant calls Shell the "quartermaster general for oil" in World War I. The group delivers oil from its fields around the world directly to distribution depots in France.

In 1915, it even carries out a covert operation that in a single night disassembles a toluol (used in TNT) refining operation in Rotterdam and moves it to England. By war's end, Shell provides 80 percent of the UK's TNT production.

World War I stimulates the rise of aviation, as dog fights and flying aces capture the attention of the world. After the war, in 1919, the group forms Shell Aviation Services and it is Shell fuel that powers Alcock and Brown's historic non-stop flight across the Atlantic that same year.

The quality of the fuel, and presumably the group's wartime efforts, so impresses King George V that he issues a Royal Warrant to Shell. It becomes the official and authorized supplier of petrol to the British monarchy – a privilege still in force.

In the 1920s, Deterding and Shell focus on "the fight for new production." In 1921, the company strikes oil on its Los Alamitos site in California, touching off an oil boom in the area.

In 1922, after almost a decade of mixed results, the company makes a 100,000 barrel per day (b/d) hit in Venezuela'a Maracaibo Basin. By decade's end, the find is Shell's largest production source.

In 1925, Shell participates in the first exploration expedition to Iraq. Three years later, in 1928, the Baba Gurger strike is made, spewing 95,000 b/d and flooding villages in the area before it is brought under control eight days later. Shell owns a 23.75 percent stake in the production.

By the end of the decade, and into the 1930s the biggest problem in the global oil industry is competition. In a foreshadowing of OPEC, Deterding spends the last years of his tenure at Shell trying unsuccessfully to create a market-sharing agreement among the major players.

In 1928, he hosts a meeting at Achnacarry Castle in Scotland that results in the "As-Is" Agreement, which sets national market shares for each company (except in the US, where such an agreement is illegal). But production continues to flood the market and it is short-lived. He tries again in 1930, reaching another agreement, which also collapses. And, again in 1934, with some success.

In his seventies, Deterding retires in 1936 and becomes something of an embarrassment to Shell. He becomes enamored of his young German secretary and Hitler's fascism, moving to Germany and dying there just before the war.

He leaves behind a leader in the oil industry. In 1938, before the outbreak of World War II, Shell is producing 580,000 barrels per day (b/d) of crude oil, just over ten percent of the total global production.

Bust and boom

With the German invasion of the Netherlands, Royal Dutch goes into exile on Curaçao. When Japan enters the war in December 1941, Shell scuttles and abandons its properties. In January 1942, company employees destroy the Balikpapan operations in Borneo, so they do not fall into enemy hands.

All the British oil companies, including Shell, place their operations under the control of the Petroleum Board, a national monopoly that controls the country's oil supplies until the end of the war. In the US, Shell is governed by the Petroleum Administration for War. The group's tanker fleet is also turned over to the war effort.

By the end of the war, 87 of Shell's ships are sunk or destroyed through enemy action. Its production fields in Romania are closed and its properties in the Far East are destroyed. At the same time demand – pent-up throughout the war years – explodes.

Shell rushes to restore its operations, increasing production everywhere it can, especially in Venezuela and Iraq. By 1947, its tanker fleet is rebuilt.

In the late 1940s and early 1950s, much energy is devoted to oil exploration in countries such as Tunisia, Algeria, Nigeria, Trinidad and off the shores of British Borneo. New strikes are made at the Schoonebeek field in the Netherlands, Colombia, and Canada.

To handle increased production, a huge construction effort is undertaken. Shell soon boasts a network of major refineries, including Europe's largest at Pernis in the Netherlands, Stanlow and Shell Haven in the UK, Rouen in France, Cardon in Venezuela, Geelong in Australia, and Bombay in India.

Three major strikes

Oil, once solely a source of lighting, is the world's most important energy resource by the last half of the 20th century, and Shell, which at times supplies as much as one-seventh of the world's oil, is a global giant in the industry.

In the post-war era, Shell integrates its operations from the upstream production of oil and natural gas into the midstream transport activities and finally, to market via the downstream manufacturing processes and marketing. Through it all, the driving force of the group remains the discovery of new sources of supply.

In 1959, NV Nederlandse Aardolie, a joint Shell and Esso venture, discovers one of the world's largest natural gas deposits in Groningen in the Netherlands – the very same province that Aeilko Zijlker left almost exactly 100 years earlier on his hard journey to Royal Dutch's first oil strike. Full-scale production begins in 1963, making Shell one of the major players in the natural gas industry.

Natural gas becomes an even more important business during the OPEC-induced oil crises of the 1970s. Oil shortages lead directly to a doubling of consumption of natural gas in Europe and by 1979, almost 15 percent of Europe's energy consumption is natural gas and LNG (liquefied natural gas). Shell and its partners supply almost 50 percent of the capacity.

The geology of the gas fields at Groningen and the rising demand for natural gas lead directly to the rich finds in the North Sea. Spurred by geological similarities between Holland and the North Sea, Shell Expro begins exploring the area for natural gas. In 1966, Shell Expro discovers the Leman gas field in the southern North Sea and soon afterward, more natural gas deposits are found in UK, Dutch, Norwegian and Danish sectors.

Natural gas is not, however, the most valuable resource of the region. In late 1969, high-quality crude oil is discovered and in 1971, Shell and Exxon tap into the huge Brent field. The Auk field is found that same year, and then the Cormorant and Dunlin fields, with Tern and Eider fields coming in the mid-1970s.

Shell's development of resources closer to home continues with the development of the large finds off the US in the Gulf of Mexico in the 1980s and 1990s. The Gulf is first tapped in the late 1940s by Kerr-Magee and development booms during the 1970s oil shortages.

In 1978, the group brings the Gulf's Cognac field in at a depth of 1025 feet – the deepest offshore strike at the time. In 1988, the Bullwinkle platform is installed, generating 44,000 b/d of oil and 100 million cubic feet per day (cf/d) of gas. In the 1990s, Auger and Mars come online and in 1997, Shell blasts past the old record by tapping Mensa in 5300 feet of water.

Shell's operating results are not so glorious, as low oil and gas prices have caused steady declines in gross revenues and profits since 1995. The late 1990s bring a period of renewed focus and reorganization for the company, which appears to be preparing itself for a fresh run in the new century.

Shell cuts costs throughout 1998, closing its corporate offices in the UK, the Netherlands, France, and Germany. It also begins pruning its chemical business and, in 1999, it joins with BASF to combine the two companies' petrochemical assets into a single producer.

The energy giant sells properties in the Gulf of Mexico for $743 billion. It invests $1 billion of the proceeds in a controlling stake in Comgas, the largest natural gas distributor in Brazil.

Shell close-up

Oil is the stock in trade of the companies of the Royal Dutch/Shell Group. Shell, as the Group is better known, has been pursuing black gold for well over a century, building in the process a company that serves as a benchmark for global operations and one of the foremost examples of a corporate structure based on alliances.

Shell is the second largest oil company in the world. In 1999, Shell recorded revenues of $105 billion and net income of $8.5 billion.

Shell is a global enterprise. The group transcends national boundaries and prides itself on its cosmopolitan nature. Currently operating in over 130 nations, Shell is one of the world's largest employers with a workforce of 96,000 people and Europe's largest employer with a workforce of 40,000 people.

The roots of Shell's globalism are long established. Until the 1950s, the crude oil that provides the life's blood of the group was simply not available in any significant quantity in Europe. The company was forced to search the world for its product. Further, Shell is itself an international network of many companies.

The Shell Group is held in partnership by Netherlands-based NV Koninklijke Nederlandsche Petroleum Maatschappij (Royal Dutch Petroleum Company) which owns 60 percent of the group and UK-based Shell Transport and Trading plc which owns 40 percent. Neither company has any operational responsibilities, but they control the leadership of the group by choosing the board of directors and rotating the chairmanship between themselves.

The group itself is composed of three holding companies: the Netherlands' Shell Petroleum NV, the UK's Shell Petroleum Company Ltd, and the US's Shell Petroleum Inc., which operates separately. The British and Dutch holding companies provide the corporate and support services for the group's far-flung network of operating companies.

The work of the holding companies is organized into three broad functions. They offer technical support functions organized around the global giant's five core businesses. They assist the group's directors in the formulation of strategy and policies. And they provide professional services in areas such as legal, human resources, and information technology.

The Shell Group includes either outright ownership or investment stakes in 1700 operating companies in over 140 countries. Each is responsible for its own success, and in those where Shell is the operating partner, the companies can draw on the knowledge and resources of the holding companies.

These companies are working in five core businesses: oil and natural gas exploration and production, and the manufacture of oil products, which together account for almost 90 percent of Shell's revenues; chemical industries; downstream gas and power generation; renewables, such as solar power and forestry; and coal.

Oil and gas exploration and production

Oil and gas is Shell's main business and the group pursues the raw materials wherever they may be found. Exploration and production employs 13,000 people and they harvest 2.26 million barrels of oil per day (b/d) and 8.21 billion cubic feet of natural gas each day (cf/d) from the earth.

In 1999, Shell's oil and gas production added up to $18.3 billion in gross revenue, including sales to other Shell operating companies. Shell realized $4.3 billion profit on these operations in 1999.

Here is a look at Shell's major oil and gas interests worldwide, by volume.

Europe

Shell's oil production in Europe totaled 620,000 barrels per day in 1999; gas production was 3.3 billion cubic feet daily. Most of Shell's European oil production is generated in the UK under a fifty-fifty joint venture between Shell UK Ltd and Esso. As operator, Shell UK is responsible for 19 percent of all oil production and 17 percent of all gas production in the UK.

The North Sea is the source of most of these reserves. Gas production comes from the southern North Sea; oil from the central and northern fields, which include the Brent field. Shell's share in the North Sea fields ranges from 10 to 50 percent.

In the Netherlands, Shell holds a 50 percent interest in natural gas and crude oil producer Nederlandse Aardolie Maatschappij BV (NAM). In Germany, Shell owns a 50 percent interest in companies Brigitta and Elwerath, which in turn formed a joint venture named BEB.

In Denmark, Shell has a 46 percent working interest in 12 fields owned by AP Moeller. In Norway, Shell is sole owner of A/S Norske Shell, which holds shares in three oil and gas fields.

In Russia, Shell also holds a 50 percent interest in Salym Petroleum Development NV, a 25 percent interest in an Arctic drilling and production facility off Sakhalin Island, and a 49 percent in Rosneft-Shell, which is participating in development of a major oil pipeline.

North America

Canada and the US comprise Shell's second largest production region, turning in 565,000 b/d of oil and 2.63 billion cf/d of natural gas. About 91 percent of this production stems from Shell Oil Company's activities in the Gulf of Mexico, California and Texas.

In the rich Gulf of Mexico offshore fields, Shell Oil's fully-owned Mensa field hit a production rate of 280 million cubic feet of gas per day. The 71.5 percent interest in the Mars field set a series of daily oil production records, and a 38 percent stake in Ram/Powell achieved its highest daily gas rate.

Shell Oil is also operating several joint ventures: it has a 36 percent stake in Altura Energy, Ltd, with production assets in west Texas and south-east New Mexico with BP Amoco and a 51.8 percent stake in Aera Energy LLC, which combines Shell Oil's California exploration and production operations with those of Mobil Corporation.

In Canada, 77.9 percent-owned Shell Canada is a major producer of natural gas, natural gas liquids and sulphur. It also produces crude oil. Ninety percent of the current production comes from Alberta. Shell Canada also has a 31 percent interest in the Sable gas field, offshore Nova Scotia.

The Middle East

Shell produces 453,000 b/d of oil and minor amounts of natural gas in the Middle East. The majority of this, 299,000 b/d, comes from the company's holdings in Oman, where Shell has a 34 percent interest in Petroleum Development Oman (PDO) and an 85 percent interest in Private Oil Holdings Oman Ltd.

In Abu Dhabi, the company owns a 23.75 percent interest in the Abu Dhabi Petroleum Company and a 15 percent interest in Abu Dhabi Gas Industries Limited. In Syria, Shell holds 60–67 percent interests in five service contracts with the Government and the state-owned Syrian Petroleum Company. Shell also has minor exploration and production interests in Yemen and Turkey.

Africa

Shell's African operations generate 333,000 b/d of oil and roughly 300 million cf/d of natural gas. In Egypt, subsidiary Shell Egypt is partner in Bapetco, a fifty-fifty joint venture with the Egypt's national oil company, which operates four fields. It also owns shares in nine exploration concessions, including a 40 percent share in the offshore Rosetta concession, and a 100 percent interest in the N.E. Mediterranean Deep Water Area.

In Gabon, the group has a 75 percent stake in Shell Gabon, which holds interests in onshore mining concessions/exploitation permits and a 42.5 percent share in the Rabi field. In Nigeria, wholly-owned Shell Petroleum Development Company of Nigeria Ltd has a 30 percent share in producing fields and the Shell Nigeria Exploration and Production Company is exploring deep-water and onshore blocks in the Gongola Basin.

Asia-Pacific

In the Far East and Pacific regions, Shell produces 247,000 b/d of oil and about 1.7 billion cf/d of natural gas. Malaysia is the leader in the region. It contributes 66,000 b/d of oil and 687 million cf/d of natural gas mainly from three wholly-owned Shell companies which have production-sharing contracts with Malaysia's state oil company Petronas, a 50 percent equity in Baram Delta PSC, and operatorships of the Jintan and Kinabalu fields.

In Australia, wholly owned subsidiary Shell Australia Limited (SAL) has a 34 percent shareholding in Woodside Petroleum Ltd and shares in Western Australian Petroleum Pty Ltd. In New Zealand, Shell holds a 25 percent interest in the large offshore Maui gas field and a 50 percent interest in the onshore Kapuni gas field.

In Brunei, a Shell company is a 50 percent shareholder in Brunei Shell Petroleum Company Sendirian Berhad, which has long-term oil and gas concession rights both onshore and offshore. In the Philippines, Shell Philippines Exploration BV is developing the Malampaya field deep in the South China Sea, which boasts 2.5 trillion cubic feet of proven gas reserves.

In China, Shell Exploration China Limited holds a 39 percent interest in a producing offshore field, and onshore and offshore exploration licenses. In Kazakhstan, operating companies have a 60 percent interest in the Temir block in western Kazakhstan and a 14.3 percent interest in offshore acreage in the north Caspian Sea. Shell is also actively exploring onshore and offshore sites in Bangladesh and Pakistan.

Latin America

Shell produces 48,000 b/d of oil and 37 million cf/d of natural gas in this region. In Venezuela, Shell has a service agreement with a subsidiary of the state oil company, Petroleos de Venezuela, for the Urdaneta West Unit in Lake Maracaibo. In Argentina, Shell has a 55 percent interest in exploration sites in the provinces of Salta and Jujuy, a 22.5 percent interest in the San Pedrito gas field, and a 40 percent interest in an oil-producing concession in Mendoza province. In Colombia, a Shell company holds a 50 percent interest in two blocks in the Caribbean Sea. And, in Peru, 57.5 percent-owned Shell Prospecting and Development Peru drilled a successful gas well.

Oil products

Shell's Oil Products businesses create refined, saleable products from the raw materials – crude oil and natural gas produced by the exploration and production companies – and market those products around the world.

Oil products businesses employ 56,000 people in refining, marketing, and transport operations. In 1999, the group's oil products companies generated $74 billion in revenues. Net profits in these businesses in 1999 were $1.53 billion.

Refining

Shell refining plants produce motor, aviation and marine fuels, liquefied petroleum gas (LPG), petrochemical feedstocks, heating oils, fuel oils, bitumens, a range of industrial/engine lubricants and other petroleum products. In 1999, the company generated a total of 2.9 billion b/d of these finished products. Oil products are created in 26 group-owned refineries operating in 17 countries, and in 33 additional refineries in 19 countries owned by associated companies.

Marketing

Shell is the world's leading seller of branded gasoline and also the sales leader in lubricants, LPG, and bitumen. The main distribution outlet for oil products is the network of 46,000 gas stations selling Shell gasoline and oil in more than 90 countries.

In terms of global market share, Shell has:

- over 20 percent of the market in 50 countries, including Australia, Malaysia and the Philippines in the Asia-Pacific region, and the Netherlands and Switzerland in Europe;
- 10–20 percent in 25 countries, including Germany, France, the UK and six other European countries, as well as Canada, Brazil and Argentina; and
- 5–10 percent in Belgium and in 10 other countries.

The Shell brand is one of the group's most valuable assets. A 1998 study commissioned by the company found that the Shell pecten, first used in 1904, is the most preferred of all oil company logos. The company continues to extend the use of its brand in its Retail Visual Identity program, which is installed at over 17,000 stations in 100 countries, to date.

Shell is also adding additional services to its sites, including its Select-brand convenience stores and shops, and car washes. By year-end 1999, the company operated 6000 convenience stores in more than 50 countries.

Transport

Shell transports its products via pipelines and tanker and gas carrier fleets. The group companies have varying shares in pipelines around the world, with its main holdings in North America and Western Europe. These include major trunk lines for crude oil and natural gas, large pipelines for natural gas liquids and LPG as well as chemicals, oil products, and carbon dioxide, and gathering lines for oil and gas production.

In 1999, Shell companies controlled transport shipping comprised of oil tankers and natural gas products carriers. The company owns and charters a fleet of 51 tankers with a capacity of 5.5 million tons. Three gas carriers give it a shipping capacity of 216,000 cubic meters.

Chemicals

The Shell Chemical Group ranks among the world's top chemical companies, producing a large number of petrochemicals and specialty chemicals. The group is currently in the process of refocusing these businesses by product groups and is divesting those chemical companies that do not strongly connect to its core competencies.

In the near future, Shell's chemical companies will be focused on major cracker products (used in the refining process), petrochemical building blocks, and large-volume polymers. The group plans to sell off and otherwise reduce its chemical product businesses from 21 to 13. The result will be, according to the company, "a set of major linked petrochemical businesses in which Group companies possess leading technologies and the proven capability to build and operate world-scale plants."

Currently, Shell is a major producer of detergent intermediates, particularly detergent alcohols, and a major supplier of base chemicals, solvents, and ethylene oxide and its derivatives. The group makes four classes of polymer products, including thermoplastics, epoxy resins, synthetic rubbers, and urethanes, and manufactures catalysts and additives. It makes 14 percent of the world's polypropylene.

Shell employs 17,000 people in its chemical companies. In 1999, chemicals contributed $13.6 billion to gross revenues, producing profits of $813 million.

At year-end 1999, Shell companies had full or majority equity interests in chemical manufacturing plants in the North and Latin America, Europe, Africa, and Asia-Pacific. The main manufacturing plants are located as follows:

- *Europe* – Shell has chemical operations in Belgium, France, Germany, Netherlands, Italy, Spain and the UK. Among the chemicals produced are catalysts, lubricating oil additives, benzene, toluene and xylene isomers, epoxy resins, styrene, ethylene oxide, propylene oxide, polystyrene, and polyethylene terephthalate (PET).
- *North America* – Shell companies run manufacturing facilities in eight states in the US, Mexico, and three provinces in Canada. It is a major producer of olefins, aromatics, phenol, detergent alcohols, ethylene oxide and derivatives, thermoplastic elastomers, epoxy and speciality resins, oxygenated and hydrocarbon solvents, polypropylene and PET.
- *Asia-Pacific* – Shell has plants in Japan, Australia, Singapore, and new ventures developing in China. These operations make polypropylene, polystyrene, and propylene oxide.
- *The Middle East* – The Saudi Petrochemical Company produces ethylene, crude industrial ethanol, ethylene dichloride, caustic soda, styrene, and methyl tertiary butyl ether.
- *Latin America* – Shell produces thermoplastic elastomers in Brazil.

Downstream gas and power generation

Shell's Downstream Gas and Power Generation Business includes the processing, sale, and delivery of natural gas and LNG by long-distance pipeline and tanker; and the development and operation of power stations. The group employs 1000 people in these businesses. In 1999, they generated $10 billion in sales and a net profit of $149 million.

Shell's major businesses in Europe include gas transmission and distribution companies in Germany, the Netherlands, Norway, and the UK. In Asia-Pacific, operations in Australia, Brunei, and Malaysia supply natural gas and LNG domestically and to major customers in Japan, Korea, and Taiwan. In Latin America, Shell has pipelines and distribution interests in Bolivia and Brazil.

In the US and Canada, Shell Oil has combined its natural gas business, with full ownership in Coral, Corpus Christi Natural Gas, and Tejas to create a single natural gas and natural gas liquids business segment. The business includes an infrastructure of natural gas pipelines in the Gulf of Mexico and natural gas transportation, processing, hub services and marketing operations.

Shell also owns interests in LNG plants in Nigeria and Oman, which supply gas to markets in Europe and Asia.

The group's interests in power generation include three percent of the committed greenfield generating capacity of the world's independent power developers outside North America. Among group holdings are ownership and investment stakes in power stations in Brazil, the UK, Mexico, Colombia, China, the Philippines, Turkey, and Egypt.

Renewables

Shell's recently formed Renewables core businesses currently includes operations in solar power, biomass or wood-based power, and forestry. The Renewables businesses address Shell's belief that renewable energy could become a major source of energy as soon as 2050.

Shell Renewables is coordinated by Shell International Renewables Ltd, based in the UK. The largest business in the group is "upstream" forestry, which harvests short-rotation, high-yield tree crops from tree plantations. Group companies own plantations in Paraguay, Chile and Argentina, and have joint-venture plantations in Congo, Uruguay, and New Zealand.

The group currently accounts for four percent of the global market in solar energy panels. Group companies manufacture, market, and sell solar photovoltaic cells and panels in the Netherlands and a second solar cell manufacturing plant is under construction in Germany. The group is also partner in a 50 percent joint-venture company with Eskom in South Africa, which is establishing a solar-based rural electrification business.

Coal

Shell's final core business is coal mining and marketing. It owns stakes in coal mining operations in Australia and Venezuela, which generated 14.2 million tons of coal for the company in 1998. Coal is marketed and sold by a number of group companies and a coal-fired power station is under construction. In 2000, Shell announced that it would sell this business.

Income statement

Year	Revenue ($m)	Net income ($m)	Net profit margin	Employees
1998	93,692.0	350.0	0.4%	102,000
1997	128,115.0	7,753.0	6.1%	105,000
1996	128,313.0	8,886.0	6.9%	104,000
1995	109,872.0	6,919.0	6.3%	106,000
1994	94,830.0	6,267.0	6.6%	106,000
1993	95,173.0	4,497.0	4.7%	117,000
1992	96,625.0	5,369.0	5.6%	127,000
1991	102,697.0	4,288.0	4.2%	133,000
1990	106,479.0	6,533.0	6.1%	137,000
1989	85,412.0	6,537.0	7.7%	135,000

1998 year-end financials

Debt ratio	9.5%
Return on equity	—
Cash ($m)	2,717.0
Current ratio	0.73
Long-term debt ($m)	6,032.0

Financial data provided by Hoover's Online (www.hoovers.com) and Media General Financial Services, Inc.

Shell contacts

The Royal Dutch/Shell Group   Phone: +31–70–377–3395
30, Carel van Bylandtlaan   Fax: +31–70–377–3115
2596 HR The Hague   URL: www.shell.com
The Netherlands

CEO: Maarten A. van den Bergh   CFO: R.M. Cox   HR: J.D. Hofmeister

Sensormatic Electronics Corporation – Boca Raton, Florida, USA

Executive snapshot

Sensormatic Electronics created the electronic asset security industry in the late 1960s and has combined technological innovation with a global reach to maintain its position at the top.

"We need to have our R&D programs focused on the right areas, products that are built and installed with quality and keen insight into what our customers want," says CEO Per-Olof Loof. "The key to this priority is to listen to our customers and then execute well."

Sensormatic backdrop

The uncontrollable urge to solve problems and an unshakable confidence in one's own convictions are hallmarks of the entrepreneurial personality. There are many corporate stories that prominently feature both qualities, but only one that also features a foot race with a shoplifter.

Running down a business concept

Ron Assaf, the founder of Sensormatic, has no trouble remembering the events of July 15, 1965. He is a store manager at a Kroger's supermarket

Future focus

Creating a new industry

The surest road to incredible fame and fortune is to invent a new product and then build a company to dominate the new industry on a worldwide basis. But that is easier said than done. There are many traps along the way to snare the unwary.

The first trap is the problem, or rather the absence of a problem that the marvelous new product you have just created is designed to solve. The combination washer/dryer invented by Bendix was a cleverly-engineered machine, but what problem did it solve? The average home had plenty of room in the basement for a washer and a separate dryer. Furthermore, with a combination machine you couldn't wash the second load while drying the first. The combination television set/computer falls into the same category. Who has ever said, "What I really want is a way to surf the web while watching television?"

The founders of Sensormatic, Ron Assaf and his cousin Jack Welch (not *the* Jack Welch), first zeroed in on a real problem, shoplifting. If they could invent something to stop shoplifting, they knew they could get rich.

The second trap is perfectionism. The need to do everything yourself. A successful entrepreneur only needs a problem and the general outline of a way to solve that problem. You can buy everything else you need. Welch got the idea of electronic tags for the merchandise and a fixed detector to sound an alarm if a thief tried to take the merchandise out the door. So the two Sensormatic founders hired university scientists to create the equipment they needed.

The third trap is money. It takes more than an idea to build a successful business. It also takes money, usually more than you had planned on. Sensormatic's founders sold franchises to raise the $3 million they needed.

The fourth trap is profits. Trying to make them too soon. The primary objective of a new company with a new idea is not to make money, but to get the idea established. "Make them an offer they can't refuse" is a good business strategy in this situation. Of the first 20 Sensormatic systems installed in retail stores, only one retailer actually paid the company anything for its system.

A number of years ago, Monsanto introduced All detergent, a low-sudsing product especially designed for front-loading automatic washers. I was privy to the marketing plan, which called for washer manufacturers to recommend the product. Some outside marketing experts were surprised when almost every manufacturer signed up for the program and shipped their front-loading washers with a box of All inside.

How did Monsanto manage that, I was asked? Easy, Monsanto made them an offer they couldn't refuse, one dollar for every machine shipped with a box of All, also conveniently supplied by Monsanto.

The fifth trap is aiming low. That is, starting at the bottom and then trying to work your way up the food chain. Small companies often think that it's easier to sell to other small companies rather than to big companies. That's not necessarily true. It's often easier to wrestle a CEO around the boardroom for a $10 million contract than it is to sell a $1000 system to a small company.

To a small company entrepreneur, the $1000 is real money which will be taken out of the company's real bank account. To a big company CEO, the $10 million is only a number on a sheet of paper. Even more important, the entrepreneur looks for a supplier's credentials. Which well-known retailers have bought this new security system?

The big company doesn't look at the situation in quite the same way. They perceive themselves to be smarter than their smaller competitors. After all, they're big, they're successful, they can dictate what products they should have and what they shouldn't have. They don't need to follow the buying habits of their less-successful competitors.

So Sensormatic, which had "sold" only one system, went right to the top. To Macy's, the biggest retailer with the best reputation. And Macy's bought the Sensormatic deal.

With the Macy's contract in hand, it wasn't hard to jumpstart Sensormatic sales with the rest of the retail industry. "If Macy's thinks it's a good idea, it must be a good idea."

(Many managers think the best way to sell a revolutionary new idea is to sell the benefits of the idea. No. The best way to sell a revolutionary new idea is to sell your credentials. The best way to sell Avis is to sell Hertz first.)

The sixth trap is greed. That is, trying to monopolize the new industry. You can't be a leader without followers. Even though Sensormatic had accumulated a number of patents on its electronic surveillance products, it wisely resisted the temptation to use the legal system to drive its competitors out of the market. The existence of competition created the legitimacy of an "industry," which greatly accelerated the use of electronic surveillance products.

Polaroid, on the other hand, sued Kodak and drove them out of the instant photography business. As a result, Polaroid suffered because instant photography never became a dynamic business.

The seventh trap is competitiveness. Companies focus so much of their efforts on competing with their competitors that they fail to recognize that the checkbook is a company's most powerful marketing weapon. Buying a competitor offers two major benefits. It increases your market share and it reduces your competition.

Over the years Sensormatic acquired dozens of competitors in the electronic surveillance industry and related fields. Their 60 percent worldwide market share would not have been possible without an aggressive acquisition program.

Filling the holes in their product line also allows Sensormatic to do deals with big retailers at the highest levels. The recent Limited deal covering 5400 stores in 11 retail business units is a good example. Few of Sensormatic's competitors would have the product line or the backup resources to handle a project of this size.

The eighth trap is leadership. That is, failing to recognize the opportunities (and responsibilities) that industry leadership confers. What should leaders do? They should lead. In other words, they should try to control the future direction of their entire industry.

This is what Microsoft has done so well in the past, with such concepts as Microsoft Office. They forced the personal computer software industry to compete on the basis of product "packages." This was good for Microsoft, and it may have also been good for users although the jury is out on this issue.

> Sensormatic is increasing its control of the electronic surveillance industry by shifting its sales efforts from retailers to manufacturers. Selling electronic tags to manufacturers greatly encourages retailers to install Sensormatic systems to read the tags. This is a strategy that only the big, dominant player can pull off.
>
> Dominating an industry on a worldwide basis is the essence of building a powerful company for the 21st century. And Sensormatic has done so by avoiding all the traps along the way.

in Akron, Ohio, when a shoplifter grabs two bottles of wine and runs. Assaf chases the thief, but loses the race.

Later, he relates the incident to his cousin, a not-so-successful inventor named Jack Welch. "Jack," says Assaf, "if you could invent something to stop shoplifting, you'd become a millionaire."

Assaf and Welch spend the next year or so coming up with ideas to stop shoplifters. None stand up to close examination until one day, Welch gets the idea to use a system of electronic tags and fixed detectors to protect merchandise. If a thief tries to take a tagged object past a detector, it will set off an alarm.

Neither man has the expertise to design such a product, so they pool their resources and hire two scientists from the University of Michigan to create the equipment. In late 1966, the prototype is ready. The pedestal-shaped detectors take up most of a room and the tag is the size of a dinner plate. Nevertheless, it works.

Throughout 1967, Assaf struggles to turn the first EAS (electronic article surveillance) system into a commercial product. He raises $3 million by selling franchise territories in the US states. By the end of the year, Sensormatic is formally established and its first system, utilizing vacuum tubes, is ready to test in the field.

In 1968, unable to find a single retailer willing to purchase or even install a free system, the company finally pays a Cuyahoga Falls, Ohio retailer $300 per month to try the system.

"It was a rather unconventional start for the founding of an industry," says Assaf, "considering you had to pay a customer to use your product."

Going pro

By 1969, Sensormatic has 20 EAS systems installed in the US, but only one store is actually paying anything for its system. That year, the company goes public and is listed on NASDAQ.

In the 1970s, with Ron Assaf as CEO and chairman, Sensormatic turns itself into a real company. It creates it first professional marketing team in 1970, when it hires several ex-IBM marketing executives to establish the department. In 1971, the company leaves Ohio and relocates to Hollywood, Florida. In 1972, Sensormatic signs up Macys, its first major retail account. The chain installs its first Sensormatic EAS system in its Herald Square, New York City store.

By 1973, the company records it first profitable year, beginning a series of record sales and earnings that will remain intact until the end of the decade. That year, Sensormatic gets its first $1 million order from the Carson, Pirie, Scott department store chain. And, in 1974, the company introduces its most widely recognized product, the Alligator Tag, a white plastic security tag that soon will find its way onto millions of soft goods.

By 1976, Sensormatic is pushing $10 million in sales. In 1977, the company reacquires the marketing rights to its products in Europe and starts building its own international sales force. Growth forces the company to build a new headquarters in Deerfield Beach, Florida in 1978.

In the early 1980s, the company hits a wall as the growth of its hard tag sales slows. The Sensormatic EAS system is a cash cow for the company with the installed base approaching 10,000 systems, but the company is reaching the limits of its market. Ron Assaf steps down as CEO and Allen Dusault is appointed.

Dusault cuts costs and the company starts a focused push to broaden its product lines so that it can offer customers complete security and loss prevention packages. It first expands into CCTV systems, creating the SensorVision brand. Sears is the first customer for the new systems. As the company returns to health, Assaf reassumes the CEO spot. By 1986, revenues are approaching $100 million.

In 1988, Sensormatic expands its EAS offerings into the hardgoods markets when it introduces the UltraMax labeling technology. One year later, the company enters the access control market when it acquires Continental Instruments Corp. and merges it with the newly formed Commercial/industrial Division. Revenues break above $150 million and Sensormatic employs 1600 people.

In the 1990s, Sensormatic drives to dominate its markets via acquisition. In 1991, Sensormatic expands its CCTV division by purchasing American Dynamics and its line of video system switchers and controllers. That year, the company is listed on the New York Stock Exchange and revenues approach $240 million. The company now employs over 2600 people.

The next year Sensormatic acquires the ALPS (Automated Loss Prevention Systems) Division of Automated Security Holdings. ALPS, once the company's biggest rival in Europe, is the leading EAS company in Europe. Revenues jump to $309 million.

In fiscal 1994, Sensormatic builds its video systems and access control businesses with a string of acquisitions including Security Tag, Inc., Advanced Entry Systems, Inc., Security Specialists of San Francisco, Inc., Robot Research, Inc., and Software House, Inc.

Sensormatic also makes an early source tagging effort with its Universal Product Protection program. UPP encourages the application of security tags and labels during the manufacturing process. The company enters a strategic alliance with Paxar Corp., a maker of clothing labels, jointly to create cloth labels with built-in anti-theft technology. Year-end revenues exceed $650 million and employee headcount hits 5500.

In 1995, Sensormatic makes a play for its largest competitor in the US, Knogo Corporation, but because of antitrust concerns, the government restricts the deal to Knogo's operations outside the US. The company also buys Case Security Ltd in the UK and Glen Industrial Communications in the US. Sensormatic is having a hard time digesting its long run of acquisitions and although total revenues grow 36 percent to almost $900 million, net income remains almost flat at $73.7 million.

Reorganization at the billion dollar level

In what has been planned as the company's first $1 billion year and Ron Assaf's well-deserved retirement from day-to-day operations, the other shoe drops. In fiscal 1996, on total revenues of just under $1 billion, the company takes $186 million worth of restructuring charges and records a loss of $97 million. In an effort to stem the losses, the company downsizes the workforce by ten percent, consolidates business units, and starts reducing manufacturing costs. Ron Assaf remains as chairman and COO Bob Vanourek is promoted to CEO. Vanourek promises continued restructuring and a return to profitability.

That same year, Sensormatic is a sponsor and the Official Electronic Security Supplier to the Olympic Games held in Atlanta, Georgia. To protect the world's athletes, the company installs the largest security system ever assembled. The company has over 400,000 installed EAS systems worldwide and counts 98 of the world's top 100 retailers among its customers.

In 1997, the restructuring and cost-cutting continues. The company belatedly breaks the $1 billion barrier, but there is little celebration as almost $50 million in restructuring charges leave Sensormatic with a loss for the year of $21 million.

At the same time, the company's source tagging efforts are paying off. Sales of source labels to manufacturers rise 50 percent to 437 million units. Kmart joins 90 other retail chains and 1300 manufacturers who are already using the company's technology. Twelve major products are launched and the company's patents rise to over 200.

In fiscal 1998, Sensormatic's total revenues drop back below the $1 billion mark on soft markets in Asia and continued restructuring. In spite of a healthy increase in operating income, $43 million in special charges leave the company with a third annual loss, this time of $37 million.

Source tagging now contributes over $30 million to the company's revenues and this year, over 650 million items get Sensormatic source tags. New product launches include the C-Cure Trac asset control system and the AD168 controller system.

In December 1998, The Limited, Inc. signs an exclusive three-year commitment to install Sensormatic's EAS technologies in its retail businesses. The Limited operates more than 5400 stores in 11 retail business units under the banners of The Limited, Express, Lerner New York, Lane Bryant, Henri Bendel, Structure, Limited Too, and Galyan's Trading Co. It also owns controlling interests in Intimate Brands, Inc., Bath & Body Works and Victoria's Secret.

In 1999, Sensormatic turns the corner and returns to profitability. With the growing use of source tags, the demand for EAS systems surges. The company expands its manufacturing capacity and starts to rebuild its workforce. CEO Bob Vanourek does not get to enjoy the comeback for long. He is replaced by Per-Olof Loof, a former NCR executive.

Sensormatic close-up

In 1997, in the United States alone, inventory shrinkage – the unexplained disappearance of goods from businesses – was pegged at $26 billion, with over 80 percent of that loss blamed on employee theft, shoplifting, and vendor fraud. Keeping the bad guys at bay is obviously a big job and that is good news for Sensormatic Electronics Corporation.

With an overall market share exceeding 60 percent, Sensormatic is the world leader in high-tech, electronic security systems for retail, commercial and industrial applications. When an alarm sounds in a retail store, airport, casino, or factory, chances are good that you are hearing one or another of the company's products at work.

Sensormatic's customers include all except two of the world's top 100 retailers, as well as more than half of the *Fortune 500* companies. The firm sells to retail, industrial, commercial, governmental, and institutional customers worldwide, virtually any business that needs to protect or control assets, information, or people. In fiscal 1999, that meant annual revenues of $1.01 billion developed by sales in over 113 countries.

Since its founding in 1966, Sensormatic has built the largest sales and service network in the industry. It employs over 1700 salespeople and maintains a network of 600 independent dealers and distributors. In addition to its world headquarters in Boca Raton, Florida, Sensormatic has a European operational headquarters in France. It has direct sales operations in 39 countries throughout North America, Europe, Asia, and South America.

Sensormatic is organized into three major sales groups by geographic locations: North American Retail, European Operations, and International Operations (which consists of the Asia-Pacific, the Middle East, and Latin America regions). In 1996, the company established a Global Source Tagging Division, which is focused on marketing security tags and labels to manufacturers – an important emerging market for the company's products.

Sensormatic also sells its products through an extensive network of independent distributors. It owns full and partial stakes in distributors in Brazil, Colombia, and Argentina. It has distribution agreements with resellers in 81 other countries located in the Middle East, Latin America, Asia, Africa and Eastern Europe.

Sensormatic's global sales are concentrated in North America and Europe, which together account for close to 90 percent of sales. Latin America and Asia-Pacific are growth markets that currently account for just over ten percent of sales.

The company's products fall into two major groups. There are retail loss prevention products and systems, which include electronic article surveillance (EAS), closed circuit television (CCTV), and exception monitoring systems that are used by retailers to deter shoplifting and internal theft. And Sensormatic's business security products and systems, which include CCTV, access control, and electronic asset protection (EAP) security systems and are used by retail, commercial, and industrial customers to protect assets, information, and people. These products can be sold as standalone systems or they can be sold in integrated packages that are designed to cover all of a customer's security and loss prevention needs.

Sensormatic manufactures its loss prevention products in factories in Florida, Ireland, Puerto Rico, and Brazil. It has a leading share in three major market segments: EAS systems, CCTV and video systems, and access control and asset management systems.

EAS systems

The main evidence of Sensormatic's EAS products are the security tags and labels that one finds on almost every imaginable consumer product. However, the re-useable hard tags and disposable labels, a wonderful source of repeat sales for the company, are just one part of larger loss prevention systems.

Sensormatic's EAS systems come in a wide variety of forms and use different technologies. A typical system consists of a detection unit, tags or labels, and a tag detacher or label deactivator. The detection units are placed at the entrances and exits to stores or at checkout lanes. They can be installed on or under floors, or hung from walls or ceilings. These units sound the alarm when merchandise affixed with the company's tags or labels passes by.

Tags and labels are available in many shapes, sizes, and configurations. Tags are removed from merchandise at checkout using a detacher and can be reused. Labels are usually passed over a deactivator at the cash register and remain on the goods. Sensormatic also makes labels that can be removed and reused with reactivation devices.

The company organizes its EAS systems by the technologies they utilize. The most popular is the UltraMax system, which was introduced a decade ago and uses a proprietary acousto-magnetic technology. The UltraMax technology is used in 15 different electronic anti-theft systems sold by the company under the brand names ProMax, FloorMax, EuroMax, MegaMax, MAX Checkout, and UltraPost.

UltraMax systems recognize hard tags and labels. The company's SuperTag is the newest hard tag available on the market. It is made of lightweight plastic that resists removal by cutting, pulling, and twisting. Sensormatic's UltraStrip labels are the smallest EAS labels available, are compatible with a wide range of packaging materials and product substances, including foil and metal, and are unaffected by moisture. Increasingly, these labels are applied as "source tags," meaning they are put on products during manufacturing and packaging processes, long before they arrive in stores.

Sensormatic uses a proprietary magnetostrictive and standard low-frequency electromagnetic technology in systems designed to protect high-theft items in supermarkets and hypermarkets around the world as well as in bookstores, libraries, liquor stores, video stores, etc. These systems include SensorStrip Checkout and SensorStrip Checkout Plus available in the Americas, and Checkout Control and Checkout Control II marketed in Europe.

The standard SensorStrip label is a thin micromagnetic wire covered in transparent tape and attached to merchandise. Items with these labels are either passed outside the system during the checkout process or are deactivated at checkout. SensorStrips can also be used for source tagging.

Sensormatic's microwave systems utilize high radio frequency technology. Microwave systems protect wide exits and are used by department stores and specialty clothing retailers. These systems are marketed under the names of MicroMax, SlimLine, and Sensormat II. Microwave systems are the most widely used technology with soft-good retailers.

Swept-RF or swept radio frequency systems utilize low radio frequency technology and are used to cover single door exits. Sensormatic markets this technology under the brand name of System One.

The company also sells two brands of "benefit denial" products, non-electronic anti-theft devices that are impossible to remove from goods without destroying or damaging the merchandise. They make stealing such a product pointless.

The Inktag product line is fastened to clothing and other soft goods in stores. There are vials of ink inside the tags that break and stain the merchandise if unauthorized removal is attempted. Inktags are sold mainly to department, specialty, discount and mass merchandise stores.

The Microlock product is used to protect items such as eyeglasses and jewelry by making it impossible to use the merchandise until the Microlock is removed. These are used primarily in department, specialty, discount, mass merchandise, jewelry, optical and drug stores.

EAS systems were the first Sensormatic's products and are still the company's stock in trade. In fiscal 1999, they contributed $548 million in revenues, 54 percent of the company's total product sales. The company's systems accounted for roughly 60 percent of the worldwide installed EAS base. Product line management is performed by the EAS Division and sales of EAS are made directly to customers through the major sales divisions.

CCTV and video systems

Sensormatic's CCTV and video systems are integrated combinations of equipment designed for safety monitoring, theft deterrence, and security surveillance. These range from simple systems that might use a single camera, monitor, and video recorder to observe a cash register to complex systems consisting of hundreds of cameras and banks of monitors and recorders all manipulated by sophisticated controllers.

Accordingly, the business customers for Sensormatic's CCTV systems range from small, independent retail stores to international chains to casinos. They are also used by governmental agencies, hospitals, correctional facilities, airports, nuclear power plants, and the list goes on and on. The company's product lines in this market segment include the following.

Indoor and outdoor video cameras are used to monitor, investigate, and record events. The most advanced cameras are the company's SpeedDome family, which feature digital and high-resolution color or monochrome features. They deliver high-resolution images of stationary or moving objects, can focus on objects at a distance in low light, as well as acquire, zoom, and focus on targets in less than one second.

The company sells a full line of video switchers/controllers, which are used to move the cameras and control the system. Their capabilities range from simple systems to increasingly complex systems that support more than 1000 cameras. Sensormatic's American Dynamics video switchers/controllers are marketed under various brand names and include high-end video switchers/controllers such as the AD2050, which can power up to 1024 cameras and 128 monitors. There is a retail-oriented View Manager family, which is used with a Touch Tracker keyboard and can control up to 96 cameras. And there is also the AD168, a new system that offers sophisticated features at a lower price.

Completing the systems are video products such as multiplexers, which allow up to 16 video inputs to be recorded on a single VCR, and video transmission systems that will remotely view stores, warehouses, and other facilities. These are sold under the SensorLink PC and HyperScan Ultra brand names.

Sensormatic's video products also include digital video systems that can search video recordings, locate and play back pre-programmed alarm events, and magnify and enhance images. These are marketed under the brand name Intellex.

In fiscal 1999, CCTV and video surveillance products contributed $292 million or 29 percent of Sensormatic's total revenues. The company's Video Products Division is responsible for these product lines. Sales are made through a distributor network, but are managed by the major sales groups.

Access control and asset management

Sensormatic's access control and asset management systems are software-based products used to monitor, protect, and track people and assets. These systems control access to facilities and track products throughout the supply chain.

Access control systems typically give people badges or smart cards that are inserted or swiped at a door reader to gain access to buildings, rooms, and other enclosures. The systems include a wide variety of features such as automatic data collection and report generation.

Sensormatic's access control systems include the C-CURE family of systems. The C-CURE 1 Plus Ultra is a high-end integrated security system that monitors and controls access with a photo imaging system. The C-CURE 800 is a mid-range system and C-Cure 750 is aimed at smaller customers. The capacity of these systems ranges from two readers with 3000 cardholders to 2048 readers with 250,000 cardholders.

Sensormatic's asset management systems are emerging as the new growth area in access control. These systems will combine asset protection and access control using RFID (radio frequency identification) technology to create a complete range of sensing and tracking solutions for people and assets.

Asset management systems use embedded-chip smart cards, which provide a miniature database that can store warranty information, time, date, and location of sale or manufacture, lease information, virtual inventory management, and reverse logistics management. The chips are attached to or embedded in employee access control badges, high-value assets, vehicles, or any other object.

In fiscal 1998, Sensormatic began test marketing its C-Cure Trac system. C-Cure Trac combines C-Cure database management and reporting with smart card readers. It is the first integrated security management system with RFID asset tracking and protection solution. In combination with C-CURE 800 software, it becomes the only system that can document the movement of stationary and portable assets and offer detailed reporting of when, where and with whom an asset left a secured area. Using transponders, C-Cure Trac can even detect the direction a cardholder and asset are moving.

Access control products contributed $45 million or four percent of the company's total revenues in fiscal 1999. The Access Control Division designs, manufactures, and supports Sensormatic's access control, integrated security management systems, and asset tracking systems.

Income statement

Year	Revenue ($m)	Net income ($m)	Net profit margin	Employees
1999	1,017.5	38.1	3.7%	5,700
1998	986.9	(37.1)	—	5,800
1997	1,025.7	(21.4)	—	6,500
1996	994.6	(97.7)	—	6,300
1995	889.1	73.7	8.3%	7,500
1994	656.0	72.1	11.0%	5,500
1993	487.3	54.1	11.1%	4,000
1992	309.9	31.5	10.2%	2,889
1991	239.2	24.7	10.3%	2,645
1990	191.3	20.0	10.5%	1,432

Stock history

Year	Stock price ($) FY High	FY Low	FY Close	P/E High	Low	Per share ($) Earns	Div.	Book value
1999	15.19	3.13	13.94	43	9	0.35	0.00	11.77
1998	20.00	11.75	14.00	—	—	(0.50)	0.00	12.06
1997	21.13	12.88	12.88	—	—	(0.29)	0.22	10.40
1996	36.50	13.63	16.38	—	—	(1.33)	0.22	11.52
1995	38.25	25.38	35.50	37	25	1.03	0.21	13.25
1994	39.25	23.60	28.75	35	21	1.13	0.21	10.95
1993	30.02	15.01	26.01	32	16	0.93	0.20	8.80
1992	20.84	13.42	18.18	—	—	0.73	0.20	6,752.58
1991	15.42	7.75	13.76	—	—	0.60	0.20	6,092.51
1990	10.01	6.59	9.42	—	—	0.48	0.09	5,563.14

1999 year-end financials

Debt ratio	32.5%
Return on equity	4.3%
Cash ($m)	209.0
Current ratio	1.91
Long-term debt ($m)	427.7
Shares outstanding (millions)	75.6
Dividend yield	0.0%
Dividend payout	0.0%
Market value ($m)	1,053.9

Financial data provided by Hoover's Online (www.hoovers.com) and Media General Financial Services, Inc.

Sensormatic contacts

Sensormatic Electronics Corporation Phone: 561–989–7000
951 Yamato Road   Fax: 561–989–7017
Boca Raton, FL, USA 33431   URL: www.sensormatic.com

CEO: Per-Olof Loof   CFO: Garrett Pierce   HR: Bruce Gant

Tellabs, Inc. –

Lisle, Illinois, USA

Executive snapshot

No product is for ever, especially in the fast-changing telecommunications arena.

"Networks of the future will surely look and behave differently than those that populate all but the most recently constructed networks today. To continue the growth we have seen in the past few years, Tellabs must address itself to the newer technologies." – Michael Birck, president and CEO, Tellabs.

Tellabs backdrop

Anyone who still refuses to acknowledge the entrepreneurial power of the workforce had better take a close look at the lesson of Tellabs. Founded in the angst of unfulfilled promises, the leaders of the company not only quickly eclipsed the fortunes of their previous employer – they turned their share of a niche market into a multi-billion-dollar slice of the global telecommunications industry.

Wescom woes

In January 1975, a good portion of Chicago area telecom equipment maker Wescom, Inc.'s operational management team are sitting in general

Future focus

Lighting the fire

What do you need to do to start a company that will become a worldwide leader in high technology?

The principles are simple, but not necessarily easy to execute. First of all, you need a unique new product to provide the spark. (You never get a second chance to make a first impression.)

Tellabs' initial spark was provided by an echo suppressor that the company sold to independent telephone operators. (Even today, 23 years after its founding, annual sales of Tellabs echo suppressors, now called echo cancellers, are more than $150 million.)

It's a pattern you see quite often. You can't build a company into a global leader without an initial "hot" product that provides the spark:

* the light bulb introduced by General Electric;
* the steel-belted radial-ply tire introduced by Michelin;
* the car radio introduced by Motorola;
* the transistor radio introduced by Sony; and
* the video game player introduced by Nintendo.

If you want to build a high-tech global powerhouse for the 21st century, don't start a company – start a fire with a unique new idea.

The second principle that can be deduced from the Tellabs story is the need to throw money on the fire. It invests enormous sums in research and development. Over 30 percent of Tellabs' employees work in R&D. This is way higher than the average company and even greater than most high-technology companies. To stay ahead of competition the typical high-tech company has to be prepared to spend heavily in this area.

The third principle is that a high-tech company needs a high-tech leader. Tellabs' founders came from telecom equipment maker Wescom where Michael Bircks was head of engineering. In the beginning Bircks was Tellabs' CEO as well as its head of research and development.

In its first five years, the company introduced on average three new products a month. To build a high-technology fire you need a combustion engineer, not a professional manager.

When I worked for General Electric the company philosophy was "A professional manager can manage anything." Twentieth-century thinking is not going to succeed in the 21st century. Tomorrow's dominant companies are going to be run by specialists:

- high-technology companies by high-tech managers;
- consumer products companies by marketing people;
- financial companies by financial people; and
- media companies by media people.

As Tellabs grew into a large company, Michael Bircks couldn't continue to be the primary source of new telecom concepts. That's not the CEO's job. His primary responsibility had to change from generating the ideas to recognizing the ideas generated by others.

This is the fatal flaw at many high-technology companies run by non-technology people. How does a professional manager recognize a good concept when it's presented?

It takes one to know one. A high-technology fire requires high-technology logs. The company's growth ultimately depends upon the ability of the corporate leader to recognize the difference between good logs and deadwood. (This is especially true in the R&D area where life-or-death technological decisions must be made frequently.)

The fourth principle is focus, a necessary attribute for all types of companies hoping to become dominant players.

Tellabs is not focused on telecommunications equipment where it would have to compete with industry leaders like Lucent Technologies and Northern Telecom. Rather it is focused on the "special services" segment of the telecom market. (Better to be a big fish in your own pond than a small fish in somebody else's big pond.)

Tellabs has, of course, acquired other companies, but not to diversity into other segments of the market, but rather to fill in the holes in their "special services" market.

The easiest way to put out a fire is to spread your logs. In other words, to diversity. The best way to make a fire burn brighter is to keep the fuel concentrated. In other words, focus.

The fifth principle is globalization. You can't fault Tellabs except for the fact that it should have gone global sooner. Less than one-third of its current business is outside the US. If Tellabs wants to fulfill its destiny in the next millennium, it is going to have to increase that percentage greatly.

A company has no choice. If you don't take your products and services into other countries around the world, companies in those other countries are doing to take their products and into your country. The best defense is a good offense.

sales manager Fred Weeks' kitchen, planning how to solve their employment problems for good.

They aren't complaining about their employer's broken pact to share profits or the misguided strategic plan any more. Instead, the band of six Wescom managers, including Weeks, engineering head Michael Bircks, controller Martin Hambel, sales manager Chris Cooney, plant manager Ronald Sproull, and advertising manager John Santucci, are working out the final details of their bid for career independence – their own company, Tellabs, Inc.

Incorporated that spring, Tellabs' first home is Weeks' kitchen and the company's founders capitalize the business with $110,000 raised amongst themselves. The company quickly relocates to more professional digs in a $600-a-month unit in a Lisle, Illinois industrial development. CEO Michael Bircks is the R&D department. On a homemade workbench, he builds the company's first product, the 7001 dial long line, that Tellabs' two-man sales force immediately begins selling to independent US phone companies.

The 7001 is a success and by year-end 1975, Tellabs has earned revenues of $312,000. The company already employs 30 people.

The founders of Tellabs know that fast-track product development and an aggressive sales force are the keys to their success. Throughout the remaining years of the decade, the company generates two or four new products *each month* and starts building the sales staff needed to get them to customers.

In 1976, growth causes the company to expand into two additional rental units. Tellabs also gains it first major contract, with Western Union. Within the year, the company moves again. This time, into its own 25,000 square foot building at 4951 Indiana Avenue in Lisle.

In 1977, the company's sales force is boosted from two to eight employees. Tellabs generates a corresponding jump in sales to $7.8 million.

By 1978, Tellabs is quickly becoming an established name in the telecom equipment "special services" sector. Its products are aimed at low profile niches, such as business telecom services and the inter-exchange market. Higher production rates and larger purchases from its suppliers are increasing the company's net profit.

The resulting revenue is invested back into the organization. In 1978, the direct sales force doubles in size and three regional sales offices open in the US. The company's operations also expand into another 20,000 square feet in Lisle and R&D spending comes in just shy of $700,000. Revenues double to $14.9 million. Tellabs' major competitor in the non-Bell special services marketplace: Wescom, Inc.

Going public

In 1979, Bob Pershing, one of Tellabs' earliest employees and a holder of a good chunk of the private company's stock, decides to move on. He cashes in, selling his shares to two venture capital firms, Greylock Partners & Co. and Sutter Hill Ventures. They get ownership stakes in the company and one seat each on the board.

Tellabs buys the buildings and land on which its headquarters is located in early 1979. It also takes its first steps outside the US, forming Tellabs Communications Canada, Ltd, a fully owned subsidiary in Mississauga, Ontario.

Sales in 1979 double yet again to $30.7 million. In December, Rockwell International files its intent to purchase Wescom, Inc., giving Tellabs' chief competitor a ready source of funding, but diluting its focus.

In July 1980, Tellabs counters with an initial public stock offering on Nasdaq. The company raises $3.1 million on the IPO and the founders retain close to 70 percent of the stock. CEO Bircks owns a 21 percent share, the largest single stake.

Tellabs sinks more cash into expansion. It leases another 36,000 square foot building in Lisle and starts construction on a new plant in Round Rock, Texas.

By year-end, Tellabs is selling over 400 individual products ranging in price from $100 to $1000. Its assemblies and systems sell for up to $20,000. Virtually all of its sales are domestic and 69 percent are generated by the company's direct sales force, which now boasts 103 employees located in five US and one Canadian sales offices. The remaining sales are made by a network of independent telecom equipment distributors that carry the company's products.

Six years old, the company has grown from 6 to 630 employees, including 48 in product development. Sales at the end of Tellabs' first year as a public company reach $43 million.

Competition mounts

In the first half of the 1980s, Tellabs' growth slows slightly as more complex and more expensive telecom equipment is cued into the company's development pipeline. The company begins to follow the early emergence of digital technology, shifting its development efforts into evolutionary products incorporating both technologies.

R&D gets a boost with the founding of the Advanced Development Laboratory in South Bend, Indiana in January 1981. Its first director is James Melsa, the former chairman of Electrical Engineering at the University of Notre Dame.

The company's fast rise to prominence and profitability has attracted some new competition. In addition to Rockwell-Wescom, General Telephone announces it will also target the special services product market

At year-end 1981, the company has 677 employees. Revenues hit $48 million and generate net profits of $7 million.

In 1982, Tellabs releases the telecom industry's first digital echo canceller, the 6921. Unfortunately, the company is depending on a vendor for the product's microprocessor and the vendor does not deliver. Finally, after lawsuits are filed late in the year, the chip arrives and Tellabs' echo cancellers become one of its best-selling product lines.

The company also releases its first statistical multiplexers. These products enable high-speed data transmission via telephone, cutting the time and cost of using leased telephone lines.

Tellabs' direct sales force is now developing 80 percent of total sales and 75 percent of orders are coming from operating telephone companies, such as the regional Bell companies. All, except for five percent, of sales come from the US.

The most significant change for Tellabs in 1982 is the government-mandated breakup of AT&T. As of January 1984, "Ma Bell," which controls 80 percent of the telephone service in the US, will have to spin off its seven regional operating companies. The newly independent companies, which until then purchased most of their equipment from AT&T's Western Electric equipment division, and new competitors in the long distance industry will create a bonanza of new sales possibilities for Tellabs. It will also attract plenty of new competition in the previously restricted market.

At year-end, the company's workforce has grown to 770 employees. Annual revenues hit $57 million, but income stays flat at $7 million.

In 1983, Tellabs extends its distribution channels. It agrees to sell select data products through Teltone Corp. and 3M's Interactive Systems Unit.

In March, Tellabs awards TIE/communications, Inc. the exclusive right to market its products outside North America. The agreement obligates TIE to achieve sales levels starting in 1986 and remains in force through 1990. If the goals are hit, TIE gets an option to extend the agreement through 1995.

In 1983, Tellabs' digital echo cancellers generate 20 percent of annual revenues. Total revenues hit $85 million and net profits rise to $12.8 million. The company has 1094 employees: 174 in the sales, support, and marketing area; 103 in product development; 778 in manufacturing and quality assurance; and 39 in administration. And a new 11,000 square foot production facility is opened in Puerto Rico.

The deregulation and digital eras dawn

In 1984, AT&T divests and the Baby Bells ring in the New Year, fundamentally altering the US telecom market. Tellabs goes to both the Winter Olympics in Sarajevo and the Summer Olympics in Los Angeles. The company builds the custom ringdown package that television's ABC uses for internal communication during its broadcasts at the two sites.

Digital is rapidly becoming the name of the game at Tellabs. The company introduces a new network-level product for systems using T1 digital transmission links. The new product combines a multiplexer for speech processing with a software-driven digital cross-connect system (DCS), and will soon become a major revenue generator. The company's echo cancellers continue to sell well, accounting for 23 percent of 1984 sales.

Late in 1984, the company signs two more OEM contracts. This time, AT&T Information Systems will market Tellabs' statistical multiplexers, data switches, and T1 multiplexers to its customers. The products are sold under its own label as part of the Dataphone II line of data communications equipment.

At year-end, Tellabs employs 1217 people. Revenues hit $95.5 million with a 50 percent gross profit margin. Net profits reach $12.8 million.

Tellabs product mix is changing. In 1985, the company's special services products account for 60 percent of revenue, and digital and data communications products – just a couple of years old – account for 35 percent of revenue.

In keeping with the growth in systems-level products, Tellabs buys a two percent stake in Sierra Semiconductor Corp. for $1 million. Sierra designs and manufactures VSLI chips, which provide the brains in Tellabs' digital systems. The investment gives the company access to microchip technology.

In 1985, Tellabs celebrates its tenth anniversary, but just misses hitting the $100 million mark, as the year runs out at $99.98 million. Profit margins, however, sink to 35 percent as the Baby Bells search for the lowest prices on equipment and new competitors enter the marketplace.

The company responds to soft margins by looking inward. It quickly adopts a just-in-time (JIT) strategy supported by a cell-based manufacturing structure and the cross training of plant employees. Inspected-in quality processes are replaced with a quality-at-the-source perspective. By March 1987, operations in Lisle are 100 percent JIT.

Tellabs pumps more dollars into R&D, spending $13.3 million in 1986. The company's digital and data products now account for 42 percent of sales. In December, the company wins a five-year contract to develop and make DS3 digital cross-connect systems for Northern Telecom, Inc.

By 1987, the international distribution agreement with TIE has died a natural death and Tellabs decides it is ready to take its products to the world on its own. It forms a new subsidiary, Tellabs International, Inc. to market outside North America. The operation records sales of $7.4 million for the year. Total revenues hit $115 million, generating net earnings of $8.4 million.

Special services (now called network access) products are no longer Tellabs' biggest sellers, as digital and data products account for 55 percent of the year's revenue. Sprint gives the company a $10 million contract for digital echo cancellers, and new products such as Crossnet multiplexers and T1 and DNX33 cross-connect systems are grabbing attention in the marketplace.

Late in the year, Tellabs announces the development of the Telemark Network Management System, a software program to control, manage, and monitor telecom networks using Tellabs products. Now, Tellabs will be the OEM contractor with Digital Equipment Corp. and Applied Computing Devices supplying the products.

At year-end, the company has 1520 employees. Sales rise to $136 million and net profits are $10.7 million.

In 1988, Tellabs reorganizes its US sales force into two segments: Public Networks and General Markets. Public Networks is organized into six regions and focuses on telecom service providers, including the Baby Bells, which generate 20 percent of the company's revenues. General Markets devotes its energies to end-users, such as utilities and businesses.

In addition to the sales reorganization, the company also creates a stand-alone customer service department to handle all technical support. Customer service personnel work from the regional sales offices, but report to Lisle.

By December 1988, the company has 1820 employees. Gross sales rebound to $155.4 million, with 58 percent coming from digital and data products. Net income rises to $13.4 million.

A piece of the old sod

By year-end 1988, Tellabs International has sales offices in the UK, Australia, and Hong Kong. In February 1989, the company creates an operational headquarters in Europe with the acquisition of telecom equipment maker Delta Communications based in Shannon, Ireland. Quickly renamed Tellabs Ltd, Delta sells digital products into the European market and adds five percent of Tellabs' 1989 sales. The Delta acquisition also adds 150 employees to the Tellabs' workforce, which now totals just over 2000 people.

In late 1989 and 1990, Tellabs begins preparing the rollout of what will be its most popular, and profitable, DCS to date – the TITAN 5500 digital cross-connect system. The company's first SONET-based system, the TITAN 5500 eats up a large portion of the $31.5 million devoted to R&D in 1990. The 5500 also sets the stage for revenue growth throughout the 1990s.

By year-end 1990, sales hit $211 million, including 12 percent from international orders, and the company employs 2127 people.

In 1991, the final chapter in the Tellabs/Wescom story is written. That year, Rockwell divests most of its Wescom telecom business to Alcatel and Charles Industries, Ltd.

Giant Alcatel swallows its portion of Wescom without a trace. Charles is a small, privately held company in which telecom equipment is only one of several diversified product lines. A few Wescom products linger in the marketplace, but for all intents and purposes, the company that provided the impetus for the founding of Tellabs, and its major competition, quietly disappears.

Closely observing effects of the AT&T breakup in the US, many countries start to deregulate and privatize their own telecommunications monopolies. Tellabs' international network expands as the business opportunities grow. In the early 1990s, the company adds offices in Belgium, New Zealand, Korea, and Mexico.

By January 1993, the company has grown to 2216 employees, with 462 of them in sales and marketing. In July, Tellabs opens its new 236,500 square foot manufacturing and R&D facility in Bolingbrook, Illinois, which also serves as headquarters of Tellabs International Inc.

In October 1993, the company acquires Finnish telecom equipment maker Martis Oy for $70 million. A privately held networking equipment company based in Helsinki, Martis brings with it the MartisDXX, a software controlled multiplexer with integral cross-connect switching. The MartisDXX is Tellabs' flagship product in Europe. In 1993, international sales are 30 percent of revenues.

Playing technological chess

As data networking technologies begin to collide with telecom, Tellabs joins the industry-wide scramble to expand its expertise with joint ventures and equity investments. In 1993, the company makes three deals to build its capabilities. Internet Communications Corporation signs on as a development partner to enhance Tellabs 300 Series packet switches and statistical multiplexers. In another deal, and in return for a 14 percent equity stake, Tellabs gets the right to use Promptus Communications, Inc.'s OASIS 1000 bandwidth manager in its network access products. Tellabs also agrees to work with TRW's High Performance Network Products to develop integrated SONET transport and asynchronous transfer mode (ATM) switching systems.

By year-end 1993, the company has 2370 employees and revenues have grown to $320 million with net earnings of $32 million. Wall Street is also taking notice and Tellabs' stock price more than triples to $69.

In 1994, Tellabs and California-based Advanced Fibre Communications form Advanced Access Labs, a fifty-fifty joint venture partnership to develop and manufacture a telephony-over-cable transport system that will be marketed under the CABLESPAN name. Tellabs cements the deal with equity investments in Advanced Fibre. In August, the company inks an OEM and technology licensing agreement with LightStream Corp. for that company's ATM switching products.

Sales jump impressively once again to $494 million and profits more than double to $72 million, as Tellabs seems to hit its stride. The company's TITAN and MartisDXX systems are generating almost three-quarters of the company's revenues. The company has 2585 employees.

On Tellabs' 20th birthday, long-time CEO Michael Bircks challenges the company to hit $2 billion in revenues by the year 2000. The company responds with a run of growth through the late 1990s that will give its stock the best five-year annualized return (91.3 percent) in the S&P 500.

In early 1995, Cisco acquires LightStream forcing Tellabs to renegotiate its access to the company's ATM switching technology. Tellabs retains its rights. The development project using Promptus' bandwidth manager is cancelled, but the agreement lives on.

With the TITAN and MartisDXX systems' continuing popularity, revenues grow to $635 million and earnings break over the $100 million mark for the first time, at $115 million. Tellabs now employs 2814.

Tellabs continues to pursue technological expansion through acquisition and development partnerships. In April 1996, the company buys Steinbrecher Corporation for $77 million in loans and cash, and turns it into the Wireless Systems Division. The purchase is intended to provide an entry into the wireless local loop market, but the products and the market never materialize.

In June 1996, the company acquires Transys Network's SONET product line for $17 million in cash. The products will add broadband access and transport technology to the TITAN digital cross-connect systems.

In December, however, Tellabs' joint venture, Advanced Access Labs, does materialize a viable product. At year-end, the CABLESPAN system for providing telephone service over cable networks is launched.

In 1996, the TITAN 5500 and the MartisDXX systems generate 80 percent of the company's $868 million in revenues. Net profits hit $175 million and the workforce expands to 3418 employees.

In early 1997, Tellabs purchases wavelength division multiplexing and optical networking technology from IBM's Thomas J. Watson Research Center. Under the agreement, the Research Center's optical network development team joins Tellabs, establishing a new R&D facility in Hawthorne, NY.

Soon after, Tellabs Oy acquires Trelcom Oy of Finland, a company specializing in digital subscriber line technology. DSL technology allows telephone operators to deliver high-quality, high-bandwidth services over existing copper lines.

Late in 1997, CABLESPAN orders start to arrive. A2000, one of Europe's largest cable operators in Europe, starts providing telephone service in the Netherlands using CABLESPAN in November. In December, MediaOne, the third largest US cable operator, selects CABLESPAN for its commercial deployment of cable telephone services.

Tellabs is fast growing out of house and home and, in 1997, undertakes a host of construction projects. Ground is broken for a new plant and research facility in Espoo, Finland in April. In June, the company starts a new 130,000 square foot addition to its Shannon, Ireland operations. In the US, a new regional headquarters for Latin America is established in Florida. And a 308,000 square foot expansion the Bolingbrook manufacturing facility is completed.

Sales during 1997 reach another all-time high as revenues cross the $1 billion mark to hit $1.2 billion. Driven by now-routine system sales, net earnings hit $263.6 million.

In 1998, Tellabs makes a play to catapult ahead with the announced acquisition of Ciena Corporation, a leader in capacity boosting optical transmission equipment. However, the $7 billion merger falls apart as Tellabs realizes that the Ciena's technological lead over the competition is not worth its hefty price tag.

More successful is the acquisition of Virginia-based Coherent Communications for $670 million in stock. Coherent brings greater depth and market share in the echo cancellation and digital speech processing businesses. And, almost immediately, it starts adding to Tellabs bottom line.

CABLESPAN continues to grow through 1998. In November, Tellabs gets a $150 million contract to provide the system to Priority Telecom for telephony-over-cable service in the Netherlands and France.

Still driven by TITAN and MartisDXX sales, revenues hit $1.6 billion in 1998 and earnings reach $590 million.

In April 1999, China Telecom chooses Tellabs' MartisDXX to upgrade and expand the service quality and capabilities of its international private leased lines networks. That same month, the company declares a 2-for-1 stock split and CEO Michael Birck issues a new challenge – "×3 by '03" or $6 billion in sales by 2003.

In May, Bircks gets a jump on the goal by announcing the acquisition of Alcatel's DSC Communications business in Europe for $110 million. DSC Communications is a leading provider of managed high-speed transport solutions based on Synchronous Digital Hierarchy (SDH) and dense wavelength-division multiplexing technology. With the addition of the business, Tellabs gets operations in Copenhagen, Denmark, and Drogheda, Ireland; sales and support offices in the UK, India, and Poland; and a stake in Fibcom India Ltd.

The acquisition spree continues with the $575 million purchase of Internet equipment maker NetCore Systems. And, in early 2000, with the $300 million acquisition of SALIX Technologies, a telecom switch maker.

Tellabs close-up

Tellabs, Inc. is a company that rises to a challenge. In 1995, CEO Michael Birck challenged the $600 million company to reach "2B by 2K" – $2 billion in annual revenues by the year 2000, and Tellabs hit the milestone one year early.

Cause for celebration? Not to Birck. In April 1999, he announced a new goal: "×3 by '03."

"Since it looks that we will achieve that objective one year early," said the CEO and co-founder of the company at the time, "it's only appropriate that we set our sights on the next goal – $6 billion in revenue by 2003."

These are heady numbers for a medium-sized player in the telecommunications equipment business, an industry that is dominated by high-profile giants, such as Lucent and Nortel. And yet, 25-year-old Tellabs has not only managed to carve out a profitable niche for itself, it has also stayed on the leading edge of an industry driven by technological change.

In 1999, Tellabs' annual revenues hit $2.31 billion and generated earnings of $559 million. To lucky shareholders who bought stock in the company during its 1980 IPO and held on, that translated to roughly an 8000 percent return on their investment.

The Lisle, Illinois-based company makes 85 percent of its revenue connecting phone calls or, more accurately, making the analog and digital systems that connect data and voice transmissions. Fully one-third of its business comes from its largest customer group, the former regional Bell telephone companies in the US. Additional customer groups include independent phone companies and other telecommunication providers, cable operators, corporate end-users, and government agencies.

Originally formed to serve US phone companies, Tellabs is in the process of expanding globally. It still generates just over two-thirds of its business in its home country and most of the remaining sales are in Europe. Its North American business is managed from its home base outside Chicago. Three regional headquarters manage the rest of the world: Singapore for Asia-Pacific; London for Europe, the Middle East, and Africa; and Fort Lauderdale, Florida for Latin America. Over 50 offices extend the company's reach into specific countries.

In January 2000, the company employed 6997 people: 2351 in manufacturing; 1747 in the sales, sales support and marketing area; 2282 in product development; and 617 in administration.

Tellabs products are assembled from standard and custom fabricated parts obtained from outside vendors. The company's major assembly facilities are located in Illinois, Texas, and New York in the US, County Clare and Shannon, Ireland, and Espoo, Finland.

Ninety per cent of 1999's sales were generated through the direct sales force. The North American sales group consists of 150 direct sales and support personnel working from corporate headquarters and six regional offices. It is organized by major customer groups.

The international sales group consists of 180 direct sales and sales support employees working from corporate headquarters, 37 regional sales offices, and three regional headquarters. It is structured geographically.

The remaining 10 percent of sales comes from a network of telecommunications equipment distributors. Distributors offer products through catalogs and trade shows. Tellabs' direct sales force supports distributors and their customers.

In the past few years, Tellabs has built a worldwide customer service staff working from regional centers in the US, Ireland, Canada, and Finland. The staff mainly supports systems customers with services including application engineering, installation, maintenance and repair, on-site training, logistics management, and 24-hour telephone and online technical support.

Over 30 percent of Tellabs' workforce is involved in R&D, a good indication of the emphasis the company places on growth for new product development and the rate of change in the industry as a whole. New product development efforts are almost entirely aimed at software and hardware using digital, SDH/SONET, wavelength division multiplexing, fiber optic, and ATM technologies.

The main R&D facilities are located in Illinois, Indiana, New York, and Massachusetts in the US, Montreal in Canada, Espoo and Oulu in Finland, and Shannon, Ireland. In 1999, Tellabs spent $303 million on research and development, one of the highest investment rates as a percentage of sales in the industry.

Major product groups

As it grows some product offerings via internal development and acquisitions, and loses others to obsolescence, Tellabs reorganizes its product portfolios. Currently, it has three main product groups.

Digital Cross-Connect Systems (DCCS)
DCCS is the home of the TITANs. First introduced in 1991, the Tellabs' TITAN family of digital cross-connect systems connects telephone calls. In the case of the flagship TITAN 5500 system, that means up to 688,000 simultaneous calls.

TITAN systems contribute 59 percent of the company's total revenues, or $1.36 billion in 1999. The SONET-based TITAN systems are the industry leader in fiber optics networks and are widely used by North American local and long-distance carriers, including six of the seven regional Bell companies. The division's major products include the TITAN 5300 Digital Cross-Connect family, the TITAN 532E and 532L, and the TITAN 5500 and 5500S.

Managed Digital Networks (MDN)

MDN's major product is the MartisDXX managed access and transport network system, used outside North America in wireless and business services.

The DXX system is integrated hardware and software products that manage voice and data networks. It is compatible with SDH (fiber optic) transmissions. DXX can be used to provide private branch exchange networking, local area network interconnectivity, leased lines, ATM-based services, and X.21 and X.25 data services. Wireless service applications include analog and digital cellular, paging as well as other public and private voice, data and messaging services.

MartisDXX sales hit $438 million during 1999, or 19 percent of the company's annual revenues. Sales growth is generated by countries with emerging telecommunications infrastructures.

Network Access Systems (NAS)

NAS is the home of a variety of products that generated $350 million in 1999 or 15 percent of revenue. They include the following.

- The CABLESPAN 2300 Universal Telephony Distribution System, which puts cable companies in the local telephone business. It is an economical way to add voice and data services to existing cable networks. The system can be managed from an integrated interface providing local and remote management, or from a PC-based Element Management System that supports multiple systems and network operators.
- The AN 2100 Gateway Exchange System, which combines echo canceller and TITAN cross-connect technology to help bridge the changeover between time-division multiplexing for transmitting separate data, voice and/or video signals simultaneously to the next-generation packet-based ATM technology.
- Tellabs' long established line of voice enhancement and echo cancellation products, which include the industry-leading products in echo cancellation and voice enhancement. The product portfolio includes: digital echo cancellers, such as the EC-8000, EC Duo

8000, and 2500 Series; the 257 T1 and 258 E1 Echo Cancellers; and the Tel/mor network management system for echo cancellers. NETS offers call-quality enhancers, including level controllers, such as Noise Reduction, Sculptured Sound and Clearcall, and compression products, such as voice compression transcoders that double the capacity of digital trunk links without compromising transmission quality. This group also includes Crossnet multiplexers, a maturing product line of time division multiplexing products.

Many of these products are sold to OEM customers through licensing and product development agreements. OEM customers include Cisco, China's Eastern Communications Company Limited, Lucent Technologies, Motorola CableComm, and Nokia.

- Element management systems (EMS), which control Tellabs' equipment. It has three major EMS products used for managing the CABLESPAN, TITAN 5300, and TITAN 5500 product. EMS software automates standard installation and service activation tasks. It provides a central control point for fault, configuration, and performance management. The products are part of Tellabs' Select solution program that offers a consultative approach to system purchases.

Income statement

Year	Revenue ($m)	Net income ($m)	Net profit margin	Employees
1999	2,319.5	559.1	24.1%	6,997
1998	1,660.1	398.3	24.0%	4,980
1997	1,203.5	263.7	21.9%	4,087
1996	869.0	118.0	13.6%	3,418
1995	635.2	115.6	18.2%	2,814
1994	494.2	72.4	14.6%	2,585
1993	320.5	32.0	10.0%	2,370
1992	258.6	16.9	6.5%	2,000
1991	212.8	6.6	3.1%	2,094
1990	211.0	8.1	3.8%	2,127

Stock history

Year	Stock price ($) FY High	FY Low	FY Close	P/E High	Low	Per share ($) Earns	Div.	Book value
1999	77.25	32.38	64.19	57	24	1.36	0.00	5.07
1998	46.56	15.69	34.28	45	15	1.04	0.00	3.54
1997	32.50	16.00	26.44	46	23	0.71	0.00	2.57
1996	23.38	7.63	18.81	73	24	0.32	0.00	1.65
1995	13.19	5.88	9.25	41	18	0.32	0.00	1.22
1994	7.00	2.73	6.97	35	14	0.20	0.00	0.84
1993	3.40	0.79	2.95	38	9	0.10	0.00	0.60
1992	1.10	0.66	1.03	22	13	0.05	0.00	0.50
1991	0.92	0.51	0.90	31	17	0.03	0.00	0.45
1990	0.63	0.35	0.63	21	12	0.03	0.00	0.42

1999 year-end financials

Debt ratio	0.1%
Return on equity	32.6%
Cash ($m)	308.4
Current ratio	6.52
Long-term debt ($m)	2.9
Shares outstanding (millions)	404.3
Dividend yield	0.0%
Dividend payout	0.0%
Market value ($m)	25,949.8

Financial data provided by Hoover's Online (www.hoovers.com) and Media General Financial Services, Inc.

Tellabs contacts

Tellabs, Inc.
4951 Indiana Avenue
Lisle, IL 60532, USA

Phone: 630–378–8800
Fax: 630–852–7346
URL: www.tellabs.com

CEO: Michael Birck   CFO: Joan Ryan   HR: Marc Ugol

Toyota Motor Corporation – Toyota City, Japan

Executive snapshot

Toyota is looking for a new challenge, but for now, expect more of the same strategy that built the company into a leader in its industry.

"We are positioning Toyota to remain a leader in the top tier of the automobile industry," says Hiroshi Okuda, chairman, Toyota Motor Corporation. "That means leading the industry in presenting customers with new possibilities in motor transport and reshaping our manufacturing and purchasing to maximize global efficiency."

Toyota backdrop

Historically, the two driving forces at Toyota Motor have been innovation and improvement. They are backed up by an impressive ability to identify market opportunities and a sense of timing that is often early, but almost never late.

The father's vision

It is not the best of times for 43-year old Sakichi Toyoda. The inventor built a small empire out of his innovative textile looms and attracted the support of one of Japan's powerful trusts, the Mitsui

Future focus

The ultimate automobile focus

Two of the defining products of the 20th century are the automobile and the personal computer. The automobile in combination with a high-speed highway system lets you explore the world physically. The personal computer in combination with the Internet highway lets you explore the world mentally.

Both products are especially significant because they are tied to the idea of personal freedom. No longer is an individual condemned to be born, grow up and die in a small geographic area. First the automobile and then the personal computer allows one the freedom to explore the world.

(Sure, the airplane also frees one from the limits of geography, but unless you particularly like duty-free shopping, you still need an automobile to do much exploring.)

While focus is a powerful business strategy, what you focus on is just as important. In many ways, the automobile is a perfect product to build a company around. First of all, it's the most expensive technological purchase an individual will ever make in his or her lifetime. Second, its economic life is relatively short so the car buyer is likely to be back in the market in a handful of years. In contrast, other expensive products like houses and jewelry have much longer lives.

As a result an automobile company can achieve enormous sales. If Toyota were an American company, for example, it would be ranked no. 6 on the latest *Fortune 500* list, ahead of IBM and right behind GE. In what other industry can a single company focused on a single product produce such substantial revenues?

Toyota is truly a global company with sales in virtually every country of the world and manufacturing facilities in dozens of locations.

In spite of its global presence, Toyota is still perceived as a Japanese brand. A Toyota might be assembled in the UK and purchased in Poland, but it's still a Japanese car. (Some products have national or regional identities; others do not. Beverage brands, for example, are usually strongly identified with an individual country. Computers only mildly so.)

Automobiles can be divided into three broad categories: Asian brands, American brands and European brands. DaimlerChrysler is competing with Volkswagen and BMW for leadership in Europe. General Motors is competing with Ford for leadership in America. But in Asia, Toyota enjoys a clear-cut leadership position. (Mixing a European identity with an American identity is one of the reasons the Daimler-Benz/Chrysler merger was ill-conceived.)

What made Toyota the leading Japanese brand? As usual, being first is the primary reason. Toyota was the first Japanese automobile company. (Nissan was second.) Henry Ford built the first mass-produced automobile in America, but lost his leadership to General Motors when he refused to launch multiple brands.

Will Nissan, Honda, Mitsubishi or Mazda ever overtake Toyota? It's unlikely. An automobile is a complex product characterized by long lead-times for both car design and production equipment design. A no. 2 or no. 3 company might easily come up with a number of better automobile concepts, but the long lead-times allow a leader like Toyota easily to copy the competitor's better approach.

(It is true, however, that both General Motors and Ford permanently lost out to Chrysler in minivans because they failed to copy the product promptly enough. If you want to maintain your leadership, you can't give the smaller company too much of a head start.)

The minivan itself is a good example of divergence, a phenomenon that has affected every industry including the automotive industry. In the beginning, the mass-produced automobile (as distinct from hand-made specialty cars) was primarily a sedan with two or four doors. Then divergence struck.

Today we have compact, intermediate and full-size cars. Sports cars, station wagons, minivans, sports-utility vehicles. In Europe you are seeing the birth of the ultra-small "city" car.

As an industry diverges, your brand should also diverge. That is, it should become two or more brands. (This is the mistake that Henry Ford made.)

Recently Toyota has handled divergence brilliantly. It was Daimler-Benz and Jaguar that pioneered the mass-produced expensive car category, followed by BMW. (Cadillacs were bigger and therefore cost more, but they were not in the same elevated price category as a Mercedes-Benz.)

Toyota decided to emulate the success of the European brands by launching an expensive Japanese car in the American market. But they didn't call the new car a Toyota Super or a Toyota Ultra. That would have been line extension.

They called the new brand "Lexus." Never underestimate the power of perception, especially with high-end brands. People buy expensive products not only because they think they are better, but also because they have an "expensive" name. A Toyota Ultra might be better, but it does not have an expensive or prestige name.

It was Honda, however, who got to the market first with the Acura. But Honda made a basic error. In addition to expensive six-cylinder Acuras, they also gave their dealers less-expensive four-cylinder Acuras to sell.

Toyota did not make the same mistake. The Lexus line consisted only of relatively expensive six-cylinder and eight-cylinder cars. As a result, Lexus (and its Nissan cousin Infiniti) achieved a reputation as true luxury cars. Acura, much less so.

Lexus today is a powerful brand in the US and one that Toyota can take worldwide as economies in less-developed countries improve.

Notwithstanding its position as the leading Japanese car company, Toyota has made some strange moves recently. It makes industrial equipment like forklifts, prefab housing and recreational boating products. It also holds stakes in three Japanese providers of telephone service.

This makes no sense. Here is a company with some 95 percent of its sales in the automotive market (if you include its finance subsidiary which mainly finances Toyota cars and trucks). The worldwide automobile business is so huge that one wonders why a company like Toyota would want to fool around with forklift trucks.

zaibatsu. But, in 1910, after a prolonged business slump following the Russo-Japanese War, he has been pushed out of his own company.

Disappointed with his country and his fate, Toyoda is touring the US. He is getting the lay of the land and considering leaving Japan for good. Toyoda is surprised by the size of the US and particularly, the many automobiles. Two years after the introduction of Ford's Model T, there seem to be cars everywhere. US automakers are already turning out 100,000 vehicles per year.

At the end of his journey, Toyoda makes up his mind. He will return to Japan; it is after all his birthplace and home. What a difference his decision will make.

On his return on January 1, 1911, Toyoda starts again. This time, instead of building looms, he buys them and makes cloth. He cannot resist the siren call of innovation, however. Unhappy with quality of the yarn he must buy, Toyoda builds a spinning mill to make his own.

By 1918, with the help of a booming war economy, the entrepreneur is back on top. He reorganizes his new companies into Toyoda Spinning & Weaving Co., Ltd. The textile maker employs 1000 workers running 34,000 spindles and 1000 looms.

In 1920, Toyoda brings his son, Kiichiro, into the business and with his help, the father develops a long-time dream, the automatic loom. The Toyodas perfect their new loom in late 1925, and in 1926 they establish Toyoda Automatic Loom Works, Ltd.

In 1929, UK-based Platt Brothers, the world's largest textile equipment maker, pays Toyoda one million yen for the rights to make the company's automatic loom. Sakichi Toyoda passes the money onto Kiichiro with one stringent condition – it must be used to develop an automobile manufacturing company.

Sakichi Toyoda's desire to build cars has been growing since his 1910 tour of the US. Since then, both Ford and General Motors have come to Japan and are successfully building and selling cars. There are three struggling Japanese carmakers, but they are building their cars by hand, not on assembly lines.

Toyoda is convinced he can beat the Americans at their own game and after an exploratory journey through the US and the UK, Kiichiro agrees. Unhappily, Sakichi never gets to see the results of the seed he has planted. In October 1930, after suffering an earlier stroke, he contracts pneumonia and dies at age 63.

The son's labor

In the months before his father's death, Kiichiro Toyoda commandeers a small space in the Toyoda Automatic Loom Works and begins working on the development of a gasoline engine. Soon he is setting up a conveyor line, machine tools, and a foundry. Toyoda is inspired by Henry Ford's book, *My Life and Work*, and advises everyone he knows to read it.

Meanwhile, in the early 1930s, the Japanese government decides a robust auto industry is essential and begins encouraging domestic companies to enter the market. In September 1933, Toyoda finds the time is right to declare his intentions. He announces he will create the prototype for a mass-produced passenger car. In November, the Automobile Department of the Toyoda Loom Works is established.

One month later, the company that will become Toyota's greatest domestic competitor, Nissan, is also founded. Kiichiro Toyoda responds by accelerating his plans and pushes Risaburo Toyoda, his adopted brother who is leader of the Loom Works, and its board to approve plans for a pilot factory and a steel mill.

An automobile, however, is a complicated machine. It takes a year and half to produce the first engine prototype, simply named the Type A. Another year later, in May 1935, the start-up's first car, the Model A1, rolls out of the shop. In August, the first truck, the G1, is complete. The operation produces 20 trucks in 1935, generating only a small fraction of the more than five million yen invested in the venture.

Nevertheless, the timing is close to perfect: Kiichiro Toyoda is paying close attention to Japan's increasingly militaristic stance. He watches as the government is raising barriers that will soon drive both Ford and GM out of Japan altogether. And when, in 1936, the government also adopts legislation that requires licensing to mass-produce motor vehicles, Toyoda is prepared.

Only two licenses are granted: one to the Toyoda Loom Works operation and one to Nissan. Toyoda now has a state-enforced franchise for making his cars and trucks.

Prospects are good, but the G1 truck is not earning a reputation for quality. There are many problems, not the least of which is a weak rear axle prone to cracking on the welds. Production, mainly of trucks, hits 1000 vehicles in 1936, but is not even nearing the breakeven point.

The problems do not give Toyoda pause. He is always looking to the future and in late 1935, purchases a 472 acre undeveloped tract of land in Koromo, a rural town east of Nagoya. In 1936, he starts planning a large production facility with all the needed ancillary operations and housing for employees. It will be, for all intents and purposes, a town devoted to the making of motor vehicles.

Toyoda estimates the cost of the new facilities at 30 million yen, a huge sum that the Loom Works cannot hope to raise. So, instead, the company decides to spin off the operation.

Again, Toyoda's timing is impeccable. In July 1937, Japan's military actions in China turn into a full-scale war, generating an immediate demand for motor vehicles. All of the company's finished inventory is purchased by the government and an additional 6000 trucks are ordered. Within the month, Toyota Motor Co., Ltd is launched, selling 240,000 shares to 20-odd investors and the Mitsui zaibatsu.

A two-edged sword

The stepped-up needs of the military drive the Japanese economy throughout the late 1930s and early 1940s. In 1938, the Koromo plant is finished ahead of schedule and immediately running at full capacity. Toyota makes 4615 vehicles, almost all trucks and buses, and turns a profit of 825,000 yen, well ahead of Kiichiro Toyoda's predictions.

In 1939, with their operations reduced to a fraction of their former levels, Ford and GM leave the country for good. Toyoda's dream of a mass-produced passenger car is put on hold as the government requires the company to restrict its production to military vehicles. Production almost triples to just under 12,000 vehicles.

The story remains the same through 1941 and the Japanese attack on Pearl Harbor. Early victories feed the Japanese economy until the first major defeat in 1942 at the Battle of Midway. As the tide of the war turns, so do Japan's fortunes.

In December 1943, the government takes over control of Toyota. It directs the company into aircraft production, an operation that never gets off the ground. Severe raw materials shortages lead to stripped-down trucks in 1944. Two headlights become one, wooden bodies replace steel, and now brakes are only installed on the rear wheels.

Understanding the seriousness of Japan's condition, Kiichiro Toyoda begins studying the history of Germany after World War I. He is already trying to determine the future of his country and company. In 1945, Koromo is partially destroyed by an American air attack. And in August, after the horrific bombings at Nagasaki and Hiroshima, Japan surrenders unconditionally.

The post-war years are just as bad. Inflation runs rampant, material shortages continue, and the occupation forces determine that the Toyoda Group, including Toyota Motor, is part and parcel of the zaibatsu system, a system it intends to destroy.

The only saving grace is the urgent need for motor vehicles in the reconstruction effort. In September 1945, General Headquarters of the Allied Forces (GHQ) instructs the company to resume truck production on a limited basis. As work slowly begins, Kiichiro Toyoda is already thinking far ahead.

"This will be the era of the small passenger car," he declares at the time. " I want research on a mass-produced passenger car begun as soon as possible." He envisions an economical car on the order of Germany's Volkswagen.

In 1946, the company makes 5821 vehicles. It is nowhere near the 16,000 units coming off the lines in 1942 and not enough to generate a profit, but Toyota is operating.

In January 1947, Toyoda introduces the prototype for the company's new car, the Model SA, to his dealer network. The company is not legally allowed to make the car, but it is ready. In June, GHQ asks Toyota for 50 passenger cars for official transport, and soon after, the company receives permission to begin making cars for the general public. Toyota is back in the automobile business.

A tenuous reconstruction

In October 1947, Toyota begins producing its Model SA car. Unhappily, Kiichiro Toyoda has vastly overestimated the market for cars. The company sells only 21 cars in 1948 and 235 in 1949. Truck sales are higher, but not high enough to service the company's debt, which grows to 782 million yen in 1948 and over one billion yen in 1949.

Then, GHQ brings in Joseph Dodge to get Japan's inflationary economy under control. A fiscal conservative, Dodge simply shuts off the money supply. The economy plunges into recession, what little cash flow the company had dries up and Toyota is, for all practical purposes, bankrupt.

Toyoda scrambles for help. A consortium of 24 Japanese banks pitch in to help the company, but only if it will radically restructure – and cut its workforce by 1600 and worker salaries by ten percent. When confronted with the plan, the workers revolt and operations slow to a standstill. The standoff continues for months until, in June 1950, Kiichiro Toyoda gives up, resigning from the company and turning control over to Taizo Ishida, president of the Loom Works.

Toyoda's sacrifice jars the workers and a settlement is reached. Over 2000 workers "retire" and on June 10, production resumes. In the same period, GHQ lifts all price and quota controls and the company is free to conduct business.

The outbreak of the Korean War at the end of June and the US decision to buy military vehicles in Japan rather than transport them from the US helps Toyota back onto its feet. In 1950 and 1951, the US buys thousands of trucks and jeeps. In 1951, the company is recording a profit and resumes paying dividends.

The early 1950s also bring a modernization effort that forms the basis for the famed Toyota Production System – a just-in-time system supported by strict process control and incremental improvement that will confound rival automakers around the world in just a few decades.

In 1952, the company is ready once again to pursue the elusive mass-produced passenger car so close to its founder's heart. Early in the year, Kiichiro Toyoda agrees to return to lead the company in the quest, but the transition never happens. In March 1952, Toyoda suffers a stroke, lapses into a coma, and dies a few days later.

It is three more years before the full-sized Crown and its deluxe version, the Crown Master start rolling off Toyota's lines. In 1957, Kiichiro's dream of an economical, mass-market car is finally realized when the Corona is launched.

In 1958, construction of a new plant to produce the Crown and Corona starts at Koromo. The entire complex is renamed Toyoda (then Toyota) City. The company is still producing three times as many trucks as cars, but it is without exaggeration, a carmaker.

Bringing cars to the world

In the 1950s, Toyota Motor Sales (TMS), the group's marketing subsidiary, begins to address exports seriously. In 1949, the company establishes its first distributorship with Taiwan's Ho Tai Company. Thailand follows in 1954.

In 1952, an order for 100 trucks from Brazil attracts the company's attention and it decides the Land Cruiser is perfect for Latin America. In the mid-1950s, distributorships and operating subsidiaries are established in Brazil, El Salvador, Costa Rica, Venezuela, Columbia, and Puerto Rico.

In 1957, TMS decides the time is ripe to enter the biggest car market in the world, the United States, and in August the first two Toyota cars are shipped to Los Angeles. In October, Toyota Motor Sales, USA, Inc. (TMS, USA) is established.

The move, however, is an unqualified disaster. The Crown, which is a hit in Japan, proves to be ill-equipped and under-powered for the US. TMS fights for a foothold in a tough market, but gives up in 1960. Export sales in the US halt and TMS, USA is reduced to a skeleton crew. Almost immediately, the company begins planning its return.

The late 1950s and early 1960s bring more sales and operating subsidiaries. Toyota establishes itself in Australia, Denmark, the Netherlands, Canada, the UK, and South Africa. By 1963, exports grow to 24,000 units annually. By 1966, they top 100,000.

In 1965, Toyota returns to the US with a vengeance. This time, it brings along a revamped Corona. The Corona is roomier than most subcompacts with a snappy engine and is priced within $200 of the Volkswagen Beetle. It is a hit in its niche and soon the US dealership network is growing. By 1967, the company is importing 37,000 cars per year and the US is Toyota's largest export market. In 1968, the Corolla is introduced and by 1970, Toyota is sending 200,000 cars per year to the US.

The same period sees tremendous expansion through the world and at home. In 1970, Toyota is the third largest automaker in the world. It builds over 1.6 million vehicles that year and revenues exceed 837 billion yen.

The worst and best of times

In the 1970s, Toyota is buffeted by world events. Recessions come and go, oil becomes a crisis – twice – and auto emissions become a legal issue in the company's main markets.

The only saving grace is that all the company's competitors are facing the same conditions. The car business is a global industry, but few automakers are as well positioned for the ensuing chaos as Toyota.

The first and worst problem is the Nixon Shock, a US-caused recession in the early 1970s, that is exacerbated by a longshoreman strike that closes US ports. Then, both the US and Japan enact tough emissions laws, forcing car companies to meet standards by a set schedule. And, hard on the heels of that development, OPEC cuts off the world's major source of oil in the fall of 1973.

During the first half of the decade, Toyota's production flattens at around two million units per year, as do revenues and profits. However, the company is looking like a gold mine compared to its competitors, which are all bleeding red ink. The company's innovative production systems and waste-free methods are keeping it afloat.

More bright spots start to appear. Auto sales in the Middle East, which is awash in oil, are booming and Toyota is already well established in the region. And, as gasoline prices soar, consumers globally quickly realize the advantages of Toyota's high-mileage vehicles.

In 1974, the Corolla is the best-selling car on earth. In 1975, the company becomes the US's leading auto importer, as Volkswagen replaces the economical Beetle with a series of uninspired new models at the worst possible time. The American carmakers are also caught flat footed and far behind in this new market for energy efficient vehicles.

The competition gets a short breather as conditions loosen in 1977 and 1978. But, in 1979, the second oil crisis erupts and US hostages are taken in Iran. As the price of gas doubles in the US, Toyota sales take off. The second crisis changes consumer buying patterns for the next decade and what they want now is exactly what Toyota makes. By 1980, Toyota is exporting almost 1.8 million vehicles annually.

In 1982, Toyota Motor Company and TMS merge to become Toyota Motor Corporation. The company also launches the Camry, which will eventually become the best-selling car in the US – an event that seems so unlikely that surely even Kiichiro Toyoda could not have imagined it.

That same year, Toyota's 50-year-long learning curve becomes a circle, as General Motors comes to it to learn to make cars more efficiently. Two years later, the first cars will roll off the assembly lines of their California-based joint venture, NUMMI (New United Motor Manufacturing, Inc.), which is built on the site of an abandoned GM plant.

In the mid-1980s, Toyota moves beyond national boundaries and currency fluctuations, and begins aggressively expanding its manufacturing capacity worldwide. It forms Toyota Motor Manufacturing in the US and chooses Kentucky for its first plant. In 1988, the first US-made Camry leaves the line.

Moving up to luxury

The mid-80s also brings another new project. In 1985, Toyota Motor president Eiji Toyoda, a younger cousin of Kiichiro who has been with the company for five decades, sends a team to the US. What, he wants to know, is the potential for a line of luxury cars? The answer to his question turns out to be one of the greatest challenges since the founding of the company.

Four years after that first foray, Toyota successfully launches its Lexus line in the US with two models, the LS 400 and ES 250. They are priced between the American and European luxury models.

The Lexus project is a textbook example of the creation and launch of a new brand. The cars themselves redefine the luxury market and change owners' expectations regarding performance and quality. And Toyota establishes a dedicated dealership network to sell them that sets new standards for customer service.

In 1990, the first full year of sales for Lexus, the company known for it economical cars sells 63,534 luxury automobiles. That is almost exactly the same number of cars as BMW sells in the US and within 15,000 units of Mercedes.

The 1990s bring increasing decentralization of manufacturing operations and a wide variety of new cars. After American carmakers pioneer the markets, Toyota belatedly expands into two new markets –

minivans and sports utility vehicles. In 1996, the 90 millionth Toyota vehicle is made.

In the mid-90s, with Lexus well established, the company starts a new project based once again on the company's beliefs about the future needs of car buyers. In December 1997, it launches the product of that thinking: Prius, a hybrid car that combines electric and gas power. The new car gets double the gas mileage of conventional cars and cuts pollutants an astonishing 90 percent under the level required in Japan.

In 1998, Toyota loses its ranking as the world's third largest carmaker when Chrysler and Daimler-Benz merge.

In 1999, Hiroshi Okuda replaces chairman Shoichiro Toyoda and Fujio Cho becomes president. The company forms a joint venture with Isuzu to manufacture buses and begins a US$800 million drive to boost its US production capacity by 200,000 vehicles per year.

Early in 2000, Toyota releases the WiLL Vi, a new sedan aimed at younger customers, and it establishes an online replacement parts business named iStarXchange. In March 2000, the company buys a 5 percent stake in Yamaha, the world's second largest motorcycle maker, and it raises its stake in Hino Motors to 33.8 percent.

Toyota close-up

Toyota Motor Corporation is a company that sets stretch goals and doggedly pursues them until they are accomplished. Using this simple technique, it has built itself into Japan's largest automaker and the fourth largest in the world.

It is a powerful competitor generating fiscal year 1999 sales of 12.7 trillion yen and profits of 356 billion yen. Toyota is associated with the influential Mitsui keiretsu (a group of companies connected by stock holdings that support and finance each other). Through its own network of just over 400 subsidiaries and affiliates, Toyota has established strong positions in all the major auto segments in almost every global market and employs over 183,000 people worldwide.

There is a problem, however. For the first time in its history, Toyota is lacking a compelling vision. It is pursuing an environmentally sound vehicle for which no major market is yet developed, and is flirting with diversification, with positions in some far afield "peripheral businesses," such as recreational boats, telecommunications, and prefab housing.

At the end of 1998, the company completed a four-year "New Global Business Plan," concentrated on increasing its overseas production capacity and increasing imports to Japan. Since then, it seems to be in search of a worthy direction. In April 1999, it announced a change of leadership. Fujio Cho, the former head of US manufacturing and most recently, executive vice-president of Corporate Planning, was promoted to company president effective June 1999.

Automotive

As Cho takes the reins, he inherits a company that is still well focused on automotive products. In fiscal 1999, Toyota generated 88 percent of its revenues, 11.1 trillion yen, from the production and sale of motor vehicles.

The company sold 4.69 million cars, trucks, and buses in 1999. Passenger cars are its major product group, accounting for 3.96 million of the total. Among the models are names such as Camry, Corolla, and Lexus, known by drivers everywhere.

International sales make up the majority of Toyota's automotive sales. The company sells cars in over 160 countries. In fiscal 1999, 2.76 million vehicles were sold outside of Japan; again, cars led the way by a large majority. The company's major geographic segments are Japan, North America, and Europe.

Japan

Japan, even given that country's prolonged economic downturn, remains the company's largest single market yielding 47 percent of revenues at just over 6 trillion yen. Toyota enjoys a 40 percent share of the Japanese market.

The company's sales coverage in Japan is comprehensive, ranging from traditional in-home visits by salespeople to recently developed US-style dealership networks. Each of five sales channels operates between 650 and 1320 new-car outlets.

It is a rather confusing mix and the company is in the process of untangling its channels to market. Toyota plans to rationalize the process by matching customer segments to their favorite models via their preferred sales channels.

The company offers a full range of vehicles in Japan. The high-end Lexus platform is sold as the Aristo. In 1998, the company also introduced the Gaia, a luxury minivan. The Progres, a full-sized passenger car, is sold in the upper-middle market.

There is a full line of station wagons, including: the Qualis; the Raum, with its sliding-door; and the midsized Caldina. Pickups and SUVs are popular in the down market. Popular models include the Harrier, a Lexus-based sport-utility vehicle, and the Land Cruiser.

The most intriguing of Toyota's Japanese models is the Prius, which swept the car-of-the-year awards when launched in December 1997. It is the world's first mass-produced hybrid car and it is a breakthrough product in terms of gas mileage and pollution reduction. If the world suffers a repeat of the 1970s oil crises, Toyota stands ready.

North America

Toyota's second largest market is North America. In fiscal 1999, sales hit 4.6 trillion yen, or 36 percent of total revenues.

The high-end in North America is the Lexus, where the ES 300 and LS 400/300 are sold through a dedicated sales channel. Under the Toyota name is the upper-end Avalon, and then, the Camry Solara and Camry – which is in a long-running battle with Ford for the title of best-selling car in the US. The sporty Celica and economical Corolla follow.

The company also sells the Sienna minivan and a variety of SUVs and pickups including the RAV4, 4Runner, Tacoma, and Tundra. In 2000, the innovative hybrid Prius is coming. NUMMI, Toyota's joint venture with GM, makes the economy class Prizm.

Toyota has aggressively built its production capabilities in North America. Production and purchasing is directed locally under the auspices of Cincinnati-based Toyota Motor Manufacturing North America, Inc. In 1998, the company made just over one million vehicles in the region.

Europe

Europe represents Toyota's third largest market with fiscal 1999 sales of 1.1 trillion yen, or nine percent of the company's total revenues.

The company has high hopes for growth in Europe following the lifting at the end of 1999 of restrictions on the number of vehicles Japan is allowed to import into the EU.

Currently, the major sellers are the Avensis and Corolla passenger cars, the company's anchors in Europe. It also sells the Picnic and Land Cruiser.

In 1999, the company is expanding into the luxury market with the Lexus IS200. And, it is introducing a new small economy car, the Yaris, which is replacing the low selling Starlet.

Yaris is powered by an efficient one-liter engine and is aimed at younger customers and females. It is produced using a newly developed modular approach, which translates to fewer parts, easier assembly, and lower cost.

In 1998, Toyota produced 170,000 vehicles in Europe, all in the UK. But, it is increasing capacity and plans to build up to 400,000 units annually by 2001.

Toward that goal, the company is building a passenger car plant in France, which will make the Yaris. It has also expanded its Burnaston, England assembly plant and North Wales engine plant. The Avensis and the Corolla are built in the UK.

The European manufacturing effort is supported by Toyota Motor Europe Manufacturing based in Brussels. Also under construction is a design center located in Cote d'Azur, France that is scheduled to open in 2000.

Other regions

The remaining portion of Toyota's automobile sales are distributed through the Middle East, Asia, Oceania, Africa, and South America. In fiscal 1999, they accounted for roughly six percent of total revenues at 852 million yen.

In Asia and Oceania, sales continue to decline year to year, and the company's operations are set at ever-lower levels. In 1998, the area produced 280,000 vehicles compared to 1997's 410,000 units.

Toyota has parts plants in Thailand, Malaysia, Indonesia, Vietnam, and the Philippines. In 1998, production was restarted at Thai vehicle plants after a two-month shut down. In Indonesia, a vehicle plant was reopened after closing because of the political unrest. The company also has vehicle plants in Malaysia, New Zealand, and Australia.

Toyota is working toward a license to build automobiles in China, but thus far is restricted to parts plants. The company and its suppliers have invested 35 billion yen in China, which it believes will develop into the world's fourth largest car market in the next decade.

Tianjin Toyota Motor Engine Co., Ltd, a joint venture with Tianjin Automobile Industrial (Group) Co., Ltd, produces engines, constant-velocity joints, and steering components for a car produced by China's Tianjin Automobile. Another venture is a wholly owned subsidiary that began producing forged parts in late 1998.

Volkswagen, Honda, and GM are all ahead of Toyota in the emerging Chinese market. Volkswagen, the most successful, owns 54 percent of that market with its Jetta and Santana models.

In the Middle East and Southwest Asia, sales are on the increase. Toyota established a joint venture in India with the Kirloskar Group that will begin production in late 1999. It will build a multipurpose vehicle aimed at families that the company is developing especially for the Indian market.

Sales in Latin America and the Caribbean are also strong. The company has seven plants in the region. A new Argentine plant came online in March 1997 and in August 1998, a second plant in Brazil began producing Corollas.

In Africa, Toyota's operations are centered in South Africa, where the company's affiliate is the market leader. Sales are around 50,000 units.

Other businesses

Toyota has a growing portfolio of diversified businesses with varying degrees of connection to the automotive industry. Together, they represented about 12 percent of Toyota's revenues or 1.5 billion yen in fiscal 1999.

The largest of Toyota's peripheral businesses is Toyota Finance Corporation, which provides sales financing for its customers. In fiscal 1999, Toyota Finance generated revenues of 573 billion yen and operated in all the company's major automotive markets.

Toyoda Automatic Loom Works, Ltd produces the industrial equipment the company sells. It makes forklifts (which account for most of the business), shovel loaders, towing tractors, and automatic-guided vehicles at plants in Japan and at joint ventures with in the US and France. In fiscal 1999, the company sold 67,348 units in this business.

The company has several ventures in telecommunications, mainly as they relate to automobiles. Toyota Mapmaster, Inc. started with partners including Aishin AW Co. Ltd, Denso Corporation, and Matsushita Communication Industrial Co., Ltd is developing car navigation systems. Toyota is also participating in ventures aimed at managing traffic through FM multiplex broadcasts and beacons, electronic tool collection, and mobile information services. It holds large stakes in three Japanese providers of cellular, domestic long-distance, and international telephone services.

Toyota owns a prefab housing business in Japan. In fiscal 1999, it produced 2941 homes. The company also operates a recreational boating company. It makes cabin cruisers in Japan and recently expanded into the US market with tournament-class ski boats.

Income statement

Year	Revenue ($m)	Net income ($m)	Net profit margin	Employees
1999	105,832.0	3,747.0	3.5%	183,879
1998	88,472.7	3,442.0	3.9%	159,035
1997	98,740.6	3,112.2	3.2%	150,736
1996	101,120.2	2,424.3	2.4%	146,855
1995	95,827.5	1,557.0	1.6%	142,645
1994	95,031.7	1,277.0	1.3%	110,534
1993	95,337.8	1,647.7	1.7%	109,279
1992	80,809.0	1,891.1	2.3%	108,167
1991	71,597.5	3,134.5	4.4%	102,423
1990	60,461.3	2,902.4	4.8%	96,849

Stock history

Year	Stock price ($) FY High	FY Low	FY Close	P/E High	Low	Per share ($) Earns	Div.	Book value
1999	58.75	40.94	57.25	30	21	1.98	0.37	29.37
1998	65.00	50.50	52.75	36	28	1.80	0.16	23.98
1997	57.88	43.25	50.50	36	27	1.62	0.33	24.15
1996	44.75	35.50	44.50	36	29	1.24	0.27	26.74
1995	45.13	34.75	39.75	56	43	0.81	0.28	31.70
1994	44.63	28.00	44.63	–	–	0.68	0.29	26,331.80
1993	31.88	21.50	28.75	–	–	0.86	0.24	23,896.99
1992	24.75	18.88	23.00	–	–	0.98	0.21	20,165.68
1991	28.52	22.27	23.75	–	–	1.62	0.19	19,691.81
1990	32.12	21.69	27.50	–	–	1.65	0.17	16,544.70

1999 year-end financials

Debt ratio	31.0%
Return on equity	7.4%
Cash ($m)	11,066.0
Current ratio	1.11
Long-term debt ($m)	24,867.0
Shares outstanding (millions)	1,880.3
Dividend yield	0.6%
Dividend payout	18.7%
Market value ($m)	107,648.6

Financial data provided by Hoover's Online (www.hoovers.com) and Media General Financial Services, Inc.

Toyota contacts

Toyota Motor Corporation
1, Toyota-cho, Toyota City
Aichi Prefecture 471–8571, Japan

Phone: 81–0565–28–2121
Fax: 81–565–23–5800
URL: www.global.toyota.com

CEO: Fujio Cho   CFO: Iwao Okijima   HR: Tadaaki Jagawa

Learning from the

Future Focus 21

As this final chapter of *Future Focus* is being written, the speculative mania that drove Internet stocks into the stratosphere in the last year or two of the second millennium is fast losing momentum. The red-hot dot com IPO market is cooling and the stocks of newly public companies that acted as if growth at any cost was somehow synonymous with profitability are in free fall.

Whether these events signal the ultimate deflation of the Internet Bubble or just a long overdue retrenchment remains to be seen. But either way, it is good to see some sensible thinking come back to the markets.

This is the perfect time to review the lessons of companies that have proven that they know how to succeed, over the long haul and through good and bad economies. The companies that begin following these examples today will be the ones that survive and succeed over the next century. The investors who begin choosing companies based on these solid values today will be the ones who prosper over the next century.

In the first chapter, we introduced four themes that have run through the *Future Focus* companies. In this conclusion, we revisit them as four calls to action for corporate success.

1. Get and stay focused

Al Ries' concept of focus is, and will remain, a cornerstone of business success. In a world where geographic borders are becoming less and less important, the pace of technological progress is accelerating, and customer expectations are ever higher, it is simply not feasible to divide your attention and resources among unrelated businesses.

The company histories that you have just read make this lesson clear. Over and over, the *Future Focus* companies experienced downturns as they diversified and grew in leaps and bounds as they narrowed their businesses down to one with an intense focus.

Focus is a never-ending job. There is an elegant simplicity to the idea of focus, but it remains an elusive target for many companies, including some of those studied in this book. Management teams change, success dulls the senses, and the siren call of new businesses is seductive.

Intel in the post-Andy Grove era, for example, is diversifying into too many new businesses. Microsoft, which may well be facing a court-ordered break-up, is too. Being focused means remaining ever vigilant against backsliding.

On the other hand, today's focus is not forever. History proves that it is not possible to choose a specific focus and simply follow it for the life of a corporation. Markets rise and fall, technology becomes obsolete, and entire industries appear and disappear. Change happens.

When the fundamentals that underlie a strategic focus change, so must a company. We've seen it in the past, such as when Intel shifted its focus from memory chips to processors. We will see it in the future. Royal Dutch/Shell, for example, has over a century of success in pursuit of fossil fuels, but is already preparing for an inevitable shift to renewable energy. So is Toyota, whose products will have to be radically altered to follow the same trend.

Managing focus is a critical leadership task. Choosing a focus and realigning your company to meet it is a tough and time-sensitive job.

It requires that you choose a business with the potential for long-term growth, and that you create products and services that can earn a top spot in that market. Think about the savvy choice to pursue telecommunications equipment made by the team of entrepreneurs that started Tellabs, and the same choice made by the already huge and diversified Nokia.

It also requires that you have the strength to withstand the pain of leaving past success behind and the pressure of the short-term losses that you are likely to incur during the transfer. Remember 3Com's decision to narrow its focus to computer networking products.

There is a price to pay for focus and it is hard work to maintain it, but focus is worth it. More important still, success in the 21st century will demand that you pay it.

2. Be innovative

The second major lesson illustrated by the histories of the *Future Focus* companies is the ongoing need to be first and fast to market with innovations. Over and over, we see businesses with a well-focused strategy succeed by offering their customers the best choices for fulfilling their needs.

Our companies show that innovative thinking can come in three major forms:

Innovation can come in the form of a new business model. Dell Computer, for instance, has grown to become one of the world's top computer makers not by making better computers, but by being one of the first and best at selling directly to end-users in the business and consumer markets.

Innovation can also come in the form of new operational and distribution processes. Witness Nucor's incredible rise to the top of the steel industry on the power of the minimill, a new kind of plant that revolutionized a stagnant market. Think about Dell's and Cisco's early success in developing a new sales channel over the Internet.

Finally and most familiarly, innovation can come in the form of new products and services. Nintendo provides a fine example as it fights a seesaw battle for leadership in the electronic games industry. The one unbeatable weapon: new games that capture the attention and wallets of players worldwide.

The *Future Focus* companies pursue innovation with a passion that is hard to match. This shouldn't come as much of a surprise – many were founded on the power of an innovative new product. Nestlés' milk products and Sensormatic's security tags are a two of the notable examples. These products created entire industries.

Coming from a heritage of innovation and also knowing that innovation is a never-ending task, these companies continue to devote a lion's share of effort and resources to research and development. They know that their position of leadership is dependent on leading change in their industries. Think of Intel and its unbeatable position in microprocessors. The company earned that position by cannibalizing its own market-leading products before its competitors could.

The *Future Focus* companies also capture innovation via acquisition. Cisco Systems, for example, has turned the art of acquisition into a science. It stays on top of the fast-changing Internet equipment industry by first buying the companies that produce the new products and technologies it needs and then expertly and efficiently folding them into its own structure.

Being focused is a tremendous enabler of innovation and it automatically confers an innovation advantage on the focused company. If you are clear about exactly what business you are in and what markets you are selling to, you are already way ahead of your diversified competitors.

The race for success belongs to those companies that can set the pace for innovation. While the other guys are still deciding which of their businesses to invest in, apply all of your resources to creating products, processes, and business models that will wow customers. Eventually, you will be the market leader.

3. Go global

To butcher a phrase from the Bard of Avon, all the world is the proper stage for a focused, innovative company. The proof lies in the fact that all but one of the *Future Focus* companies are international businesses.

Once you have built a focused business, the easiest way to grow it is to expand into new geographic markets. Where would Applied Materials be today if it hadn't expanded the markets for its chip fabrication equipment first to Japan and then into the nations that are home to all of the major semiconductor producers? The US chipmakers alone could never have provided the sales that the company needed to grow into a $4 billion business.

Use global expansion as a hedge against the vagaries of politics and the regular downturns that all national economies suffer. HSBC provides a striking example of both circumstances. The bank's operations were almost completely suspended during World War II but through global expansion and a move of headquarters, it managed to negotiate the return of its former home base (Hong Kong) to China with hardly a tremor. HSBC has also used its expansion into major regions throughout the world to lower its risk during regional downturns, such as the recent recession in Asia, its former stronghold.

Finally, build the value of your brands by making them known throughout the world. Global business means global brands. Follow the examples of Heineken and Nestlé and turn the products and services that you have worked so hard to create into global icons.

Ultimately, major companies have little choice except to go global. In his commentaries, Al Ries says that if you don't expand into new geographic markets, competitors in those markets will expand into yours. Nucor, the one *Future Focus* company that is the exception to the global rule, supports the statement: in 1999, the company sagged under the pressure of millions of tons of foreign steel that were dumped on the US market.

The threat of foreign competition is not the most important reason to go global, however. As with any other company, the success of a focused company requires growth. Some of that growth can and will come from expanding into the domestic market, but the greatest growth will come from expanding the domestic market into an international one.

Lastly, with you or without you, the move to a global economy is progressing. The economic barriers between countries are falling. As a result, most industries are becoming international in nature. If you do not follow the markets, your company will end up a very small fish in a big pond.

It all adds up to one critical action for long-term business success: become a big fish in a big pond, go global.

4. Be prepared for hard times

It would be nice to able to tell you that if your company is focused, innovative, and global, your road to success will be straight and smooth. It would be nice, but it would not be true. Business growth is cyclical and as the *Future Focus* companies prove, even the best corporations stumble and fall.

There are three great lessons among our 21 companies and it is well worth taking a few minutes to consider them.

Remember that every success carries with it the seeds of its own destruction. Consider Microsoft's relentless competitiveness, which has helped it earn a spot as one of the great business successes of all time, but it has also led the company to a critical juncture in its history. Its seeming inability to back away from a battle caused a federal judge to find the company guilty of monopolistic behavior and, as a result, it could be forced to split itself apart.

Take heed of storm warnings and be ready to adjust your speed and heading quickly. Applied Materials, for example, operates in a highly cyclical business. Management knows this and on several occasions, has stemmed the potential for large losses by quickly cutting its workforce and consolidating facilities. Growth stops, but the company securely rides out the storm.

Be willing to accept short-term pain for long-term gain. Over and over, we have seen *Future Focus* companies pay a stiff price for getting a narrower focus. In each case, businesses are sold, employees are laid off, and restructuring costs are incurred. Performance suffers in the short term, but the long-term rewards are worth it.

There is a silver lining to the hard times cloud. Every tough market and rough competitor and disastrous business development that you take on and survive can make you stronger. You don't have to be right every time. Sometimes being wrong is the best way to learn how to approach the future.

Be prepared for the inevitable hard times. Navigate them with skill and keep moving forward.

A few last words before you go to back to work: stay focused, pursue innovation, and grow your company into a name known worldwide. Face every challenge head on, accept failure as part and parcel of business growth, and keep learning. Those are the lessons of the *Future Focus* companies and the keys to 21st-century business success.

Index